FRENCH LITERATURE
AND ITS BACKGROUND

6
The Twentieth Century

FRENCH
LITERATURE
AND ITS
BACKGROUND

EDITED BY

JOHN CRUICKSHANK

6

The Twentieth Century

OXFORD UNIVERSITY PRESS

LONDON   OXFORD   NEW YORK

1970

Oxford University Press

LONDON OXFORD NEW YORK
GLASGOW TORONTO MELBOURNE WELLINGTON
CAPE TOWN SALISBURY IBADAN NAIROBI DAR ES SALAAM LUSAKA ADDIS ABABA
BOMBAY CALCUTTA MADRAS KARACHI LAHORE DACCA
KUALA LUMPUR SINGAPORE HONG KONG TOKYO

*First published as an
Oxford University Press paperback by
Oxford University Press, London, 1970*

PRINTED IN GREAT BRITAIN

Contents

Introduction

THIS is the last of six volumes appearing under the collective title *French Literature and its Background*. It covers the period extending roughly from the 1890s to the early 1960s (from the 'Modern Movement' to the 'Nouveau roman') and involves some slight overlap with the previous volume in the series, *The Late Nineteenth Century*.

The problem of what to put in and what to leave out, together with that of the degree of importance to be given to various writers and literary movements, proved particularly difficult in the case of the twentieth century. Within the limits set, choices had to be made and these have resulted in an overall pattern which will prove acceptable to some readers, while others may well want to disagree. Some may regret that Colette or Simone de Beauvoir have been omitted, that Apollinaire and Céline receive relatively brief mention, and that existentialism is not separately discussed as a background movement. In fact, there is no shortage of books on these topics and our own aim here, as in the previous volumes, has not been to provide complete coverage of twentieth-century writing in France. We have thought it more useful to attempt to stimulate discussion and to challenge our readers rather than give them a comprehensive, all-or-nothing, narrative.

Among the less orthodox chapters are 'The Birth of the Modern', 'Gide', 'Catholic Humanism', and 'Theatres of Escape', all of which adopt a personal approach to ideas and writers frequently presented in rather different terms. The only authors who are the subject of entire chapters are Proust, Valéry, and Gide, though other important figures are dealt with in a more dispersed way. Thus Claudel is discussed from different viewpoints in three chapters, 'Theatre of Heroic Grandeur', 'Catholic Humanism', and 'Poetry and Collective Experience', while Sartre receives attention both in 'The Novel of Action' and in 'Revolt and Revolution'. As regards the general background of ideas, this is outlined in terms of developing aesthetic doctrines, the impact of the First World War, the Catholic revival, surrealist theory, the experience of the Occupation, and the general ideological debates focused in the quarrel between Camus and Sartre. Since a number of excellent books have already been written on Camus and Sartre separately, it seemed useful here to bring them together in terms of significant contrast and conflict.

As in all previous volumes, a six-column 'Chronology' has again been provided. This should enable readers to relate major works of twentieth-century French literature to historical events, to works in a variety of other literatures, to the main composers and painters of the period, to books of literary criticism and aesthetic theory, and to a selective list of more general and varied writings from Freud's *The Interpretation of Dreams* to *La Pensée suavage* of Lévi-Strauss.

I should like to take this opportunity of thanking my thirty-five fellow contributors for making these six volumes possible. The life of a general editor is not an easy one, but my collaborators in this enterprise ensured that it was stimulating and (often) enjoyable. I am grateful for all they have taught me.

JOHN CRUICKSHANK

University of Sussex
November 1969

1. The Birth of the Modern: 1885-1914

THE problem to be dealt with in this chapter can be formulated quite simply: the years 1885-1914 saw the birth of the modern movement in the arts. What are the specific features of the movement, and how are we to account for its emergence?

Three points have to be made before we start. First of all we must be clear that from one point of view our inquiry is nonsensical. There is no specific thing called 'modernity' which we can extract from the variety of individual works of art and hold up for inspection. Every modern artist worth his salt is good precisely because he has found his own individual voice and because this voice is distinct from that of his fellows. And yet it cannot be denied that something did happen to art, to all the arts, some time around the turn of the century, and that Proust, Joyce, Picasso, Klee, Schoenberg, and Stravinsky, for all their manifest individuality, do have something in common. Before we plunge into a study of individual artists and works it may be useful to have a frame of reference, a set of common assumptions, which will stop us asking the wrong kinds of question or looking for the wrong sorts of answer.

This leads to the second point, which is that such an inquiry is far more than an academic exercise, the reconstruction of the past for its own sake. Although more than half a century has passed since those decisive years, the majority of people who are interested in the arts have still not come to terms with what happened then. The indiscriminate abuse of Picasso and Schoenberg may have ceased, but it has merely given way to equally indiscriminate praise. Great artists create their own posterity, said Proust; but though it may be fashionable to enthuse over the latest *avant-garde* music and painting, there is everywhere—among professional reviewers as well as academic critics—a real failure to understand the premisses upon which the great artists of the turn of the century based their works.

And until such an understanding has been arrived at, the serious artists of today, who are their heirs, are bound to be misjudged—though not necessarily to go unrecognized. It is thus of paramount importance for us today that we should make sense of the great change that came over the arts at the turn of the century.

The third point is merely a reminder of a historical fact which, if rightly interpreted, should serve as a guide and a warning throughout this investigation. Although the First World War effectively marks the break between the world of the nineteenth century and our own—both in the minds of those who lived through it and of those of us who read about it in the history books—the modern revolution in the arts did not take place during the war or immediately after it, but a decade or so before it. This should make us wary of too facile an identification of art with the culture and society out of which it springs. For, paradoxically, while artists have always been ahead of their times, art has always fulfilled the same basic needs, and men have not fundamentally altered since the days of Homer. It is with the changing *forms* of art and not with what one might call the furniture of art—the props and backdrops which it borrows from the world around it—that we will be concerned in the pages that follow.

The modern movement in the arts cannot be understood in isolation. It must be seen as a reaction to the decadent Romanticism that was prevalent in Europe at the turn of the century. Some of the theoreticians of modernism, such as T. E. Hulme in England, tried to argue that it was nothing other than a wholesale rejection of Romanticism and all it stood for, and a return to a new classicism. Looking back at those pre-war decades from our vantage-point in the mid-century, however, we can see that the matter was considerably more complex than Hulme suggests; that it was more a question of redefining Romanticism, of stressing some of those aspects of it which the nineteenth century had neglected and discarding some of those it had most strongly emphasized, than of rejecting it outright. If we are to understand what the founders of modern art were doing it will be necessary to grasp the premises and implications of Romanticism itself.

Romanticism was first and foremost a movement of liberation—liberation from religious tradition, political absolutism, a hierarchical social system, and a universe conceived on the model of the exact sciences. Reason and scientific laws, the Romantics felt, might allow man to control his environment, but they formed a sieve through which the living, breathing individual slipped, and which retained only the dead matter of generality. What man had in common with other men, what this landscape had in common with other landscapes, was the least important thing about them. What was important was the uniqueness of men and the uniqueness of everything in the world around us, be it a leaf, a sparrow, or a mountain range. There were moments, they felt, when man was far from the distractions of the city and of society, and when the reasoning, conceptualizing mind was still, when life seemed suddenly to reveal itself in all its beauty, mystery, and terror. In such moments man felt himself restored to his true self, able to grasp the meaning of life and of his own existence. It is to experience and express such moments, both in our lives and in our art, that we should strive, for these are the moments when we throw off the shackles of generality and are restored to our unique selves.

The function of art thus becomes that of digging deep down into those areas of the mind and of the world which lie beyond the confines of rational thought and ordinary consciousness; and the hero of Romantic art becomes none other than the artist himself, who is both the explorer of this unknown realm and the priestly mediator between it and his audience. Something of this is suggested by August Wilhelm Schlegel, who is most probably responsible for introducing the term 'Romantic' as a description of the age:

Ancient poetry and art is rhythmical *nomos*, a harmonious promulgation of the eternal legislation of a beautifully ordered world mirroring the eternal Ideas of things. Romantic poetry, on the other hand, is the expression of a secret longing for the chaos . . . which lies hidden in the very womb of orderly creation . . . [Greek art] is simpler, cleaner, more like nature in the independent perfection of its separate works; [Romantic art], in spite of its fragmentary appearance, is nearer to the mystery of the universe.

Schlegel, it is true, is not here talking only of the nineteenth century; he is contrasting the whole 'modern' or Christian era with the Classical age of Greece and Rome. But his stress on the transcending impulse of Romanticism, on the aspiration towards the mystery of the universe, is taken up by Baudelaire nearly half a century later, in a discussion of the 'Salon' of 1846: 'Qui dit romantisme dit art moderne, — c'est-à-dire intimité, spiritualité, couleur, aspiration vers l'infini, exprimées par tous les moyens que contiennent les arts.'

But here a curious contradiction begins to emerge, a contradiction that lies at the heart of the whole Romantic endeavour, and that was to determine its future course. One final quotation, from the theologian Schleiermacher, will bring it out into the open:

> I am lying in the bosom of the infinite universe, I am at this moment its soul, because I feel all its force and its infinite life as my own. It is at this moment my own body, because I penetrate all its limbs as if they were my own, and its innermost nerves move like my own. . . . Try out of love for the universe to give up your own life. Strive already here to destroy your own individuality and to live in the One and in the All . . . fused with the Universe.

Romanticism had begun as a movement of rebellion against the arbitrary authorities of the eighteenth century and its abstract laws, a rebellion undertaken in the name of the freedom of the individual. But this freedom, which, as we saw, involves the suppression of the tyrannical intellect, now appears to be synonymous with the loss of individuality as most men conceive it; thus the ultimate freedom, according to the Romantic logic, is death.

Where consciousness itself is felt to be an imprisoning factor, keeping man from his true self, freedom must lie in transcending it. Yet the only times we escape from consciousness for more than a brief moment are in sleep, under the influence of alcohol and drugs, or in madness, while the only total escape is death; hence the key place accorded by Romanticism to dreams, to various forms of addiction, to madness, and to the death-wish. In all these cases the result is, of course, extremely ambiguous. The freedom from consciousness and from social convention does often result in deeper insight, but it results also in the destruction of the individual. Hence the general tone of Romantic art and literature is one of melancholy gloom, for there seems to be no way of resolving the contradiction.

This pull between freedom and annihilation is even easier to discern in the sphere of art itself. The task of the poet, as the Romantics saw it, was to communicate those moments of visionary intensity which only he could experience, moments in which the meaning and value of life were revealed to him. But the poet's only means of expression is language, and language belongs almost by definition to the realm of consciousness and of social intercourse. For language, as Plato had already noted, only exists at a certain degree of abstraction and universality; it takes for granted that there is some sort of social agreement as to the referents of words: we can use the word 'tree' or 'man' only because we all agree roughly what these two words stand for. But if we feel that what is important is the individuality, the 'instress' as Hopkins called it, of this tree or this man—what essentially differentiates it from all other trees or men—then clearly words are going to be a hindrance rather than a help. How then are we to express this insight? The Romantic poet finds himself struggling to express by means of language precisely that which it lies beyond the power of language to express. He is a man desperately trying to get away from his own shadow.

Only one poet in the nineteenth century was fully aware of the implications of the Romantic endeavour, and was prepared to accept and try to overcome them. In Rimbaud's famous letter to Paul Demeny of 15 May 1871, we can see that he had fully understood the problem and had decided on a radical solution:

Donc le poète est vraiment voleur de feu.

Il est chargé de l'humanité, des *animaux* même; il devra faire sentir, palper, écouter ses inventions; si ce qu'il rapporte de *là-bas* a forme, il donne forme; si c'est informe, il donne de l'informe. Trouver une langue; — du reste, toute parole étant idée, le temps d'un langage universel viendra! Il faut être académicien — plus mort qu'un fossile — pour parfaire un dictionnaire, de quelque langue que ce soit. Des faibles se mettraient *à penser* sur la première lettre de l'alphabet, qui pourraient vite ruer dans la folie!

Cette langue sera de l'âme pour l'âme, résumant tout, parfums, sons, couleurs, de la pensée accrochant la pensée et tirant. Le poète définirait la quantité d'inconnu s'éveillant en son temps dans l'âme universelle: il donnerait plus — que la formule de sa pensée, que l'annotation *de sa marche au Progrès*! Énormité devenant norme, absorbée par tous, il serait vraiment *un multiplicateur de progrès*!

The failure of this ideal can be traced through the poems themselves, and forms the explicit content of *Une Saison en enfer*. And, indeed, how could he succeed? What he desires is not communication but communion, the direct and total contact of one person with another through a language so charged that it will act without needing to pass by way of the mind at all. Such a language can never be more than a Utopian dream, for to give words the meaning we want them to have, regardless of the socially accepted meaning they already have, is tantamount to abolishing language altogether. When Rimbaud recognized this, with admirable logic, he gave up writing poetry.

But just because he was so ready to push the premisses of Romanticism to their ultimate conclusion, Rimbaud remains one of the key figures of the nineteenth century, marking for ever one of the two poles within which modern art is to move. His contemporaries (Mallarmé excepted—but see below), both in England and in France, chose a somewhat less arduous and therefore less interesting path. They tried to solve the problem by making their verse approximate as closely as possible to their own conception of music—which had, naturally enough, become for the Romantics the artistic language *par excellence*, since it appeared to have none of the disadvantages of speech. To this end they made their verse as mellifluous as possible, stressing its incantatory qualities, smoothing out all harshness of diction, minimizing its referential content, and rigidly excluding all forms of wit and humour for fear these would break their fragile spell. The result was aptly described by T. S. Eliot in a famous essay on Swinburne:

Language in a healthy state presents the object, is so close to the object that the two are identified. They are identified in the verse of Swinburne only because the object has ceased to exist, because the meaning is merely the hallucination of meaning, because language, uprooted, has adapted itself to an independent life of atmospheric nourishment.

So, as with Rimbaud, we see the normal function of language being denied and words taking on an independent meaning. But here the meaning is not just independent of general usage, but of the poet's own will into the bargain. The result is not insight into the mystery of the universe but empty cliché, not the articulation of what lies beyond the confines of rationality, but simple reflex, the verbal equivalent of the canine dribble. For language has a way of getting its own back on those who try to step over it in this manner, and just as the Romantic dreamer found that he escaped from the bonds of his intellect at the cost of his life, so the Romantic poet, trying to escape from the bonds of language, found himself its prisoner, uttering platitudes in the voice of a prophet.

But if the poets dreamt of living in a world freed from the stifling restrictions of language, and looked with envy to the composers, these, had the poets but known it, were no freer than themselves. For if language is not natural, that is, if words are not inherently expressive, as Rimbaud had thought, the same is true of music. Although Hoffmann wrote enthusiastically about the inherent qualities of a chord of A flat minor, the truth of the matter is that music is nearly as conventional as speech. We find it difficult to grasp music which is distant from us in space or time (Indian or Japanese music, or Gregorian chant, for instance); to know when it is 'cheerful', when 'sad'. Musical instruments, too, have different and highly specialized functions in other societies, and so are associated with different things than they are for us. It is only through frequent hearing, through a familiarization with its 'language', that we can come to appreciate Indian music; the composer, no less than the poet, works in a language which is largely the product of convention, and according to rules to which he voluntarily submits in order to master the world of sounds. Thus, when the initial impetus of Romanticism starts to peter out, we find a development in music parallel to that we traced in poetry—a slackening of formal control, a loosening of the harmonic texture, and the emergence of a soulful, cliché-ridden style that strives to lull the listener into a trance as the music struggles to express the world of the infinite which Baudelaire had urged the artist to seek with every means at his disposal. Naturally enough the piano, instrument of the half-echo, the indefinite, the suggestive, becomes the favourite of artist and public alike. And in music, as in poetry, the attempt to express everything, the totality of experience, unfettered by the rules and limitations of convention or consciousness, leads to its own destruction. More than any of the other arts Romantic music is imbued with the melancholy which stems from the knowledge that to achieve its goal is to expire.

The apotheosis of Romantic art, as all his contemporaries recognized, is to be found in the operas of Richard Wagner. These vast music-dramas seemed to be the perfect answer to Baudelaire's plea for a work of art that would make use of all the arts, thus finally lifting the spectator into the realm of the infinite, the very heart of the mystery of the universe. And we are fortunate in possessing a critique of Wagner by one of the few men who was really aware of the implications of Romanticism because he was so much of a Romantic himself: Friedrich Nietzsche. Nietzsche's analysis of the 'decadent' style sums up some of the points already made:

> What is common to both Wagner and 'the others' consists in this: the decline of all organizing power; the abuse of traditional means, without the capacity or the aim that would justify this; the counterfeit imitation of grand forms . . .; excessive vitality in small details; passion at all costs; refinement as an expression of impoverished life, ever more nerves in the place of muscle.

But Nietzsche is not content with a simple catalogue of Wagner's characteristics: he wants to understand what lies behind this, and to try to account for Wagner's enormous popularity. He sees first of all that for Wagner music is only a means to an end: 'As a matter of fact his whole life long he did nothing but repeat one proposition: that his music did not mean music alone. But something more! Something immeasurably more! . . . "Not music alone"—no musician would speak in this way.' And he explains what this 'more' is: 'Wagner pondered over nothing so deeply as over salvation: his opera is the opera of salvation.' And this, thinks Nietzsche, is the source of Wagner's power, that what he offered was nothing less than the hope of personal salvation to a Europe—and especially a Germany—bewildered by the rapid social and technological changes of the previous forty or so years: 'How intimately related must Wagner be to the entire decadence of Europe for her not to have felt that he was decadent!' And again: 'People actually kiss that which plunges them more quickly into the abyss.' We remember that Schlegel had already talked about a 'secret longing for the chaos . . . which lies hidden in the very womb of orderly creation', and that this longing was nothing other than the Romantic desire for a total and absolute freedom. Nietzsche's suggestion that with Wagner this longing spills out of the realm of art into that of politics and society allows us to glimpse the connection between decadent Romanticism and the rise of totalitarianism. The cataclysmic events of the first half of the present century would have occasioned him little surprise.

What Nietzsche particularly objects to in Wagner is precisely the fact that by trying to turn his music into a religion he debases both music and religion; by trying to turn the entire world into a music-drama, drawing the audience up into the music until they shed their dull everyday lives and come into contact with the heart of the mystery, he dangerously distorts both the life of every day and the nature of art; by blurring the outlines between life and art he turns art into a tool and life into an aesthetic phenomenon, that is, into something which is to be judged entirely by aesthetic criteria and where the rules of morality no longer apply. In so doing Wagner is typical of decadent Romanticism in general, of Huysmans and Swinburne and all those who took to heart Axël's dictum that, as for living, our servants can do that for us. The end of the nineteenth century is the great era of the *poète maudit*, of the dandy, of the Romantic agony. It marks the final bankruptcy of the Romantic revolt.

But even as Wagnerism swept through Europe and Nietzsche sank into his final madness the reaction to Romantic decadence had already begun. This did not take the form of a movement in the sense that surrealism, say, was a movement, with polemical manifestos and self-appointed leaders and spokesmen. It was not even a movement of like-minded men holding the same beliefs about human liberty and the function of the artist in society, as

Romanticism, in its early phases, had been. Proust and Joyce met once and barely spoke to one another; Schoenberg loathed Stravinsky; Eliot was more interested in Laforgue than in Mallarmé or Valéry; and Kafka ignored them all. Yet it is easy for us today to see that all these artists were united by one common attitude, albeit a negative one: they all insisted on the *limitations* of the sphere of art. More than that, they all stressed, in the art itself, that what they had created was only art and nothing more: that a painting was nothing except a series of brush-strokes on a flat canvas; that music was nothing except certain notes played by certain combinations of instruments; that poetry was nothing except a grouping of words on the page; that prose fiction was fiction and not reality.

Since the Romantics had regarded art as simply a means to a transcendental end, they naturally tended to see all the arts as more or less interchangeable—it doesn't matter what train you take since they're all going to the same place. The insistence on the part of the moderns that their work was art and not something else, their stress on the particular *medium* in which they were working, was not meant to be a denial of art but rather a reassertion of its crucial function. Art, they argued, was not a means of piercing the sensible veil of the universe, of getting at the 'unknown', as Rimbaud and others had claimed, for there was nothing beyond the world that lay all round us. The whole mystery was there, right in front of us, where everybody could see it—except for the fact that normally men are too blind or lazy to do so. What most of us tend to do in front of the world, of ourselves, of works of art, is to neutralize what is before us by reducing it to something we know already. Thus we are for ever shut up inside our preconceived notions, reacting only to that which makes no demands that we should really see. As Giacometti put it:

Où y a-t-il le plus de monde? Devant le 'Sacre de Napoléon'. Pourquoi les gens regardent-ils justement ce tableau? Parce qu'ils imaginent d'abord assister à la scène, y participer. Ils deviennent des 'petits Napoléons'. En même temps le spectacle devient l'équivalent de la lecture d'un roman.

Like the library novel, it becomes an excuse for daydreaming. The modern artist, on the other hand, holds that the work of art is meaningful precisely because it reveals to us the 'otherness' of the world—it shocks us out of our natural sloth and the force of habit, making us 'see' for the first time what we have looked at a hundred times but never really noticed. Art is not a key to the universe but a pair of spectacles, as Valéry, echoing Proust's Elstir, points out:

Nous devinons ou prévoyons, en général, plus que nous ne voyons, et les impressions de l'œil sont pour nous des signes, et non des *présences singulières*, antérieures à tous les arrangements, les résumés, les raccourcis, les substitutions immédiates, que l'éducation première nous a inculqués.

Comme le penseur essaie de se défendre contre les *mots* et les expressions toutes prêtes qui dispensent les esprits de s'étonner de tout et rendent possible la vie pratique, ainsi l'artiste peut, par l'étude des choses informes,[1] c'est-à-dire de forme *singulière*, essayer de retrouver sa propre singularité . . .

Art, then, does not feed us information, nor does it give us a glimpse of a world beyond or above this one. What it does is to open our eyes by removing the film of habit which we normally carry around with us. It does this by shocking us into awareness through its insistence on itself as an object in its own right, irreducible to anything we could see or think in the normal course of affairs. The cubist picture, for instance, teases the eye as we follow shape after shape on the canvas, always on the verge of understanding it, yet never quite allowed to do so. And because we cannot step back and say: 'Ah, yes, a mandolin, a glass of wine, a table', etc., we go on looking at the canvas and in time learn to accept its own reality instead of reducing it to our own preconceived idea of what a mandolin or a glass of wine looks like. Thus Braque can say: 'le tableau est fini quand l'idée a disparu', and Valéry, elsewhere in the essay on Degas quoted earlier: 'Regarder, c'est-à-dire oublier les noms des choses que l'on voit.' Proust's whole novel can be seen as an attempt to substitute the object for the name, to render the uniqueness of the feeling by recreating it rather than simply by naming it.

An art of this kind clearly makes the spectator work. It does not, like Wagnerian opera, claim to provide a passport to salvation, nor,

[1] A lump of coal, a handkerchief thrown anyhow on to a table.

like the 'Sacre de Napoléon', allow each of us to indulge his day-dreams. What it does claim to do is to recreate within the willing reader or spectator the liberating experience of the artist himself. When Picasso said, of his famous sculpture of the bull's head made out of the seat and handlebars of a bicycle, that the whole point would be lost if the viewer, through excessive familiarity with it, were to see *only* a bull's head, he neatly illustrated this aspect of modern art. What is important is not the finished product, but the *process*. Picasso wants us to be aware of the fact that what is in front of us is not a bull's head but a man-made object. The product is not there to be contemplated for its own sake but to stimulate the viewer's own perception and to allow him to relive the act of creative discovery for himself. In the same way Proust's novel does not so much tell a story as create within the reader the potentiality for telling the story Marcel is about to set down as the work ends. Thus, paradoxically again, the artist's very acceptance of limitation, his open acknowledgement of the medium in which he is working, leads beyond art to alter the very life of the reader or viewer.

We have been looking at the modern revolution in the arts as a reaction to decadent Romanticism, but if we look at it in a larger perspective it becomes clear that this reaction entailed a radical break with four centuries of the Western artistic tradition. Shifts in taste and in forms of expression had occurred at regular intervals in those four centuries, of course, but these were really modifications within a fixed framework. Romanticism, by trying to give full expression to the individual, burst this framework and so made it possible for the moderns to step out of it and see that the frame enclosed not the whole universe but only a restricted area of it. Perhaps a more accurate way of describing the change would be to say that what the artists of the previous four centuries had taken to be the limits of the universe were now discovered to be only the limitations imposed by spectacles they had not realized they were wearing. It is not by chance that the birth of the modern coincides with the discovery or rediscovery of Japanese art, African sculpture, Romanesque painting, the musical instruments of the Far East, and the poetry of the troubadours. This was no simple widening of the cultural horizons; it was the momentous discovery that what had been taken as *the* way of seeing was really only one way among many; that perspective and harmony, far from being in each case a datum of experience, were almost as conventional as the sonnet form and, unlike the latter, were the product of certain metaphysical assumptions which began to emerge in the West at the time of the Renaissance.

All art, since the Renaissance, had been based on the twin concepts of expression and imitation. In an earlier chapter[1] I suggested why these two should always go hand in hand, and why they should have emerged as the primary criteria of art at the time when medieval notions of analogy could no longer be accepted. It seems appropriate to conclude this brief analysis of modernity by looking at it from the point of view of each of these concepts in turn.

The artist expresses himself and he imitates external reality. For three centuries there was an uneasy compromise between these two notions, until the Romantics, by stressing the first of these aspects to the exclusion of the second, brought the hidden assumptions of both out into the open and showed how unsatisfactory they both were. Writing again about the 'Salon' of 1846, Baudelaire quotes at some length from the German Romantic writer, E. T. A. Hoffmann. The passage, as will readily be seen, is central not only to Baudelaire's whole aesthetic, but to that of Romanticism in general:

Ce n'est pas seulement en rêve, et dans le léger délire qui précède le sommeil, c'est encore éveillé, lorsque j'entends de la musique, que je trouve une analogie et une réunion intime entre les couleurs, les sons et les parfums. Il me semble que toutes ces choses ont été engendrées par un même rayon de lumière, et qu'elles doivent se réunir dans un merveilleux concert. L'odeur des soucis bruns et rouges produit surtout un effet magique sur ma personne. Elle me fait tomber dans une profonde rêverie, et j'entends alors comme dans le lointain les sons graves et profonds du hautbois.

The implicit belief behind this passage is that individual sights,

---

[1] i.e. Chapter 1 ('From Analogy to Scepticism') of *French Literature and its Background: 1, The Sixteenth Century.*

sounds, smells, and tastes touch each one of us in the same way and are themselves interchangeable. In other words, that each speaks a natural language. In a similar way the poet has simply to reach down into himself and pour out what he feels, while the reader allows this to enter into his own soul. We have seen how this grossly over-simplified view of the poetic process led to the breakdown of art into a series of utterances so individual that they no longer made sense, or else turned into the banal expression not of vision but of cliché. This failure showed the moderns that the work of art is not simply the expression of some inner feeling, but the creation of a structure which will 'hold' this feeling for the poet as well as for the reader. Hence the insistence on the impersonality of the poet, the radical distinction between the artist and the man made by Proust and Rilke and Eliot. For the artist *qua* man is no different from the reader; the difference lies in the fact that he is a craftsman who can 'catch' the fleeting sensation and make it communicable in the form of a poem or a painting. The work of art, to use a famous phrase of Archibald MacLeish, no longer says, but *is*.

This is really only another way of making the point discussed earlier about the modern artist's emphasis on the limitations of his medium. To draw these two together it may be useful to look at the change from Romanticism to modernity from a slightly different point of view, that of the change from a view of art as magic to a view of art as game.

The Romantic artist, as we saw, be he Rimbaud or Wagner, claimed, in some way, to be a magician. He claimed, that is, that words and sounds hide within themselves certain magical pro-perties over which the artist alone has power. Through this power the artist can confer salvation upon the rest of mankind. The reader or listener has simply to submit to the words or sounds in order to shed the pains and frustrations of daily living and to emerge reborn. The consequences of such a view were quickly seen by Nietzsche in connection with Wagner, and his description of the Wagnerian style can be paralleled in all the other arts: there is everywhere a solemnity, a pompousness, the stifling feeling of a magical ritual no longer quite under control. In contrast to this view, the moderns sought to instil the notion of art as a game. The work of art does not offer permanent salvation, its function is to increase the reader's own powers of imagination. This requires his active participation and he can, if he wishes, withdraw from the game—no one is forcing him to take part. If he agrees to go on, however, he must abide by the rules laid down by the artist. Again it is not a matter of what the work is saying, but rather of what it is doing. This notion of art as game, moreover, lays stress on the essential modesty of the modern artist, and his awareness that though art has a supremely important place in life, it is helpless to change the world. The rediscovery of the hieratic and stylized arts of other periods and cultures, we must remember, went hand in hand with the rediscovery of genres and forms of art which had not been considered serious enough to form part of the mainstream of European art: the puppet-play, the shadow-play, children's games of all sorts, used to such good effect by Jarry and a little later by Stravinsky, Picasso, Satie, and Debussy. The latter's *Jeux*, a ballet performed by the Diaghilev company in Paris in 1913, and one of the most subtle and inventive works of the period, is 'about' nothing other than a game of tennis!

If all art is a game with its own rules—something that happens between the author and the reader, viewer, or listener—then what is important is the mastery of convention, not the accuracy with which either external reality or the author's own emotions are depicted. And this leads us to the final and most obvious aspect of the modernist revolution: its break with four centuries of mimesis.

Because all Western art since the Renaissance had been essentially an imitation of reality, it was necessarily anecdotal. Paintings have been concerned with subjects such as coronations, battles, weddings, landscapes, and so on. Novels have told stories, and so have all but the shortest lyrical poems. But, as the Romantics realized, to tell one story, to describe one scene, is at once to cut out the possibility of telling a lot of other stories, of describing quite other scenes. Why should the artist paint this rather than that? Why should the novelist tell this story rather than that, put in this incident rather than another? It is not enough to say: 'Because he feels like it', since this feeling is itself in need of justification—why does he feel like it? Since everything is possible, everything is equally arbitrary, as the hero of Kafka's *The Castle* recognizes:

> It seemed to K. as if at last those people had broken off all relations with him, and as if now in reality he were freer than he had ever been, and at liberty to wait here in this place usually forbidden to him as long as he desired, and had won a freedom such as hardly anybody else had ever succeeded in winning, and as if nobody could dare to touch him or drive him away, or even speak to him; but—this conviction was at least equally strong—as if at the same time there was nothing more senseless, nothing more hopeless, than this freedom, this waiting, this inviolability.

The problem already haunted the Romantics, and we find its echoes everywhere in their poetry. But so long as they held to any expressive theory of art they could never solve it, however hard they tried to blur the outlines of their fictions, their music, their painting, until it merged with the surrounding world. The paintings of Cézanne mark the decisive break, and his phrase 'Je pars neutre' is the key one for this aspect of modernist aesthetics. What he meant was that he tried to paint, eliminating the inevitable personal slant in both subject and object, seeking instead to discover the general laws of light and space in the scene before him, rather than reproducing that particular scene on his canvas. Proust, whose design is similar, makes the point again and again in *Le Temps retrouvé*: he is not interested in imitating a flat reality but in drawing out the general laws inherent in love, in perception, in speech. And thinking perhaps of a Cézanne and of one of those society portraits even more popular then than now, he says:

> Si l'un dans le domaine de la peinture, met en évidence certaines vérités relatives au volume, à la lumière, au mouvement, cela fait-il qu'il soit nécessairement inférieur à tel portrait ne lui ressemblant aucunement de la même personne, dans lequel mille détails qui sont omis dans le premier seront minutieusement relatés, deuxième portrait d'où l'on pourra conclure que le modèle était ravissant tandis qu'on l'eût cru laid dans le premier, ce qui peut avoir une importance documentaire et même historique mais n'est pas nécessairement une vérité d'art.

In other words the work of art does not convey a fixed meaning from the artist to the reader or viewer: rather, it creates an object which did not exist before in either the one or the other, an object which both gives joy and uncovers a truth about the world hitherto hidden. The work of art becomes necessary rather than arbitrary because it is rather than simply tells. The words in a novel by Joyce, Virginia Woolf, Proust, Robbe-Grillet, Claude Simon, do not enclose a content which the reader simply takes in as he takes in a telephone message, they live and function within the whole work, asking the reader to reactivate them within himself as he reads. Ultimately we cannot extract a meaning from the painting or poem or novel, the meaning is the work itself, to be re-experienced every time the reader or viewer wishes to renew the experience.

It might be thought that the search for an art of total potentiality, an art of laws rather than things, would lead to a complete abstraction. Certainly the danger is there and one could say that, if Rimbaud forms one of the poles within which modern art moves, Mallarmé forms the other; for both took to their limits the implications of the Romantic revolt. To go too far in the direction of one or the other is to burst the bonds of art; it leads to either total noise or total silence, either total randomness or total organization. The artist then either plunges in and relies on the honesty of his gesture, on the spontaneity of his response to the paint he handles or the words or notes he puts down, or he organizes his work so rigidly that it might as well be—and often is—produced by a machine. Both points of view are prevalent in so-called *avant-garde* circles today, and both would have been anathema to the great modern revolutionaries, since both do away with the artist's most precious possession, his individual freedom of choice. As we have seen, this is a limited freedom, and to imagine that it is total is to lose what little there is. But it is essential to maintain it if art is going to survive.

Two quotations from painters would seem to sum up admirably the central features of the modernist movement. The first is from Picasso, who, it will be remembered, broke away from the strict cubism of his early period when he felt he had subjected himself sufficiently to its discipline. Talking to his friend, the photographer Brassai, he said:

I always aim at the resemblance. An artist should observe nature but never confuse it with painting. It is only translatable into painting by signs. . . . But such signs are not invented. To arrive at the sign you have to concentrate hard on the resemblance. To me surreality is nothing and never has been anything but this profound resemblance, something deeper than the forms and colours in which objects present themselves.

The second is from the English painter, Francis Bacon:

Art is a method of opening up areas of feeling rather than merely an illustration of an object. . . . A picture should be a re-creation of an event rather than an illustration of an object; but there is no tension in the picture unless there is the struggle with the object.

The preceding pages are an attempt to sketch out some of the characteristics and implications of the modernist revolution and to account for its sudden outbreak at the turn of the present century. Inevitably we have been involved in a discussion which has moved backwards and forwards from the sphere of history to that of aesthetics—inevitably because modernism is first and foremost a rethinking of the whole field of aesthetics as it had been seen in the West since the time of Plato and Aristotle. But this is not to say that this was a mere revolution in the theory of art, for, if the moderns have grown more modest than the Romantics in their view of the function of the artist, they are even more firmly convinced of the crucial place of art in human life.

It has also been necessary, as a matter of strategy, to make the division between the Romantics and the moderns sharper than it really is. For however much the modernist movement is a reaction to a decadent Romanticism, its basic assumptions are still the Romantic ones: a refusal to rely on any external system of values, moral or epistemological, the attempt to discover and communicate the uniqueness of the individual and of each object. If the modern artist frequently harks back to the wit, irony, and sophistication of the eighteenth century, it is always a wit tinged with anguish, an irony that is mainly self-protective, a sophistication that has in it the stoic desire for evil to destroy itself mixed with the gnawing certainty that it is far more likely to destroy the good.

Finally, this chapter has deliberately not been confined to French artists because the modern movement was above all an international one. More specifically, and again in implicit reaction to Romanticism, it was an urban movement, one whose exponents are to be found in all the great cosmopolitan centres of Europe: Vienna, Munich, Prague, and especially Paris. It was to Paris that the painters and sculptors who formed the backbone of the movement came; in Paris that Proust, Valéry, and Joyce published their work; in Paris that Diaghilev's Russian Ballet burst upon the world as the modernist answer to the Wagnerian *Gesamtkunstwerk*. For this reason the modernist revolution has affected the cultural life of France more than that of any other country. In England and Germany the public remembers the leaders of the movement much as they remember all their classical writers—distant and embalmed, standard editions and dreary hours in the classroom. Only in France are they still the mentors of every aspiring artist, the source of all that is most alive in the intellectual life of the country. The history of French literature in the twentieth century is the history of the fortune of one or other of the modernist discoveries. And such was the richness and importance of these discoveries that we are only now beginning to realize their full implications.

NOTE

The best introduction to 'modernism' is to be found in certain major modern novels, particularly those of Proust and Thomas Mann, but also those of Joyce, Virginia Woolf, Musil, Broch, etc. Other key texts are: T. S. Eliot, *The Sacred Wood* (1920), Valéry's essay 'Poésie et pensée abstraite' (a lecture delivered in Oxford in 1939 and reprinted in *Variété V* (1944)), and Hofmannsthal's 'The Letter of Lord Chandos' (first publ. as 'Ein Brief' in 1902; transl. in Hugo von Hofmannsthal, *Selected Prose*, publ. in the Bollingen Series XXXIII in 1952). A selection of views by modern painters on their art is to be found in G. Charbonnier, *Le Monologue du peintre* (1959), and R. L. Herbert (ed.), *Modern Artists on Art* (1964). To these should be added Brassai, *Conversations avec Picasso* (1964), and Françoise Gilot and Carleton Lake, *Vivre avec Picasso* (1965). Important views by modern composers on music will be found in Schoenberg, *Letters* (1964), and the conversations between Stravinsky and Robert Craft: *Stravinsky in Conversation with Robert Craft* (a Pelican book of 1962 containing *Conversations with Igor Stravinsky* (1958) and *Memoirs and Commentaries* (1959)), *Expositions and Developments* (1962), and *Dialogues and a Diary* (1968). A varied selection of texts on 'modernism' by writers, painters, and musicians will be found in H. M. Block and H. Salinger, *The Creative Vision: Modern European*

Writers on their Art (1960); R. Ellmann and C. Feidelson, *The Modern Tradition* (1965); J. Cruickshank, *Aspects of the Modern European Mind* (1969).

Criticism. Even a selective bibliography of interesting secondary works would quickly reach enormous proportions. The following books are in the nature of a few tentative suggestions:

R. Barthes, *Le Degré zéro de l'écriture* (1953);

M. Blanchot, *L'Espace littéraire* (1955) and *Le Livre à venir* (1959);

M. Butor, *Répertoire* (to date 3 vols.: 1960, 1964, 1968);

G. Hartman, *The Unmediated Vision: an Interpretation of Wordsworth, Hopkins, Rilke and Valéry* (1966);

F. Kermode, *Romantic Image* (1957);

W. Mellers, *Caliban Reborn: Renewal in Twentieth-Century Music* (1968);

D. Mitchell, *The Language of Modern Music* (1963; paperback 1966);

Marthe Robert, *L'Ancien et le nouveau: de Don Quichotte à Franz Kafka* (1963).

2. Proust

EIGHT words emerge from the silence, hang for a moment in the air, then die away: 'Longtemps, je me suis couché de bonne heure.' Perhaps they settle in some corner of the reader's mind, to be re-activated later by an allusion; but other sounds, other words, fill up the silence, and to all intents and purposes they disappear. Yet the black print holds them prisoner, thirty-five letters on the white page. Or does it? Since they make up not the statement of a logical proposition but the utterance of an individual person it is not enough to check the words in the dictionary; we have to ask not: 'What do these words mean?' but: 'What do these words mean when spoken by this person?' And why does he break the silence with them and with no others? Who is he, this 'I' who goes to bed so early? Marcel, we say, reading on, and perhaps Marcel Proust, but is that really an answer? What is the relation between the name Marcel and the voice that speaks, between the name and its owner?

This is not only our problem as readers; it is primarily Marcel's own. The three thousand three hundred pages that follow provide the most subtle, tenacious, and profound exploration of it that has ever been undertaken, as the 'I' of that opening sentence unfolds in search of its own identity. We must try to map out some of the central features of that quest.

Appropriately enough the novel opens in the hinterland between sleep and waking, where the self first takes consciousness of itself:

Quand je m'éveillais au milieu de la nuit, comme j'ignorais où je me trouvais, je ne savais même pas au premier instant qui j'étais; j'avais seulement dans sa simplicité première le sentiment de l'existence comme il peut frémir au fond d'un animal; j'étais plus dénué que l'homme des cavernes; mais alors le souvenir — non encore du lieu ou j'étais, mais de quelques-uns de ceux que j'avais habités et où j'aurais pu être — venait à moi comme un secours d'en haut pour me tirer du néant d'où je n'aurais pu sortir tout seul; je passais en une seconde par-dessus des siècles de civilisation, et l'image confusément entrevue de lampes à pétrole, puis de chemises à col rabattu, recomposaient peu à peu les traits originaux de mon moi. (I. 5–6)[1]

There are thus four stages in the journey from sleep to waking life. First there is sleep itself, a purely negative experience of non-being, 'néant'; then comes the sheer animal sensation of pure being; only after this do images and memory begin to return, still dependent on the body, on the physical disposition of the limbs, a memory which takes no account of strict chronology but indiscriminately jumbles impressions from the whole of the sleeper's past life, any one of which might correspond to the present reality; and finally, after this, full consciousness returns, bringing with it the recognition of which room he has in fact been sleeping in, what has happened the day before and what he has to do that day. His 'moi' has been recomposed and he can now get up.

Sometimes, when we arrive in a new town, or move into a new room, we experience an analogous sensation to that of waking up, but spread out over a longer period of time. The strangeness, the newness of everything around us, makes it difficult for us to get our bearings, but eventually we always triumph over these circumstances, just as eventually we are always able to get up and go about our daily tasks. What makes it possible for us to do this is not consciousness itself, but habit, which tends to go hand in hand with consciousness:

L'habitude! aménageuse habile mais bien lente, et qui commence par laisser souffrir notre esprit pendant des semaines dans une installation provisoire, mais que malgré tout il est bien heureux de trouver, car sans l'habitude et réduit à ses seuls moyens, il serait impuissant à nous rendre un logis habitable. (I. 8)

But here we begin to discern a curious quality of habit: it makes the room habitable by effectively sealing us off from it, by reducing it from this unique room to a room I know and therefore take for granted, cease to see. Habit allows us to go about our business in

---

[1] All references are to the three-volume Pléiade edition of *A la recherche du temps perdu*.

the world only by reducing everything to its most general terms; it is not truth but a cliché of the mind which we take to be truth. Thus it is only when Marcel hears his grandmother's voice over the telephone, divorced, that is, from the rest of her person which he has so long taken for granted, that he feels he is hearing it for the first time: the frail voice of an old woman. Again, it is only because he surprises her in the house before she has had time to prepare herself for the encounter with him, to put on the face to meet the faces that we meet, that he realizes that he has before him a crazy old woman and not some abstraction of habit called his grandmother.

Habit, then, has two aspects. On the one hand it renders the room habitable and makes it possible for us to go about our daily tasks; but it does this at the cost of reducing everything to a generality. We tame the world around us by adapting everything in it to some prior generalized notion that we have of things, so that to live in the world of habit is to live shut up in a private world, incapable of noticing what goes on around us—since everything that happens is immediately neutralized by being related to what we already know. But is it even really we who know? Habit deadens our response to the world by deadening our awareness of ourselves. The individual himself becomes a ghost who is given consistency only by the way other people think of him; and as the way other people think of us differs according to their social status, political views, and private desires, we become phantoms with as many different selves as there are people who know us. The 'moi' that Marcel so elaborately recomposes as sleep gives way to consciousness seems only to exist by reason of the space he occupies:

Or, comme le moi vit incessamment en pensant une quantité de choses, qu'il n'est que la pensée de ces choses, quand par hasard au lieu d'avoir devant lui ces choses, il pense tout d'un coup à soi-même, il ne trouve qu'un appareil vide, quelque chose qu'il ne connaît pas, auquel pour lui donner quelque réalité il ajoute le souvenir d'une figure aperçue dans la glace. Ce drôle de sourire, ces moustaches inégales, c'est cela qui disparaîtra de la surface de la terre. (III. 466)

Is the self then made up of nothing but stray thoughts on the one hand and a strange face seen in a mirror on the other? Most people keep their minds turned firmly away from such dizzying reflections, but for Marcel to find an answer to these questions is more than personal curiosity, it is an ineluctable necessity. For if the world of habit is the true one, then we are indeed nothing and less than nothing, we have no self at all. But obscurely he feels that this is not the case, that we live in time as well as in space, and that therefore each one of us is a unique individual because each one has a unique past which reflects upon his present. The very awareness of the gap between the random thoughts and the stranger's face suggests that there has been a time when the gap was not there. Once again sleep and waking provide a paradigm case, but now the progressive stages of waking can be read not as a recovery of the self but as a loss of the self:

Alors du noir orage qu'il nous semble avoir traversé (mais nous ne disons même pas *nous*) nous sortons gisants, sans pensées: un 'nous' qui serait sans contenu. Quel coup de marteau l'être ou la chose qui est là a-t-elle reçu pour tout ignorer, stupéfaite jusqu'au moment où la mémoire accourue lui rend la conscience ou la personalité? . . . Certes, on peut prétendre qu'il n'y a qu'un temps, pour la futile raison que c'est en regardant la pendule qu'on a constaté n'être qu'un quart d'heure ce qu'on avait cru une journée. Mais au moment où on le constate, on est justement un homme éveillé, plongé dans le temps des hommes éveillés, on a déserté l'autre temps. Peut-être même plus qu'un autre temps: une autre vie. (II. 981-3)

Instead of a gulf, a 'néant' from which the self is rescued, is not sleep perhaps the true home of the self, like that sea from which mankind first emerged at the dawn of time, 'notre milieu vital où il faille replonger notre sang pour retrouver nos forces'? But if that is so, how can a waking man re-enter that other life and yet remain awake enough to know it?

Just as the first thought on waking up is the consciousness of separation, which is also the consciousness of self, so there is in each individual life a moment when the self becomes conscious of itself as unique—and this too is the result of loss, separation. Thus Marcel's first memory, beyond which he cannot go, is of his mother's kiss withheld. The kiss, which he compares to the host at mass, is the tangible symbol of communion with the world; it reflects a universe in which there is no distinction between the self and other people or between the self and nature. It is because his mother withholds her kiss (because Swann is coming to dinner) that Marcel is forced to recognize that his desires and those of other people do not always match; that other people, even those who are closest to us, have thoughts and desires which we can never discover. This is his very earliest memory, to which, on waking up, he always returns, yet not out of morbidity, but because this awareness of separation is nothing other than the self's first awareness of itself. The kiss withheld is but the earliest demonstration of the law that our only consciousness of unity, of a fullness of being, comes when we no longer possess it; for, possessing it, we are not conscious of it: the only paradise is paradise lost.

How then to regain the lost paradise? The force of habit is bent upon making us forget the loss by making us forget ourselves, but for Marcel the smooth surface of daily life ruled over by the goddess of habit is too frequently wrenched apart by intimations of another life, another and more meaningful state of being, for him ever to be completely at his ease in it. The story of his childhood and youth is the story of these intimations, and how he responded to them. But before we examine these there is one more example of the consciousness of loss, something that Marcel insists on a good deal, which we ought to consider.

The imagination of childhood is entirely subjective, projecting its reveries upon the world as the magic lantern projects the story of Gilbert le Mauvais over the walls of Marcel's room at Combray. Implicit in it is the belief that simply to know the name of a person is to know the person, and that by possessing the former we automatically possess the latter:

Les mots nous présentent des choses une petite image claire et usuelle comme celles que l'on suspend aux murs des écoles pour donner aux enfants l'exemple de ce qu'est un établi, un oiseau, une fourmilière, choses conçues comme pareilles à toutes celles de même sorte. Mais les noms présentent des personnes — et des villes qu'ils nous habituent à croire individuelles, uniques comme des personnes — une image confuse qui tire d'eux, de leur sonorité éclatante ou sombre, la couleur dont elle est peinte . . . (I. 387–8)

B

Thus the name of 'Parme' seemed to him to be 'compact, lisse, mauve et doux', and he imagined the houses as having similar characteristics; 'Florence' he imagined 'semblable à une corolle, parce qu'elle s'appelait la cité des lys'; and as for Mme de Guermantes, descendant of that Geneviève de Brabant whose image the magic lantern projected on the walls of his room, 'je me la représentais avec les couleurs d'une tapisserie ou d'un vitrail, d'une autre manière que le reste des personnes vivantes'. But the imagination cannot survive the confrontation with reality. Just as Marcel became aware of himself as a distinct being at the same time as he became aware of the impossible distance between himself and other people, so here he becomes aware of other people when he recognizes how little they resemble what his imagination has made of the names they bear. Like Troilus forced to acknowledge Cressida's faithlessness by the evidence of his eyes, Marcel watches Mme de Guermantes in church and tries to reconcile the name with the person:

'C'est cela, ce n'est que cela, Mme de Guermantes!' disait la mine attentive et étonnée avec laquelle je contemplais cette image qui naturellement n'avait aucun rapport avec celles qui, sous le même nom de Mme de Guermantes, étaient apparues tant de fois dans mes songes, puisque, elle, elle n'avait pas été comme les autres arbitrairement formée par moi, mais qu'elle m'avait sauté aux yeux pour la première fois, il y a un moment seulement, dans l'église. (I. 175)

And yet the name goes on casting a glow over the person, even after Marcel has got to know Oriane and found her to be as shallow, frivolous, and vain as the rest of her sex. It is as though however often he learned the lesson that the Name is really no less arbitrary, no less a label, than the word, it still retains something of its old power. For most of us habit so dulls the senses that we accept the fact that a name is merely a label, helpful for identifying people, and no more; we live among people whose appearance and even whose place and function in life are simply the projection of our own imaginations, helped on by a few hints from reality. But if, like Marcel, we feel that there must be a relation between the person's name and himself, that he must have an essence which we can, if we make a sufficient effort, grasp, then the gap between what must be and what appears to be will force us to recognize that we live among people who change every day, who appear under a different guise every time we see them. It is because Marcel is so much more concerned with who and what people really are that he is so much more aware that they are not any one thing. Saint-Loup, for instance, first appears as a haughty and insolent aristocrat who would never dream of speaking to Marcel; immediately afterwards he is the most loyal and considerate of friends, and a republican steeped in Nietzsche and Proudhon; then the jealous lover of the actress Rachel; then a cruel husband and a homosexual who keeps mistresses as a cover for his real desires; and finally he is the only character in the novel killed in combat, a hero and a patriot. It is because Marcel is so aware of the gap between the arbitrariness of the imagination and its lack of relation to reality that the world he describes seems often to have no more centre to it than an onion. The imagination is not opposed to habit and the intellect: these merely cloak the subjective nature of the imagination.

Marcel's fascination with the aristocracy can now be understood, for only among the old families of France does the name still seem to stand for something real, to be more than a mere label. Marcel takes a peculiar pleasure in finding himself in the same room as people whose names are also the names of places, not because he is a snob but because only here does the name seem to adhere to the thing. (Similarly Marcel's interest in etymologies reveals the desire to trace a place-name back to its origin and see how it sprang from the physical nature of the place.) Marcel's need to believe that the Name reflects the person is a metaphysical need, for if it does, then by grasping the name, by turning over in our minds and on our tongues the syllables, feeling their weight and colour, we can fully know the person. But this, as he is to discover, can never be other than an illusion, shattered for the first time by the kiss withheld, and doomed to be shattered again and again as he gets to know a person or a place. The name 'Guermantes' is, in fact, the only stable thing about that family, and all the more deceptive for that, since the more we insist on an identity between the name and the object, the more bitter will our disillusion be. By a final irony it is none other than Mme Verdurin who comes to bear that sacred name when she marries the senile prince.

But there are moments when a reverse process takes place, and it is not the illusion of our imaginations that is brought home to us, but the illusion of what we normally take for reality. Just as habit makes us look at something without seeing it, so it makes us recall something without remembering it. We recall what happened but we do not remember what we felt: we look at our past as though it was that of someone else. And, in a sense, it is. Because the body is like a vase we tend to think that what it has experienced or thought is permanently present in it; but that is not the case. We die daily and our new self knows nothing of the old selves. And yet the old selves inhabit our body, they leave their trace, 'les jambes et les bras sont pleins de souvenirs engourdis', and these memories may accidentally be revived. So, when Marcel bends down to undo the buttons of his boots he suddenly feels the presence of his grandmother flooding through his limbs. It is his body that relives the moment when she had first helped him off with his boots, so many years before that his mind had forgotten the incident. And now Marcel realizes that his grandmother, who had been dead for so long, had never been dead to him at all, because he had never felt her as alive. So that, paradoxically, it is only when he becomes conscious of her presence, of her as a living person rather than an abstraction, that he becomes aware of her death.

> Ce qui nous rappelle le mieux un être, c'est justement ce que nous avions oublié (parce que c'était insignifiant, et que nous lui avons ainsi laissé toute sa force). C'est pourquoi la meilleur part de notre mémoire est hors de nous, dans un souffle pluvieux, dans l'odeur de renfermé d'une chambre ou dans l'odeur d'une première flambée, partout où nous retrouvons de nous-même ce que notre intelligence, n'en ayant pas l'emploi, avait dédaigné. . . . Hors de nous? En nous, pour mieux dire, mais dérobée à nos propres regards, dans un oubli seul que nous pouvons de temps à autre retrouver l'être que nous fûmes. . . . Au grand jour de la mémoire habituelle, les images du passé pâlissent peu à peu, s'effacent, il ne reste plus rien d'elles, nous ne le retrouverons plus. (I. 643)

Ordinary memory is the memory of habit, of the intellect, which smooths out the specific in favour of a generalized view of the past.

It is always those senses which are the furthest removed from the intellect (smell, taste, touch) which reawaken our past selves. Thus it is only when Marcel tastes the *madeleine*, not when he sees it, that the whole of Combray floods through his mind and senses, Combray not as he consciously remembered it, but Combray as it felt when he lived in it. And he explains this by saying that he had probably seen *madeleines* between that time and this, so that they too had taken on the familiar, generalized look of habit. Taste and smell, however, remain uncorrupted.

The *madeleine* episode occupies a key position in the structure of the novel, since without it there would have been no Combray, no two 'ways', and therefore no book. But if involuntary memory is the most striking reminder that the life of habit and the intellect is not the only life, it is far from being the sole reminder. Marcel himself, at the end of the novel, distinguishes between memories and impressions, and the opening volumes give many examples of the way in which the external world—a hawthorn bush, the reflection of the sun in water, certain trees—seem suddenly to strike at our imagination, causing us the same thrill of pleasure, the same wrenching of habit, as does the influx of involuntary memory.

Particularly interesting is a scene which takes place in one of Marcel's walks towards Méséglise, when he suddenly sees the sun reflected in the water and his heart leaps in his body:

> Et voyant sur l'eau et à la face du mur un pâle sourire répondre au sourire du ciel, je m'écriai dans tout mon enthousiasme en brandissant mon parapluie refermé: 'Zut, zut, zut, zut.' Mais en même temps je sentis que mon devoir eût été de ne pas m'en tenir à ces mots opaques et de tâcher de voir plus clair dans mon ravissement.
>
> Et c'est à ce moment-là encore — grâce à un paysan qui passait, l'air déjà d'être d'assez mauvaise humeur, qui le fut davantage quand il faillit recevoir mon parapluie dans la figure, et qui répondit sans chaleur à mes 'beau temps, n'est-ce pas, il fait bon marcher' — que j'appris que les mêmes émotions ne se produisent pas simultanément dans un ordre préétabli, chez tous les hommes. (I. 155)

Here, as with involuntary memory, the joy felt by Marcel seems to be dependent on a chance object and yet, if he is to get anything lasting out of it, to be equally dependent on his making sense of the encounter. Instead of responding with simple inarticulate cries of pleasure he should have tried to see more clearly 'dans mon ravissement'. But the different reactions of Marcel and the peasant to the same scene also show that it is not enough to react by saying that it is a beautiful day—such words too are opaque, no more expressive of what he really felt than the inarticulate 'zut'. In a sense, then, Marcel is as much outside his sudden sensation of joy as is the peasant, and will remain so unless he can say something more meaningful about it than either 'zut' or 'beau temps'.

But however hard he tries, Marcel never seems to be able to 'make sense' of his experience before these natural phenomena, and consequently they always slip away and disappear, leaving nothing more than the memory of an encounter, but not the feel of it. Even when he succeeds in putting down on paper what he has felt on seeing the three spires on the ride to Martinville, he fails to convey why it is that he reacts as he does, while in the other two major instances, that of the hawthorn bush and that of the three trees at Hudimesnil, the pleasure of perception is accompanied by a keen sense of frustration: 'Le sentiment qu'elles éveillaient en moi restait obscur et vague, cherchant à se dégager, à venir adhérer à leurs fleurs' (I. 139), he says about the first, while of his last glimpse of the three trees he says: 'dans leur gesticulation naïve et passionnée, je reconnaissais le regret impuissant d'un être aimé qui a perdu l'usage de la parole, sent qu'il ne pourra nous dire ce qu'il veut, et que nous ne savons pas deviner' (I. 719). These natural objects seem to be gesturing towards us, but it is in vain that we try to interpret their gestures. Marcel knows that if only he could understand what they were trying to say, if only he could somehow 'hold' these trees, that hawthorn bush, in his consciousness, 'hold' them as they first appeared to him in that breath-taking moment, he would hold a secret more precious than any other, the secret of life itself. But the longer he goes on looking at them the more certain he is that the feeling will fade, that habit and its deadening effect will take over, that he will see in the scene no more than had the peasant.

It is thus not surprising that the frustrated longing before a land-scape or a natural object should be followed by the desire for a

woman who will embody this landscape but who will be easier to
possess:

Mais si ce désir qu'une femme apparût ajoutait pour moi aux charmes
de la nature quelque chose de plus exaltant, les charmes de la nature, en
retour, élargissaient ce que celui de la femme aurait eu de trop restreint.
Il me semblait que la beauté des arbres, c'était encore la sienne, et que
l'âme de ces horizons, du village de Roussainville, des livres que je lisais
cette année-là, son baiser me la livrerait . . . la passante qu'appelait mon
désir me semblait être non un exemplaire quelconque de ce type général:
la femme, mais un produit nécessaire et naturel de ce sol. (1. 156-7)

Here already we see what Marcel is later to call the pathological
aspect of love, the reason why all love is an aberration since it is
always in search of something other than the beloved. The desire
for a woman is the desire for a possessable incarnation of the landscape, and is thus the direct outcome of his failure to 'grasp' it by
himself. But is a woman easier to possess than a landscape? Physically no doubt she is, but since it is not just her body that is desirable, mere physical possession is hardly sufficient: 'Je savais que
je ne posséderais pas cette jeune cycliste, si je ne possédais aussi ce
qu'il y avait dans ses yeux. Et c'était par conséquent toute sa vie
qui m'inspirait.'

But since a woman's name does not yield her essence, the desire
for a woman only makes her inaccessibility more obvious. No less
than natural objects, women emit signs which we strive to interpret
but never with any guarantee of success, while their essence remains
hidden from us. Marcel's first encounter with Gilberte sets the
pattern for all his later relationships with women. He has lingered
behind his family on the walk through Swann's property, and she
seems to have done the same, for suddenly the two children come
face to face across an alley bordered by flowers. He fixes her with a
look which, he says, would have liked to 'toucher, capturer,
emmener le corps qu'il regarde et l'âme avec lui'; then his look
changes to one of beseechment, begging her mutely to acknowledge his presence. She in turn glances round to see if his father
and grandfather are watching, then

elle laissa ses regards filer de toute leur longueur dans ma direction, sans
expression particulière, sans avoir l'air de me voir, mais avec une fixité

et un sourire dissimulé que je ne pouvais interpréter d'après les notions que l'on m'avait données sur la bonne éducation que comme une preuve d'outrageant mépris; et sa main esquissait en même temps un geste indécent, auquel, quand il était addressé en public à une personne qu'on ne connaissait pas, le petit dictionnaire de civilité que je portais en moi ne donnait qu'un seul sens, celui d'une intention insolente. (1. 141)

And then she is called on, leaving him with nothing but her name and a series of gestures which he interprets as best he can according to the code he thinks he should use. As we learn at the very end of the novel, he interprets wrongly.

Who is Gilberte? Who is Albertine? What is the relation between the name and the woman who bears it? The metamorphoses through which they pass are even more dizzying than those of someone like Saint-Loup, simply because Marcel is more aware of them, more tormented at the discrepancy between their old selves and their new selves, between what he had taken them to be and what he now sees they are. But whenever Marcel imagines that he has understood them he ceases to love them, which means he ceases to see them; understanding here, as with the room in which he wakes up, is simply another word for the reassertion of habit. The syndrome of habit as it relates to love is easy to trace and impossible to escape from: since what has drawn the lover in the first place is the beloved's 'otherness', for her to lose this is equivalent to losing his love; but to maintain it is to cause him unbearable anguish in the knowledge that there is a portion of her life that he does not know. Thus when Marcel has finally made up his mind to break with Albertine, since he is beginning to find her a bore and an imposition, she reveals to him her friendship for Mlle Vinteuil, with its lesbian implications, and so sets the whole complex cycle of desire and frustration in motion once again. And, in a parallel peripety later in the novel, it is just when he finally decides to let her go free and himself travel to Venice (where he may forget her as he forgot Gilberte, by an effort of the will) that he learns of her escape, and all the old love and anguish flood back into his body no less powerfully and spontaneously than had his childhood in Combray on tasting the *madeleine*. The conscious mind can never forestall the senses, we can never imagine what true joy or suffering will be like since its characteristic is that it comes to us from outside us.

The desire to possess the beloved is thus bound to be frustrated. He may keep Albertine a prisoner in his house, but then either she bores him because, as a prisoner, she has ceased to embody the freedom of the sea which was what he longed to possess in her, or he realizes that even as a prisoner she retains her liberty, however much he may caress her: 'Je sentais que je touchais seulement l'enveloppe close d'un être qui par l'intérieur accédait à l'infini.' Even the kiss, which had seemed to the child Marcel to be the sign of a total communion, and which, a little later, he thought would yield up to him the essence of Roussainville, is now seen to be nothing but a mockery, a final affirmation that the union of two bodies is far from being the union of two souls.

But women, unlike trees, can talk, and so, we would think, make it possible for the lover to know them in their essence, as they really are, rather than the changing creatures they appear to the senses. But that is to forget the encounter with the peasant on the road to Méséglise, and Marcel's realization that words are inadequate to convey private sensations. Because he kisses her Albertine thinks Marcel loves her, but he, less naïve, recognizes that her saying she loves him does not necessarily mean that she does so. And because Marcel is so desperate to find out the truth, he is rewarded with nothing but lies. For what is the truth? In normal social intercourse, we do not demand of people that they justify their actions and testify to the truth of what they say. Marcel is aware of this when he goes out into society—the words of Mme Verdurin, of Norpois, of Charlus are, no less than their gestures, to be interpreted according to a code rather than implicitly believed. But when it comes to a woman one loves, what is the code? For in reality Albertine is not concealing anything from Marcel; he is only trying to find something she herself does not know she has. When he probes and questions her, she answers the first thing that comes into her mind, or else what she thinks he wants to hear. The past is not something fixed and stable which she can call up at any time. Prodded by Marcel, Albertine's memory wanders over her own past, inventing, remembering, or unconsciously mingling memory and invention.

Marcel's anguish lies not so much in the revelation of suspected relationships as in never being able to know for certain if she is telling the truth or not. That is why it is only when she is asleep that he feels he does to some extent possess the real Albertine:

> En fermant les yeux, en perdant la conscience, Albertine avait dépouillé, l'un après l'autre, ces différents caractères d'humanité qui m'avaient déçu depuis le jour où j'avais fait sa connaissance. Elle n'était plus animée que de la vie inconsciente des végétaux, des arbres, vie plus différente de la mienne, plus étrange, et qui cependant m'appartenait davantage. (III. 70)

The more 'other' the beloved becomes, the further she gets from the social images we have of her, the more she appears to be—in some mysterious way—oneself. Eve rose out of Adam's rib; Marcel may be in love with Albertine because she incarnates the sea, but the sea itself is only an incarnation of something else, of that which is totally other only because it was once totally himself:

> Dans les personnes que nous aimons, il y a, immanent à elles, un certain rêve que nous ne savons pas toujours discerner, mais que nous poursuivons. . . . Du reste, à cause justement de cet individuel auquel on s'acharne, les amours pour les personnes sont déjà un peu des aberrations. (III. 839)

But what is it we desire? When Marcel first catches sight of Gilberte he mutely pleads with her to acknowledge his presence, and later he muses over an encounter with Albertine: 'Si elle m'avait vu, qu'avais-je pu lui représenter? Du sein de quel univers me distinguait-elle?' What Marcel ultimately longs for is to possess that look from another universe without its ceasing to be other. This is why homosexual love is seen as being so much more primitive, so much less distorted by society than heterosexual love; for here at least there is a frank acknowledgement that the sexual partner is both other and oneself. If love is only the effort of the self to incarnate desire so as to possess itself, then there is no difference in kind between Charlus asking to be beaten more viciously in Jupien's male brothel as the German planes swoop down over wartime Paris (the horrific scene that forms the nadir of the novel) and Marcel's own efforts to possess the women he loves. The former is simply more blatant, less disguised by social and moral codes. Unlike the society of the Faubourg St. Germain, that of the invert does not merely appear to be, but really is closer to the primitive roots of man, made up as it is of the original hermaphrodites, men and women who are each both man and woman.

But every kind of love which looks for satisfaction from the object of its love is doomed to failure. Like the three trees at Hudimesnil, the women in Marcel's life beckon mutely and disappear, and soon the soothing hand of habit softens the pain of loss, and the self that loved joins the myriads of other dead selves in the recesses of the body, only to be briefly resurrected by a chance encounter, an unexpected word, a smell, a taste.

The failure of love seems to presage the failure of Marcel's quest, a quest all the more confusing in that Marcel has only fitfully understood his goal. In relation to Names and love, it was an attempt to incarnate a dream at the same time as to understand the world; in relation to the flashes of involuntary memory, of the encounters with nature and with women, it was the attempt to possess, and thereby make sense of, the sudden gaps that appeared in the smooth surface of habit. At the end of the novel Marcel seems as far from achieving one of these aims as the other. But this is not quite true, for in the meantime he has come to understand the nature of art and learnt how to apply its lessons to himself.

Among the many desires felt by the young Marcel is the desire to write. But this is subject to a double frustration: on the one hand he feels himself to be inadequate, without the powers of description, or the ability to think of a subject about which to write. On the other hand his experience with the peasant makes him aware of the fact that words are mere labels, generalizers, unable to convey anything except the tired life of habit. Art then seems pointless, the mere prolongation of the meaningless life of habit, the minute reproduction of a world that is all surface. But, as he comes to see, while this may be true of fiction, it is decidedly not true of music:

. . . cette musique me semblait quelque chose de plus vrai que tous les livres connus. Par instants je pensais que cela tenait à ce que ce qui est senti par nous de la vie, ne l'étant pas sous forme d'idées, sa traduction littéraire, c'est-à-dire intellectuelle, en rend compte, l'explique, l'analyse, mais ne le recompose pas comme la musique où les sons semblent prendre l'inflexion de l'être, reproduire cette pointe intérieure et extrême des sensations qui est la partie qui nous donne cette ivresse spécifique que nous retrouvons de temps en temps et que, quand nous disons: 'Quel beau temps! quel beau soleil!' nous ne faisons nullement connaître au prochain, en qui le même soleil et le même temps éveillent des vibrations toutes différentes. (III. 374-5)

In music there is no distinction between form and content, between word and meaning, for the sound is its meaning, both abstract and concrete at the same time. But music is a language without issue, and if the composer can reveal to himself and others that 'pointe intérieure et extrême des sensations' which is the sole source of joy, what is the artist whose tools are poor words to do?

The answer is to be given in the climactic series of revelations of involuntary memory which begin the coda of the novel. The law of being, as Marcel had experienced it, said that we only understand that which we no longer feel, that we only desire that which we can never know. But now he discovers the real law of the lost paradise: it is not till something has been lost that it can really be found. Involuntary memory does not just call up a moment of the past, but something common at the same time to the past and the present, and thus more essential than either. Living through an experience we cannot grasp it with our consciousness, and when we do it means it is gone. But with involuntary memory it is both present to the senses and to the mind:

Mais qu'un bruit, qu'une odeur, déjà entendu ou respirée jadis, le soient de nouveau, à la fois dans le présent et dans le passé, réels sans être actuels, idéaux sans être abstraits, aussitôt l'essence permanente et habituellement cachée des choses se trouve libérée et notre vrai moi, qui, parfois, depuis longtemps, semblait mort, mais ne l'était pas entièrement, s'éveille, s'anime en recevant la céleste nourriture qui lui est apportée. Une minute affranchie de l'ordre du temps a recréé en nous, pour la sentir, l'homme affranchi de l'ordre du temps . . . situé hors du temps, que pourrait-il craindre de l'avenir? (III. 872-3)

This is why Marcel could never think of a subject about which to write; to believe that truth rests in the subject is to go along with the falsehoods of habit. For incidents are always arbitrary, whether

Marcel were to invent them or simply write about those in his own
life, since the incidents in his own life are so much a matter of
chance. Had he never known Swann he would never have gone to
Balbec, had he not gone there he would never have met Saint-Loup
and Charlus and Albertine, his whole life would have followed a
different path. And what if Mlle de Stermaria had turned up when
he waited for her, or he had met the chambermaid of Mme Putbus?
We begin to understand the cause of the anguish felt by the young
Marcel that evening in Combray when his mother withheld her kiss.
Not only are other people opaque, their innermost selves and
desires hidden from us, but our own realization that we are ourselves
and no other is also a recognition that for everything that happens
to us a million possibilities are ruled out. That is the reason for
Marcel's dissatisfaction with realist art, with intellectual conversation, with friendship: it merely yields the possible, the world
of meaningless incidents, the world of habit. Music, on the other
hand, appears to have that ineluctable quality which is the mark of
authenticity and, by understanding the nature of involuntary
memory, Marcel begins to see how he too might write a work of art
that would be authentic, necessary, and therefore true:

> Et déjà les conséquences se pressaient dans mon esprit; car qu'il
> s'agît de réminiscences dans le genre du bruit de la fourchette ou du
> goût de la madeleine, ou de ces vérités écrites à l'aide de figures dont
> j'essayais de chercher le sens dans ma tête où, clochers, herbes folles,
> elles composaient un grimoire compliqué et fleuri, leur premier caractère
> était que je n'étais pas libre de les choisir, qu'elles m'étaient données
> telles quelles. Et je sentais que ce devait être la griffe de leur authenticité.
> Je n'avais pas été chercher les deux pavés inégaux de la cour où j'avais
> buté. Mais justement la façon fortuite, inévitable, dont la sensation avait
> été rencontrée, contrôlait la vérité du passé qu'elle ressuscitait . . .
> (III. 879)

What he has been looking for all his life is not outside him; but it is
not simply inside him, in the psyche, the imagination, for these too,
as we saw, are characterized by their arbitrariness. We have seen
Marcel trying to make sense of his feelings in front of objects, places,
women. Now he realizes that the truth will only reveal itself by a
creative act, for 'le livre aux caractères figurés, non tracés par nous,

est notre seul livre. Non que ces idées que nous formons ne puissent être justes logiquement, mais nous ne savons pas si elles sont vraies.'

The role of art, the role of Marcel's novel, is now apparent. It must reveal and make sensible the laws under which his life could be lived, however different the people and places he might have known; it must create that state of being which is prior to any event and action we undertake, that being 'qui serait sans contenu' because it would be all potentiality. But what is this being except the self asleep, or the self on the threshold of sleep, feeling only 'dans sa simplicité première le sentiment de l'existence comme il peut frémir au fond d'un animal'? For sleep is not only a 'néant', it is, rather, the fullness of time, for 'un homme qui dort tient en cercle autour de lui le fil des heures, l'ordre des années et des mondes'. But sleep itself is only that because it is the time, as we saw with Albertine, when the body comes into its own, more animal than human, more vegetable than animal. Even when memories begin to appear to the sleeper who is waking up, these are still dictated by the body:

> Mon corps, trop engourdi pour remuer, cherchait, d'après la forme de sa fatigue, à repérer la position de ses membres pour en induire la direction du mur, la place des meubles, pour reconstruire et pour nommer la demeure où il se trouvait. Sa mémoire, la mémoire de ses côtes, de ses genoux, de ses épaules, lui présentait successivement plusieurs des chambres où il avait dormi . . . (I. 6)

But already here the choice is limited by what the body has lived through, no longer master of all possibilities as was the state of pure sleep or the first instant of waking up. And we see now that the relation of these two stages is the same as that of involuntary memory and of art. We see too the particular significance of Swann's role. For if it is because of him that Marcel's life takes the path it does, his love affair with Odette also plays a crucial role in revealing to Marcel that his own lifelong search is not the result of mother-fixation or persistent ill health, but is rather a permanent, almost a biological factor, prior to the individual, common to mankind. Without Swann Marcel would have thought himself unique. As it is, delving down beneath the generalities of social life to 'ces mondes que nous appelons des individus et que sans l'art nous ne connaîtrons jamais', he arrives at the fundamental laws of the body which are both unique and common to all mankind.

But before Marcel can sit down and write or translate the book of himself, one final revelation awaits him. That is the discovery that the man who is 'affranchi de l'ordre du temps' does not, as he had at first thought, live in a kind of eternity. The final law that he has to learn is that his freedom from time is only the ability to understand time, to grasp it with his senses and his consciousness as he had grasped the essence of Combray. For if the body exists in a timeless realm, it also moves steadily from birth through maturity to death. The body does not live according to clock time, but it grows and flowers and decays, this body, my body, the only one I possess. That is the last and hardest lesson, and when Marcel has learnt it, seeing the passage of time on the faces of all those he had known in the past, he finally realizes that the time has come for him to begin the novel that will allow him to bring together the name Marcel and the self that bears that name.

Marcel's novel is an attempt to make conscious the whole of the body, to resurrect all the dead selves, and to catch in words the very movement of time itself as that body moves towards death. What Marcel had never been able to 'catch' in the flashes of involuntary memory, in the joyful perception of the sunlight reflected in water, in Gilberte or Albertine, he finally catches in words. But they are words cunningly wrought into a work of art, a formal structure, and their meaning is inseparable from it. It is up to the reader to let the words echo in his mind, from the first sentence to the last, as they echo in the mind of the man who sits in his cork-lined room, night after night and day after day, writing himself into the total consciousness of himself. But if the reader does this, a strange phenomenon will occur, for 'en réalité chaque lecteur est, quand il lit, le propre lecteur de soi-même. L'ouvrage de l'écrivain n'est qu'une espèce d'instrument optique qu'il offre au lecteur afin de lui permettre de discerner ce que, sans ce livre, il n'eût peut-être pas vu en soi-même' (III. 911). As Vinteuil's music led Marcel to the final consciousness of all his senses, so Proust's book will lead the willing reader.

NOTE

MARCEL PROUST, 1871–1922, was born of a Catholic father and a Jewish mother into a family of solid Parisian bourgeois. From an early age he was afflicted with asthma, which made him something of an invalid all his life. He discovered, too, that he had homosexual inclinations which, unlike Gide, he found it impossible to justify. After brilliant but half-hearted studies at the Lycée Condorcet and the university, he began to frequent the salons of the aristocratic Faubourg Saint-Germain, and to publish slight essays on art, literature, and society life, meanwhile secretly working on a huge novel which he abandoned before it was complete. In 1905 his mother, probably the only person he ever whole-heartedly loved, died, and in the following year Proust moved to 102 Boulevard Haussmann, where he shut himself away from the world and devoted himself to *A la recherche du temps perdu*. *Du côté de chez Swann* was published by Grasset in 1913 at his own expense after being turned down by several publishers, but by the end of the war the tide had turned and he was awarded the Prix Goncourt for *A l'ombre des jeunes filles en fleurs*. He died with his novel still growing under his hands and his reputation firmly established.

Editions. Proust was a one-book man, whose whole life was an apprenticeship for the writing of *A la recherche*. Nevertheless, it would be wrong to take him at his word and imagine that he idled away his early years. Apart from *Les Plaisirs et les jours* (1896), and the translations of Ruskin which appeared in 1904 and 1906, he wrote *Jean Santeuil* (3 vols.) and *Contre Sainte-Beuve*, both of which have been published since the war, in 1952 and 1954 respectively. *A la recherche* presents editing problems of fearsome dimensions as a result of Proust's method of adding to the bulk of his manuscripts any thoughts or scenes that later came to mind. As a result the Pléiade edition in three volumes (ed. P. Clarac and A. Ferré, 1954) is far more complete than the original fifteen-volume Gallimard edition, and is likely to remain the standard edition for a long time to come.

Criticism. It is virtually impossible to write badly about Proust for the same reason that it is virtually impossible to write really well about him: *A la recherche* provides the best commentary on its own aims and achievements. Notable recent criticism includes the two essays by M. Butor, 'Les "moments" de Marcel Proust' and the brilliant 'Les œuvres d'art imaginaires chez Proust' (reprinted in Butor, *Essais sur les modernes* (1964)); and G. Deleuze, *Marcel Proust et les signes* (1964). Other suggestive studies are those by Samuel Beckett, *Proust* (1931), and L. Bersani, *Marcel Proust: the Fictions of Life and of Art* (1965). The standard biography is now G. Painter's two-volume *Marcel Proust: a Biography* (1959 and 1965), though this lacks the genuine understanding of its subject displayed by A. Maurois's *A la recherche de Marcel Proust* (1949). A recent, succinct introduction is Adèle King, *Proust* (1968).

3. Paul Valéry

'Je jouis sans fin de mon propre cerveau', wrote Valéry in a poem composed as early as 1887; but opposed to these intellectual inner forces by which he was to be attracted throughout his life were emotional outer forces from which he was not always able, and indeed not always willing, to isolate himself. 'J'ai dû commencer vers l'âge de neuf ou de dix ans', he suggested, 'à me faire une sorte d'île de mon esprit, quoique d'un naturel assez sociable et communicatif.' Consequently Valéry found himself on the frontier between the inner world and the outer world, the mind and the senses, the conscious and the unconscious.

But although Valéry, looking back on his life, was able to recognize that these two sides of his nature had existed in him from an early age, it was not until he was in his twenties that he became aware that they were fundamentally in conflict. The episode generally known as the 'nuit de Gênes', which marked the climax of his difficulties, occurred on 4 October 1892 when a stormy night in Genoa seemed to him the very symbol of the struggle going on within him between two different selves. It was the inner self, the conscious self, the intellectual self which won and Valéry decided that his destiny lay in the exploration and development of the powers of his mind, rather than in the writing of poetry, which seemed to him at this stage an essentially emotional activity, largely dependent on and appealing to the senses. He was soon to invent, in 1894, the character of Monsieur Teste, whose name of course derives, significantly, from 'tête' and of whom he says, in a striking metaphor, that 'son âme se fait une plante singulière dont la racine, et non le feuillage, pousserait vers la clarté', a phrase which admirably defines Valéry's own deeply introspective attitude during the twenty years of virtual silence which followed.

A comparison is often made between Valéry and Descartes, to

whom he was later to devote several essays, for the latter went through a similar crisis and reached a similar solution. Descartes's statement, 'Je pris un jour résolution d'étudier en moi-même', could equally well be applied to Valéry, whose M. Teste 'fait de ses yeux un usage étrange, et comme intérieur'. Furthermore, Valéry also shared at this time Descartes's obsession with the idea of finding a method by which to make the optimum use of the infinite potentialities of the human mind. His *Introduction à la méthode de Léonard de Vinci*, written in the latter part of 1894 and the early part of 1895, is in fact far more concerned with method than it is with Leonardo da Vinci, about whom Valéry really knew very little. What he admired was the capacity he attributed to Leonardo, and which was epitomized in the latter's motto, 'Hostinato rigore', for patiently and carefully tracing the hidden relationships between things, thus attaining universal knowledge. M. Teste too, in *La Soirée avec Monsieur Teste*, published in 1896, 'était arrivé à découvrir des lois de l'esprit que nous ignorons', and the volumes of the *Cahiers* dating from this period have as a recurrent theme the way in which the mind works, the mechanics of thought. In fact, Valéry was far more interested in scientific than in literary matters at this time, as is evidenced by the books on mathematics and physics he is known to have studied and by his friendships with leading scientists of the day who paid tribute to his grasp of fundamental scientific ideas even though he was inevitably lacking in specialized technical knowledge.

Yet Valéry, like M. Teste, still had another side to his character. Mme Teste, in a later part of the Teste cycle, the *Lettre de Mme Émilie Teste*, writes:

Quand il me revient de la profondeur, il a l'air de me découvrir comme une terre nouvelle! Je lui apparais inconnue, neuve, nécessaire. Il me saisit aveuglément dans ses bras, comme si j'étais un rocher de vie et de présence réelle, où ce grand génie incommunicable se heurterait, toucherait, s'accrocherait, après tant d'inhumains silences monstrueux.

Valéry's own 'return from the depths', his renewed desire to make fresh contact with the world of the senses and the emotions after his long years of silence and intellectual introspection, began to make itself felt in 1912 when he was persuaded to gather together some of his early poems with a view to publishing a volume of verse. The revision of these lines written some twenty years before was begun with reluctance and even with a feeling of hostility towards something he now regarded as completely alien to him. But gradually Valéry was recaptured by the pleasure of writing poetry, by the delight of experiencing 'ces commencements de l'état chantant, ces printemps intimes de l'invention expressive'. Although this was, in a sense, a renewal of the creative urge of his adolescence and early youth, there was, however, a difference in that Valéry's second, conscious self, assiduously developed over so many years, could now stand back and watch his unconscious self at work. It is this conscious awareness of the activities of the unconscious that forms the fundamental theme of the poem, at first intended to be of a mere thirty or forty lines, which Valéry began to write in 1912 to add to his early verse and which slowly grew, as he worked on it for the next four or five years, to more than five hundred lines.

The title of this work was originally to have been the simple and more or less self-explanatory one of *Psyché*, but since this had already been chosen by his friend Pierre Louÿs for a novel he was writing, Valéry looked round for something else and finally decided on *La Jeune Parque*, a title which admirably conveys the implication that the young woman whose thoughts and feelings are explored in the poem is symbolic of the complex web of intimate thoughts and feelings that have woven the destiny of the poet and that weave the destiny of man in general. Her awakening to the realization that within her 'une secrète sœur brûle' can reasonably be equated initially, whatever the wider implications of this complex and difficult poem may be, with Valéry's own awakening to the realization that within him a sensitive poet still existed; the temptations and hesitations she experiences probably reflect Valéry's own uncertainties during these years when he was re-examining his position; and her willingness, at the end of the poem, to face the wind, the sea, and the sun, which Valéry so vividly remembered from his younger days at Sète, no doubt has its equivalent in his decision to abandon the exclusively intellectual ambitions of M. Teste and to make a place as well for the world of the senses.

It is not therefore surprising that the twenty poems that Valéry selected from among his considerable amount of early verse to make up the *Album de vers anciens* in 1920 should, for the most part, reflect the two sides of his nature which, he now realized, had, in an ill-defined way, existed subconsciously in his early years and which he now no doubt wished consciously to emphasize. Thus the heroines of 'Féerie' and 'Même féerie' (separate versions of a poem originally entitled 'Blanc') and 'Au bois dormant' express Valéry's aspiration towards a non-sensual world, although at this early stage in his development it is of a vaguely mystical rather than a clearly intellectual nature. Similarly 'Narcisse parle', whose theme of self-contemplation attracted Valéry as early as 1890, already seems to hint at the long years of introspection which were to follow. 'César' too, which may be an early poem although it was added to the *Album de vers anciens* only in 1926, expresses the admiration for mastery and control which gave rise to the essay on Leonardo da Vinci and to the creation of M. Teste:

> César, calme César, le pied sur toute chose,
> Les poings durs dans la barbe, et l'œil sombre peuplé
> D'aigles et des combats du couchant contemplé,
> Ton cœur s'enfle, et se sent toute-puissante cause.

On the other hand, 'Naissance de Vénus' (originally 'Celle qui sort de l'onde'), 'Fragment' (later entitled 'Épisode'), 'Hélène', and 'Baignée' can be seen to herald *La Jeune Parque* by the way in which the heroines of these poems all feel the awakening of the senses symbolized by the sea. Similarly, in a poem written in 1891, 'La Fileuse', whose title may well have taken on an added depth of meaning after that of *La Jeune Parque*, lines such as:

> Mystérieusement l'ombre frêle se tresse
> Au fil de ses doigts longs et qui dorment, filée,

must have acquired a new and symbolic significance for Valéry once he had realized that the rational, methodical processes of the conscious mind were not, after all, capable of achieving everything and that the potentialities of the unconscious too had to be acknowledged.

Although the *Album de vers anciens* is therefore not untypical of Valéry, despite the inevitably derivative nature of some of these early poems, it is the later volume, *Charmes*, published in 1922 and made up of twenty-one poems written in the years immediately following *La Jeune Parque*, which is much more openly and consciously concerned with the way in which the intellectual and emotional sides of one's nature, the mind and the senses, the inner world and the outer world, have their contribution to make to the creative process.

By far the best known of these poems is 'Le Cimetière marin', begun when Valéry was writing *La Jeune Parque* and first published in 1920, which reaches much the same conclusion as the earlier, less overtly personal poem. The famous final cry in 'Le Cimetière marin': 'Le vent se lève! . . . il faut tenter de vivre', as the poet finds renewed vitality in the exhilarating feel of the sea breeze blowing over the tombs in the cemetery at Sète, could well belong to *La Jeune Parque* whose heroine also stands facing the sea:

> L'être contre le vent, dans le plus vif de l'air
> Recevant au visage un appel de la mer.

Otherwise, however, the two poems are rather different and might be said to reach the same conclusion from opposite directions: the one deals evocatively with the symbolic heroine's slow awakening to the knowledge of the temptations of life to which she finally and willingly submits, while the other analyses the way in which, until the final revolt against inaction, Valéry has succumbed to the opposite temptation of contemplating eternity and waiting for death.

'L'Abeille' also makes a plea in favour of the outer world providing the necessary stimulus to creative activity. The image of the bee's sting for which the heroine of the poem asks so insistently is clearly related to that of the serpent's bite which awakens the heroine of *La Jeune Parque*. Both have those erotic overtones which form the obvious way of symbolizing the notion of contact with the sensual world and which constantly recur in Valéry's poetry. Moreover, the 'vierge de sang' as she is described in the last lines of the earlier poem, whose breast is raised to the burning rays of the sun, awaiting the 'doux et puissant retour du délice de naître', is not unlike the heroine of 'L'Abeille' with her urgent appeal:

> Quelle, et si fine, et si mortelle,
> Que soit ta pointe, blonde abeille,
> Je n'ai, sur ma tendre corbeille,
> Jeté qu'un songe de dentelle.
>
> Pique du sein la gourde belle,
> Sur qui l'Amour meurt ou sommeille,
> Qu'un peu de moi-même vermeille
> Vienne à la chair ronde et rebelle!

One might even add a parallel between these verses and two lines from the end of 'Le Cimetière marin', however different this essentially masculine poem may otherwise be:

> Brisez, mon corps, cette forme pensive!
> Buvez, mon sein, la naissance du vent!

But although 'L'Abeille', like *La Jeune Parque* and 'Le Cimetière marin', may be concerned with the poet's realization that the mind cannot remain turned in on itself but must recognize the importance of the senses, it can also be regarded more specifically as a plea in favour of poetic inspiration and in this sense it can be linked with several other poems in *Charmes* which deal with the role of the unconscious in poetry. In 'La Pythie', for example, the uncontrolled delirium against which the high priestess of Apollo, possessed by a demon in the form of the serpent that figures so often in Valéry's work, has struggled in vain, is suddenly transformed in the last two verses into 'une voix nouvelle et blanche'. This is clearly symbolic not only of Valéry's profound mistrust of inspiration in the days of *La Soirée avec Monsieur Teste* and the *Introduction à la méthode de Léonard de Vinci*, but also of his later admission that one must come to terms with the irrational and that, once one does so, its suggestions can be directed into true creative channels:

> Belles chaînes en qui s'engage
> Le dieu dans la chair égaré.

In 'La Dormeuse' and 'Le Vin perdu', on the other hand, there is no suggestion of a struggle against the workings of the unconscious. These two admirable sonnets simply recognize that a secret and silent activity is constantly going on in the mind, just as it is within the sleeping girl of the first poem, and that a forgotten idea can suddenly bear fruit in the most unexpected way, just as the drop of wine carelessly flung into the ocean in the second poem dissolves into the water and then, in the last two lines, has a sudden and astounding fertilizing effect as huge figures leap up from the waves like Venus rising from the sea. 'Les Grenades' and 'Palme' repeat this theme using the parallel images of a slowly ripening fruit in the one case and, in the other, of a tree whose hidden roots are constantly at work, offering the reassurance that, as Valéry himself had found:

> Chaque atome de silence
> Est la chance d'un fruit mûr.

But although ripeness is all, it is not easy to seize the right moment when the fruits of these unconscious activities are ready. Several poems deal with this difficulty: 'Le Sylphe' in a light-hearted fashion, as Valéry compares inspiration to a whiff of perfume and teases his future exegetes on the errors of interpretation to which its suggestions may give rise; 'La Ceinture' in a much more serious vein, as he feels a half-formed idea slip away from him like a cloud at sunset being overtaken by the oncoming darkness; 'Poésie' in a gentler manner, as the muse of poetry reproaches him for having tried to force the flow of inspiration; and 'Les Pas' in a moving and tender way, as Valéry waits like a lover for the supreme moment when the future poem which he can feel taking shape will finally come to him.

In other poems, however, Valéry gives an increasingly active and positive role to the conscious mind. 'Intérieur' merely expresses his gratitude that the burden imposed on it should be eased, assuming that this is the sense of the image of a woman quietly and unobtrusively looking after a house and leaving its master's meditations undisturbed:

> Une esclave aux longs yeux chargés de molles chaînes
> Change l'eau de mes fleurs, plonge aux glaces prochaines,

Au lit mystérieux prodigue ses doigts purs;
Elle met une femme au milieu de ces murs
Qui, dans ma rêverie errant avec décence,
Passe entre mes regards sans briser leur absence,
Comme passe le verre au travers du soleil,
Et de la raison pure épargne l'appareil.

But in 'Aurore', the opening poem, no doubt significantly, in *Charmes*, he awakens from sleep and advances into his own soul 'tout ailé de confiance', adopting a commanding attitude towards the ideas that have been slowly forming during the night. Similarly in 'Cantique des colonnes', the underlying feminine quality of the columns is masked and disciplined by their outer coldness and rigidity; and in 'L'Insinuant' the slow and deliberate seduction of Eve by the serpent no doubt symbolizes the patient and pains-taking completion of a poem by conscious rather than unconscious processes. In 'Le Rameur' the same kind of persistence is revealed by the poet as he rows doggedly upstream, refusing to be dis-tracted by the scenes around him, and in 'La fausse morte' his refusal to abandon even the most wearisome poetic task suggests an infinite capacity for taking pains.

But whether Valéry is resolving to make contact with the sensual world, or urgently pleading for inspiration, or patiently waiting for the unconscious mind to do its work, or observing its activities, or subjecting it to the control of the conscious mind, or allowing the latter to take over completely, he is constantly preoccupied in *Charmes* with the fundamental problem of poetic creation. The poet must resist the temptation, as he declares in 'Au Platane', to lament his own impotence, but must instead cultivate a ceaseless awareness of what is going on around and within him which he can then accept, control, and develop. Despite the sadness and bitterness that this endless process of self-examination and self-analysis can bring with it, as in 'Fragments du Narcisse' or in the lines preceding the conclusion of 'Ébauche d'un serpent' when Eve has been tempted into tasting the fruit of the tree of knowledge, it ultimately leads to triumphant results, as in the latter poem which ends on an optimistic note with the affirmation, repeated in 'Ode secrète', that this substitution of knowledge for ignorance is the equivalent of the substitution of being for non-being. In other words, the power to create springs from knowledge of oneself and from recognition of the contribution that the conscious and the unconscious both have to make to the creative process.

Valéry extends his fusion of these two forces into the sphere of form as well as that of content. There is no doubt that he was by nature an extremely gifted poet, capable of writing with very little conscious effort. Early in his career he produced more than eighty poems in the year 1889 alone and in 1891 he wrote to Gide that an isolated line of poetry had come to him in his sleep: 'Assise la fileuse au bleu de la croisée', which then grew to half a dozen verses within the space of a few days. 'La Pythie', too, is known to have started from a single unconscious line: 'Pâle, profondément mordu', and Valéry repeatedly stated that 'Le Cimetière marin' began simply as a rhythm, that of the ten-syllable line divided into two groups of four and six syllables, which suggested itself to him long before he had any idea of what the subject of the poem was to be. But there is no doubt too that after his return to poetry at the time of *La Jeune Parque* he also became one of the supreme practitioners of conscious artistry. Whereas in the *Album de vers anciens* his verse had flowed easily into largely conventional moulds—over half the poems are in sonnet form and over three-quarters of them are in alexandrines—he exercises a much greater technical virtuosity in *Charmes*. An unusual and elaborate pattern of ten-line verses is adopted in four long and important poems, 'Aurore' and 'Palme' being in seven-syllable lines and 'La Pythie' and 'Ébauche d'un serpent' in eight-syllable lines. The ten-syllable lines of 'Le Cimetière marin' are grouped in verses of six lines and though there are half a dozen sonnets they show considerable variety, 'La Dormeuse' being in alexandrines, 'Le Sylphe' in five-syllable lines, and 'L'Abeille', 'La Ceinture', 'Les Grenades', and 'Le Vin perdu' in octosyllabic lines, each with a different rhyme scheme. In fact, only the first and last poems of *Charmes*, 'Aurore' and 'Palme', have precisely the same form, no doubt in order to give an impression of balance to the volume. The remaining nineteen poems all differ from one another in their structure to a greater or lesser degree.

As well as within *Charmes* as a whole there is ample evidence within individual poems of the patient and subtle craftsmanship which Valéry must have exercised in order to give his poetry its unique wealth of connotations and overtones. To choose just two obvious examples among many, the replacement of the liquid consonants and the exclusively feminine rhymes of the quatrains of 'L'Abeille', which have been quoted above, by the sharper sounds and exclusively masculine rhymes of the tercets undoubtedly adds to the impact of the poem as an appeal for creative stimulus:

> J'ai grand besoin d'un prompt tourment:
> Un mal vif et bien terminé
> Vaut mieux qu'un supplice dormant!
>
> Soit donc mon sens illuminé
> Par cette infime alerte d'or
> Sans qui l'Amour meurt ou s'endort!

Similarly 'Les Grenades' is generally agreed to refer not only to the principal image in the poem of ripe pomegranates, but also to the subsidiary images of grenades and the city of Granada which thread their way through the poem in words evocative of war or royal palaces and reinforce the impression of ideas bursting from a powerful mind:

> Dures grenades entr'ouvertes
> Cédant à l'excès de vos grains,
> Je crois voir des fronts souverains
> Éclatés de leurs découvertes!
>
> Si les soleils par vous subis,
> O grenades entre-bâillées,
> Vous ont fait d'orgueil travaillées
> Craquer les cloisons de rubis,
>
> Et que si l'or sec de l'écorce
> A la demande d'une force
> Crève en gemmes rouges de jus,
>
> Cette lumineuse rupture
> Fait rêver une âme que j'eus
> De sa secrète architecture.

Individual lines too bear witness to Valéry's skill at matching flawless 'vers donnés' with equally flawless 'vers calculés', to use his own terms. Among the latter one is naturally tempted to class those numerous lines in which, putting into practice his own definition of poetry as 'cette hésitation prolongée entre le son et le sens', he makes a characteristic and audacious use of assonance and alliteration. 'Je hume ici ma future fumée', in 'Le Cimetière marin', is one of a host of celebrated examples, as is his description of a sleeping girl: 'Dormeuse, amas doré d'ombres et d'abandons', and the dramatic opening lines of *La Jeune Parque*:

> Qui pleure là, sinon le vent simple, à cette heure
> Seule avec diamants extrêmes? . . . Mais qui pleure
> Si proche de moi-même au moment de pleurer?

With such poetry, however, it is as impossible to distinguish between what has been consciously worked out and what has been unconsciously suggested as it is to distinguish between its intellectual and its emotional appeal. The earlier conflict between the two sides of Valéry's nature has been resolved and has produced in *La Jeune Parque* and in *Charmes* a unique kind of poetry of an extraordinarily rich and complex nature, both in its origins and in its effects.

No sooner had Valéry completed *Charmes*, however, than his patron M. Lebey died in February 1922, a few months before the actual publication of the volume. This meant that Valéry was obliged to think of ways and means of earning a living and the obvious method, which he promptly adopted, was to capitalize on the enormous literary reputation he had acquired over the course of the previous few years. He had, indeed, already begun the endless round of lectures and speeches and the vast output of essays, articles, and extracts from his *Cahiers* which were to occupy the remainder of his life. These—despite the penetrating nature of some of his studies, such as those of Descartes and Baudelaire, the interest of his comments on Mallarmé in particular, and the acuity of many of his remarks on creative writing—are hardly of the same importance as his poetical work.

One is naturally tempted to assume that Valéry was thus prevented by force of circumstances from writing poetry and that he would otherwise have continued to do so. But one can also perhaps take the view that these multiple activities fall into place as part of the pattern of Valéry's life. If his poetry is the recognition of the fact that the mind cannot, as he had at first believed, remain turned in on itself, but must turn outwards to the world, it seems logical and inevitable that he should then have put this principle into practice. In this sense, therefore, the latter part of Valéry's life could be considered as complementary to his poetry and even as a response to the closing lines of *La Jeune Parque* and to the injunction given in 'Le Cimetière marin': 'il faut tenter de vivre'; although it is true that Valéry frequently complained about this new life as a public figure into which he was plunged.

This is not to say, however, that Valéry's work during this period is unrelated to what preceded it; on the contrary he is still concerned with the same fundamental issues. This is particularly true of his four dialogues, the first of which, *Eupalinos ou l'architecte*, commissioned in fact as early as 1921, is clearly linked to his life-long interest in architecture and to an essay 'Paradoxe sur l'architecte', written thirty years before, which had ended with the sonnet 'Orphée', reprinted in the *Album de vers anciens*. The theme of the alliance of the conscious and the unconscious, mind and body, work and inspiration runs through the dialogue, rising to a climax in the final prayer of Eupalinos:

Mon intelligence mieux inspirée ne cessera, cher corps, de vous appeler à soi désormais. . . . Nous agissions chacun de notre côté. Vous viviez, je rêvais. Mes vastes rêveries aboutissaient à une impuissance illimitée. Mais cette œuvre que maintenant je veux faire . . . puisse-t-elle . . . surgir uniquement de notre entente.

L'Âme et la danse, also published in 1921, is a hymn in praise of movement as a means of combating 'l'ennui de vivre . . . cet ennui enfin qui n'a d'autre substance que la vie même et d'autre cause seconde que la clairvoyance du vivant'. The echo of 'Le Cimetière marin' in these lines is even more noticeable in the statement that 'parmi toutes les ivresses, la plus noble et la plus ennemie du grand ennui, est l'ivresse due à des actes'. *L'Idée fixe*, published some ten years later in 1932, although written in a humorous vein, also revolves round similar basic themes—that the mind is engaged in a constant and intense activity, obsessed not so much with any particular 'idée fixe' as with what is redefined as a general 'idée omnivalente' ('j'aime la pensée', wrote Valéry elsewhere, 'comme d'autres aiment le nu, qu'ils dessineraient toute leur vie'); that there exists in man a kind of vague potential, for which the term 'implexe' is created; that man is 'à la fois capable de raisonnement minutieux, de rigueur soutenue, de doutes et de réserves — et d'autre part sujet aux impulsions, esclave de ses détentes'. Finally, in the *Dialogue de l'arbre*, which dates from 1943, two years before Valéry's death, the two sides of his nature can again be seen, symbolized this time by the two speakers, Lucrèce, the thinker, and Tityre, the man of feeling, who decide to join forces: 'Faisons entre nous l'échange de ta connaissance de cet Arbre avec l'amour et la louange qu'il m'inspire.'

The two unfinished plays, one, *Le Solitaire*, of a mere twenty or so pages, the other, *Lust*, five times that length, which Valéry sketched out very rapidly in 1940 on the theme of Dr. Faustus, also reveal that his thoughts still ran along the same lines. The very choice of subject—a man who aspires to universal knowledge— recalls Valéry's admiration for Leonardo da Vinci and his creation of M. Teste; but just as the latter, in the *Lettre de Mme Émilie Teste*, emerges from his meditations and clings to his wife as if to 'un rocher de vie et de présence réelle', so Faust turns towards Lust, the 'demoiselle de cristal', and in a moving hymn to life declares that:

Le moindre regard, la moindre sensation, les moindres actes et fonctions de la vie me deviennent de la même dignité que les desseins et les voix intérieures de ma pensée. . . . C'est un état suprême, où tout se résume en vivre.

Thus Valéry remained convinced, until the end of his life, of the need to maintain that reconciliation of thought and action, of the mind and the senses, of the inner world and the outer world which, after the early period of conflict between the two, he had achieved in the years between 1912 and 1922 and which had formed the subject of *La Jeune Parque*, the *Album de vers anciens*, and *Charmes* during that fertile decade.

NOTE

PAUL VALÉRY, 1871–1945, was born and bred in the town of Sète on the Mediterranean coast. He moved to Paris in 1894 and in 1900 accepted a position as private secretary to a wealthy businessman. He remained in this unexacting post for more than twenty years, able to devote much of his time to intellectual pursuits. After the death of his patron in 1922 Valéry, who was by then acknowledged as the outstanding poet of his generation in France, earned his living as critic, essayist, and lecturer.

Works. Valéry's poetical work consists chiefly of the *Album de vers anciens*, published in 1920 but made up, as the title indicates, of poems written some thirty years before; *La Jeune Parque*, published in 1917 and inspired by the reawakening of Valéry's interest in poetry, which had lain dormant for many years; and *Charmes*, published in 1922, the product of his maturity as a poet. His vast amount of prose work includes the *Introduction à la méthode de Léonard de Vinci* (1895) and *La Soirée avec Monsieur Teste* (1896), several volumes of essays, reminiscences, commentaries, and occasional writings, mostly published under the apt title of *Variété* between 1924 and 1944, a number of dialogues, and two unfinished sketches on the theme of Dr. Faustus under the title of *Mon Faust* (1940). For fifty-one years, from 1894 until his death, Valéry set down the raw material of his ideas every day in his *Cahiers*.

Editions. The two volumes of Valéry's *Œuvres*, published by Gallimard in the Pléiade edition in 1957 and 1960 respectively, have superseded previous editions. The twenty-nine volumes of the *Cahiers* were published in a facsimile edition between 1957 and 1960.

Criticism. Recent general studies include those of A. W. Thomson, *Valéry* (1965), Agnes Mackay, *The Universal Self, a Study of Paul Valéry* (1961), J. Charpier, *Essai sur Paul Valéry* (1956), and F. Scarfe, *The Art of Paul Valéry* (1954). F. E. Sutcliffe has examined *La Pensée de Paul Valéry* (1955) and N. Suckling *Paul Valéry and the Civilized Mind* (1954). W. N. Ince has analysed *The Poetic Theory of Paul Valéry* (1961) and J. Hytier *La Poétique de Valéry* (1953). P. O. Walzer has covered *La Poésie de Valéry* (1953), C. G. Whiting the earlier poetry only in *Valéry, jeune poète* (1960), and J. R. Lawler the later poetry only in *Lecture de Valéry, une étude de 'Charmes'* (1963). The study of the *Cahiers* has begun with Judith Robinson's *L'Analyse de l'esprit dans les Cahiers de Valéry* (1963). Edmée de la Rochefoucauld summarizes and comments on the contents of the *Cahiers* in the three volumes of *En lisant les Cahiers de Paul Valéry* (1964, 1966, and 1967).

4. The First World War and the Literary Consciousness

WITH the benefit of more than fifty years of hindsight, one can now clearly see that beneath the social glitter and cultural ferment of *la belle époque*, the underlying mood of the nation was essentially anti-intellectual, chauvinistic, and increasingly bellicose. The writers who most accurately expressed this mood and, indeed, helped to incite it were those who, in spite of repeated defeats for the nationalist cause from the Boulanger fiasco onwards, continued to affirm their faith in the Church and the Army and consistently urged their youthful readers to seek in war the surest proof of their manhood. In this respect, the most representative and influential writer of the age was Maurice Barrès.

At the outset of his literary career, in the novels of his *culte du moi* phase, Barrès professed a lofty contempt for those of his fellow men who were unable to appreciate his sensitivity and share his Romantic aspirations. His *Cahiers* (published posthumously, 1929–57) and his private correspondence reveal that he remained at heart an agnostic who felt that 'l'univers et la vie, d'eux-mêmes, sont un chaos'. Nationalism provided him with a cause which gave sense and purpose to his own life, and he served it with all the fervour and dedication of the convert. His views and their implications are most succinctly expressed in *Les Amitiés françaises* (1903), in which he re-enacts some of the practical lessons he devised for the moral education of his son. The boy is warned of the evils of rationalism, he is taken to such sacred national shrines as Lourdes and Domrémy, and he is indoctrinated with the heady *mystique* of the war to be waged for the lost provinces of Alsace and Lorraine:

— Nous affirmons, nous jurons que nous allons nous exercer, refaire, choisir le bon moment et prendre notre revanche.

— Tu es sûr que les Français reviendront vainqueurs?
— J'en suis certain: je te l'ai déjà dit.
— Mais jamais tu ne m'as dit quel jour.
— Le jour que tu seras grand.

One of the most striking converts to this doctrine of recapturing the glories of France's military and religious past was Ernest Psichari who was, ironically enough, a grandson of Renan. He found the contemporary world repellent in all its aspects and became a professional soldier. His literary testament is to be found in three novels based on his army experiences in North Africa and can be fairly summed up in two short quotations: 'Nous voulons que la grande aventure serve à notre santé morale, à notre perfectionnement' (*Terres de soleil et de sommeil*, 1908); and 'Les canons sont les réalités les plus réelles qui soient, les seules réalités du monde moderne' (*L'Appel des armes*, 1913). His life and works established him as the epitome of a whole generation of idealistic nationalists. He was converted to Catholicism in 1913 and killed in action in the very first weeks of the war.

The most significant portents of all, however, are to be found in the works of Charles Péguy, most particularly in those which reveal his attitudes and allegiances as they evolved from 1905 onwards. In 'Notre Patrie', an essay published in *Les Cahiers de la quinzaine* in November of that year, he described the effect on the population of Paris of the Kaiser's bellicose posturing over the Tangier incident:

Ce n'était pas une nouvelle qui se communiquât de bouche en bouche, que l'on se communiquât, latéralement, comme les nouvelles ordinaires.... En réalité c'était en lui-même que chacun de nous trouvait, recevait, retrouvait la connaissance totale, immédiate, prête, sourde et immobile et toute faite de la menace qui était présente. . . .

The realization that war was inevitable provided Péguy with the crusade he had been seeking ever since the Dreyfus Affair had degenerated from a campaign for absolute justice into a squalid political squabble. The chance to defend France against unwarranted aggression appealed to his sense of justice, his love of the French Army, and his burning patriotism, instincts which he was rarely able to enlist in the service of a single cause. From 1905 onwards, he was therefore committed to an ideological course which was to alienate him from his former Dreyfusard comrades-in-arms and draw him ever closer to the right-wing forces to whom, at the turn of the century, he had been so implacably opposed. By August 1914, even, before any official proclamation to close the ranks, *L'Action française* and *Les Cahiers de la quinzaine* were united against the common enemy.

Against this background of dynamic nationalism, it is now clear how out of sympathy with the spirit of the age were those writers who were committed to the belief that the world could be remoulded by humane and peaceful means. Romain Rolland's *Jean-Christophe* (1906-12), declaring his faith in the redemptive powers of Art, and Martin du Gard's *Jean Barois* (1913), expressing his high hopes in the panacea of rationalism, would seem to have been less in harmony with the mood of their day than Georges Sorel's *Réflexions sur la violence* (1908) with its scorn for the individual and for democratic procedures and its eulogy of brute force.

Yet it would be wrong to interpret the infectiousness of this pre-war patriotism as craven surrender to atavistic instincts. The militant patriots of the Right had something else in common not only with each other but also with the humanists whose attitude to life was, in all other respects, diametrically opposed to theirs: they all subscribed to a veritable cult of heroism.

In his *Cahiers* Barrès recognized that twentieth-century man had inherited from his ancestors those pugnacious instincts which centuries earlier had ensured the survival of his tribe; but he argued that nobler qualities had been handed down as well:

Par-dessous une couche d'habitudes pacifiques, nous avons de ce résidu héroïque et brutal dans le sang. Et en même temps, nous avons dans le sang une hérédité d'héroïsme moral; nous avons dans le sang des quantités de saints, catholiques, idolâtres, indifférents, des gens qui se sont oubliés, sacrifiés pour autrui, qui ont fait sans bruit, tout seuls, des choses admirables.

In *Terres de soleil et de sommeil* Psichari declared that he was

c

proud to keep burning within himself 'cette petite lampe d'héroïsme, si vacillante aujourd'hui, et de retrouver . . . un peu de l'antique passion des dominateurs et des conquérants'. Romain Rolland proclaimed in the Preface to his *Vie de Beethoven* (1903): 'L'air est lourd autour de nous . . . le monde étouffe. — Rouvrons les fenêtres! Faisons entrer l'air libre! Respirons le souffle des héros.' Heroes, he went on to explain, were in his view the world's great creative artists who triumphed over all their personal difficulties and adversity and found joy through suffering.

This cult of heroism in France was not confined to a handful of men of letters. The spectacular acclaim which greeted *Cyrano de Bergerac* on its première in 1897, and which won Rostand his place in the Académie Française at the phenomenally early age of thirty-three, suggests how widespread was the public appetite for *panache*. A striking similarity may be noted between the defiant boast of the dying Cyrano: 'Que dites-vous? . . . C'est inutile? . . . Je le sais! Mais, on ne se bat pas dans l'espoir du succès! Non! non, c'est bien plus beau lorsque c'est inutile!', Romain Rolland's declaration in the Preface to his play, *Aërt* (1897): 'Je n'ai pas besoin d'espérer pour entreprendre et de réussir pour persévérer', and Péguy's affirmation in *L'Argent suite* (1913): 'Nous ne savons pas si nous serons heureux, mais nous savons que nous ne serons pas petits.'

Péguy, in fact, believed that the chief distinguishing characteristic of the French was their highly developed sense of the heroic. In *Notre Jeunesse* (1910), the most lyrical of all his essays, he declared:

Quand une grande guerre éclate, une grande révolution, cette sorte de guerre, c'est qu'un grand peuple, une grande race a besoin de sortir; qu'elle en a assez; notament qu'elle en a assez de la paix. . . . Notre affaire Dreyfus ne peut s'expliquer que par un besoin, le même, par un besoin d'héroïsme qui saisit toute une génération, la nôtre, par un besoin de guerre, de guerre *militaire* et de gloire militaire, par un besoin de sacrifice et jusque de martyre, peut-être (sans doute), par un besoin de sainteté.

Péguy's diagnosis seemed amply confirmed by the great bulk of the replies to the survey conducted in 1913 by Henri Massis and

Alfred de Tarde under the title, *Les Jeunes Gens d'aujourd'hui*. They were able to report that the youth of France was patriotic and anti-intellectual to a degree and impatient to express its heroic ardour in action. On the evidence of this survey, Péguy clearly voiced the aspirations of a whole army of Frenchmen and, indeed, of Europeans when, in that same year, he composed his noble liturgy, *Prière pour nous autres charnels*:

> Heureux ceux qui sont morts pour la terre charnelle,
> Mais pourvu que ce fût dans une juste guerre,
> Heureux ceux qui sont morts pour quatre coins de terre,
> Heureux ceux qui sont morts d'une mort solennelle. . . .

When, in 1914, the armies marched so exultantly to the battle-fields, even the peace-loving Romain Rolland was at first able to recognize the appeal which war could exercise over the young men of his day:

> Comme vous nous vengez des années de scepticisme, de veulerie jouisseuse où nous avons grandi, protégeant de leurs miasmes notre foi, votre foi, qui triomphe avec vous sur les champs de bataille! Guerre de 'revanche' a-t-on dit. De revanche, en effet, mais non comme l'entend un chauvinisme étroit; revanche de la foi contre tous les égoïsmes des sens et de l'esprit, don absolu de soi aux idées éternelles.[1]

But Rolland was very quick to realize that Europe had been engulfed in a cataclysm of appalling dimensions and that a civilization which had taken centuries to build was in mortal peril. Martin du Gard, likewise, all too readily saw through the propagandists' claim that the French were fighting to defend civilization against barbarism; in his view, expressed as early as November 1914 in a

---

[1] There is, *mutatis mutandis*, a striking and surprising similarity between the sentiment expressed in these lines from *Au-dessus de la mêlée* (1915) and that expressed in Rupert Brooke's often quoted sonnet 'Peace' (1914):

> Now, God be thanked who has matched us with His hour,
> And caught our youth, and wakened us from sleeping,
> With hand made sure, clear eye, and sharpened power,
> To turn, as swimmers into cleanness leaping,
> Glad from a world grown old and cold and weary,
> Leave the sick hearts that honour could not move,
> And half-men, and their dirty songs and dreary,
> And all the little emptiness of love!

number of still unpublished letters to his friend Marcel Hébert, both sides were equally barbarous and equally guilty of betraying the cause of Humanity.

Rolland and Martin du Gard at this stage formed a tiny minority. The overwhelming majority of the intelligentsia, as well as the masses in each of the belligerent nations, were wholly convinced that their lives were worth sacrificing 'dans une juste guerre'. Chauvinistic enthusiasm in France produced some remarkable conversions: Antole France, who as recently as 1912 had trenchantly denounced fanaticism and mob-rule in *Les Dieux ont soif*, tried to join the Army in 1914 at the age of seventy; in 1891 Rémy de Gourmont had declared in *Le Joujou Patriotisme* that he would not lift a finger to recover Alsace and Lorraine:

Personnellement, je ne donnerais pas, en échange de ces terres oubliées, ni le petit doigt de ma main droite: il me sert à soutenir ma main, quand j'écris; ni le petit doigt de ma main gauche: il me sert à secouer la cendre de ma cigarette;

in 1915 he publicly recanted and pledged his unstinted support for La Ligue des Patriotes, which was by then presided over by Maurice Barrès.

The bellicose mood was sustained in France, as in each of the other warring nations, by writers too old to fight. Barrès became the foremost French jingoist of the day and throughout the war produced a daily column for *L'Écho de Paris*. After the war, fourteen volumes of these articles were published under the title *Chroniques de la Grande Guerre* and Barrès persisted in maintaining that they were the most beautiful books he ever wrote. They now seem by far the most expendable, so much hollow rhetoric and over-elegant phrase-making. The same is true of the many volumes of patriotic French poetry produced in the course of the war; even the best of these, such as Francis Jammes's *Cinq Poèmes pour le temps de la guerre* (1916), *Les Ailes rouges de la guerre* (1917) by Verhaeren, or *Le Vol de la Marseillaise* (1919) by Rostand, only serve to demonstrate that great public events almost invariably produce bad verse. Claudel's war poetry is typical of the genre. In 'Le précieux sang' he urges the troops on towards martyrdom:

> Si vraiment il y a une source en nous, eh bien, c'est ce que nous
>   allons voir!
> Si ce vin a quelque vertu,
> Et si notre sang est rouge, comme vous le dites, comment le savoir,
> Autrement que quand il est répandu?
> Si notre sang est vraiment *précieux* comme vous le dites, si vraiment il
>   est comme de l'or,
> S'il sert, pourquoi le garder?
> Oublieux, de tout ce qu'on peut acheter avec, pourquoi le réserver
>   comme un trésor,
> Mon Dieu, quand vous le demandez?

The bombast of lines such as these and of the more often quoted 'Tant que vous voudrez, mon Général' is not rendered more palatable by the knowledge that shortly after they were written, Claudel was safely ensconced behind his ambassador's desk in Buenos Aires.

Apollinaire's war poetry has lasted rather better, indeed it is arguably the only French poetry of the 1914-18 war which is now readable at all. Unlike the best war poetry of Sassoon, Owen, or Rosenberg, it is neither bitter nor angry; its most remarkable quality is its childlike innocence, and this is true of poems written after months of active service. He finds the experience of war exhilarating:

> Ah Dieu! que la guerre est jolie
> Avec ses chants ses longs loisirs
>   ('L'Adieu du cavalier')

and delights in an artillery barrage as though it were a spectacular firework display:

> Comme c'est beau toutes ces fusées
> Mais ce serait bien plus beau s'il y en avait plus encore.
>   ('Merveille de la guerre')

Military combat also serves as a powerful aphrodisiac, heightening his sexual desire and at the same time providing him with the imagery to express it. Thus, in 'Chef de section', he elaborates in some detail the analogy between his mistress and a military fortress, each to be taken by a well-mounted assault, while in 'Fête' the after-glow of bursting shells at once makes him think of the body of his distant beloved:

> . . . Deux fusants
> Rose éclatement
> Comme deux seins que l'on dégrafe
> Tendant leurs bouts insolemment
> IL SUT AIMER
> > quelle épitaphe . . .

Apollinaire was not the only French writer of distinction to treat the war less as a subject worthy of study in itself than as a vivid back-cloth before which he or his characters could act out their private dramas. *Les Silences du Colonel Bramble* (1918) by André Maurois is memorable not as an evocation of life in the front line but as an amiable *exposé* of the peculiarities of the English national character; the subject of *L'Équipage* (1924) by Joseph Kessel is not really the war in the air but the conflict between comradeship and rivalry in love. In *L'Exil* (1915) and *Le Songe* (1922) by Montherlant and in Cocteau's *Thomas l'imposteur* (1923) the true focus of attention is not the clash of battle but the catalytic effect of the *idea* of war on the aspirations and inner fantasies of the hero. The same is true of the most accomplished French work so far written about the Second World War, Saint-Exupéry's *Pilote de guerre* (1942).

The most comprehensive rendering in French of the actual experience of combat is the series of four novels by Maurice Genevoix now available in a single volume under the title *Ceux de Verdun* (1915–22): the narrator seems so close to the events he so graphically records that it is difficult to decide whether one is dealing with an authentic journal or fiction cleverly disguised as *reportage*. Photographic accuracy is not, however, what the contemporary reader now demands of First World War fiction, and he is therefore likely to respond rather more enthusiastically to works where the author's viewpoint is more heavily accentuated—the profound compassion of Duhamel's *Vie des martyrs* (1917) and *Civilisation* (1918), two sets of vignettes based on his observations as a doctor in the Army Medical Corps, or the anger and pity of *Le Feu* (1916) by Henri Barbusse or *Les Croix de bois* (1919) by Roland Dorgelès.

Le Feu made the greatest impact of any work of First World War fiction written by a serving French soldier. It is certainly not a flawless work—a particularly jarring note is struck in the final chapter in which the narrator turns preacher and delivers a sermon on the new society to be built out of the ruins of the old—but its well-organized structure and clusters of images most vividly convey Barbusse's disgust at the horror and waste of war: 'Honte à la gloire militaire . . . aux armées . . . au métier de soldat qui change les hommes tour à tour en stupides victimes et ignobles bourreaux.' Writing twenty years later, Jules Romains enjoyed the benefits of greater leisure and greater distance from the events he set out to describe; his two novels devoted to the great battles of 1916, *Prélude à Verdun* (1937) and *Verdun* (1938), have been widely praised for presenting a panoramic view of events both at the Front and in Paris, but the gain in scope has been achieved at the cost of intensity; the reader is not involved with Romains's large cast of characters as he cannot fail to be with the doomed members of Barbusse's small squad. In these two books, as in the other twenty-five of the series devoted to *Les Hommes de bonne volonté*, Romains seems not so much an authentic novelist as a literary journalist, albeit of a very high order.

Barbusse's violent denunciation of the horrors of war was matched in a different medium by Romain Rolland. He was working in Switzerland in the summer of 1914 and elected to stay on there throughout the conflict, devoting most of his energies to Red Cross work for the prisoners of war on both sides. In a series of articles and open letters, nearly all first published in *Le Journal de Genève*, he protested vehemently against any behaviour on either side which degraded the cause of common Humanity; he protested not only against such German atrocities as the destruction of Louvain and of Rheims Cathedral but also against jingoists, French as well as German, whose propaganda was intensifying the atmosphere of fratricidal hatred. He was especially severe on the intellectuals who all too willingly allowed their talents to be enlisted in the chauvinist cause, a charge which Julien Benda was to renew with considerably more pungency after the war in *La Trahison des clercs* (1927).

Rolland's campaigning did not go unrecognized. As the casualty-lists lengthened, he was encouraged by an increasing amount of private correspondence from ordinary citizens as well as from some of the world's foremost intellectuals, and he was publicly rewarded for his stand by the award of the Nobel Prize in 1916. But he was at the same time violently denounced by self-styled patriots of both sides, by Barrès and Massis especially and, no less predictably, by their German counterparts.

Rolland accepted his lonely eminence inevitably with sadness but also with barely disguised relish. A sense of isolation seems to have been as vitalizing to him as the prospect of combat was to Péguy. Although his doctrines were diametrically opposed to those of Barrès and of Psichari, he shared their Romantic feeling of being cut off from ordinary men. From childhood on, he was always self-consciously a solitary, and his resolution to act single-handed is clearly stated in his *Mémoires*:

> Ne jamais faire partie d'un groupe, d'une association politique. . . . Je suis et je veux demeurer libre. Et si je fais la guerre, en marge d'un camp, je la ferai, seul responsable de moi seul.

Rolland steadfastly adhered to this principle throughout his career. Although his sympathies were all for Dreyfus, he did not publicly commit himself to his cause; *Clérambault* (1925), a novel in which he transposed his wartime attitudes, was at one stage to have been sub-titled '*L'un contre tous*', and he has left his own image of his sense of loneliness in the Preface to the posthumously published *Journal des années de guerre* (1952):

> J'étais seul, en face d'un monde possédé de haine et de fureur guerrière. Par la brusque explosion d'outrages contre mon attitude, par la riposte, moins nombreuse, mais audace et fidèle, de ceux qui la défendirent, je me trouvai, sans l'avoir voulu, incarner la cause de l'Europe, au-dessus de la mêlée, sacrilège des nations.

By choosing to remain in isolation throughout the conflict, Rolland was able to act a role similar to that of his favourite real-life heroes, Beethoven, Michelangelo, and Tolstoy, and to that of Jean-Christophe, the eponymous hero of his ten-volume *roman fleuve*. He depicted all of them as lonely figures perpetually at odds with turpitude and iniquity. Jean-Christophe, clearly meant to be seen as an exemplary hero, now looks suspiciously like unconscious self-caricature: his views are as sincere as they are noble, but because of excessive earnestness and gaucheness, he unfailingly makes more enemies than is strictly necessary for the good of his cause. If Rolland's strategic objectives now seem wholly admirable, his tactics still appear to have been inordinately ill-considered: his attack on the corruption and pretentiousness of the cultural life of pre-war Paris, sustained throughout *La Foire sur la place* (1908), now seems needlessly shrill and over-insistent; the tactlessness of the title of the collection of his protest articles, *Au-dessus de la mêlée* (1915), so strongly, but wrongly, suggesting Olympian aloofness, was later bitterly regretted by Rolland himself.

Even had Rolland been a master of tact and diplomacy, bitter conflict would have been inevitable between himself and the spokesmen for the nations waging total war. Rolland was utopian in hoping that the nations could implement his pleas, that they would unite in the name of universal brotherhood, and he was anachronistic in believing that war could still be fought by a code of gentlemanly rules. The time was long since past when opposing generals could offer each other the honour of firing the first shot or when scholars could continue to visit enemy countries while their professional armies fought for mastery on some isolated battlefield. The vituperation provoked on all sides by *Au-dessus de la mêlée* was a conclusive demonstration of the barbarous depths to which the civilized nations of the West had sunk, a point made with telling force at the end of Duhamel's ironically entitled *Civilisation*, when a group of African stretcher-bearers are shown standing silent and wide-eyed, surveying human bodies mangled and pulped by the end-products of centuries of European culture.

In the restless years immediately following the Armistice, writers who reflected on the legacy of the war found little occasion for rejoicing. So much seemed to have been swept away by the

cataclysm that the general mood was one of numbed bewilderment
rather than euphoria. This is nowhere better expressed than in
La Crise de l'esprit, the moving essay Valéry wrote in 1919, depicting the European intellectual as a Hamlet of the modern age, brooding on the battlements of a vast new Elsinore stretching from the
North Sea to the Alps:

> Il y a des milliers de jeunés écrivains et de jeunes artistes qui sont
> morts. Il y a l'illusion perdue d'une culture européenne et la démon-
> stration de l'impuissance de la connaissance à sauver quoi que ce soit;
> il y a la science, atteinte mortellement dans ses ambitions morales, et
> comme déshonorée par la cruauté de ses applications; il y a l'idéalisme,
> difficilement vainqueur, profondément meurtri, responsable de ses
> rêves; le réalisme déçu, battu, accablé de crimes et de fautes; la convoitise
> et le renoncement également bafoués; les croyances confondues dans les
> camps, croix contre croix, croissant contre croissant; il y a les sceptiques
> eux-mêmes, désarçonnés par des événements si soudains, si émouvants,
> et qui jouent avec nos pensées comme le chat avec la souris — les scepti-
> ques perdent leurs doutes, les retrouvent, les reperdent, et ne savent
> plus se servir des mouvements de leur esprit.

A few years later, in *La Tentation de l'Occident* (1926), Malraux
described Europe as a 'grand cimetière où ne dorment que des
conquérants morts', and claimed to speak for a whole generation
when he concluded: 'Il n'est pas d'idéal auquel nous puissions nous
sacrifier, car de tous nous connaissons les mensonges, nous qui ne
savons point ce qu'est la vérité.'

For most writers, however, the ideologies of *la belle époque* were
not so readily discounted, and even the most discredited of them
somehow survived the war, though often in drastically modified
form. The taste for military glory finally lost its appeal in the
carnage of Verdun in 1916, and on the Chemin des Dames in the
following year, but after the war men could still be found eager to
prove themselves as heroes. In his *Chant funèbre pour les morts de
Verdun* (1924), Montherlant claimed that war brought out the best
as well as the worst in man:

> Il faut faire une paix qui ait la grandeur d'âme de la guerre.... J'appelle
> une paix où nous provoquerons, systématiquement, toutes les occa-
> sions du courage et de l'oubli de soi. Cette paix-là sera autre chose que

l'absence de guerre. Elle aussi, elle parlera aux imaginations et aux cœurs. Elle suffira à cette faim d'héroïsme qui fait venir les larmes aux yeux.

His enthusiasm for football and for bull-fighting, like Malraux's expeditions through the Cambodian jungles or Saint-Exupéry's active role in pioneering airmail routes over the Atlantic and the Andes, can all be seen as attempts to find substitutes for martial dangers in times of peace.

The post-war preoccupations of a number of other writers were consistent with, and, to a significant degree, conditioned by their experience of the 1914-18 war. The sense of outrage it left with Céline provoked the monumental nihilism of his *Voyage au bout de la nuit* (1932); the communism of Barbusse is already clearly visible in embryo in *Le Feu*, with his growing conviction that the humble soldier has been tricked into laying down his life by and for the corrupt powers-that-be; Drieu la Rochelle's fatal flirtation with fascism was clearly not unconnected with the sense of power he experienced when he led a bayonet charge in September 1914 and which he later recalled in *La Comédie de Charleroi* (1934): 'J'étais un chef. Je voulais m'emparer de tous ces hommes autour de moi, m'en accroître, les accroître par moi et nous lancer tous en bloc, moi en pointe, à travers l'univers.'

Alain's experience of military power and his reaction to it were markedly different; in *Mars ou la guerre jugée* (1921) he claimed that the most important lesson he had learned from his years of service at the Front was that the urge to wield arbitrary power over other men was the most insidious and pernicious of all human instincts and was, in fact, the basic cause of all wars:

Tout pouvoir aime la guerre, la cherche, l'annonce et la prolonge, par un instinct sûr et par une prédilection qui lui rend toute sagesse odieuse. Autrefois, je voulais conclure, trop vite, qu'il faut être assuré de la paix pour diminuer les pouvoirs. Maintenant, mieux instruit par l'expérience de l'esclave, je dis qu'il faut réduire énergiquement les pouvoirs de toute espèce, quels que soient les inconvénients secondaires, si l'on veut la paix.

Throughout the inter-war years, Alain lost no opportunity of inciting *les citoyens contre les pouvoirs*: the considerable influence he was able to exert both as a deeply revered schoolteacher at the Lycée Henri IV and as a widely-read journalist and sage should clearly be counted as one of the several factors which brought about the débâcle of 1940.

A no less important factor in this respect was the mood of militant pacifism which inevitably became deeply rooted in a land as ravaged by war as France. It found its most eloquent literary expression in the 1930s in Giono's novel *Le Grand Troupeau* (1931), Giraudoux's play *La Guerre de Troie n'aura pas lieu* (1935), and Roger Martin du Gard's novel *L'Été 1914* (1936)[1] which was awarded the Nobel Prize in 1937. Given the political situation in Europe at this time, it seems evident that, like Romain Rolland twenty years before him, Martin du Gard won his prize for his unequivocal condemnation of war. In the traditional speech of acceptance in Stockholm, he acknowledged this by emphasizing the pacifist message of his novel:

> En ce moment exceptionellement grave que traverse l'humanité, je souhaite — sans vanité, mais de tout mon cœur rongé d'inquiétude — que mes livres sur l'Été 1914 soient lus, discutés, et qu'ils rappellent à tous (aux anciens qui l'ont oubliée comme aux jeunes gens qui l'ignorent ou la négligent) la pathétique leçon du passé.

The inevitable corollary of violent hatred of war was reluctance or refusal to recognize the growing menace of Nazism. Martin du Gard made his position all too clear in a letter to his friend, Marcel Lallemand, in September 1936:

> Suis dur comme fer *pour la neutralité*. Principe: tout, *plutôt que la guerre! Tout, tout!* Même le fascisme en Espagne! Et ne me poussez pas, car je dirais: oui . . . et . . . même le fascisme en France! . . . Il faut avoir totalement oublié *ce qu'est* la guerre pour un peuple, le mal suprême, la souffrance à la $N^{ème}$ puissance. Rien, *aucune épreuve, aucune servitude*, ne peut être comparée à la guerre, à tout ce qu'elle engendre. Avez-vous si courte mémoire? Le 'partisan' étouffe-t-il en vous l'"humain'? *Tout:* Hitler, plutôt que la guerre!

Giono declared as late as 1939: 'Si l'Allemagne nous attaquait, que faire? — Réponse: refuser d'obéir à la guerre. Que peut-il

---

[1] The seventh volume of Martin du Gard's *roman fleuve* entitled *Les Thibault* (1922-40).

arriver de pire si l'Allemagne envahit la France? Devenir Allemands?
Pour ma part, j'aime mieux être Allemand vivant que Français
mort.' There could scarcely be a more dramatic contrast with the attitudes expressed by Barrès and Péguy at the end of *la belle époque*.

But bellicose patriotism was not the ideology which was most
damaged by the First World War. The revelation of the savage
forces just beneath the civilized surface of modern Europe provided
a specially traumatic shock to those writers who at the turn of the
century professed their optimistic belief in the essential goodness
of Man. This shock can be measured with dramatic clarity in the
works of Martin du Gard. In *Jean Barois*, first published in 1913,
several notable victories are recorded for the liberal humanist
cause: after the bitter and prolonged campaign to reopen his case,
Dreyfus is rehabilitated and released; Jean Barois himself is recon-
verted to Catholicism because of his fear of death but the leader of
the rationalists, significantly called Luce, faces death with the serene
confidence that Good will inevitably triumph:

> Ma raison me prouve que notre vie n'est ni un mouvement à vide, ni
> une simple occasion de souffrir, ni une course au bonheur individuel;
> elle me prouve que mes actes collaborent au grand effort universel; et
> partout elle me fait découvrir des motifs d'espérer! Partout je vois la vie
> naître de la mort, l'énergie naître de la douleur, la science naître de
> l'erreur, l'harmonie naître du désordre. . . . Et en moi-même, ces évolu-
> tions-là se produisent tous les jours.

Martin du Gard's faith in the innate nobility of Man did not
survive the First World War: Jacques Thibault, who is sometimes
taken to be the exemplary hero of the Thibault chronicle, dedicates
his life and finally sacrifices it to the ideal of peaceful social revolution, but to the end he remains bitterly aware that human nature is
ineradicably flawed. In *Les Thibault*, the counterpart to Luce is the
brilliant surgeon, Dr. Philip, the 'privileged' character through
whom Martin du Gard voices his own views most directly; in
Épilogue (1939) he answers Luce from across the gulf of one world
war and on the very brink of another:

> Nous avons cru que l'humanité, adulte, s'acheminait vers une époque
> où la sagesse, la mesure, la tolérance, s'apprêtait enfin à régner sur le

monde. . . . Où l'intelligence et la raison allait enfin diriger l'évolution des sociétés humaines. . . . Qui sait si nous ne paraîtrons pas, aux yeux des historiens futurs, des naïfs, des ignorants, qui se faisaient d'attendrissantes illusions sur l'homme et sur son aptitude à la civilisation? Peut-être que nous fermions les yeux sur quelques données humaines essentielles? Peut-être, par exemple, que l'instinct de détruire, le besoin périodique de foutre par terre ce que nous avons péniblement édifié, est une de ces lois essentielles qui limitent les possibilités constructives de notre nature? — une de ces lois mystérieuses et décevantes qu'un sage doit connaître et accepter?

Younger liberal humanists carried their pessimism even further and declared that the basic concept of Man himself was no longer viable. In a newspaper interview in 1926, given on returning from his first hazardous journey to the Far East, Malraux declared that 'l'objet de la recherche de la jeunesse intellectuelle est une notion nouvelle de l'homme'; his attempt to find an adequate formulation was to prove the dominant theme of all his novels and culminate in the colloquium on the Idea of Man in *Les Noyers de l'Altenburg* which he composed in 1941. Two years afterwards, in a letter written just before his death, Saint-Exupéry declared that once the Second World War was won, the survivors would be confronted with a much more pressing problem, 'celui du sens de l'homme. Et il n'est pas proposé de réponse et j'ai l'impression de marcher vers les temps les plus noirs du monde.'

It would clearly be wrong to attribute the modern humanists' malaise exclusively to the impact of the First World War. The traditional bases of humanism were in any event being gravely eroded by the effects of spectacular advances in science and technology, by the challenging new ideas of anthropologists and sociologists, and, most particularly, by the revolutionary theories of Freud. At the same time, the effect of the war should not be underestimated either. It provided its own irresistible impulse to forces which were already dynamic, brutally stripping away illusions and confronting Man with the frailty of his body and the fragility of his beliefs. Man has, ever since, been left to come to terms with the daunting conclusion that the principal cause, as well as the principal victim, of war is Man himself.

NOTE

MAURICE BARRÈS, 1862-1923, was born in Lorraine but moved to Paris while still young. He combined a literary career with very active involvement in politics and served for some years as a right-wing *député*. He exerted considerable influence over the young in the opening years of the century to the extent of being hailed as 'le Prince de la Jeunesse'.

CHARLES PÉGUY, 1873-1914, came from very humble stock in Orléans which instilled in him his lifelong concern for the hardships of the poor and a passionate love of traditional (i.e. rural and provincial) France. He won a scholarship to the École Normale Supérieure but did not stay long enough to complete his academic qualifications. Instead he devoted himself to vigorous pamphleteering in *Les Cahiers de la quinzaine*, his most cherished causes being socialism, Dreyfus, and Joan of Arc, on whom he wrote two vast poems. He was killed at the head of his troops in the first Battle of the Marne.

ROMAIN ROLLAND, 1866-1944, came from a bourgeois family in central France and, like Péguy, studied at the École Normale Supérieure. He was a close friend of Péguy's and his novel cycle *Jean-Christophe* first appeared serially in *Les Cahiers de la quinzaine*. His abiding interests were music, best expressed in a massive study of Beethoven, and humanitarian idealism, which inspired his best novels and a prolific correspondence with fellow intellectuals from all over the world.

ROGER MARTIN DU GARD, 1881-1958, came from a prosperous middle-class background. After attending the École des Chartes, where he developed his life-long interest in history, he devoted his life to writing and, throughout his career, deliberately shunned publicity. He was a very close friend of Gide, of whom he wrote a particularly revealing study and with whom he conducted a voluminous correspondence.

Modern Editions. Publication of a new complete edition of the works of Barrès began in 1965 under the imprint of Au Club de l'Honnête Homme; seven volumes, including all the novels, have so far appeared. The *Cahiers*, in fourteen volumes, (1929-57), are still essential reading. There are two editions of Péguy's works which do not completely overlap: the Gallimard *Œuvres complètes* (20 vols., 1917-55), and three volumes in the Bibliothèque de la Pléiade: *Œuvres poétiques*, edited by Pierre Péguy (1948), and *Œuvres en prose 1898-1908* (1959) and *Œuvres en prose 1908-14* (1957), both edited by Marcel Péguy. Romain Rolland's *Jean-Christophe* is available either in a single volume or in the Livre de Poche series in three volumes. Other important works are the *Mémoires et fragments du journal* (1956), *Journal des années de guerre, 1914-19* (1952), and the invaluable series of *Cahiers Romain Rolland* (1948 onwards), consisting, for the most part, of volumes of correspondence. The articles which originally constituted *Au-dessus de la mêlée* have been reissued with *Les Précurseurs* under the title *L'Esprit libre.* The most convenient edition of Martin du Gard's works is the two-volume Pléiade *Œuvres complètes* (1955) with a preface by Camus. Editions are being prepared of his voluminous correspondence and of his unfinished last work *Le Journal du Colonel Maumort.*

Criticism. Good surveys of the intellectual climate in the first decade of the century will be found in A. Goldberger, *Visions of a New Hero* (1965), R. Griffiths, *The Reactionary Revolution: the Catholic Revival in French Literature, 1870–1914* (1966), and M. Tison Braun, *La Crise de l'humanisme* (1958). The most exhaustive study of French fiction of the First World War is J. Norton Cru, *Témoins* (1929), and his very much shorter *Du témoignage* (1967).

The best studies of the main authors under review are as follows: on Barrès: J. Domenach, *Barrès par lui-même* (1954), P. de Boisdeffre, *Maurice Barrès* (1962), and J. Vier, *Barrès et le 'culte du moi'* (1958); on Péguy: D. Halévy, *Péguy et les Cahiers de la quinzaine* (1941), R. Rolland, *Péguy* (2 vols., 1944), A. Dru, *Péguy* (1956), and M. Villiers, *Charles Péguy: a Study in Integrity* (1965); on Rolland: J. B. Barrère, *Rolland par lui-même* (1962), R. Cheval, *Romain Rolland, l'Allemagne et la guerre* (1963), and R. Wilson, *The Pre-War Biographies of Romain Rolland* (1939); on Martin du Gard: R. Gibson, *Roger Martin du Gard* (1961), D. Boak, *Roger Martin du Gard* (1963), R. Robidoux, *Roger Martin du Gard et la religion* (1964), and D. Schalk, *Roger Martin du Gard: the Novelist and History* (1967); a penetrating chapter on *Jean Barois* will be found in V. Brombert, *The Intellectual Hero* (1962), which also provides further useful information on the intellectual background. The very important *Gide–Martin du Gard Correspondance* (ed. J. Delay) was published in 1968.

5. Theatre of Heroic Grandeur: Claudel and Montherlant

CLAUDEL and Montherlant belong to different generations. Claudel wrote his main plays between the 1890s and the 1920s. Montherlant, having established his reputation as a novelist and essayist during the inter-war period, began his public career as a dramatist during the Second World War. Both have increasingly emerged, thanks to some memorable productions of their work by Barrault and others, as two major figures in the twentieth-century French theatre. They have recently been called 'les frères ennemis', and this is a particularly apt description in so far as it suggests that they share certain fundamental features but also exhibit radical differences.

Both writers have given many of their plays a historical or partly mythical setting and seem to be particularly attracted, where dramatic material is concerned, by the attitudes and conflicts of fifteenth- and sixteenth-century Spain. They belong to a richly rhetorical and poetic tradition, using a 'theatre of language' to convey exaltation and grandeur, passion and heroism. From this point of view, they clearly stand apart from the more fashionable trends and movements of more recent French—and European—drama. Yet they too, in different ways, challenge or reject the assumptions and beliefs of their audiences. They express their own forms of dissent through the unfashionable medium of 'costume tragedy' and their work has the appearance, though certainly not the substance, of convention at a time when rhetoric and tragic grandeur are deeply suspected by their fellow-playwrights. They remain equally remote from the desperate buffoonery of Jarry, the ironic intellectuality of Giraudoux, the laconic aridity of Beckett.

Neither Claudel nor Montherlant can be accused of offering an easy optimism in their theatre. On the contrary, the passion and exaltation which they convey are most often associated with heroic renunciation or nihilism. In *L'Annonce faite à Marie*, Anne Vercors expresses a typically Claudelian view when he exclaims:

> Est-ce que le but de la vie est de vivre? Est-ce que les pieds des enfants de Dieu sont attachés à cette terre misérable?
>
> Il n'est pas de vivre, mais de mourir! et non point de charpenter la croix, mais d'y monter et de donner ce que nous avons en riant!
>
> Là est la joie, là est la liberté, là la grâce, là la jeunesse éternelle! . . . (IV. ii)

The authentic voice of Montherlant is similarly heard in the words of Jeanne la Folle, in *Le Cardinal d'Espagne*:

> Aujourd'hui je suis du monde du rien. Je n'aime rien, je ne veux rien, je ne résiste à rien . . . plus rien pour moi ne se passera sur la terre, et c'est ce rien qui me rend bonne chrétienne, quoi qu'on dise, et qui me permettra de mourir satisfaite devant mon âme, et en ordre devant Dieu, même avec tout mon poids de péchés et de douleur. Chaque acte que je ne fais pas est compté sur un livre par les anges.

These two quotations serve as a reminder that most of Claudel's plays, and several of Montherlant's, are primarily concerned with religious ideas. Nevertheless, they approach Christianity from very different points of view. Claudel writes from within the Catholic faith. His conception of life lived in the continuing presence of divine providence makes immense demands on human beings. The positive and proselytizing nature of his belief is expressed in plays that are sometimes too obviously edifying. Montherlant, although he shows an impressive, imaginative sympathy for the more heroic aspects of Christianity, lacks personal belief. The solitary and often self-divided characters of his tragedies reach out towards an absolute—but an absolute expressed as nothingness or death, rather than in terms of Christian hope.

In keeping with this distinction, Claudel's plays seem primarily theological and do not always carry conviction at the psychological level. By contrast, the emphasis in Montherlant's theatre is distinctly psychological whereas the theological implications are sometimes confusing or obscure. These differences emerge particularly clearly in the way the two dramatists regard human love. With Claudel, it is a stepping-stone to love of God; with Montherlant, it is most often a blind and egotistical passion offering no exit from the self. In this as in several other ways, and with due allowance made for differences of period, Claudel and Montherlant stand in a relationship to one another not unlike that of Corneille to Racine in the seventeenth century.

The theatrical success of Claudel's plays, written in the first place with little hope of stage production, is all the more remarkable in that they represent in almost every respect—as already suggested— a complete reversal of twentieth-century trends. Not only are they composed in a poetic idiom highly lyrical, often flamboyant and exuberant, sometimes solemn and grandiloquent, rhetorical to excess, but they also bring back to the French theatre a histrionic heroism of behaviour not seen since the time of Corneille. Moreover, except in early works such as *Tête d'Or* and the first version of *La Ville*, the playwright takes it upon himself to show a quasi-divine point of view, God's ordering of the lives of men and women in suffering and renunciation, so that He alone may be loved. There is no means of explaining away the events without recourse to the supernatural. Claudel forces the reader or spectator to face, if not to accept, a world permeated with the elements of the Catholic faith, a post-Tridentine triumphal Catholicism, with no mitigation of the simplest pieties. A dead child is brought back to life in *L'Annonce faite à Marie*; her guardian angel informs the heroine of *Le Soulier de satin* of God's plan concerning her, though it is only fair to add that the moon, the constellation of Orion, and the double shadow formed by the momentary meeting of the hero's and heroine's shadows all have their commentary to make, as well as statues of saints in a Bohemian church. Such is in fact the form the poet's exuberantly creative fantasy sometimes takes. Nevertheless, the basic issue is always vital, the meaning that our lives have, that our loving relationships have, the question of our ultimate destiny. Hard decisions have to be taken. In *L'Otage* a decision is taken by the heroine which goes so completely against her nature that she becomes utterly exhausted. No doubt, the theatrical success that Claudel has achieved is due in part to the quality of his language, in part to the intense seriousness of his preoccupations, in part to the very fact that he stands alone, out of his time, witnessing to religious values which are no longer fashionable, indeed despising all fashionableness, all moderation, utterly uncompromising.

In the course of the theological explanation which the guardian angel conveniently provides for Prouhèze in the eighth scene of the Third Day of *Le Soulier de satin* (omitted from the stage version), we find one of the basic notions on which Claudel's drama is based:

Pour les uns l'intelligence suffit. C'est l'esprit qui parle purement à l'esprit.

Mais pour les autres il faut que la chair aussi peu à peu soit évangélisée et convertie. Et quelle chair pour parler à l'homme plus puissante que celle de la femme?

The power of woman over man, the power of her physical beauty over his senses, is a basic factor in Claudel's work. He is one of the greatest love poets, expressing in vividly original imagery the deep call of man's earthy nature, the full impact of another human being whom one loves, 'Quelqu'un d'humain comme moi dont la présence et le visage hors la laideur et la misère de ce monde ne sont compatibles qu'avec un état bienheureux' (*Le Soulier de satin*, First Day, scene vii). But the force of physical love, or even its mere memory, weighs the soul down in its spiritual aspiration, so that the fourth of the great odes, 'La Muse qui est la grâce', where the poet is called upon to give himself wholly to God, to burn up his earthiness in a blaze of divine light, ends with a despairing return to the earth:

Qui a mordu à la terre, il en conserve le goût entre les dents.

Qui a goûté le sang, il ne se nourrira plus d'eau brillante et de miel ardent!

Qui a aimé l'âme humaine, qui une fois à été compact avec l'autre âme vivante, il y reste pris pour toujours.

Quelque chose de lui-même désormais hors de lui vit au pain d'un autre corps . . .

The 'evangelization of the flesh', to which Prouhèze's guardian angel refers in the passage quoted above, is a long and painful process, to which the whole of Claudel's drama bears witness. From 1905, when he wrote *Partage de midi*, immediately following the termination of an intense love affair which marked him irrevocably, until 1924, when he completed *Le Soulier de satin*, we find one fundamental theme in his dramatic production: the reconciliation of human love with love of God, or rather, the slow transmutation of human love into love of God, the 'evangelization of the flesh'. *Partage de midi*, the most lyrical of Claudel's plays, written in the white heat of passion not yet spent, makes the transmutation too abruptly, for the poet has not yet himself fully lived this transmutation, this making of his love for a woman the same thing as his love of Christ crucified; but Mesa's soliloquy when abandoned by Ysé shows that he understands Christ's love of man, each man, in the light of his own love of Ysé:

> Ah! je sais maintenant
> Ce que c'est que l'amour! et je sais ce que vous avez enduré sur votre croix, dans ton Cœur,
> Si vous avez aimé chacun de nous
> Terriblement comme j'ai aimé cette femme, et le râle, et l'asphyxie, et l'étau!... (Act III)

Obviously dissatisfied with a conclusion which is from the dramatic point of view gratuitous, a too clear determination to achieve at whatever cost to plausibility a fully redemptive pattern which is in reality an apotheosis of romantic love, a marriage of two souls predestined in eternity—moreover an eternity which seems to consist only of this shared life of two beings totally absorbed in one another—Claudel went on writing various permutations of his fundamental theme. Nearly always we have two beings who love one another but who must be prevented from achieving a happy union because God, understood as a jealous Being apart Who brooks no sharing, would thus be excluded. Suffering, apparent betrayal, separation, and, ultimately, renunciation are necessary elements in *L'Otage*, where other factors are also involved, in *L'Annonce faite à Marie*, *Le Père humilié*, and *Le Soulier de satin*. In this last-named play Claudel finally achieved what he evidently considered to be a satisfactory solution to this problem of seemingly irreconcilable loves, since *Le Soulier de satin*, though not the last of Claudel's plays, is the last dealing specifically with this theme. It is, moreover, his most ambitious work, being a baroque vision of the sixteenth century, centred on Spain as the major world-power and at the same time the power-house of a militant, triumphal Catholicism, and embracing all Europe, Africa, and America. In this play the transformation of human love into love of God is the work of a whole lifetime and not the disconcertingly sudden operation of unseen Grace that it is in *Partage de midi*. In the twenty years that have passed since the writer himself experienced the ending of a relationship of which he felt compelled to seek the meaning in the context of a divine providential plan concerning himself, his once passionate view, embodied in *Partage de midi*, has now become an intricate scheme of theological justification in which are involved the whole communion of saints, the living and the dead, the happy and the unhappy.

Adultery is a necessary element in *Partage de midi*, rendered as inevitable as possible by circumstances; the narrow confines of the ship in which Mesa and Ysé can hardly avoid one another, their uprootedness, the equatorial heat, their approaching middle age, Mesa suffering from a sense of failed religious vocation, Ysé from being married to a man who has not satisfied her deeper needs. There is thus, as she says, 'une certaine totalité de moi-même / Que je n'ai pas fournie . . .' (Act II), but which she will finally, through Mesa's agency, spend in a supreme gift, the willing sacrifice of life itself. Meanwhile she is to send her husband to his death, abandon her children and afterwards Mesa himself, while pregnant with his child, which she eventually murders. Claudel blackens the case as much as possible against the adulterous lover, so that God's forgiveness of the woman who loves may be shown as boundless. When Ysé unexpectedly rejoins Mesa, to be blown up with him in the besieged Chinese citadel, his explanation of the evil she has done is that 'l'amour . . . a tout fait'; evil brings with it a good which must not be lost. Even more disconcerting, perhaps, is the lovers' consent to one another in a pact evidently more binding than the conjugal union, a kind of synthesis of all the sacraments in one: 'la puissance indestructible / De tous les sacrements en un seul grand par le mystère d'un consentement réciproque . . .'. Earlier, Ysé has characterized the death they heroically await as 'Plus rien que l'amour à jamais, plus rien que l'éternité avec toi!' Yet the final words of Mesa are a lyrical affirmation of man's feeling of strength in himself, reminiscent of the sun-god hero of Claudel's first full-length play, *Tête d'Or*, who dies in similar self-assertion. He is 'la forte flamme fulminante, le grand mâle dans la gloire de Dieu, / L'homme dans la splendeur de l'août, l'Esprit vainqueur dans la transfiguration de Midi'. This transfiguration seems indeed of a very different order from that of the Gospels.

The merit of *Partage de midi* lies, not in the redemptive plan which brings Ysé back to Mesa's side without psychological or other explicable motivation so that she may be reconciled with him and therefore, through his identification of *eros* with *agape*, with God, but in the lyrical intensity of the passion of the lovers, the searing anguish of their adulterous love, the overwhelming bitterness of Mesa's reproaches to Ysé in the third act and the deep suffering serenity of Mesa's return to God when struck down and abandoned in the citadel. This can be seen as a drama of romantic love, straying from the nineteenth into the twentieth century, in which the lovers ultimately sacrifice all for one another, awaiting death in the confident certainty of an ulterior satisfaction which will more than compensate them for the guilt feelings which have blighted their earthly happiness. Eventually, however, as we have seen, a stronger theological framework was to be provided, involving not only the avoidance of adultery, but the hardship of separation and the bitter necessity of renunciation.

Vast as is the canvas and widely embracing the scope, *Le Soulier de satin*, the complex and definitive resolution of Claudel's problem of reconciling *eros* and *agape*, is not the most dramatically effective of his works. Even in the shortened stage version it is far too long. Moreover, the presentation on the stage of the theological explanation of the action, in the guise of a crudely materialized guardian angel, tends to alienate the spectator's sympathy from the protagonists, for they are thus seen, not as struggling human beings uncertain of their destiny, but as manipulated puppets of an omniscient deity lacking in compassion. The device of a desperate letter of appeal taking ten years to reach the recipient, during which time irrevocable events in favour of the lovers' separation take place, ranks among the more grotesque elements that this play often deliberately exploits. The transmutation of love is, none the less, worked out in terms more psychologically and theologically acceptable than elsewhere in Claudel's work. There is immense poignancy in Prouhèze's soliloquy after the first attempt by Rodrigue to entice her away from her African post:

> Oui, je sais qu'il ne m'épousera que sur la croix et nos âmes l'une à l'autre dans la mort et dans la nuit hors de tout motif humain!
>
> Si je ne puis être son paradis, du moins je puis être sa croix! Pour que son âme avec son corps y soit écartelée je vaux bien ces deux morceaux de bois qui se traversent!
>
> Puisque je ne puis lui donner le ciel, du moins je puis l'arracher à la terre.
>
> Quand je le tiendrai ainsi par tous les bouts de son corps et par toute la texture de sa chair et de sa personne par le moyen de ces clous en moi profondément enfoncés,
>
> Quand il n'y aura plus aucun moyen de s'échapper, quand il sera fixé à moi pour toujours dans cet impossible hymen, . . .
>
> C'est alors que je le donnerai à Dieu découvert et déchiré pour qu'il le remplisse dans un coup de tonnerre, c'est alors que j'aurai un époux et que je tiendrai un dieu entre mes bras! . . .
>
> Il a demandé Dieu à une femme et elle était capable de le lui donner, car il n'y a rien au ciel et sur la terre que l'amour ne soit capable de donner! (Second Day, scene xiv; scene xi in the stage version)

Though it may seem hardly necessary, in the light of such a deep realization of the meaning of love, for Prouhèze to wait a further ten years and be prompted by her guardian angel before asking Rodrigue to relieve her of her promise of herself to him, this passage of time emphasizes the difficulty of reconciling the body to this privation, the slowness of the 'evangelization of the flesh'.

This 'evangelization of the flesh' seems absent from *L'Otage*, so bitter for the heroine is the renunciation of human love. Claudel even confers on his heroine in the last act a nervous movement of the head which symbolizes her refusal to accept the situation into which she has been argued, her marriage with Turelure, undertaken to secure the Pope's supposed safety. The value of Sygne de Coûfontaine's sacrifice of her cousin's love remains equivocal. For one thing, it is not really a question of the Pope's safety but of whether he remains in Bourbon hands or falls into Turelure's. In the brilliantly sharp dialogue between Abbé Badilon and Sygne (Act III, scene ii), a masterpiece of cruelty, the priest in effect equates the Pope with God, his safety with his remaining a monarchical pawn. Employing the utmost sophistry of argument, he yet contrives to throw the onus of decision on Sygne:

> Et vous, que pour sauver le Père de tous les hommes, selon que vous en avez reçu vocation,
> Vous renonciez à votre amour et à votre nom et à votre cause et à votre honneur en ce monde,
> Embrassant votre bourreau et l'acceptant pour époux, comme le Christ s'est laissé manger par Judas,
> — La Justice ne le commande pas. (III. ii)

The priest clearly implies, however, that love requires this distortion of Sygne's nature. Once she has made her decision, he glosses over the intolerable hardship involved:

> 'O mon enfant, certes la joie est grande que je réserve à mes saints, mais que dites-vous de mon calice?' Il est facile de mourir,
> Il est facile d'accepter la mort, et la honte et le coup sur le visage et l'inintelligence, et le mépris de tous les hommes.
> Tout est facile excepté de Vous contrister.
> Tout est facile, ô mon Dieu, à celui qui Vous aime
> Excepté de ne pas faire Votre volonté adorable . . . (III. ii)

The rest of the play reveals how hard it is to accept sacrifice and what a total absence of joy there is for Sygne. If, however, one were to take the absolutist view of the priest, who makes no allowance for ordinary human nature, one would no doubt argue that the play reveals how little love, love of God, Sygne really has.

In the original version of this play, the priest asks Sygne's forgiveness, when she is at the point of death, for 'ce mal que je vous ai fait, . . . / Afin que Pierre soit sauvé et que votre couronne soit parfaite' (Act III, scene ii). Sygne's exhaustion hardly bears effective witness, however, to the priest's claim that his arguments were furnished 'Sur l'ordre de Dieu, mon maître . . .'. Her final effort to make the sign of the cross, in the original version of the play, is plainly meant to imply her ultimate acceptance of her frustrated life, though in the variant that Claudel wrote for the denouement, the movement she makes is less explicit and therefore remains ambiguous. Indeed, the excellence of the play lies in its deep ambiguity. Turelure, for all his unscrupulous expediency as a man gaining power through the Revolution, is sensitive to the course of history, 'l'homme du possible' (Act II, scene i), whereas Sygne's cousin, who brought the pope to Coûfontaine in the first place, is shown as clinging to a dead past. Claudel no more oversimplifies the historical than the personal issue, the problem whether Sygne has indeed fulfilled God's purpose or merely made a misguided sacrifice of her own and her cousin's lives, responsible as she is for the latter's spirit of rebellion.

L'Otage is one of only two plays by Claudel which are fully tragic. The other is *Tête d'Or*, poetically the richest of Claudel's plays, the first version being written when he was only twenty-one, before his symbols became too obvious, his meaning too edifyingly clear. The exaltation and exultation of youth, the determination to conquer the world, inspire this work, though the spirit of conquest, which Turelure and Rodrigue also embody, comes to its usual violent end. Sun symbolism pervades the play in the contrasting dualism of inner sun of Grace and physical sun of nature, foreshadowing Claudel's later dichotomy between divine and human love, but embracing them both in one unifying symbol. The dying Tête d'Or, whose own head of golden hair is an obvious sun symbol, ecstatically celebrates his union with the appropriately setting sun, which he clasps on his chest like a wheel: 'Poitrine contre poitrine, tu te mêles à mon sang terrestre! . . . / O lion, tu me couvres! O aigle, tu m'enserres!' (Part III, second version). To be offset against this glorification of nature is the dying hero's merciful act in unnailing the crucified princess from the tree, an unmistakable salvational symbol. In this self-questioning play by a young man anxious to elucidate the riddle of life, Claudel provides no categorical answer. He was to do so, however, two years later, in *Le Repos du septième jour*, where at the end the new emperor dons pontifical vestments, the sign of his Christian conversion. The second version of *La Ville*, written one year later still, in 1897, presents in the final act the new leader of the new city embracing Christianity, the solution to all the social ills of the past, without, be it said, the play's indicating how this ideal is to be practically achieved. The creed recited by Cœuvre, poet and finally bishop, declares the Church to be 'catholique, infaillible et exclusive'. The encounter with 'Ysé' three years later was to convince the poet that Christianity involves difficulties in practical application not solved by a mere proclamation of belief, but it was also to turn his attention away from the social problem which had been at least envisaged, especially in *La Ville*. Passionate love, he was to find, was as exclusive as he considered the Catholic Church to be.

Too often Claudel's plays are unambiguous representations of the working of the divine will of which the author seemingly knows all the secret interplay. *L'Annonce faite à Marie*, for instance, is really a pseudo-medieval mystery play, demonstrating on a heroic scale how saintliness may unexpectedly be imposed on a girl who only wants to live a life of domestic happiness. As always, spiritual growth is accomplished in intolerably hard conditions, lack of sufficient love from others, the foregoing of the beloved, leprosy, blindness, segregation, and ultimately death by violence at the hands of the sister who has suffered from the jealousy of being a younger child, less favoured in looks and nature. The flesh is 'evangelized' through the slow corruption of leprosy, though Violaine's body is indeed finally healed in readiness for death. As always, too, spiritual action is interdependent: the major events of the world, the influence of friends, the life of cloistered nuns, all are interlocked in a spiritual exchange. The play has great beauty in its serene simplicity, but such a hugely edifying demonstration of God's harsh providence hardly involves the reader or spectator very fully in the human vicissitudes, for, ultimately, there is little that is human. The human tragedy of the married life of Jacques, Violaine's former fiancé, and Mara, her jealous homicidal sister, is only glimpsed, overshadowed by the exemplary self-sacrifice of Violaine.

Despite the failings, Claudel's achievement is immense, both as poet and as poet-playwright. He is a writer unique in the twentieth century, unique as a passionate love poet who is at the same time deeply committed to the Christian faith. The very harshness, the rigidity, the absolute and exclusive nature of that faith, make for his particular quality as a dramatist of heroic renunciation, seen most uncompromisingly in *L'Otage* and *L'Annonce faite à Marie*. Woman was always for him of deeply religious significance, ever since he read, at the age of eighteen, the eighth chapter of Proverbs, soon coming to see in the Woman evoked there the figure of Wisdom and eventually the Mother of Christ. The impact of one particular woman merely added a further dimension, albeit an agonizingly enigmatic one for him, to a religious meaning in womanhood that he had long before perceived. While he is the dramatist of denied satisfaction, he is also the dramatist of feminine apotheosis. Mesa is indeed the spiritual superior and instructor of Ysé, but Violaine and Prouhèze firmly point the way heavenward to the bewildered and earthbound males left broken behind.

It has been said that Christianity, because of what has been called its 'dialectic of salvation', represents an essentially dramatic view of the world which might readily suggest to a writer like Claudel the appropriateness of theatrical expression. Curiously enough, Montherlant's much more secular viewpoint and different outlook also point towards dramatic possibilities. One of the most persistent features of his thought is an emphasis on the multiplicity of life and on the fact that human instincts and human experience are compounded of conflicting and contrasting elements which must be embraced within a wider unity. This is the doctrine of 'totalisme' or 'syncrétisme et alternance' which holds that the qualities of tenderness and cruelty, humility and pride, self-restraint and self-indulgence, are all desirable as manifestations of life and should be equally acceptable. In an essay of 1923 Montherlant writes:

... que je vive toutes les vies, toutes les diversités, et toutes les contradictions du monde, avec intensité et détachement. . . . Tout pouvoir pour tout vivre, tout vivre pour tout connaître, tout connaître pour tout comprendre, tout comprendre pour tout exprimer.

Such a statement does much to explain Montherlant's resolutely non-sectarian outlook and his general opposition to systematization and dogma. It also suggests one way in which he has been attracted by the theatre, since to create plays is an obvious means for a writer to 'live' confrontation and multiplicity through diverse and contrasting characters. The dialectical nature of Montherlant's outlook on life finds a natural expression in the dialectic of theatrical drama.

Although he wrote *L'Exil* in 1914 and *Pasiphaé* in 1928, Montherlant first arrived as a major French dramatist—suddenly, if not wholly unexpectedly—with the success of *La Reine morte* in 1942. The authentic Montherlantian note was at once struck in this play of psychological and moral dilemma. Set in Portugal, it concentrates on the seventy-year-old king, Ferrante, who is disillusioned by life and claims that action is pointless, yet has to deal with the fact that his son Don Pedro, destined for reasons of state to marry the Infanta of Navarra, is already secretly married to Inès de Castro who is expecting his child. In the third and final act, as a subtle understanding and friendship develops between them, Ferrante gives the order for Inès to be killed. He himself dies shortly afterwards addressing his companions:

> Messieurs, je ne sais comment l'avenir jugera l'exécution de doña Inès. Peut-être un bien, peut-être un mal. . . . O mon Dieu, dans ce répit qui me reste, avant que le sabre repasse et m'écrase, faites qu'il tranche ce nœud épouvantable de contradictions qui sont en moi, de sorte que, un instant au moins avant de cesser d'être, je sache enfin ce que je suis. (III. viii)

Ferrante's problem concerning his identity, together with his consciousness of acute moral conflict, makes him the forerunner of a series of dramatic heroes and heroines that includes Alvaro (*Le Maître de Santiago*), Malatesta (*Malatesta*), Sœur Angélique de Saint-Jean (*Port-Royal*), and Cisneros (*Le Cardinal d'Espagne*). Ferrante is at once sympathetic and egotistical, generous and cruel, strong and weak. The other main characters in the play reflect aspects of his personality—the Infanta his logic, Don Pedro his vacillation, Inès his tragic vocation, Coelho and Gonçalvès (two members of his court) his Machiavellian qualities—and all, like Ferrante himself, are portrayed with impressive psychological insight.

La Reine morte is typical, then, of the 'théâtre de caractères' which Montherlant describes himself as offering to the public. The element of heroic grandeur emerges from the experience of his main characters as they struggle with some enormous inner crisis in a manner that recalls the heroes and heroines of Corneille and Racine. It is this struggle and this crisis, whether surmounted in victory or experienced as ultimate defeat, which give his plays their rich, spiritual dimension so that they serve Montherlant's own theatrical aim: 'passer à l'universel par le plus violemment ou le plus pauvrement particulier'.

At the same time, it is also typical of Montherlant that he matches the tragic inevitability inherent in his dramatic material with a tightly woven and closely organized theatrical structure. He does so in a way that recalls Racine's 'action simple, chargée de peu de matière', and this is true of virtually all his plays from *La Reine morte* to *La Guerre civile*. *Le Maître de Santiago*, first performed in 1948, is an obvious example of 'strong' drama derived from 'slight' matter. The play is set in Avila in the early sixteenth century. The main character, Don Alvaro, master of the chivalric Order of Santiago, seeks salvation through total renunciation of the world in a way that recalls Ferrante. His daughter Mariana is in love with Jacinto whose father, Don Bernal, belongs to the same Order and will only agree to the marriage if Alvaro will go to the New World and obtain a rich dowry for his daughter by this means. Despite his high, contemplative ideals Alvaro has almost been tricked into reluctant agreement when Mariana reveals the deception to him, renounces her desire to marry, and joins her father in lofty, heroic self-sacrifice. In the opening scene of the play Mariana had said of Alvaro: 'Pour mon père, seul est important, ou plutôt seul est essentiel, ou plutôt seul est réel ce qui se passe à l'intérieur de l'âme.' In the final scene she confirms her determination to share her father's *askesis* and concludes: 'Je sais qu'une seule chose est nécessaire, et qu'elle est celle que tu disais . . .' Once again, on the way to this conclusion, Montherlant reveals a series of psychological insights as he shares with his audience a searching exploration of pride, loneliness, suffering, self-deception, world-weariness, and spiritual ambition.

In both *La Reine morte* and *Le Maître de Santiago* a father is prepared to sacrifice his daughter or daughter-in-law. These are
instances, along with such plays as *L'Exil* and *Fils de personne*, of
that obsession with Abraham's sacrifice of Isaac which Montherlant
notes in his own work. In each case, too, sacrificer and sacrificed
become joined together in a strange complicity which introduces a
note of disturbing moral ambiguity. Perhaps on this account, some
critics have held Alvaro to be a monster of egotism, a determined
opponent of all obstacles to his personal grandeur, a fanatic who
lacks charity, humility, and every other saintly attribute. Nevertheless, this reaction seems to be insensitive to the moral nuances that
characterize Montherlant's work. He himself is frequently his own
best commentator, as when he writes of Alvaro:

> Je n'ai pas fait d'Alvaro un chrétien modèle, et il est par instants une
> contrefaçon du chrétien: presque un pharisien. Il reste en deçà du
> christianisme. Il sent avec force le premier mouvement du christianisme,
> la renonciation, le *Nada*; il sent peu le second, l'union, le *Todo*. L'Islam
> imprègne l'Espagne de cette époque: la religion d'Alvaro consiste
> presque toute, comme celle des Mores (ou celle de l'Ancien Testament),
> à révérer l'infinie distance de Dieu: Allah est grand. Mais l'Incarnation?
> mais l'intimité tendre avec un crucifié? mais 'Emmanuel' ('Dieu avec
> nous')?

This passage is revealing because it suggests the inadequacy of one
particular critical commonplace frequently applied to Montherlant
—that his plays, even when they contain Christian subject-matter,
are totally devoid of any truly Christian spirit. It is clear, on the
contrary, that his attitude is a complex one and that he is especially
sensitive to what is perhaps a severe and unpopular element, but
undoubtedly an authentic one, within Christian teaching: the need
to renounce the world in order to follow Christ. It is this element of
withdrawal and asceticism in Montherlant's thought which has
most readily, and justifiably, encouraged commentators to speak of
his Jansenism.

'Jansenism' is an appropriate term with which to describe the
subject, as well as the spirit, of Montherlant's most obviously religious play, *Port-Royal* (1954). The action is set in the convent of
Port-Royal in Paris in August 1664. Telescoping two historical

visits by Archbishop Péréfixe into one, the play describes the unsuccessful resistance by the Port-Royal nuns to the Archbishop's demand that they sign the formulary condemning as heretical five propositions derived from Jansen's *Augustinus*. Montherlant himself interestingly describes *Port-Royal* as a rewriting of *Le Maître de Santiago*. He means by this that the conflict between the nuns and the worldly Archbishop of Paris is essentially the same as that between Don Alvaro and Don Bernal. Historically, purity and compromise of this kind have always been in opposition to one another within the Christian tradition. As Montherlant puts it, 'la race des durs' and 'la race des doux' have been regularly warring factions deriving their justification from a common Christian source. And he adds: 'Cette race [des intransigeants], la mauvaise conscience des chrétiens de la compromission la persécute incessamment sur la terre.' It is the spectacle of this persecution that we are offered in *Port-Royal*; it is sharply revealed in the exchanges between Sœur Françoise and the Archbishop, particularly when she exclaims:

En tout endroit où le christianisme est pris au sérieux un peu plus, qu'ailleurs, on appelle jansénistes ceux qui le prennent ainsi, et on les traite en maudits et en pestiférés

and the Archbishop counters:

De là cette rigueur qui . . . fait paraître au monde la vertu trop pesante, l'Évangile excessif, le christianisme impossible. Le monde est déjà si près de trouver le christianisme trop austère — et vous y ajoutez! Que deviendrons-nous quand tous se détournent d'une religion rendue impraticable?

Port-Royal is a play of great richness at both the spiritual and human levels. It serves as the vehicle for a crucial religious debate which, apart from its ultimate doctrinal origins, also possesses a general moral reference taking it beyond the limits of Catholic theology. Characteristically, Montherlant responds to both conflicting elements in the debate. It is typical of his own position— and no doubt also an indication of his particular qualifications to turn this historical subject-matter into a genuinely dramatic confrontation—that he should have written to Philippe de Saint Robert in 1958: 'Je reste de tout cœur avec les religieuses jusqu'au bout;

cependant, si j'avais été archevêque de Paris en 1664, j'aurais fait mon devoir, comme Péréfixe.'[1] At the same time the nuns, whose resistance gives rise to the whole drama, are portrayed in essentially human terms and are not mere puppets mouthing set phrases in a theological debate. On stage it is not always possible to distinguish them visually as they move backwards and forwards in their white habits with a scarlet cross embroidered on the scapular. But their speech individualizes them at once: the serenity of Mère Agnès; the pure Jansenist intransigeance of Sœur Françoise; the early rigidity of Sœur Angélique dissolving, under pressure, into anguished doubt about her faith; the betrayal by Sœur Flavie. One of the difficult lessons emerging from the play—a lesson peculiarly appropriate to its subject—is the suggestion that once the nuns are tempted to try to win their case on Péréfixe's own terms, rather than to justify themselves by faith alone, a certain deterioration sets in.

The familiar Montherlantian theme of heroic spiritual struggle is central to another of his most impressive plays, *Le Cardinal d'Espagne* (1960). With this tragedy we return to sixteenth-century Spain and in Cardinal Cisneros we meet a character in the elevated tradition of Ferrante and Alvaro (Aralo says of Cisneros: 'Il est Castillan: tout ce qui n'est pas dur l'exaspère'). However, there is an important difference. While Ferrante and Alvaro represent an ideal of renunciation for which they fight against other characters in the same play, Cisneros is above all a self-divided individual embodying the essence of *alternance*. One element in his nature prompts withdrawal into religion through reaction to the vanity of life; the other seeks and enjoys power, particularly the power of life and death over his fellow men. The Queen, Jeanne la Folle, brutally reveals his contradictions when she says: 'Vous vous êtes enfui vers les cloîtres parce que vous aimiez trop le pouvoir. . . . Vous, vous composez. . . . Vous, vous vivez dans la comédie.' Prior to his death Cisneros comes to a realization, though not a resolution, of his contradictory nature and confesses: 'Je ne veux pas ce que j'aime, et je veux ce que je n'aime pas.' The Cardinal lives his contraditions at a heroic, almost superhuman, level. His strength

---

[1] Philippe de Saint Robert, *Montherlant le séparé* (Paris, 1969), p. 88.

D

and his weakness are equally on a grandiose scale. His tragedy is summed up by Montherlant in seven words: 'Cisneros a deux passions, et meurt déchiré.'

Le Cardinal d'Espagne is thus a tragedy of human blindness, of inadequate self-knowledge. It is a perfect example of Montherlant's own definition of the tragic element in his plays: 'Le tragique dans mon théâtre est bien moins un tragique de situation qu'un tragique provenant de ce qu'un être contient en lui-même.' Once again, the structure skilfully matches the subject and Montherlant has written an analysis of its three acts in terms of the three *tercios* which make up the inevitable and preordained progress of the bull-fight to the final moment of truth, the resolution of conflict in death.

There has not been space to comment on all Montherlant's 'costume' plays—*Malatesta* (1946) and *La Guerre civile* (1965) are also worth study—and his plays with modern settings such as *Fils de personne* (1943) and *La Ville dont le prince est un enfant* (1951) have been ignored for the purposes of this chapter. It was the rich, heroic vein in his theatre that we were concerned to discuss, and one general point about it remains to be made. Montherlant's most impressive characters, like those of Claudel, are drawn on a grand scale. In evil as in good they approach superhuman dimensions. Inevitably, therefore, certain critics have complained that the heroic grandeur of these characters works against their ability to engage the emotions of the audience. It is sometimes suggested that Montherlant's plays are static, remote, hieratic, and lacking in naturalness. Apart from the fact that this is distinctly not the impression made on many readers and theatre audiences, the criticism is one which seems to mistake the nature of the tragic in art. Distortion, stylization, and heroic projection are essential, in some measure, to any art attempting to give us insights that we cannot normally expect to have in ordinary day-to-day contact with experience. Great tragedy of the kind which Montherlant offers has never been solely a matter of emotional identification with characters on a stage (any more than it has been in the case of Racine, or Greek tragedy). It has always required, beyond the psychological level, the intellectual apprehension of certain qualities or a set of circumstances bringing unavoidable disaster to the characters in question. Emotional experience inevitably accompanies this intellectual illumination, but two separate things—art and life—are involved. Great tragic plays are not simply windows through which we observe life directly. They shape and pattern the life which is their subject-matter so that they take us, momentarily at least, beyond normal 'life' in that sense. It is this shaping and patterning which enables us to experience the exaltation, aesthetic in its original impulse, which comes from the fact that we have foreseen and accepted, on some universal human level, a form of inevitable disaster.

NOTE

PAUL CLAUDEL, 1868-1955, after holding various consular posts, became ambassador in turn to Japan, the United States, and Belgium. He was elected to the Académie française in 1946. His literary work was thus written in his spare time. His life and his writing were much influenced by his conversion to Catholicism, which took place in 1886, though he was not received into the Church until 1890. During the last twenty years of his life he devoted himself increasingly to biblical exegesis.

Works. Claudel's best-known plays, many of which have two published versions, are *Tête d'Or* (1890 and 1901), *La Ville* (1893 and 1901), *La Jeune Fille Violaine* (1926 and 1901),* *L'Annonce faite à Marie* (1912), *L'Échange* (1901 and 1954), *Le Repos du septième jour* (1901), *Partage de midi* (1906), *L'Otage* (1911), *Le Pain dur* (1918), *Le Père humilié* (1920), *Le Soulier de satin* (1929 and 1944), *Cinq Grandes Odes* (1910). Among his numerous other works are translations of plays by Aeschylus and odes by Coventry Patmore. Several volumes of his correspondence have been published, that with André Gide receiving most attention.

Editions. The plays have been grouped in two volumes, *Théâtre* by J. Madaule in the Bibliothèque de la Pléiade (1947-8, second volume re-edited in augmented form, 1966, by J. Madaule and J. Petit). These two volumes were followed by the *Œuvre poétique* (1957) and *Œuvres en prose* (1965), the texts of the latter established and annotated by J. Petit and C. Galpérine, both volumes in the Pléiade edition. Nearing completion are the *Œuvres complètes*, of which twenty-six volumes have been published since 1950, various scholars preparing different volumes. A critical edition of *La Ville*, established by J. Petit, appeared in 1967.

* This play has two versions, written in 1892-3. The first version was published as late as 1926, whereas the second version had appeared in 1901.

Criticism. P.-A. Lesort, *Paul Claudel par lui-même* (1963), is an indispensable introduction to both man and work. Studies of the plays include J. Madaule, *Le Drame de Paul Claudel* (1947), J. Bastien, *L'Œuvre dramatique de Paul Claudel* (1957), and Gabriel Marcel, *Regards sur le théâtre de Claudel* (1964). More particularized studies include E. Beaumont, *Le Sens de l'amour dans le théâtre de Claudel* (1957), J. Boly, *'L'Annonce faite à Marie', étude et analyse* (1957), P. Brunel, *'Le Soulier de satin' devant la critique* (1964), P. Brunel, *'L'Otage' de Paul Claudel ou le théâtre de l'énigme* (1964), C. Cattaui, *Claudel, le cycle de Coûfontaine et le mystère d'Israël* (1968), M.-M. Fragonard, *'Tête d'Or', ou l'Imagination mythique chez Paul Claudel* (1968), J. Petit, *Pour une explication du 'Soulier de satin'* (1965), J. Kempf and J. Petit, *Études sur la 'Trilogie' de Claudel, 1, L'Otage* (1966), *2, Le Pain dur* (1967), *3, Le Père humilié* (1968), M.-L. Tricaud, *Le Baroque dans le théâtre de Paul Claudel* (1967), Yvette Bozon-Scalzetti, *Le Verset claudélien — une étude de rythme — (Tête d'Or)* (1965). *Claudel: A Reappraisal,* ed. R. Griffiths (1968), also contains studies of certain plays. Eight issues of the *Cahiers Paul Claudel* have appeared, the first of these being wholly concerned with *Tête d'Or* (1959), and the last comprising G. Gadoffre's *Claudel et l'univers chinois.* Five issues of the *Revue des Lettres Modernes* have been devoted to Claudel, articles on the plays appearing in *Paul Claudel 2, le Regard en arrière* (1965), *Paul Claudel 3, Thèmes et images* (1966), *Paul Claudel 4, l'Histoire* (1967), and *Paul Claudel 5, Schémas dramatiques* (1968). Five issues of the *Cahiers canadiens Claudel* have also been published.

HENRY DE MONTHERLANT was born in Paris in 1896 and has become one of the most versatile and independent French writers of this century. His early enthusiasms, of which he has written extensively, include bull-fighting, football, athletics, and Roman civilization. He was wounded in both World Wars and in the inter-war period spent much time travelling outside France, particularly in North Africa. Primarily known as a novelist and essayist before the Second World War, he has since established a major reputation as a dramatist. In 1963 he was elected to the Académie française.

Works. Two Pléiade volumes of collected works extend as far as the 1950s: *Théâtre* (ed. J. de Laprade, 1954) and *Romans et œuvres de fiction non théâtrales* (ed. R. Secrétain, 1959). To the former should be added *Brocéliande* (1956), *Don Juan* (1958), *Le Cardinal d'Espagne* (1960), and *La Guerre civile* (1965). Novels to be added to the second Pléiade volume are: *L'Histoire d'amour de 'La Rose de sable'* (1954) (the complete novel, *La Rose de sable*, was published in 1968), *Le Chaos et la Nuit* (1963), and *Les Garçons* (1969). Among Montherlant's many volumes of essays special mention may be made of *La Relève du matin* (1920), *Aux fontaines du désir* (1927), *Mors et vita* (1932), *Service inutile* (1935), *L'Équinoxe de septembre* (1938), *Le Solstice de juin* (1941), *Textes sous une occupation* (1953). Two collections of 'notebooks' are: *Carnets: 1930–1944* (1957) and *Va jouer avec cette poussière* (*Carnets: 1958–1964*) (1966).

Criticism. Some of the most illuminating comments on Montherlant's drama are to be found in the many notes, prefaces, postscripts, etc., which he himself has written in connection with almost all his plays. Major studies of his theatre as a whole are J. de Laprade, *Le Théâtre de Montherlant* (1950), and J. Batchelor, *Existence and Imagination: the Theatre of Henry de Montherlant* (1967). Books on individual plays include M. de Saint-Pierre, *Montherlant, bourreau de soi-même* (1949), C. Paulus, *Témoignages du théâtre: 'Le Maître de Santiago' ou l'extase sans Dieu* (1951), J. Datain, *Montherlant et l'héritage de la Renaissance* (1956), and B. Mondini, *Montherlant du côté de Port-Royal: la pièce et ses sources* (1962). Among the many general studies of Montherlant's work special mention should be made of M. Mohrt, *Montherlant, homme libre* (1943), J. N. Faure-Biguet, *Les Enfances de Montherlant (de neuf à vingt ans)* (1948), Jeanne Sandelion, *Montherlant et les femmes* (1950), P. Sipriot, *Montherlant par lui-même* (1953), G. Bordonove, *Henry de Montherlant* (1954), H. Perruchot, *Montherlant* (1959), Nicole Debrie-Panel, *Montherlant, l'art et l'amour* (1960), J. de Beer, *Montherlant ou l'homme encombré de Dieu* (1963), J. Cruickshank, *Montherlant* (1964), R. B. Johnson, *Henry de Montherlant* (1968), P. de Saint Robert, *Montherlant le séparé* (1969).

6. Gide

GIDE loved paradox, he was proud to think of himself as a creature of paradox, and paradox occurs throughout his life and work. One such paradox is that, while he considered himself an esoteric writer speaking to a limited audience, and for much of his career did not appeal beyond such an audience, he frequently adopted the manner of a proselytizer or prophet who seeks a wider public. Whether he sought it or not, Gide eventually found his wider public. In the latter part of his life, with his major production behind him, alternately hailed as the liberator of youth or decried as its corrupter, Gide was generally recognized as an immensely important figure.

His influence and appeal can be measured in terms of the number of ordinary readers who bought his books and in terms of young writers who were influenced by him. Both Sartre and Camus, who were to occupy for a later generation a position similar to Gide's, have admitted his influence. Camus has stated that his view of classicism derived directly from Gide's view of it as *romantisme dompté*, whilst Sartre has written that his whole generation was dominated by the dual influence of Proust and Gide. Even when unstated, his influence on both these men is sometimes apparent. The use of *conscience* as a key-term in Camus's thinking, exploiting the word's ambiguity in French to stress alternately intellectual awareness and moral conscience, is highly reminiscent of its similarly ambiguous function in *Le Prométhée mal enchaîné*. The mischievous might even suggest that Camus based Grand's style on the poetic prose of, say, *La Tentative amoureuse*. Equally, Sartre's claim that the fatherless son has an advantage over other boys, since his development is not inhibited by the daunting example of a father, although rooted in personal experience often reads like a revised version of Gide's apologia for the bastard or *natural* child, who is free from the artificial constraints of family and tradition. In fact, it is an interesting coincidence—perhaps more than co-incidence—that Gide, Camus, and Sartre figure among the significant number of one-parent children who have made a distinguished contribution to twentieth-century French literature.

However, as Gide himself noted, the influence of one writer on another rarely takes the form of encouraging the latter along the path mapped out by the former, but more often drives him in protest against his mentor along quite a different path. Thus, Camus and Sartre have both on occasion indicated where they differed from Gide. Camus felt obliged to point out that his own early sensualism had nothing to do with Gidian *ferveur*. Sartre has more than once explained why he outgrew the initial influence of Gide. But his most compelling rebuttal of any claim that Gide's relevance extends beyond a historically and socially limited group is in the characterization of his hero Mathieu Delarue (*Les Chemins de la liberté*), which is worth considering in some detail.

There seems little doubt that Mathieu was conceived along deliberately Gidian lines. In *sincérité* and *disponibilité*, Sartre has given him two of Gide's key-expressions to justify his attempt to live a life free of commitments to any save himself. The account of his earliest attempts to 'be himself' have the same quality of childish petulance as Lafcadio's *punte*. Mathieu, in fact, comes to us as a kind of ageing Lafcadio, when the first thrill of revolt is beginning to wear thin and he is forced to take stock of his achievements. At the same time, Sartre is at pains to show us that while claiming to remain independent of any system, Mathieu, by accepting a state salary and trying to behave like a gentleman, subscribes to the values of the society and class to which he belongs. Far from being presented as a heroic effort to discover his true nature and follow it in defiance of social taboos, Mathieu's adventure is shown as an empty sham. Thus, within Gide's own lifetime, the type of character which he used to portray revolt and authenticity had been stood on his head to become the prototype of moral timidity and bad faith.

Whatever reservations one has about the full implications which Sartre would seem to have us read into the characterization of

Mathieu, it serves as an early example of the rejection of Gide's values by the kind of restless inquiring mind which previously had welcomed them, and helps to define historically the comparative neglect from which Gide's work now suffers. To complete the historical perspective, it is necessary to consider how Gide's great reputation came about. Although generally thought of as a twentieth-century author, Gide published a considerable amount in the 1890s and a fair proportion of his major literary works had appeared by 1914. Yet Gide broke through to a wide public in the 1920s. The publications of that period which enabled him to do so were the first public edition of *Corydon* (1924), *Si le grain ne meurt* (1926), and, in the same year, *Les Faux-Monnayeurs* and a re-edition of *Les Nourritures terrestres*, which the reading public had almost totally ignored when it first appeared in 1897 and continued to ignore for nearly thirty years. Thus Gide, novelist, dramatist, essayist, and—to take into account a slim volume of verse and his early attempts at poetic prose—poet, found fame largely on the strength of a novel (incidentally his only piece of prose-fiction which Gide called by that name), two essays, and a book of personal reminiscence. Furthermore, all four works, particularly the last three, treat with varying degrees of outspokenness and emphasis, but always sympathetically, the then controversial subject of homosexuality.

The fact that Gide got through to a wide public in the 1920s, largely as the propounder of views which were at the time extremely daring, points to a major difficulty facing the modern reader of his work. Apart from whether or not his views on homosexuality have any relevance today, there is a broader question affecting the critical approach to Gide's work. From his non-imaginative writing there emerged, and quite properly, the picture of a man prepared to speak out courageously on behalf of a misunderstood and socially oppressed minority, a man prepared to state unpopular views publicly. This reputation spread to his imaginative writing, so that we are asked to consider Gide's work as a lifelong struggle for self-identity, undertaken by a man keenly aware of the obstacles placed in his path both by society and the contradictions in his own personality; but a successful struggle, so that his work is seen as an intricate complex of tension and counter-tension between opposite and equal forces, moulded into a satisfactory artistic pattern of harmony embracing dissonance. There was of course the obverse picture of the shameless degenerate, forever washing filthy linen in public. But both pictures share the common feature of identifying the man with his work and judging one largely in terms of the other.

All of this tends to get in the way of a reader anxious to make a clear critical appraisal of Gide. Facts about a writer's life and personality can often suggest the most useful critical approach to his work, but should never be allowed to swamp the critical process. Criticism of Gide has undergone a lot of swamping. For instance, we are sometimes invited to look upon *La Porte étroite* as a successful attempt by Gide to purge himself of a tendency towards mysticism. Whether we applaud this as a successful attempt to eradicate a debilitating habit, or deplore it as a deviation from the path of true righteousness, we should not imagine that in so doing we have even begun to make a critical assessment of the book. Equally, there is no doubt that Gide's treatment of homosexuality in his literary works is more outspoken than Proust's. Some might even agree that Gide was right to conclude that by depicting the admirable sides of homosexual relations in *A la recherche* in heterosexual terms and leaving only the comic and the grotesque in homosexual terms, Proust betrayed their common cause. But it does not necessarily follow that Proust's monumental novel is thereby a lesser or less lasting achievement than anything Gide wrote. The ultimate test for a work of literature is not whether its author was courageous or cowardly to have written it, but whether it is well written. It is a test which has been applied all too rarely to the work of Gide.

There is no doubt that many of Gide's ideas have dated. Thanks in a large measure to his own efforts, the world has no further need of Gide the agitator for a more enlightened approach to homosexuality. Equally, in a permissive age Gide's broader appeals for self-liberation have lost their power to shock, stimulate, or even interest. Would-be Nathanaëls are hard to come by these days when it is rare to find an undergraduate with the patience to read *Les Nourritures terrestres* right through, let alone adopt it as his *vade mecum* for life. But the fact of a writer's ideas dating need not date his work. For instance, Christians no longer put to death co-religionists of alternative persuasions. Yet we can still read Voltaire on the subject, because the manner of his writing—but equally the rigour of his thinking—stimulate an enthusiastic response.

The same quality of rigour is rarely to be found in Gide, whose thinking, though invariably original, brilliant, vital, versatile, is frequently, in the last resort, muddled. One such example of muddle is to be found in his treatment of the bastard. For all his celebration of such a person's good fortune, Gide never shows us an out-and-out bastard with no father, no name, no security. Bernard (in *Les Faux-Monnayeurs*) is the child of a married woman and her lover, brought up with his brothers and sister in the belief that his mother's husband is his father. The novel begins when, as an adolescent, Bernard discovers the truth about himself. The discovery in no way disturbs him, but reassures him by relieving him of the need for any remorse for having always disliked his 'father'. Bernard makes the immediate decision to leave his family, but having done so, soon finds a very adequate adoptive father in Édouard. Lafcadio (in *Les Caves du Vatican*) is even more comfortably cushioned against the practical and psychological inconveniences of illegitimacy. He is illegitimate in the technical sense that his mother was not married to his father, but no other. After a childhood spent with his mother and a series of 'uncles' in the fashionable spas of Europe, Lafcadio stumbles on to the identity of his aristocratic father. Moreover the father, within the limits of convention, acknowledges his son and arranges that after his death, which follows almost at once, Lafcadio will be handsomely provided for. Here history or at least literature repeats itself, for the homeless Moll Flanders, whose adventures were one of the few books to have passed through Lafcadio's hands, crowned an early life of vicissitude with a rich inheritance. Likewise, the financial security of Bernard's early life derived in part from his 'father's' salary, in part from a comfortable inheritance from his mother's parents.

Altogether Gide has given us an unusual pair of bastards. They are never in the position of having no family or background; it is their own choice, not an accident of birth, which cuts them off from their families. True, Lafcadio is never integrated into family life as Bernard is, but he assumes moral responsibility for the decision which prevents formal recognition by his father. 'Occupons-nous à liquider notre passé', he remarks after his meeting with Juste-Agénor, and again, on learning of his father's death: 'Apprêtons-nous à nous éloigner de lui davantage'. Instead of giving us characters without family ties, Gide has given us characters so placed in relation to their families as to be able without difficulty to reject the disadvantages of being tied to a family, while retaining the advantages which belonging to a rich bourgeois or aristocratic family provides. In selecting his two chief bastards, Gide shows the same social predilections as Oscar Molinier when choosing his sons' friends. Such predilections are natural in a right-thinking Establishment man, but disappointing in an iconoclast who thereby remains rooted in the tradition which he seeks to question. Moreover, by arranging for Lafcadio's Figaro-type discovery of his lordly antecedents, Gide draws uncritically on a long-established literary tradition. So, for all his technical bastardy, Lafcadio has a clear if unexciting pedigree: by social preference out of literary convention.

It might be objected that illegitimacy, though an important and recurring theme in Gide's work, still only represents a small part of the whole. But there are good reasons for stressing its importance. Unlike homosexuality, it is still a live social issue today and could in theory bridge the thought gap between Gide and contemporary readers. Furthermore, Gide's treatment of the subject raises points relevant to the whole of his thinking and writing. All of Gide's main characters reveal their creator's inability or unwillingness to think beyond the social group whose assumptions and values he purported to challenge. They all spend their time between Paris, fashionable spas, and country estates; should they venture further afield, it is to places which contemporary fashion had pronounced exotic. They all enjoy a comfortable income, preferably unearned. Even Boris, the least favoured of Gide's bastards, had he survived his grandfather, would have come into a small unearned income. At the same time, Gide's preoccupation with theft, invariably of an anodine variety, and counterfeit coins pays oblique homage to the importance of property and money. The automatic assumption of moneyed ease stands out most glaringly as Ménalque's account of his wild bohemian wanderings, which the author repeats in his own name, reaches its climax:

> A cinquante ans, l'heure étant venue, je vendis tout, et, comme mon goût sûr et ma connaissance de chaque objet ne m'avait fait possesseur de rien dont la valeur n'eût augmenté, je réalisai en deux jours une fortune considérable. Je plaçai cette fortune toute entière de façon que j'en pusse perpétuellement disposer. Je vendis absolument tout, ne voulant rien garder de *personnel* sur cette terre; pas le moindre souvenir d'antan.

This passage is an untidy compromise between monastic renunciation of worldly goods and attachment to bourgeois affluence, which, combined with the evangelistic tone elsewhere (for example 'il quitta tout pour me suivre'), reads like a sermon on the text: 'Sell all and keep every penny for yourself'. The Ménalque of *L'Immoraliste* presents the same uneasy amalgam of revolt and conformity. He explains his belief in individualism and hatred of imitation, while dressed in tails at a formal reception. He is said to have led a life of adventure and exploration, as a result of which the Minister for the Colonies has entrusted him with a special mission. But the nearest he gets to adventurous individualism in the reader's presence is to turn his back on a fellow guest. Altogether, he comes across to a present-day reader not as a genuine adventurer but rather as a gentleman got up as a Malraux hero for a fancy dress ball.

Gide's account of his own early religious and moral development in *Si le grain ne meurt* shows him similarly rooted in conventional attitudes:

> La morale selon laquelle j'avais vécu jusqu'à ce jour cédait depuis peu à je ne savais trop encore quelle vision chatoyante de la vie. Il commençait à m'apparaître que le devoir n'était peut-être pas pour chacun le même, et que Dieu pouvait bien avoir lui-même en horreur cette uniformité contre quoi protestait la nature, mais à quoi tendait, me semblait-il, l'idéal chrétien, en prétendant mater la nature. Je n'admettais plus que morales particulières . . . de sorte que tout effort pour se soumettre à

une règle commune devenait à mes yeux trahison; oui, trahison, et que j'assimilais à ce grand péché contre l'Esprit 'qui ne serait point pardonné', par quoi l'être particulier perdrait sa signification précise, irremplaçable, sa 'saveur' qui ne pouvait lui être rendue.

In short, while claiming to recognize only personal ethics, Gide makes no attempt to redefine such concepts as God, nature, duty; and while questioning the validity of the Christian ideal, leans heavily for his meaning on the implied connotations of salt losing its savour and explicit reference to the Holy Spirit. The true Gide devotee would perhaps find here an example of harmony embracing dissonance or, possibly, a master-stroke by the master of paradox and irony. Others might be forgiven if they see nothing more than a half-hearted and muddled attempt by Gide to think his way out of traditional values.

The inadequacy of Gide's attempts to think clearly, and free of contemporary assumptions, need not invalidate his writing. Great literature has been produced by authors whose thinking remained rooted in the assumptions, contradictions, and prejudices of their age. The real test is whether the writing has satisfying artistic shape. For instance, it might be argued that in the fictional context where Lafcadio and Bernard appear, we are not intended to consider the social and psychological aspects of illegitimacy; that their realization of illegitimacy, followed by the token period of pennilessness which both undergo before falling on their feet again, is symbolic of a spiritual development, whereby they make a break with their past and assume responsibility for their own destiny, rather as Michel's stripping off his clothes and removing his beard (in *L'Immoraliste*) is symbolic of his break with the past and previous values.

The argument would soon falter. First, in neither of the two later cases is the break as radical as Michel's. Thanks to his father's death-bed largesse, Lafcadio continues to live the life to which his successive 'uncles'' largesse had accustomed him. The break is even less radical in Bernard's case. After only the briefest hiatus, he goes from the tutelage of his legal father to that of Édouard. His links with his academic past and all it stands for by way of conventional values remain firm. Although he misses taking his *baccalauréat* by leaving Paris with Édouard, he continues to work for it and passes brilliantly at the autumn examination. What sort of a rebel is it, today's young will ask, who never even questions the examination system?

There are more general reasons why Lafcadio's and Bernard's illegitimacy and their attitudes towards it cannot be taken as an adequate symbol of some other kind of development. Michel's drama is enacted against a sketchily drawn, forever shifting social background, made up largely of rented houses and hotel rooms. The other characters, and Michel's relationship with them, are equally sketchily drawn. So in the absence of any firm social framework it is easy to read Michel's journeyings as an allegory of a spiritual pilgrimage. This is not the case with the later works, where social background is amply depicted, newspaper items and—in the case of *Les Faux-Monnayeurs*—historical figures worked into the narrative and several leading characters and their relationships with each other fully depicted. In works where social and psychological factors play an important part, we are bound to consider a social and psychological phenomenon like illegitimacy in its own terms.

Although the larger-than-life quality of character and narrative in *Les Caves du Vatican* perhaps discourages serious consideration of the social issues it raises (and questions relating to illegitimacy do not dominate throughout), this is not so with *Les Faux-Monnayeurs* where marriage, family life, and variations on them are the main themes. Within this framework, illegitimacy is given special emphasis. Just as the story opens with Bernard leaving his family, so it closes with him returning to his 'father' and brother. For good measure, Gide includes a second bastard in Boris and although his death thins the illegitimate ranks, with Laura pregnant by her former lover reinforcements are on their way as the story ends. Gide underlines the importance of these factors when he makes Édouard remark: 'L'avenir est aux bâtards. . . . Seul le bâtard a droit au naturel', to which Vincent adds botanical confirmation: 'Les bourgeons qui se développent naturellement sont toujours les bourgeons terminaux . . . les plus éloignés du tronc familial.' And in fact the main story concerns the efforts of Bernard and Olivier to branch out from the family tree.

Thus the basic structure of the book implies thematic contrasts between legitimate/natural children and dependence/independence of family. But one is bound to conclude that these contrasts do not find adequate artistic expression. As has already been indicated, Bernard is not natural enough, in Gide's sense of being without family ties, to lend himself to satisfying contrast with Olivier. By including Boris, a much more natural child, having been brought up only by an unconventional mother, Gide holds out the promise of a more interesting contrast. But Boris is never developed and the promise remains unfulfilled.

Much the same must be said of the second element of contrast. There is a static contrast between the adults with families and the independent adults, but the search for independence by the younger protagonists is never satisfactorily pursued, since they move from dependence on their family to dependence of some other kind: Bernard, from his family, to Édouard, and back to his family; Olivier, from his family, to Passavant, to Édouard. Again, Gide teases us with the inclusion of genuinely independent characters who are never allowed to figure prominently. The anarchical Strouvilhou and Cob-Lafleur are simply caricatural sketches. Sarah, with her feminist views and deliberate espousal of free love, is a far more independent spirit than Laura, who drifts into a love affair and an unwanted pregnancy and then relies largely on the initiative of others to resolve her difficulties; equally, Armand, with no money, no protector, and fierce scorn for his parents' values, is more independent in every way than either Bernard or Olivier. Yet neither he nor Sarah are more than perfunctorily developed.

There is one further broad structure to the book, where Gide stimulates and disappoints his readers' expectations. The story is set in 1896 when the Dreyfus Affair was under way. There can, of course, be no question of criticizing Gide for not dealing with the Affair, in the way that Sartre criticized Flaubert for not dealing with the Commune, however useful it might appear as material for an author concerned with the individual in relation to the community. If Gide chooses to let the family stand for the community and makes his choice work artistically, all well and good. But Gide does not so choose; he falls between two stools by writing mainly about the family, but raising, and failing adequately to deal with, the broader issue of the individual in relation to society as a whole. Édouard makes a statement about the individual and his milieu in an image which extends Vincent's earlier statement about tree-trunks and buds: 'Les romanciers nous abusent lorsqu'ils développent l'individu sans tenir compte des compressions d'alentour. La forêt façonne l'arbre.' Gide gives us some indications of how the pressures of the social forest help shape his protagonists. Most obviously he shows us the individual in relation to the judiciary and, although lawyers get a poor write-up, the system they represent is not seriously challenged. More interestingly, there is indirect reference to the Dreyfus Affair, by way of reference to Maurras and the *Action française*, Barrès's candidature, and in the description of the Nationalist meeting which Bernard attends. Not unexpectedly, he rejects the invitation to bury his individuality in the idea of the nation and the conclusion is implied that any collective movement is a danger to the individual. But this, without adequate consideration of those who at that time were countering the Nationalists' claims, by asserting the rights of the individual, is an unsatisfactory resolution of the problem Gide has unearthed. Furthermore, once issues arising from the Dreyfus Affair have been raised, given the basic themes of the book, it is difficult to find any artistic justification for the greater emphasis which Gide ultimately gives the author and first performance of *Ubu Roi*. All in all, Gide's treatment of *compressions d'alentour* represents an annoying loose end rather than an interesting new dimension to the novel.

There are further points of detail which also produce loose ends. For instance, the suggestion is made in the book that boys need a father-figure, but that natural fathers are unsuited to the task. The evidence, however, is ambiguous to say the least. Bernard and Olivier prefer Édouard to their fathers; but Édouard is a writer and the boys are both budding writers, whereas their fathers are both lawyers; are we to conclude that the situation would be unchanged if the boys were budding lawyers; or are we perhaps meant to understand that sensitive intelligent lads are necessarily budding writers and need a writer-father? The relationship between Bernard and his 'father' is fraught with ambiguity, culminating at

the point where Bernard 'follows his heart' and returns to him, ill
and abandoned by his wife. What impulse of the heart prompts the
return? Is it sympathy for a sick person or natural affection for a
non-natural father, given freer rein now that the mother is absent?
Finally, what is one to make of Pauline's assertion to her half-
brother that he would have been a better father to her boys than
their real father? Surely only a very silly woman would place much
reliance on the good influence on her children of an uncle who
choked with emotion at the mention of a favourite nephew's name.
Even if one gives Gide the benefit of the doubt and assumes that
each of the many ambiguities in *Les Faux-Monnayeurs* is the result
of deliberate paradox, one must still conclude that he abuses a
stylistic feature to the point of irritating his reader. Moreover, the
thematic untidiness of the book is emphasized by contrast with
the formal neatness of the overall structure, ensured by the ubi-
quitous, diary-writing Édouard, tying all the stray ends of the
plot together with the help of some startling coincidences.

One stylistic weakness of *Les Faux-Monnayeurs* crops up throughout Gide's work. Commenting on his diary account of his first meeting with Georges, Édouard notes that it would be better recounted
from the point of view of the child. One agrees and extends the
criticism to Gide's treatment generally of young characters in the
book, who are viewed rarely from the inside, almost always through
the eyes of an adult: Bernard and Olivier, mainly through the eyes
of their parents and Édouard; Boris, through the eyes of La Pérouse
and Sophroniska. In fact, the only young characters to be developed
are those who have a close relationship with an adult, through
whose eyes they can then be described. This obviously creates an
imbalance in the account of the relationship that emerges.

The same imbalance occurs elsewhere. In *Isabelle*, Casimir is
seen through the eyes of Gérard, the first person narrator: likewise
Gertrude in *La Symphonie pastorale* comes to us through the first
person narrative of the pastor. In his version of the Prodigal Son,
Gide imagines a younger brother; but in the exchange between
Prodigal and younger brother, the main stress is on the way in
which the former's attempt to influence the latter helps him to
clarify his own viewpoint. *La Porte étroite* shows us the attempt of

young people, recorded by themselves, to forge their destinies without reference to their elders. But the whole attempt is undertaken in terms of Christian values acquired from their elders and is, moreover, set in motion by the adultery of Alissa's mother, followed by the pastor's sermon and the apocalyptic vision it conjures up in Jérôme's mind, which colours the whole of his subsequent conduct. So, to that extent, the young characters remain a projection of adult behaviour and attitudes.

Les Caves du Vatican, where a third person narrator treats all characters with equal objectivity, is refreshingly free from this distorting perspective. In fact, the young are presented not as immature or inferior versions of their elders, but as a distinct and superior species. The older characters usually suffer some physical defect, often of a disfiguring kind: Anthime is half-crippled with sciatica and has a large wen on his neck; Julius suffers from insomnia; Amédée is of doubtful virility, bronchitic, and, for much of the story, covered with flea-bites, mosquito-bites, and a pimple on the chin. The young, on the other hand, are all physically perfect specimens: Julie is 'une gracieuse fille', Beppo 'un svelte adolescent', Lafcadio 'un beau jeune homme blond'.

However questionable as an intellectual proposition, Gide's version of the generation gap provides an artistically effective framework in which to develop his themes. The two half-brothers are contrasted as the man of letters and the man of action—dramatically a far more imposing contrast than, for instance, the 'good guy' writer and the 'bad guy' writer of *Les Faux-Monnayeurs*. Within each camp, thought and action are related to physical attributes. The Freemasonry-Roman Catholicism struggle is shown as a suitable activity for the elderly—two rigid systems appealing equally to people whose joints, along with their mental processes, have stiffened; a struggle which, because they stand quite outside it, enables the young to mock and exploit their elders. Equally, the mental flexibility of the young finds expression in physical agility: the ability to assume disguises, scramble up walls or drainpipes, toss old gentlemen out of trains. Like the basic situation, narrative development often rests on the contrasting features of young and old coming into contact. Anthime, whose agnosticism withstands the onslaught of adult reproaches, is largely shamed into conversion by the show of disapproval which his iconoclasm produces in Beppo and Julie. Similarly, the flea-bitten Amédée is drawn into the railway carriage, from which he is eventually thrown, by the youthful grace of Lafcadio.

By maintaining perfect formal balance throughout, Gide maintains equal balance between the themes of conformity and individualism. Lafcadio's 'gratuitous act' is just as much a caricature of individual freedom as Julius's return to the ways of officially rewarded conformity is a caricature of consistency and serves to delineate rather than resolve his moral dilemma. Lafcadio's action, it is argued, has placed him in criminal society, which is just as coherent a social system as the society whose laws he has broken. Must Lafcadio resort to servile acceptance of the code of conduct which each group seeks to impose on him, or will he continue his search for a personal ethic? Thus the story ends, quite literally, on a question mark. Moreover, the question mark has been effectively contrived, unobscured by a number of subsidiary question marks, which might or might not be intended to be there.

Considering his work as a whole, Gide emerges as an artist forever seeking after new modes of thought and new forms of expression, but lacking the intellectual rigour and artistic power fully to achieve either. Édouard compared a work of literature to a voyage into uncharted waters, where the traveller must forge ahead out of sight of the shore. Subject as he was to the assumptions of his day, Gide's literary voyages hardly fit the comparison. But neither, clearly, was Gide content to cruise gently in home waters. He seems more in the way of a mariner who sets forth boldly for the high seas, but forgets to unmoor his craft. Gide has perhaps unfairly suffered for having been hailed as a writer 'ahead of his times', which eventually invites the conclusion that he has lapsed behind the times, and was doubly unfortunate to have become fashionable in the twenties, an age which, as Brasillach pointed out, by its efforts to remain resolutely up to date, dated faster than any other. It would be absurd, following what has been called the filter-view of criticism, whereby literary appraisal is thought to become gradually sounder as time goes by, to assume that Gide's present fall from favour represents his permanent place in literature. The most one can say is that the present position is comprehensible and signs of a shift to a position more favourable to Gide, slight. Meanwhile, those of us who come willy-nilly under Gide's spell must, like the master, accept our anomaly, follow our bent, and hope it leads upwards.

NOTE

ANDRÉ GIDE, 1869-1951, was brought up by his mother and her Scots ex-governess Anna Shackleton after his father's death in 1880. Educated variously, with interruptions for illness, at the Protestant École Alsacienne, by private tutors, and in state *lycées*, Gide's first interests were music and natural history. His literary talent emerged in his last years at school where he met Pierre Louÿs, who introduced him to Symbolist circles and doctrine (*Le Traité du Narcisse* (1891)). Following a tubercular attack, he visited Tunisia 1893-4 and enjoyed his first sexual encounters (*Si le grain ne meurt* (1926)). In 1895 he married his cousin Madeleine, the marriage remaining unconsummated (*Et nunc manet in te* (1951)). By now an established figure in literary circles, Gide embarked on the most fruitful period of his career, punctuated with brief interludes of travel abroad including the Congo 1925-6 (*Voyage au Congo* (1927); *Le Retour du Tchad* (1928)). In the early thirties Gide toyed with Communism (*Les Nouvelles Nourritures* (1935)) and campaigned as an anti-Fascist militant (*Littérature engagée* (1950)), but a visit to Russia in 1936 confirmed his break with the Left and politics (*Retour de l'U.R.S.S.* (1936); *Retouches à mon Retour de l'U.R.S.S.* (1937)). Following his wife's death in 1938 Gide undertook further extensive travel in 1939. After the Armistice he broke with the now collaborationist *Nouvelle Revue Française*, which he had helped found in 1908, and spent 1942-5 in North Africa. Of the last twenty years of his life, only the trilogy *L'École des femmes*, *Robert*, *Geneviève* (1929-36) and *Thésée* (1946) bear comparison with his previous work. He won the Nobel Prize in 1947.

Editions. There is no complete edition of Gide's works. The Gallimard *Œuvres complètes* (15 vols., 1932-9) was not resumed after the war. Of other partial collections the Pléiade *Romans, Récits et Soties* (1958), though omitting *Les Cahiers d'André Walter* (1891), is most valuable, as are *Journal 1889-1939* (1951) and *Journal 1939-1949: Souvenirs* (1954) in the same edition. The Gallimard *Théâtre* (1942) includes *Saül, Le Roi Candaule, Œdipe, Perséphone*, and *Le Treizième Arbre*. The *Théâtre complet*, published by Idea et Calendes (8 vols., 1947-9), is complete and includes Gide's translations and adaptations.

Single works are mostly available in Gallimard editions, with the notable exception of *Et nunc manet in te*, Ides et Calendes, 1951.

Gide's main fiction, along with *Les Nourritures terrestres suivi de Les Nouvelles Nourritures*, are available in the Livre de Poche edition; *Dostoïevsky* is available in the Collection Idées.

The most interesting of Gide's published correspondence is with Jammes 1893-1938 (1948), Claudel 1899-1926 (1948), Valéry 1890-1942 (1955), and Rilke 1909-26 (1952).

Criticism. Biographical and critical studies include J. O'Brien, *Portrait of André Gide* (1953), and W. Fowlie, *André Gide: his Life and Art* (1965). J. Delay, *La Jeunesse d'André Gide* (2 vols., 1956), is the most penetrating biographical study of Gide, tracing his development up to the time of his marriage. Of predominantly literary studies J. Hytier, *André Gide* (1938), is still rewarding and Germaine Brée, *Gide* (1963), offers an acute, arguably over-generous, appraisal. Works concentrating on particular aspects of Gide, but of considerable general interest, are G. I. Brachfeld, *André Gide and the Communist Temptation* (1959), and Catharine H. Savage, *André Gide: l'Évolution de sa pensée religieuse* (1962)—also very useful for its full bibliography of books and articles on Gide. G. D. Painter, *André Gide: A Critical and Biographical Study* (1951), and G. W. Ireland, *Gide* (1963), are helpful introductory works, the latter containing an excellent bibliography.

7. Surrealism

IF the surrealists had remained true to their early promises they would have left no trace behind them either of literature or of art. In an interview with Roger Vitrac in the spring of 1923, André Breton said that he was going to give up writing altogether since he had found all modes of expression to be meaningless. 'Seul tout le système d'émotions est inaliénable', he affirmed. One of the editors of *La Révolution surréaliste*, Pierre Naville, stated categorically that there could be no such thing as surrealist painting. They meant that by committing their experience to paper or canvas they were bound to betray its authenticity. The life of the mind was vital, indeterminate, and in a perpetual state of flux. Formal expression in whatever medium of communication externalized what could only be subjective and destroyed this essential indeterminacy. As the libraries and museums show, however, the surrealists went on to find satisfactory answers to their own anguished questionnaire: 'Pourquoi écrivez-vous?' Their repudiation of art may have been a last burst of dadaist nihilism. In 1923 Breton was already putting distance between himself and the dadaists and he did not keep up his ostentatious self-denial. Nevertheless, the significance of surrealism can only be properly understood in the context of a crisis of confidence in the meaning and purpose of art that had been building up since the 1890s.

Dadaism was less a war-machine aimed at the demolition of cultural certainties dating back to the Enlightenment than a postmortem confirming that they had already suffered their demise. Relativity and quantum theories, the insights of Bergson and Nietzsche, recognition of the role of chance in causation, and the psycho-analytical discoveries of Freud had all helped to shatter the idea of a familiar and dependable Nature and of a wholly self-conscious and rational Man. Matter was dissolved into energy and motion: a universe of becoming. Concepts of relation and lines in movement replaced the stable points by which men were accustomed to take their bearings. It was, as Egon Friedell wrote, 'the end of reality'; or rather the substitution of a convenient fiction for the concept of reality as an absolute. The Nietzschean philosophy that man must create his own values, that he can ignore the fate of the rest of society and should scorn the slave morality of Christianity was propagated to the young in France by Barrès and Gide. The disintegration of matter, space, time, and morality was reflected in all the arts. Poetry, the novel, music, and architecture alike were invaded by what R. L. Delevoy has called 'the aesthetic of discontinuity'. Fauvism, cubism, and their successors had progressively 'de-realized' the real to the profit of the artist's subjective imagination and freedom. Paintings ceased to be windows on a world reproduced according to the laws of Euclidean perspective and became autonomous signs. Artists now saw their task as being to present the world ('donner à voir') rather than to represent it. Since chance was a constitutive element in the structure of the universe, it too was allowed to intervene in the process of creation.

The discredit of the old order of verities was carried a stage further by the débâcle of bourgeois values in practice during the First World War. As science put itself at the service of the holocaust, art at that of hysterical propaganda, reason at that of sophistry, and language at that of mystification, the war made even the excesses of Jarry's Père Ubu look like innocent games. As ideologies and institutions one by one fell in ruins in this Verdun of the mind, the question whether or not literature and art could come to terms with an incoherent universe became more and more insistent. A sickness had touched both poetic and discursive language. Surrealism was born in the last spasms of what had become a pathological condition of language dating back to Rimbaud through Mallarmé, Apollinaire, the futurists, and dadaism, a condition in which poetry oscillated between esotericism and delirium. If, as Breton had told Vitrac, the only thing man could now rely on with confidence was his consciousness of himself, on 'the whole system of the emotions', then how could language or art enable one man to communicate with his fellows? As the universe became more incoherent so the artists' cyphers became more hermetic. Authentic art in these circumstances, Tristan Tzara proclaimed in his *Manifeste Dada 1918*, could only be the product of a supreme egoism such that any work would almost certainly be meaningless to all but the author himself. The destruction of established semantic codes had reached the point where it was no longer worth putting pen to paper. The only logical recourse for the writer was suicide or else the austere silence of a Valéry or a Duchamp which Breton himself had vowed to keep in 1923.

What was at stake was a reason for living as well as a reason for writing. When, however, Jean Hytier reproached the author of 'La confession dédaigneuse' for not committing suicide, André Breton replied: 'Si je possède à quelque degré le sentiment tragique de la vie, concevrait-on qu'il me détourne d'exalter ce qui me paraît exaltable?' Even in the sound and the fury of dadaist iconoclasm, Philippe Soupault, Louis Aragon, Paul Éluard, and Breton himself, the nucleus of the future surrealist group who edited the ironically titled review, *Littérature*, were looking around them to see what could be salvaged from the wreckage. They felt reservations about Jacques Vaché's blanket judgement on the 'inutilité théâtrale (et sans joie) de tout'. Something of value did remain, wrote Breton: 'Parmi tant de disgrâces dont nous héritons, il faut bien reconnaître que la plus grande liberté d'esprit nous est laissée.' This freedom of the imagination he had already experienced himself, when, in the autumn of 1918, he and Soupault had made their first experiments with the psycho-analytical technique of automatic writing. Abandoning conscious critical control and creating a vacuum in the mind, they had acted as simple recording machines of whatever their unconscious might dictate. The resulting texts, which they later published as *Les Champs magnétiques* (1921), were astonishing for the abundance of sparkling new images they contained. The young editors of *Littérature* believed that they had hit upon the source of poetic inspiration, the key to the imagery of Lautréamont and Rimbaud, for instance, that had so far eluded them.

It was as if an unknown or disregarded constituent of the human mind was at last finding expression: an element just as real as, perhaps more real than, the conscious, rational mind. Furthermore, the unconscious was still innocent and intact. It did not share in the discredit of the other faculties whose information about reality had been proved by the new science to be so misleading. Thus, in the middle twenties, the surrealists wrote up the findings of their descents into the unconscious as if they were part of a scientific project, laying out the first numbers of *La Révolution surréaliste* like a specialist academic quarterly. They hotly repudiated any suggestion of a literary 'alibi' for what they were doing and denied that it could have anything in common with 'art' in the accepted sense of the word. When they gave the name of 'poetry' to the outpourings of the unconscious, to the stuff of dreams, to the messages relayed to them through the medium of hypnotic trances, to the fruits of the multitude of methods they had for soliciting the marvellous, they were defining poetry in an entirely original way. It was no longer 'un moyen d'expression' but 'une activité d'esprit'. It had suddenly become a route towards knowledge about the human condition and at last could really 'lead somewhere'. It was no longer just a civilized way of making the leisure hours more agreeable but a source of possible solutions to the problems of life, 'une véritable poésie du Cogito'. At the cost of redrawing the frontiers of poetry so that they extended over the whole continent of experience not sealed off by the iron curtain of common sense, the surrealists had found the answer to their question: 'Why do you write?'

Surrealist methods of making audible the interior murmur gave rise to a purified, innocent language and silenced the old rhetoric. Surrealist texts and paintings recorded the mind in movement, the fluidity of consciousness itself. The initial effect of these records of 'la vie immédiate' of the mind was to penetrate and disorientate the reader or spectator rather than to please him. Benjamin Péret described 'les tulipes plus méchantes qu'un foie pourri' and Desnos 'les pierres en bois d'ébène les fils de fer en or et la croix sans branche'. Dali and Buñuel opened their film *Un Chien Andalou* with intercutting shots of a cloud passing the moon and a razor passing through a girl's eye. The surrealists set language free from the host of literary connotations which hampered the expression of new and original thoughts. At the same time, they set about refurbishing the corroded powers of the imagination by giving new significance to utterly banal and devalued symbols from the past. Max Ernst, in his collages for *La Femme 100 têtes* (1929) for instance, rearranged nineteenth-century engravings so that the lions' heads from the arms of Consulate chairs came disturbingly to life. The old semantic clichés of the poster, the proverb, the riddle, and the scrapbook were taken to pieces and reassembled to produce startling and unfamiliar messages.

The surrealists converted the distrust that was sapping traditional notions of reality into credit for the freedom of the mind and poetic imagination. Here lay the essential difference between their aims and those of the dadaists. The latter had used very similar techniques to those adopted for *Les Champs magnétiques* but solely for destructive purposes: to demonstrate 'le peu de réalité'. Spontaneity for Tristan Tzara had meant strangling a nascent image rather than bringing it to successful birth. The surrealists, on the other hand, were intoxicated with the potentialities of the image and saw in its light intermittent flashes of a new and better world beyond. The language that issued from their mouths during the 'époque des sommeils' had little more than respect for the dictionary and the laws of syntax in common with normal, referential, discursive, and logical speech. Yet in phrases such as 'L'huître du Sénégal mangera le pain tricolore', produced collectively in the game called 'Cadavre exquis', or 'Sur une aiguille de chemin de fer j'ai vu se poser l'oiseau splendide du sabotage' from Breton's *Poisson soluble*, the surrealists found signs of a vast extension of the significant. Sentences which were logically nonsensical were nevertheless endowed with a powerful meaning. It even seemed possible that (as Péret had said when he prompted Breton's invention of another game, 'L'un dans l'autre'): 'Tout peut se définir à partir de tout.'

But what sort of solution did this provide to 'the crisis of reality'? In its insistence on keeping faith with chaos, in its refusal to tamper with or 'improve' the messages of an unfettered imagination, to elaborate anything approaching a finished work, surrealism was an acute symptom rather than a cure for the crisis. Its exploitation of the submerged resources of the individual psyche was the ultimate in subjectivity. Roger Shattuck is thus right to say in *The Banquet Years*, that, although the rug had been pulled from underneath the artists' feet and they had to dance to keep their balance, both dadaists and surrealists had accomplished the feat of acting as if this was exactly the way they wanted things to be. But what separated the surrealists from the dadaists was the former's search behind the evident chaos for new principles of coherence. The surrealists pointed to the dual nature of the unconscious itself, mediating between man's body and his consciousness, uniting man the machine and man the free subject. Did it not thus hold out some promise of permitting the eventual reconciliation between the subjective and objective worlds, between *res cogitans* and *res extensa*?

In the apparently nonsensical babbling of the unconscious the surrealists found hints of an order unknown to Aristotelian logic in which phenomena might be ordered and classified according to analogical principles. The instrument of research into this superior order or 'surreality' was nothing else than the basic element of poetry itself: the image. In the poetic image two entities from totally different realms of reality might be juxtaposed and, thanks to the sudden illumination of the 'déclic analogique', perceived as one. In a powerful image the two entities might be seen to fuse and become a unity, to cause what Nicolas Calas has called 'la sensation d'un objet non-perçu — ce serait une forme à laquelle la matière fait défaut'. Furthermore the brightness of the image, its intensity and suggestiveness, was often in direct proportion to the apparent incongruity of the entities brought together. For as Éluard wrote in *L'Amour la poésie*: 'Les ressemblances ne sont pas en rapport. Elles se heurtent.' In these moments of verbal hallucination in which common-sense notions of contradiction were temporarily blotted out, the surrealists witnessed revelations of a reality which transcended the confusion of the positivists' universe and was, in effect, more real. That is why they called analogy and the poetic image 'la plus grande conscience possible du concret'.

Affirming as they did that the key to man's mental prison was the untrammelled free play of analogies, the surrealists attributed immense power to the word and to the manipulation of language by the imagination. Some, like Michel Leiris, even fell victim for a time to a jejune solipsism, believing that reality could be changed simply by expressing it differently—that it was not an external fact to which men had to submit but an internal projection. As Philippe Soupault put it in 1924: 'Vos limites sont en vous-mêmes et vous les imaginez.' Like the primitive and the alchemist, the surrealists have resorted to incantation using words like talismans with magic powers over the world. Trusting in the guarantee of the principle of linguistic equivalence and the structure of language itself, they have credited words with the power of changing and controlling things. In their less lyrical moments, however, they have modified the claim that 'the imaginary is real' to 'l'imaginaire est ce qui tend à devenir réel'.

Clearly if poetry was the royal road to 'knowledge' as the surrealists claimed, this could not be 'un savoir' in the commonly accepted sense of the term. The very words which the surrealists used to describe the effectiveness of an image—'intensity', 'suggestiveness', 'force'—showed that it was judged not by the conviction it carried in the mind but by the 'shock' it caused to the whole sensibility. By 'knowledge' the surrealists meant not so much abstract ideas as affective experience. In this they were entirely consistent, for the unconscious which they had set out to rehabilitate was the seat of the libido, of preconscious desire, as well as the source of imaginative inspiration. Side by side with imagination, the second of the twin arches supporting the structure of surrealist theory was desire. And by desire they meant not merely sexual passion, Eros, Thanatos, and Ananke, but a whole hierarchy of yearnings down to humble and transitory caprice of which the conscious mind barely becomes aware. The surrealists were seeking to overcome the age-old dichotomy besetting Western man that Siegfried Giedion has diagnosed as the divorce between thinking and feeling.

The surrealist aesthetic was defined in terms of desire. Beauty was not something to be passively contemplated or recollected in tranquillity; it caused a physical response, 'un choc affectif', a 'frisson' which Breton likened to the sensation of 'une aigrette de vent aux tempes'. Thus for the surrealist there was only a difference of degree between his emotional reaction to a work of art and his reaction to the woman he loved. Desire, by definition, implies movement towards its object; it cannot be static. In the same way, for the surrealist, art, poetry, dreams, symbolic objects—all the various sublimations and enrichments of desire—had to convey this same sense of movement. This is what Breton meant when he concluded *Nadja* with the dictum: 'La beauté sera convulsive ou ne sera pas.'

Just as they believed that the imaginary tends to become real, so the surrealists felt that there were links between subjective desire and the course of events. Freud had already shown how desire projected itself into dreams; the surrealists found evidence that it could also project itself into waking life. Events which looked at first sight like simple coincidences or mere chance revealed on further examination signs of a mysterious complicity between the unconscious and external phenomena. The surrealists classified these events under the heading of Hegel's term known in French as 'hasard objectif': '. . . cette sorte de hasard à travers quoi se manifeste encore très mystérieusement pour l'homme une nécessité qui lui échappe mais qu'il éprouve vitalement comme nécessité.' The happenings described by Breton which occurred during his walks around Paris in the company of Nadja, Chirico's prophetic portrait of Apollinaire with a circle on the forehead where the poet's later trepanation was to be made, the symbolic correspondence between objects found at the Marché aux Puces and a sculpture on which Giacometti was working (described in Breton's *L'Amour fou*): all these seemed to suggest that the external world was capable of replying to the most secret workings of the mind. The surrealists kept themselves in a state of readiness or expectancy, which at times degenerated into wishful credulousness, for these manifestations of 'hasard objectif'. They believed that this 'comportement lyrique' removed obstacles in the path of desire and facilitated its consummation in the real world. The surest evidence in their view of 'la pénétrabilité de la vie subjective par la vie substantielle' was that of love for one woman. In 'l'amour électif' destiny and choice were reconciled, external necessity and subjective desire became one and the same.

As the free expression of the imagination coupled with desire, poetry had acquired a new dynamic and became an adventure into life itself. It could begin to answer Rimbaud's challenge: 'changer la vie'. It was no longer a luxury commodity produced by linguistic technicians for the consumption of a cultivated élite. 'Le sur-réalisme', as an early handout proclaimed, 'est à la portée de tous les inconscients.' Or to quote Breton's essay, 'Le message auto-matique': 'Le propre du surréalisme est d'avoir proclamé l'égalité totale de tous les êtres humains normaux devant le message sub-liminal, d'avoir complètement soutenu que ce message constitue un patrimoine commun dont il ne tient qu'à chacun de revendiquer sa part. . . .' Poetry, after an immense extension of its meaning, had broken out of the limited field of 'literature' and had become the home of all men's liberty. And liberty, like beauty, was not some-thing that could be quietly savoured in the chimney-corner; it was a 'force vive entraînant une progression continuelle', perpetually asserting itself in the achievement of desire. Thus, as the poet revealed the world as it might be, so men would endeavour to con-vert the possible into the real. The poet was leading the struggle to raise reality to the level of men's dreams.

Surrealism implied not simply a revolt against traditional modes of literary expression but an attack on a whole social order and its system of values. As Breton wrote in an early number of *La Révolu-tion surréaliste*: '. . . derrière l'amoralité du style . . . nous dénonçons l'amoralité de l'homme.' In the course of its much-vaunted techno-logical progress, the Christian and capitalist society of Western Europe had caused disastrous impoverishment to man's affective life and had upset the necessary equilibrium between the mind and the emotions. Because they apparently served no useful purpose to the analytic sciences which were ever extending man's control over nature, vital human faculties were ignored or left undeveloped or even deliberately crippled in childhood by the educational system. Society denounced the world of the imagination as nonsense or fantasy. Desire was qualified by pejorative epithets like lust, sloth, or 'primal instincts'. Private man had been sacrificed to public man and subjective needs to economic and political 'necessity'. The surrealists reversed this order of priorities by putting the pleasure principle before the reality principle (and by pleasure they did not mean the soft and padded comfort going under the name of 'le bonheur'. which men had been fobbed off with in miserly recompense for the loss of the living force of desire).

In turning on a world to which their sense of human dignity forbade them to adapt, the surrealists extended their sympathy indiscriminately to everything that might undermine the common-sense explanations of the materialists and the ready-made creeds of the 'bien-pensants'. They endorsed all kinds of anti-social behaviour—crime, suicide, and drug-addition—as expressions of instinctive human freedom. Éluard demanded the release of the insane from the asylums: 'Qu'on le sache bien, c'est nous qu'on enferme quand on clôt la porte des asiles: la prison est autour d'eux; la liberté, la liberté est à l'intérieur.' The surrealists esteemed the mentality of the primitive who did not make hard-and-fast distinctions between the subjective and objective worlds. They looked back nostalgically to childhood when thought was as fluid and unformed as in dreams and life was still full of infinite possibility. In short, surrealism was deliberately and totally scandalous: 'the spirit of demoralization' had made its home in the surrealist castle. Aragon proclaimed himself a poisoner and a disease-carrier and went on: 'Nous sommes les défaitistes de l'Europe. Nous réveillons partout les germes de la confusion et de la malaise. . . . Nous sommes les agitateurs de l'esprit. Nous sommes ceux qui donnent la main à l'ennemi.'

The surrealists were not satisfied for long with simply shocking the bourgeois. They soon realized that it was not enough merely to express reality in new words or to see it with the eyes of Dali's 'paranoiac-critical method' in order to change it. The power of social and economic determinism was too great to permit the liberation of man under the existing régime. It was necessary to couple the Rimbaldian watchword with that of Karl Marx: 'The philosophers have only *interpreted* the world in different ways; the point is to change it.' A number of the surrealists joined the French Communist Party and the majority participated in the successive 'front organizations' that the Party set up for intellectuals and artists in the thirties. But the claims of spiritual regeneration and social revolution have always been difficult to reconcile and relations between the surrealists and the political militants were stormy. For one thing the former were not prepared to make any concessions to expediency and tended to equate the art of the possible with base compromise. They could not admit the need for intermediary stages between existing society and the total revolution of their dreams. Naturally they were soon disillusioned by developments in Russia under Stalin. The surrealists produced nothing remotely resembling what is commonly thought of as 'revolutionary art'. Slogans, didacticism, brawny proletarians, exhortations to healthy plain-living and plain-loving of the socialist-realist school were all conspicuously absent from surrealist poetry and painting. In the thirties their preoccupation was precisely the defence of artistic freedom against inroads upon it from the totalitarianisms of both left and right. Their attitude to poets like Louis Aragon, who broke with surrealism to become a full-time party worker, was summed up in Benjamin Péret's ironic comment in *Le Déshonneur des poètes* (1945): 'En définitive, l'honneur de ces "poètes" consiste à cesser d'être poètes pour devenir des agents de publicité.'

Surrealism's efforts to come to terms with Communism may have owed something to the coincidence of its birth with the Russian Revolution. The surrealists were looking for an effective force to challenge the established order in France and the French Communist Party was the only credible one to hand. But there was never any real understanding. The Communists probably divined that the task of disrupting society was made much harder if at the same time one repudiated the institution of language in which alone one could make one's intentions understood. The surrealists were unwilling when it came to the point to exchange the libertarian ethic of the rebel for the unquestioning obedience of the militant. Since their rupture with the Communists, the surrealists have returned to the utopian roots of socialism, and especially to the ideas of Charles Fourier.

The nature of a society based on surrealist principles still remains extremely problematical. It is not clear how society could be organized on the pleasure principle in the event of its being found that one man's pleasure was the coefficient of the suffering of others. The surrealists tended to beg this question by talking about desire in the abstract without specifying whose desire was at stake. Perhaps, like most anarchists, they believed that desire took vicious forms only in a society that was itself corrupt and perverted. For all their political agitation, the surrealists' chief preoccupations have remained individualistic; their aim is still to 'réhabiliter l'étude du moi'. When the surrealists today are questioned about the efficacy of their collective action, 'Que faire? . . . comment faire?' etc., they reply with an ethical imperative for individuals: 'Comment ne pas faire.' This 'exercise du non', they claim, is a task sufficient unto the day.

In certain respects the surrealist group was a prefiguration of what society to come might be: the Golden Age in microcosm. For its members did not express the surrealist spirit in books and paintings only, but in everyday living. Surrealism was, in effect, a way of life. With its 'sacred' time and place of meeting, its rituals and self-instituted codes, the group strongly resembled what J. Huizinga, in *Homo Ludens*, has described as a game situation. In a world which was unacceptable, the group offered the surrealists a haven in which affairs could be regulated according to their desires. Paul Éluard has recalled the spirit of comradeship and generosity that presided at sessions when the group were at work (or play?) together making 'Cadavres exquis':

Plus aucun souci, plus aucun souvenir de la misère, de l'ennui, de l'habitude. Nous jouions avec les images et il n'y avait pas de perdants. Chacun voulait que son voisin gagnât et toujours davantage pour tout donner à son voisin. La merveille n'avait plus faim.

At the same time, as in all secret societies, members of the group had to be ready to submit to a rigorous discipline. Breton has said that there is nothing with which it is more dangerous to take liberties than with liberty itself and he consequently demanded a high degree of 'asepsie morale' of anyone who sought to co-operate in the surrealist 'entreprise de transmutation de la vie'. The merely curious and the titillation-seekers were either turned away at the threshold or 'excommunicated' when their lack of dedication came to light. Sharing in the essential ambivalence that characterizes all things surrealist, the group was at once a clan of socially irresponsible

E

escapists or absentees *and* a social movement in embryo that continually threatened to erupt into the world at large.

It should be evident from this brief survey of surrealist ideas that the central ambition of the movement has been to discover some unitary principle or totality behind the atomization of modern life. Encouraged by the scientists' dissolution of the Aristotelian distinctions between identity and difference, sequence and simultaneity, the surrealists went one step further and posited synthesis. By giving voice to the unconscious they sought to establish links between the rational and the irrational elements of man's nature. Thanks to the analogy and the poetic image, they revealed common ground between entities normally presumed to be utterly strange to one another. In their researches into dreams they found evidence of 'un tissu capillaire' which made dream and waking life into 'vases communicants'. As members of the surrealist group they sought to combine the tasks of 'interpreting man' and of 'transforming the world'. Taken together these add up to a truly Promethean project to bring to light and to life powers in men's minds that will enable them to master the overwhelming complexity of existence and to re-establish existence again on a human scale. As Maurice Blanchot has put it:

Le surréalisme est à la recherche d'un type d'existence qui n'est pas celui du donné, du tout fait. . . . Et en même temps il est en recherche d'un événement absolu où l'homme se manifeste dans toutes ses possibilités, c'est-à-dire comme l'ensemble qui les dépasse.

In their determination to substitute an open for a closed rationalism, it was natural that the surrealists should adopt a dialectical framework. The idea that every thesis conjures up its complementary antithesis, that it is relations between things rather than things in themselves which are important, that there is an upward spiral of transcendence relating and ordering the various categories of existence was eminently suitable for expressing the fluid character of surrealist thought. In the *Second Manifeste* (1929), Breton defined the 'point suprême', the still centre of the whirlpool of the surreal, in dialectical terms:

Tout porte à croire qu'il existe un certain point de l'esprit d'où la vie et la mort, le réel et l'imaginaire, le passé et le futur, le communicable et

l'incommunicable, le haut et le bas cessent d'être perçus contradictoire-
ment. Or c'est en vain qu'on chercherait à l'activité surréaliste un autre
mobile que l'espoir de détermination de ce point.

It must be said, however, that in applying the dialectic, the surrealists were sadly lacking the necessary rigour. Most of the time
they only achieved a sort of syncretism, a balance between opposites,
or what Sartre called a perpetual 'papillotement' between subject
and object, the real and the imaginary. The surrealists' 'point
suprême' was very different from Hegel's Absolute Idea. It
possessed meaning less for reason than for intuition. It was an
affective perception rather than a logical concept. The sensation
of the 'point suprême', which all the creative powers of surrealism
were devoted to stimulating, was one of the highest tension at which
the mind, as though energized by an alternating current, momentarily held in suspense the greatest number of apparent contradictions. The surreal was not a state or a place that could be
conquered and occupied. It was a point that could be approached in
varying degrees of proximity at privileged moments of illumination.
Thus, although the surrealists were convinced that poetry could
'lead somewhere', they still felt that it was better to travel, hopefully
or desperately according to temperament, than to arrive.

In the foregoing pages an attempt has been made to give a
succinct answer to the question: 'Qu'est-ce que le surréalisme?'
It is not possible in the space of one chapter to describe individual
works and it would in any case be invidious to single out 'masterpieces' by members of a movement that has denounced the sacro-
sanctity of personal authorship as a superstition. Surrealism has
had to be treated here as 'une seule pensée' overlooking the opposing
temperaments, the divisions between 'mystiques' and 'politiques',
and the great differences of emphasis on fundamentals found, for
example, in Aragon, Éluard, Péret, Artaud, and Dali. The adoption
of a synchronic approach has precluded any account of the evolution of surrealism with its astonishing powers of self-renewal and
succession of methods for breaking through to the 'other side' of
reality: from dreams, hypnotic trances, and automatism in the early
twenties, to researches into sexuality, 'hasard objectif', the simula-
tion of the speech of the insane, paranoia-criticism, surrealist

objects, 'l'humour noir' in the thirties. After so many unavoidable omissions it is perhaps most useful to conclude with a few general remarks about the originality of surrealism, to indicate the peculiar quality of its achievement and to relate it once more to the theme of the crisis in language with which this survey opened.

How original was surrealism? A case could be made out for seeing it as a backward-looking phenomenon rather than a revolutionary one. In their insistence on the recuperation of *lost* powers, in their veneration of the savage mind, it could be argued that the surrealists were rejecting the whole syndrome of scientism, pragmatism, and specialization on which modern civilization depends. On a different level, did not surrealism sponsor a literary school of painting quite contrary to the main currents of modernism, and did not Dali and Magritte, for instance, revert to the stalest academic techniques? The surrealists themselves were not reticent about acknowledging their debt to a long line of spiritual ancestors. They published lists of writers from the past as 'recommended reading': Sade, Rimbaud, Nouveau, Lautréamont, Jarry, Roussel—side by side with still longer lists of great names 'à ne pas lire'. Breton even went so far as to admit that surrealism could be called the tail-end of Romanticism, adding 'mais alors la queue tellement préhensile'.

On closer examination the case that surrealism was reactionary collapses. Though they might indulge in daydreams of the mongol hordes watering their horses in the fountains of the Place de la Concorde, they did not await the obliteration of Western culture so much as a reconciliation of Western modes of thought and being with all that was valuable in the primitive mentality. Far from turning their backs on the technological age, the surrealists were marvellous poets of the urban environment. Drawing their inspiration from window-displays, hoardings, the cinema, the latent eroticism of crowded city streets, they helped to acclimatize men to surroundings that had previously seemed coldly prosaic and inhuman. They traversed the labyrinth of modern Paris in search of phantoms and familiar spirits, creating a new mythology to replace the mummified symbols of the pre-industrial age. As for the objection that the painting style of some surrealists was retrograde—the choice of a reassuring, meticulously naturalistic technique was deliberately made to fortify the shock effect of the bizarre images themselves and to enhance the spectator's sense of the interpenetration of two realities: of dream and of waking life. Again the surrealists' plea to be understood in the context of a literary heritage dating back to the Romantics was not a bid for respectability but just one more provocation. The writers from the past whom the surrealists claimed as kindred spirits were one and all either ignored or despised, condescendingly patronized as 'maudits' or condemned as immoral or insane by the cultured public of the twenties. Indeed it has been one of the greatest achievements of the surrealists to shape the modern sensibility so that whole dimensions of art and literature from the past that had previously been disregarded are now recognized and appreciated.

Another of surrealism's achievements, and one of which the full consequences cannot yet be determined, was its synthesis of different modes of language, the poetic and the critical, in one 'écriture unique'. Despite their readiness to put their trust in so many manifestations of the irrational, the surrealists never lapsed into a nebulous mysticism. They have been at pains to demonstrate that there is nothing supernatural about the surreal, that it is contained within reality as an 'au-delà immanent' demanding only an awakening of man's consciousness to be perceived. In order to express this message, surrealism had to coin a new mode of discourse which *simultaneously* led the prosecution in the trial of realism and exalted and exemplified the powers of the imagination. Despite their intoxication with the infinite possibilities open to language once it becomes self-sufficient and ceases to be an instrument of social exchange, they made every effort to be coherent and convincing. In the *Manifeste* of 1924, for instance, Breton took to task the criteria of logical discourse but at the same time furnished definitions, analysed, and expounded. He wrote a poetic work in which poetry is described as the negation of reason and at the same time succeeded in communicating rationally as philosopher, critic, and historian.

Surrealism then has refused to dodge the issues involved in the 'end of reality'. Its obvious contradictions are the concomitant of its very lucidity and of its insistence that all the options must be

left open. It perseveres in the search for fresh equivalences behind
the chaos of discontinuity but it refuses to allow any of the diversity
and richness of life to be sacrificed in the process.

As a cultural phenomenon itself, the surrealist movement presents the same ambiguous face to the world as does the idea of the
surreal and the language in which the surrealist enterprise has been
expressed. The surrealists promised 'le nettoyage définitif de
l'écurie littéraire', yet the inclusion of a chapter on the movement
in a volume such as this shows that it has been gathered willy-nilly
into the literary fold. The surrealist movement is not dead—its
periodicals succeed one another with healthy regularity and the
group still states its position on every burning issue from Vietnam
to teenage promiscuity. Nevertheless, it is hard not to talk about it
in the past tense. Surrealism still resides on the margin, sapping
traditional conceptions of art and reality, but these have now
absorbed its virus and assimilated it along with all the other new
values and new aesthetics that go to make up modernism. Perhaps
Maurice Blanchot should have the last word on the situation of
surrealism today: 'Le surréalisme s'est-il évanoui? C'est qu'il n'est
plus ici ou là: il est partout. C'est un fantôme, une brillante hantise.
A son tour, métamorphose méritée, il est devenu surréel.'

NOTE

The appearance of André Breton's *Manifeste du surréalisme* in October 1924 is
usually held to mark the inception of the movement. Justifiable alternatives
would be the period known as the 'époque des sommeils' in 1922, or the autumn
of 1918 when Breton and Soupault carried out their first experiments with automatic writing. Enjoying a remarkably long life, and despite the recent death of its
founder and guide, the surrealist group is still active today. Centred in Paris, the
movement acquired world-wide ramifications, particularly in the thirties. Its
membership, which has included individuals from all walks of life, except
perhaps the clergy, has changed from one decade to the next. If a list limited
arbitrarily to twenty names had to single out those who contributed most to
surrealism during the 'heroic period' between the wars, this should no doubt
include: Paul Éluard, Louis Aragon, Benjamin Péret, Philippe Soupault,
Antonin Artaud, Luis Buñuel, Salvador Dali, Robert Desnos, Michel Leiris,
André Masson, Jean Miro, Max Ernst, René Char, Raymond Queneau, Alberto

Giacometti, René Crevel, Man Ray, Tristan Tzara, Jacques Prévert, and Yves Tanguy.

Works. The best introduction remains Breton's *Manifeste du surréalisme* (1924) and his short essay *Introduction au discours sur le peu de réalité* (1927). The essays collected in *Les Pas perdus* (1924) plot the early evolution of surrealist ideas. Among the works by Breton that convey the essence and tone of surrealism in its purest form are *Nadja* (1927), *L'Amour fou* (1937), and *Arcane 17* (1946). Aragon's *Le Paysan de Paris* (1926) records the surrealists' search for the marvellous in everyday life while the savagely brilliant essay, *Traité du style* (1928), expresses their disgust at the 'miserable mental expedient' that currently went under the name of reality. His prophetic essay, *La Peinture au défi* (1930), is a landmark in the history of modern art. Other works that exemplify various characteristics of the surrealist state of mind are: Éluard, *Capitale de la douleur* (1926), *L'Amour la poésie* (1929), and *Donner à voir* (1939); Péret, *De derrière les fagots* (1934) and *Je ne mange pas de ce pain-là* (1936); Desnos, *La Liberté ou l'amour* (1927) and *Corps et biens* (1930); and Crevel, *Le Clavecin de Diderot* (1932). The liveliest impression of surrealist activity 'sur le vif' is afforded by the group's reviews: *Littérature* (1919–24), *La Révolution surréaliste* (1924–9), *Le Surréalisme au service de la révolution* (1930–3), *Minotaure* (1933–9), *Médium* (1952–5), *Le Surréalisme même* (1956–9), *La Brèche* (1961–5) and, today, *L'Archibras.* Maurice Nadeau has assembled a large number of occasional broadsheets, manifestos, and memoranda put out by the group over the years. These are to be found in the second volume of his *Histoire du surréalisme* (1945–7).

Criticism. M. Raymond, *De Baudelaire au surréalisme* (1933); J. Monnerot, *La Poésie moderne et le sacré* (1945); F. Alquié, *Philosophie du surréalisme* (1955); M. Carrouges, *André Breton et les données fondamentales du surréalisme* (1950); J. Gracq, *André Breton* (1948); A. Gavillet, *La Littérature au défi* (1957); C. Courtot, *Introduction à la lecture de Benjamin Péret* (1965); M. Jean, *A History of Surrealist Painting* (1960); A. Kyrou, *Le Surréalisme au cinéma* (1963).

For invaluable exchanges of views and for suggestive ideas on a number of subjects raised in this chapter, I should like to acknowledge my debt to Roger Cardinal, author of an excellent but as yet unpublished doctoral thesis, *The Conception of Love in French Surrealism*, and to René Lourau who is preparing a book entitled *La Sociologie du surréalisme*.

8. Catholic Humanism

IN one of the chapters of his *Port-Royal* (Book III, ch. 15) Sainte-Beuve imagines a 'colloquy' between Pascal and Molière, in the gardens of the Hôtel de Longueville, presenting them as the protagonists of Christianity and humanism. 'Chose remarquable! à chaque pas d'abord que fait l'entretien, ces deux hommes sont d'accord.' By the end of the seventeenth century, no *entretien* of that kind was possible, and for the next two hundred years both Christianity and humanism had withdrawn into closed worlds, despite the abortive attempts of the Romantics to break down barriers. What has been called 'le renouveau catholique' has little or nothing to do with its predecessors in the early nineteenth century. It was a spontaneous resumption of the colloquy, and communication was re-established between poetry and religion.

This renewal is perhaps best seen in the setting of the symbolist movement. Indeed, if one takes Valéry's analysis of the symbolist movement as roughly correct, one could say that it is incomplete if lopped of its religious pendant, just as the Catholic renewal becomes parochial or political if wrenched from its intellectual context. The symbolist movement was a double event, the rejuvenation of poetry and religion—and this is nowhere more convincingly brought out than in Valéry's essay 'Existence du Symbolisme' (published in Vol. I of the Pléiade edition of his works).

The movement, he says, began in 1886—a convenient moment from which to date the *renouveau*: Claudel's religious experience occurred in 1885, Blondel conceived his philosophical work in 1886, and Péguy called the year 1881 the beginning of the modern world.

Symbolism, Valéry declares, was 'une sorte de révolution dans l'ordre des valeurs'. The poets, Verlaine, Rimbaud, Mallarmé,

Laforgue, Villiers, revolted against critics and public and demanded of their readers a sort of collaboration. They disdained success (it is Valéry speaking) and admired those who suffered: Poe, Baudelaire, Wagner (*sic*). They accepted 'le rénoncement', which meant 'chercher par une voie dure, et même douloureuse, à s'édifier, à se construire', and this asceticism in the realm of art becomes the condition of the very life of the artist and of the production of his work. Their work is personal and they are not a school: 'L'esthétique les divisait; l'éthique les unissait.' The religious parallels which he goes on to draw provide the context in which the sources of the Catholic movement can be seen:

Jamais les puissances de l'art, la beauté, la force de la forme, la vertu de la poésie, n'ont été si près de devenir dans un certain nombre d'esprits la substance d'une vie intérieure qu'on peut bien appeler 'mystique', puisqu'il arrivait qu'elle se suffît à elle-même, et qu'elle satisfît et soutînt le cœur de plus d'un *à l'égal d'une croyance définie*. . . . Je le dis en connaissance de cause: nous avons eu, à cette époque, la sensation qu'une manière de religion eût pu naître, dont l'émotion poétique eût été l'essence.

Whatever may be thought of Valéry's aestheticism ('Jamais plus haute n'a paru la Tour d'ivoire'), each feature he describes is seen to be repeated, as in a looking-glass, in the Catholic revival: the repudiation of the traditional past, the renunciation of success, the demand for collaboration, the rejection of the classicism of the Parnasse in favour of a romantic aesthetic, an intense concern with ideas, with the inner life, with asceticism and mysticism. And because the movement was entirely spontaneous in each individual, it is a mistake to look for a school or a clique. But the parallels which help Valéry to build his ivory tower could also bear a different interpretation and in the place of his aesthetic theology there arose a theological aesthetic.

The way for the revaluation of all values was prepared by Sedan and the Commune. The massive certainties of the mid century crumbled under the impact of military defeat and social unrest. The real *débâcle* was in the intellectual field, and the over-confident world of Renan and Taine could not survive the questioning of a generation which was both intellectually curious and spiritually starved. Moreover, the generation which came to maturity about 1886 was one of the most gifted France had known: Proust and Péguy, Gide, Valéry and Claudel, Matisse and Rouault, Bergson, Blondel and Debussy. But before they could establish their rights, the conventional attitudes and alignments held in place by the political structure of the country had to be undermined. The period between 1870 and 1890 is the age of 'Affairs', of endemic crises, a sort of interregnum. The change began in 1894 when a Jewish officer on the General Staff, Alfred Dreyfus, was arrested on a charge of treason. The Dreyfus Case blew up into the Dreyfus Affair, and *l'Affaire* grew into *la révolution dreyfusienne*. The whole fabric of French life began to alter. The proletariat came into political existence, there was a growing, united Left—and Catholicism was split in two.

The victory of the dreyfusards gave the Radicals under Combes the support of the new socialist parties, and the opportunity to abrogate the Concordat with the Vatican: the Church was disestablished, Catholic schools closed, the religious orders exiled. It was the end of political Catholicism. Simultaneously, the Modernist Controversy exploded and centring on the historicity of the Bible forced Catholics to re-examine the foundations of their belief—no longer solely in the traditional, abstract, Greek (Aristotelian) terms of the past but in historical, Jewish (Pauline) terms. From opposite quarters Catholic thought was focused and reorientated by the fact of Judaism—and it is no coincidence that so many Catholic writers were stirred by their debt to Judaism: Bloy, Péguy, Maritain, Marcel. The contrast and interplay of Greek and Jewish forms of thought was instrumental in transforming certain unexamined assumptions: whatever others might say, Catholics could no longer see the Church as Graeco-Roman and Mediterranean, or subscribe to the historical absolute of a 'European Culture'. Like the classicism of the Parnasse, the old Catholic classicism of Bonald and Maistre (restated by Maurras) was a thing of the past.

But so complete a revolution, touching the French tradition on the nerve, and reversing the rationalism and positivism of the eighteenth and nineteenth centuries, was not allowed to proceed by default. The immediate reaction to the Dreyfus Affair was the formation of the *Action française* under the leadership of Charles Maurras. It dominated the Catholic scene until its condemnation in 1926. It was royalist in politics, classical in taste, Roman Catholic in religion, and it gained the support of all thinking conservatives whether Christian or atheist. Its influence can be seen in the pages of Belloc, T. S. Eliot, Irving Babbit, and Wyndham Lewis. Its intellectualism was austerely presented by Julien Benda (*Les Sentiments de Critias*, *La Trahison des Clercs*), and its 'cultural' panache was always more important than its motto suggests ('la politique d'abord').

Thus, until 1918, when the *union sacrée* had in certain respects completed the *révolution dreyfusienne*, the innovators among the Catholics had lived under a cloud—regarded as disloyal to the Church in the hour of its disestablishment, and as spreading the poison of Modernism. In retrospect it is easy to group them into a school; but they were unknown to one another and to the great world. Claudel was in China, Blondel in Aix-en-Provence, Péguy and Bloy struggling against poverty. They had either no knowledge of or no interest in each others' work and were exempt from the dangers of a clique. There was really only one point on which all agreed: the necessity of beginning with a *mea culpa* for the sins and errors of a Christianity which had never known the need or the wish to revive the *entretien*, and which had regarded power, wealth, prestige, and authority as the best means of communication. Blondel wrote in his *Lettre sur l'apologétique* (1896):

Nous avons donc, en France, et dans les pays catholiques, assisté depuis des siècles à cet étrange spectacle de voir ce qui était donné comme 'le tout de l'homme' soustrait à l'étude franche, à l'art sincère, à la pensée vivante.

This admission, in whatever form it was made, opened the way to the future and outlined the scope of the work to be done.

Léon Bloy (1846–1916) is the John the Baptist of the movement, the voice of one crying in the wilderness of the Third Republic. Bloy broke completely with the old diatonic system in which Church and State were as tonic to dominant, the two poles of a stable harmony; and he did so as effectively as Debussy in music. He threw the rubbish of tradition out of the window and the new order of values owed nothing to Bonald, Maistre, Lamennais, Veuillot, Barbey, or Huysmans. He was *Le mendiant ingrat*, *Le pélerin de l'Absolu* in the tradition of Verlaine and Rimbaud.

What Bloy introduced, like a time bomb, into Catholicism was the Absolute, the drastic realism of an uncompromising spirituality. Everything becomes a symbol of the Absolute: a stinking Jewish beggar is Abraham, the father of the faith; a penny given to a beggar drops into the hand of God. The truth can only be reached through exaggeration. And if he fulminates against the bourgeois society that rejected him, his fiercest scorpions are reserved for the clergy, for the Catholics, for Brunetière, Bourget, Coppée. The wild violence of his denunciations is a valid expression of Christianity's incompatibility with the world of *Bouvard et Pécuchet* and *la belle époque*. His tactics are those of the reformer, not altogether different after all from the technique of so circumspect and systematic a thinker as Kierkegaard, out to demolish 'established', complacent Christianity. One cannot help wondering, indeed, what Bloy would have made of Kierkegaard's last pamphlets if his Danish wife had introduced him to them on their visit to Copenhagen. But however fantastic he becomes, his work retains an undiluted existential core (and a superb *vis comica*) which only a platitudinous criticism can fail to see, and which gave him his influence on the future through Maritain, Bernanos, Béguin, Mounier, and Rouault. The latter left an unforgettable lithograph of the man who never understood his painting, but had served to inspire it.

Bloy spoke like a prophet of 'the one thing necessary'; but it is Charles Péguy (1873–1914) who incarnates the ideas and ideals, the aims and aspirations of the movement as a whole. He is not its prophet, but its missionary: 'c'est une renaissance catholique qui se fait par moi.' He was neither talented nor original in the ordinary sense, and he was ordinary to the point of eccentricity. Though by training a *normalien*,[1] he remained an autodidact, so that his very

[1] i.e. Péguy was a student at the École Normale Supérieure in Paris. Normale has traditionally contained a student intellectual élite recruited by a fiercely competitive examination and working for the *agrégation*.

knowledge seems spontaneous—or as Romain Rolland prefers to say, he is more profoundly autobiographical than Jean-Jacques himself. There is nothing 'literary' in his pages, so that in a sense one could say there is no difference between his poetry and his prose. Everything he wrote, without a correction, without a suppression for the most part, was published in the series he founded and sunk his little capital in: *Les Cahiers de la quinzaine*. It is a sort of tape-recording (with all the defects that implies) of his inner life, his self-education, the whole human experience of poverty, love, work, and sickness unfolding into a 'mystique' that ultimately formed into a *croyance définie*.

The disconcerting aspect of the *Cahiers* is not the *longueurs* of his drumming, repetitive style, or the unforeseeable parentheses, as tortuous as those of Proust, and always winding back to the main theme; nor is it the *faits divers* which provide him with stepping-stones (for example an official visit by Alfonso XIII) the relevance of which is too often lost. The baffling thing is the level, the plane on which he writes and which is neither that of philosophy, psychology, sociology, aesthetics, nor even of politics. All philosophies worthy of the name, he says, are a journey of discovery, and he is 'un bon français de l'espèce ordinaire'; so that just as Bloy disconcerts by overplaying his hand, Péguy presents the major problems of life on a common-sense level and leaves the reader to transpose them, or at least to supply the connecting links. Bergson said, truly enough, that Péguy had understood his philosophy more fully than he himself, and Étienne Gilson came down on Péguy's side when Péguy defended Bergson against Maritain's criticisms; but the terms in which Péguy wrote are so distant from those of the professional philosopher that a casual reading of the *Cahiers* easily fails to bring out his full meaning. The fact, for example, that the Dreyfus Affair occupies a central position in his work does not lighten the task of abstracting his philosophy.

This is strikingly apparent in regard to his return to the Church. Péguy always refused to admit that he had been 'converted' either morally or intellectually. He had not, he writes, 'changed sides', like Renan. He denied nothing of his past, least of all *his* socialism (more radical than appears). He had simply stuck to his guns; he left the Church as a young man because he found that the Catholics cheated, and he broke with the Socialists when they cheated (and supported Combes against the Church, against freedom). The *Cahiers*, he maintained, united all those who did not cheat—Jews, Socialists, Protestants, and Catholics—on a level where honesty remained 'open' to the possibility of faith. And he called the process not conversion but *approfondissement*. It is impossible to 'date' his conversion, and all that is known is that at a certain point he attained to a new vision: he became a poet. The form and content of his work changed: he had discovered his mission, the sources of a renaissance. The contradictions which he had honestly accepted at the outset were reconciled: on the one hand *La Cité harmonieuse* (his socialism was not an order but a harmony); and on the other hand *Jeanne d'Arc*, the hero and the saint. The natural order he had discovered through the 'Affair' was completed by the supernatural order of charity he had discovered through Jeanne; but what had caused an explosion in Bloy was for Péguy the source of harmony:

> Et l'arbre de la grâce et l'arbre de nature
> Ont lié leurs deux troncs de nœuds si solennels,
> Ils ont tant confondu leurs destins fraternels
> Que c'est la même essence et la même stature.
>
> (*Ève*)

'Le tout de l'homme' implies for Péguy the junction of the temporal and the eternal, not in some theory or metaphysic but, as in Kierkegaard, in the *instant* of existence, which is the meeting-point of time and eternity.

Péguy's thought was ripened in contact with Judaism: through his practical experience of the Affair and his friendship with Bernard Lazare (*Notre Jeunesse*) and through his study of Bergson (the *Note Conjointe*). From these two sources he derived two of his principal categories, *la mystique* and *la politique*, the 'open' world of the individual, and the closed world of social pressures—an example of how he foresaw Bergson's intellectual development and the ideas expressed thirty years later in *Les Deux Sources de la morale et de la religion* (1932). 'Tout commence en mystique et finit en politique': everything begins with an original intuition and in lived truth, and ends in politics. That is the danger which a mystique must face unless it is to turn in upon itself and be false to itself. Contemplation leads to action and must become incarnate in the temporal. The notion of incarnation completes the notion of *mystique* and is the organizing idea which unifies his politics, his ethics, his aesthetics, and his theology.

To Péguy, Catholicism is not 'a' fixed and defined tradition or culture, but the possibility of tradition, of an *entretien*. That is why Péguy could 'inherit' the past, from Michelet and Bergson, the Middle Ages and Socialism, and feel himself the heir of Monarchy, Revolution, and Republic, because he could share their *mystiques* without subscribing to their *politiques*. As a result he has been called by some a nationalist and conservative, by others a socialist and progressive, and by Romain Rolland, who felt the paradox, an anarchist. What he rejected was an 'intellectual' synthesis or system, the false 'orders', the closed tyrannies which do not spring spontaneously from the depths of the individual, from life itself: he is not imprisoned either by the past or by the (planned and ordered) future. It is the inner life, to recall Valéry's expression, that determines the outward harmony, and that is the source of freedom, of what Bergson was to call the 'open' morality which is the basis of democracy.

Péguy's influence on Catholic thought can perhaps be explained by saying that while he totally rejected the notion of Christendom in its old form (roughly speaking that of the *Action française*) he only broke with that tradition in order to give it new life—for the task of Christianity as a mystique must always be to communicate with, and if possible inform, the new forms of life, or art, society, philosophy. It can never be a closed world or a private world, what Chateaubriand called 'le cercle fermé de Bossuet'.

This is not the place to discuss the achievement of Claudel (1868-1955), an achievement which may tempt some future critic to say that the greatest poet of the period was 'Claudel, hélas!' But there are elements in Claudel's aesthetic which reveal a degree of agreement with Péguy which are not always stressed enough. What Jacob Burckhardt says of Rubens—like Claudel a successful diplomat—can surely be said of him: 'It is extraordinarily fortunate for the Catholicism of the north to find so great, so willing and so happy an interpreter who was fired with enthusiasm for its great religious figures.' His response to Rubens illustrates very well the starting-point which he shared with the innovators of his generation:

Le Vice-roi — C'est Rubens qui conservera la Flandre à la chrétienté contre l'Hérésie! Ce qui est beau réunit, ce qui est beau vient de Dieu, je ne puis l'appeler autrement que catholique. . . . Qu'ont voulu ces tristes réformateurs sinon faire la part de Dieu, réduisant la chimie du salut entre Dieu et l'homme à ce mouvement de foi . . . à cette transaction personnelle et clandestine dans un étroit cabinet. . . .

Le Chapelin — Je n'aurais jamais cru que Rubens fût un prédicateur de l'évangile.

Le Vice-roi — Et qui donc mieux que Rubens a glorifié la Chair et le Sang; cette chair et ce sang même qu'un Dieu a désiré revêtir et qui sont l'instrument de notre rédemption.

(*Le Soulier de Satin*, Deuxième Journée)

Beauty, in Claudel's aesthetic, is not only an access to the inner life, as in Valéry; it is a revelation of being, not to be separated from the good and the true. Just as Péguy was inspired by Bergson and Michelet, Claudel was inspired by Rimbaud and Mallarmé: 'Tout ce qui vient à moi, butin de la rime' ('Ode jubilaire pour le six-centième anniversaire de la mort de Dante'). Like all the Catholic writers who launched the *renouveau catholique*, the *mea culpa* Claudel calls for is the recognition of a latent Jansenism and Manichaeism which, like the error of the Reformers, consisted in limiting Christianity to the good and the true—to a two-dimensional world and ultimately a closed world, 'un étroit cabinet', a private religion without symbols, *incommunicado*. For Christianity can only avoid the alternative of Jansenism or an official religion where power and authority are in the final resort the substitutes for communication, if it embraces the aesthetic sphere, the sphere of feeling. 'Le tout de l'homme' is neither an ivory tower (Valéry) nor a narrow cell from which beauty is excluded.

Bloy, Péguy, Claudel, Jammes, Max Jacob, and Bernanos are examples of the Catholic movement as it rediscovered 'un art sincère'. However, nothing is more calculated to conceal the real character of the *renouveau* than to study them in isolation, that is, apart from the 'pensée vivante' and the 'étude franche' which emerged at the same time. What they had to say, often in the most idiosyncratic forms, was defined by the philosophy and theology and scholarship which developed at the same time. No doubt their work would, in the end, have borne fruit; but simply as a matter of fact some of the decisive conflicts within the Church were resolved in other fields. In a sense, the crucial battle (between the innovators and the *Action française*) was first decided in the field of philosophy. Maurice Blondel (1862-1949) did for Catholic philosophy and theology what Bergson did for philosophy in general: he liberated it. *L'Action* (1893) may be lacking in the graces of Bergson's books, but went with relentless accuracy to the heart of the problem: the inadequacy of traditional apologetics. Very crudely stated, the argument of *L'Action* is that a sufficiently comprehensive analysis of the human spirit, which must therefore embrace action as well as thought, far from imprisoning man in his own subjectivity, reveals the necessity of a succession of decisions (action) which lead, by the force of their own dialectic, to the frontier of the transcendent, to the point at which 'l'option religieuse' presents itself. Blondel's dialectic has certain analogies with that of Kierkegaard: both, for example, begin with an either-or, presenting an alternative between the aesthetic sphere (the ivory tower) and the ethical sphere, and developing the argument up to the point at which the religious option is the condition for the survival of the 'open' world, which is at first simply the transcendent, as yet undefined by Christianity.

Although the 'either-or' as presented in this form might seem to exclude the aesthetic sphere, Blondel's argument is on the contrary the source of a new approach to the problem of the relation of natural and supernatural, and as a result of his work Catholic theology (so long influenced by a submerged Jansenism) underwent a transformation parallel to the discoveries of Péguy and Claudel. One of the principal results of this change was the rediscovery of the spiritual writers and mystics of the past, in particular of the seventeenth century in France—a school which had fallen into oblivion ever since the condemnation of Fénelon had left the Jansenists and the authoritarian Church of Bossuet, with its reliance on power and prestige, masters of the field.

It was at this point that 'l'étude franche', an honest scholarship, left its deepest mark. The work of Henri Bremond, for all its defects, deserves mention. Not only was his monumental *Histoire littéraire du sentiment religieux en France du dix-septième siècle à nos jours* responsible for making this central aspect of the history of Christianity known in wider circles; Bremond related religion and culture and stressed the vital nature of their *entretien* in *Prière et Poésie* and a number of polemical articles and brochures. Bremond, it could be said, repeated in the field of history and criticism what Péguy and Claudel were saying in their own way. When he quoted Fénelon saying 'la poésie est plus utile et plus sérieuse qu'on ne croit' it can be seen that Valéry's definition of the symbolist movement was being taken in a realist sense. What Bremond had to say is not so very far from Proust's polemic: *Contre Sainte-Beuve*. But it must be remembered that when Bremond says 'le romantisme est le retour à la tradition constante du genre humain en matière de poésie' (the thesis of *Prière et Poésie*), he was not writing in the country of Coleridge and Keats. From a purely literary standpoint, the conflict between the *Action française* and the new school of Catholic writers was between the so-called classical tradition, and a romanticism which in France had not, until then, reached maturity.

Although the *Action française* enjoyed its greatest prestige during the decade after the First World War, its authority was no longer unchallenged. The writers of the pre-war period were being discovered, and their isolated achievements were consolidated, diversified, and criticized. The condemnation of the *Action française* in 1926—so utterly unexpected—was the end of an epoch, a decisive date in the intellectual history of France.

What had been a spontaneous movement became, after the war, a conscious renewal, the first nucleus of which was provided by Jacques and Raïssa Maritain—godchildren of Bloy. Their house at Meudon was the centre from which their influence radiated into unexpected quarters, and for the first time a *croyance définie* was no bar to intellectual communication. *Art et scolastique* met a wide response at the time of Stravinsky's 'classical' period, and the author of *Anti-moderne* was wholly modern in taste. The 'cercle d'études thomistes' which the Maritains organized expressed the intellectualist mood of the moment, the revulsion against Bergsonism, vitalism, and 'philosophies of life', not excluding the more existentialist thought of Blondel. Among those who attended these meetings were Rouault, Henri Ghéon, and the young Emmanuel Mounier. This grouping—if the word is not too definite—though sharing the intellectualist and classical principles of the *Action française*, abhorred its anti-semitism, and at the most condoned its politics. The condemnation of the *Action française* in fact released the Maritains from a false position which Maritain himself frankly acknowledged in *La Primauté du spirituel* (1927)—as opposed to 'la politique d'abord'—and was followed by the same author's *Humanisme intégral*.

The extent of the change in the ethos of Catholicism was only fully revealed on the outbreak of the Civil War in Spain when a number of Catholic intellectuals sided with the anti-clerical Republic. Bernanos, formerly a royalist and, in roughly the same sense as the Maritains, a follower of Maurras, wrote *Les Grands Cimetières sous la lune*. The 'opening to the left' in Catholicism may be dated from this moment and was to lead to the worker-priest experiment. The die-hard conception of Christendom, of France as a 'Catholic country', which Péguy and Blondel had undermined, ceased to carry conviction; and in the place of that traditional outlook it became usual to think of *France pays de mission*!

From 1930 onwards, the *entretien* which had begun in the aesthetic sphere was diverted into a dialogue with Marxism. The name which will always be associated with this development is that of Emmanuel Mounier (1905–51). Like Péguy, to whom he owed so much, Mounier gave up a secure academic career to found a journal —*L'Esprit*—the very title of which is significant. The intellectual centre of gravity which had for so long rested on 'the prophets of the past' (Barbey d'Aurevilly), among the works of Bonald, Maistre, and Bossuet, lost its appeal and Mounier fed his readers on a strong diet of Freud, Marx, and Kierkegaard—in the light of which the ideas of Blondel, Teilhard de Chardin, Laberthonnière became highly relevant. The 'social Catholicism' which Blondel had encouraged, the labours of Marc Sangnier, by which François Mauriac had been moved and which he described in a novel, had come to fruition. But although the strong political and social bias of the period—so necessary for the re-education of Catholics, and in harmony with the example given by Péguy—is the most obvious manifestation of the renewed vitality of Catholicism between the wars, it was only the visible part of the iceberg, and in part a very desirable reaction against the stolid conservatism of the past. In the long run, the renaissance which Péguy had felt in his bones remained unchanged. The source, even of the social Catholicism of the time, and of the readiness for communication between Christian and communist, was the same: an attitude of mind which cannot be defined in political terms only, being dependent not on a *politique* but on a *mystique*, which implies that the essential, the centre of gravity, is not to be found in a 'dialogue' but in the recovery of a renewed and fuller understanding of Christianity. Mounier's successor as editor of *Esprit*, Albert Béguin, will be remembered not by his often premature or immature political judgements, but by his work as a critic, by his studies of Balzac, Bloy, Péguy, and by *Le Romantisme et le rêve*, a remarkable study of the parallels between the German Romantic writers and the symbolists.

The legacy of the innovators is to be found therefore not so much in the political and social campaigns which made the headlines, but rather in the critical, philosophical, and theological work which led up to the Second Vatican Council when the renaissance which Péguy, Bloy, Blondel, and Claudel had worked for was, as it were, canonized and made into the norm. This would no doubt be more apparent if the very considerable theological work done in the last fifty years and the accompanying philosophical developments were better known in this country. The Catholic philosophy which has been successfully transplanted across the Channel—Maritain, Gilson, and Marcel—is hardly representative, partly because it is too exclusive, partly because more recent work is ignored. The impression given that Maritain and Gilson are 'representative' while Marcel is a lone rider is almost the reverse of the truth—and it is significant that both Maritain and Gilson have, for no valid reason, failed to find appointments in France, and have lived one in the United States, the other in Canada. There is a much closer relationship between Gabriel Marcel's work and the numerous writers who derive in one sense or another from Blondel.

If one looks for an underlying unity in the *renouveau catholique* which began somewhere around 1885, hand in hand with the symbolist movement, it would lie not in any formal agreement, but in the fact that 'l'éthique les unissait', in the new stress given to the 'inner life', and consequently in what would now be described as a more existential thought. This is the factor which liberated Catholicism in France so that what was united on the plane of ethics was free, on the plane of art, to express itself spontaneously and in a way that had been impossible as long as unity was thought to derive solely from an external tradition. They might be divided regarding their aesthetics, but not regarding the importance of the aesthetic sphere.

NOTE

A good deal of bibliographical information relevant to the above chapter will be found elsewhere, particularly in the Note to Chapter 11 of the previous volume, *The Late Nineteenth Century* (pp. 194-7). This same note contains biographical and bibliographical details for Bloy, Péguy, and Claudel. The items listed below therefore represent no more than a highly selective list of some additional texts.

Primary sources. Raïssa Maritain, *Les Grandes Amitiés: souvenirs* (1941); H. Massis, *Évocations: souvenirs 1905-1911* (1931) and *L'Honneur de servir* (1937).

Criticism and history. The Catholic Revival is dealt with in J. Calvet, *Le Renouveau catholique dans la littérature contemporaine* (1927); A. Dansette, *Histoire religieuse de la France contemporaine* (revised ed. 1965); E. Fraser, *Le Renouveau religieux d'après le roman français de 1886 à 1914* (1934); R. Griffiths, *The Reactionary Revolution: the Catholic Revival in French Literature 1870-1914* (1966); abbé Maugendre, *La Renaissance catholique dans la littérature du XXᵉ siècle* (1962); M. Ozouf, *L'École, l'Église et la République, 1871-1914* (1963).

For the post-war period and relations between Marxism and Catholicism see G. Fessard, *De l'actualité historique* (1960).

On the 'Modernist' controversy see H. Daniel-Rops, 'Une crise de l'esprit: le Modernisme', *La Table Ronde*, Nov.-Dec. 1962. Also, the part played by Maurice Blondel in these debates is discussed by E. Borne, *Passion de la vérité* (1962), H. Bouillard, *Blondel et le christianisme* (1961), and J. Lacroix, *Blondel: sa vie et son œuvre avec un exposé de sa philosophie* (1963).

Other essential reading includes Blondel's own works and H. Bremond's *Pour le romantisme* (1923) and *Prière et poésie* (1926).

9. Poetry and Collective Experience: Péguy, Claudel, Saint-John Perse

SINCE the 1880s real 'schools' of writers have almost disappeared from the Parisian literary scene. This is particularly so with poetry because poets have in this century not only asserted the essentially individualistic nature of their art, but have abandoned their former position at the head of the aesthetic fashion world to novelists, and even, more recently, to philosophers and critics. It is therefore necessary to cut across the various *manifestes* and *arts poétiques* in order to pick out general trends, at the risk of associating individuals who saw themselves as outsiders, or even bracketing them for reasons they themselves might have objected to. Claudel and Cendrars, Saint-John Perse and Jules Romains, or Apollinaire, Péguy, and Supervielle appear divided by country and class, by political and religious belief, by character and vocation, even by the outward appearance of their writing. Yet they are distinguished within the movement of French poetry in that their inspiration is based on the outside world and the French, European, or human community as a whole, rather than on individual experience. Even the labels publishers and week-to-week chroniclers have applied to them—'intégraliste', 'épique', 'unanimiste', 'futuriste', 'simultanéiste', 'socialiste'—show clearly a breadth of outlook essentially alien to the lyrical mode, which had usually been the medium of even the most mystically ambitious of the Romantics and symbolists. We find this intention clearly expressed, too, in the experiments and innovations of their prose and verse.

The new rhythm of life in France and modern Europe generally has had a profound influence on the outlook and ambitions of poets.

Geographically they have become scattered and mobile, and modern communications have appreciably lessened the call of Paris for intellectuals and artists. Publishing is centred there as exclusively as before, but it is no longer as essential to frequent certain salons or cafés to establish one's reputation or communicate with other artists. This change has had two opposite effects on literary horizons. A first group of poets, and some novelists too, have remained attached to their province or home town, and made it the subject of their writing: Jammes and Reverdy, amongst the poets, found inspiration in retirement, one in Béarn, the other in Anjou. Others, however, while publishing their works in Paris, have travelled and lived outside France: Claudel and Saint-John Perse have spent the better part of their lives abroad as diplomats; Cendrars and Aragon were both profoundly marked by journeys to Russia. There has also been a growing cosmopolitanism within artistic circles: the old contacts between Paris and other centres such as London, Berlin, Copenhagen, Vienna, and more recently New York, interrupted since the late eighteenth century by the outbreak of national Romanticism in Europe, have been re-established. Paris has also attracted poets from many other parts of the world, who have written in French: Apollinaire, half Polish and half Italian, Supervielle, a Uruguayan of Basque ascendance, Césaire and other negro writers.

The new, lesser status of poets has also broadened their experience. None can remotely hope to live off their poetry alone, and the detached life of the literary gentleman of independent means is increasingly rare. For most, whether teachers, diplomats, or clerks, literature is a spare-time activity. Some find a germane occupation, in journalism or publishing, or in the French cultural relations service. But in all these cases, political and social awareness cannot fail to be of a different, more detailed and involved kind: the relative decline of lyrical poetry coincided for a while in the early part of this century with an increased participation of poets in politics. It is perhaps no accident that two major figures, Claudel and Saint-John Perse, as well as Paul Morand, issued from the Quai d'Orsay, professionally aware of the world scene before they became poets; or that others, such as Péguy or Romains, have also participated as journalists and novelists in the invasion of *belles-lettres* by the literature of everyday experience.

Poetry has also been sensitive to broader cultural changes, affecting the status of the printed word. The publishing revolutions of this century did not affect it until very recently, but the growth of broadcast and recorded forms of communication immediately tended to blur the frontiers between 'poetry' and a host of other media such as the popular song or the radio programme. Poets have tried to react against the confused popularization that might rate them in the same status group as the radio compère or the professional rhymester in a publicity agency—yet at the same time to achieve modernity by bringing within the scope of their genre certain facts of contemporary experience. The 'modernists' of 1910 sensed that poetry would have to develop in an entirely new way, to parallel the changes in modern life. Apollinaire, for instance, wrote at the time:

L'esprit nouveau qui s'annonce prétend . . . hériter des romantiques une curiosité qui le pousse à explorer tous les domaines propres à fournir une matière littéraire qui permette d'exalter la vie sous quelque forme qu'elle se présente.

Explorer la vérité, la chercher, aussi bien dans le domaine ethnique, par exemple, que dans celui de l'imagination, voilà les principaux caractères de cet esprit nouveau. . . .

Les poètes font aujourd'hui l'apprentissage de cette liberté encyclopédique. Dans le domaine de l'inspiration leur liberté ne peut pas être moins grande que celle d'un grand journal quotidien qui traite dans une seule feuille des matières les plus diverses, parcourt les pays les plus éloignés. On se demande pourquoi le poète n'aurait pas une liberté au moins égale et serait tenu, à une époque de téléphone, de télégraphie sans fil et d'aviation à plus de circonspection vis-à-vis des espaces.

La rapidité et la simplicité avec lesquelles les esprits se sont accoutumés à désigner d'un seul mot des êtres aussi complexes qu'une foule, qu'une nation, que l'univers n'avaient pas leur pendant moderne dans la poésie. Les poètes comblent cette lacune et leurs poèmes synthétiques créent de nouvelles entités qui ont une valeur plastique aussi composée que des termes collectifs.

For the first time the electric telegraph and the telephone brought events from all over the planet together in newspapers once a day and even, during the inter-war period, several times a day in special editions. France, and more widely Europe and the Western world, literally lived every day together. With mass communications came mass ideals: exacerbated patriotism, developing, after 1918, into an uneasy internationalism, in reaction, though not always successfully, against the dangers of patriotism.

As Apollinaire also points out, collective entities were more and more common. In France, as in Britain slightly before and in other industrialized countries a little while after, the focus of everyday life was beginning to switch from the smaller family unit to larger communities of people. Nowadays, almost everyone regularly identifies himself with an office, a factory, a university, the other travellers on the same train, the other members of a society or union, the other readers of a newspaper. This important feature of urban life, far more influential on people's minds than their narrowing prospect of green fields, was bound to permeate through to the structure of literary inspiration as much as the strident colours and rhythms of modern posters and machines. It was first represented in the novels of Zola, where the preoccupations of the individual, at war with the social group in the early nineteenth-century novel, were finally lost amongst those of the group.

One can only attempt a rough explanation of why these trends affected poetry specifically in the first decade of this century, since the social processes they reflect have been more or less continuous since 1850. Perhaps the gusts of political and social commitment that entered literary circles during and after the Dreyfus Affair helped to set up as examples such enormously influential writers as Péguy and Barrès, and their idealistic appeals to large numbers of socially involved readers. Péguy is the first example of a phenomenon that our century knows only too well: the poet read primarily because of the ideological position he is known to have (in this case patriotic and Catholic—Aragon is another, opposite, instance) rather than for the immediate appeal of his verse.

Not only has this 'information explosion' emphasized the individual's consciousness of his wider cultural allegiances; modern ideas have changed the very type of human experience to which poetry has traditionally applied itself. Lyrical verse becomes increasingly difficult to write when one can no longer talk plausibly of an individual without referring to his fellows, his history, and his environment. The predominant trends shaping contemporary thought suggest that we do not understand ourselves fully, as many earlier artists had believed they could, without reference to past experiences still alive in our subconscious, or perhaps even, so the Jungians say, to experiences of our ancestors and of the human species as a whole. Furthermore, the individual, we are told by sociologists, is always related in unexpected ways to his class or group. These must be seen, as they were by Lévy-Bruhl, as a stage in an anthropological story, where curious echoes of primitive existence influence modern attitudes. We must even take into account, in talking of our 'selves', the links between our species and other natural phenomena, remembering the constant cross-interpretation that has linked biology and physics in our century. Lyrical poetry has not disappeared, and individuals such as Valéry have been strongly exposed to the kind of influences enumerated and yet have chosen to construct a poetic universe of their own— but they can only do so by deliberate choice.

Nor is it possible, as it still was in the time of the symbolists, for a poet to entrench himself with an entirely clear conscience in the opinion that his alchemy of language is a privileged activity, in some way more noble than that of science: anthropology, archeology, psychology, and linguistics have combined to investigate the mysteries of words, and the poet must absorb their findings if he is to retain his authority. Only by in a sense 'keeping ahead of them' can he avoid being swallowed up in some general communication theory.

Yet many intellectuals between 1900 and 1930 were as disappointed as Brunetière who, in a famous essay of 1896, had talked of 'la faillite de la science'. Scientific inquiry had not offered the set of easy material explanations of the world that the mid nineteenth century had hoped for, but had instead stretched out of the grasp of the amateur observer into a maze of complexity and conjecture. Mathematical physics itself was undergoing a crisis, as the theories of Einstein and Planck cast doubts on two essential elements of its reckonings: absolute time and geometrically arranged matter. If science too rested on uncertainty, if the answers it gave were as closely linked as all other fields of knowledge to the way an individual had phrased his question, then literary and religious expression could hope to reclaim its status as an anthropomorphic and anthropocentric means of inquiry into man's condition and his place in the world. During this period many writers found themselves agreeing with Bergson, who held that the human mind is able to disturb as well as comprehend the best materialistic explanations. He encouraged a return to a more arrogant view of man's superiority, as well as a trend towards even more individualistic types of expression.

On the other hand, in a world constantly enlarged and complicated by the various advances of science and technology and yet never pieced together by any one theory, poets can also see themselves as interpreters, translating these bewildering realities into human terms. As the frontiers of knowledge explode they must, if they are to perpetuate the romantic ideal of leadership, attempt first an encyclopaedic, then a synthetic survey, similar to the 'descriptions of the world' written after the great voyages of discovery of the fifteenth and sixteenth centuries. Claudel's special interest in Columbus the map-maker is significant; like Saint-John Perse, he is attempting to encompass our world within a system of poetry lest its frontiers recede beyond the speed of human comprehension.

French poetry in the nineteenth century had only been partly sensitive to this trend. The Romantics and the symbolists had been aware of the spread of industrialized urban life, but rather to deplore the passing of an old order than to hail a new one. Their belief in progress sometimes led them to an epic vision of the evolution of mankind, but theirs was not such a puzzling world: as yet only the historical dimension had been added to it, and Hugo's *Légende des Siècles* and the miniature epics of Leconte de Lisle and Heredia were illustrations of mankind's improvement (or their author's nihilism, its counterpart) throughout the ages. They were still concerned moreover with individuals, even where the latter were supposed to be representative of collective experiences.

Émile Verhaeren illustrates the turn towards more mundane sources of inspiration. After early lyrical poetry searching for symbolic counterparts to his complex depressions in the sad and ghostly monotony of his native Belgian plains, Verhaeren suddenly discovered socialism, and from 1885 began to see the modern city in a new light. It became a place of achievement, of work in common, of social transformation, though its material possessiveness remained frightening: Verhaeren coined the phrase 'villes tentaculaires', and its long-standing popularity amongst architects and economic planners illustrates the continued exorcizing power of the poetic word:

> Tous les chemins vont vers la ville
> Du fond de brumes
> Là-bas, avec tous ses étages
> Et ses grands escaliers, et leurs voyages
> Jusques au ciel, vers de plus hauts étages
> Comme d'un rêve, elle s'exhume.
>
> Là-bas,
> Ce sont des ponts tressés en fer
> Jetés, par bonds, à travers l'air;
> Ce sont des blocs et des colonnes
> Que dominent des faces de gorgonnes;
> Ce sont des tours sur des faubourgs
> Ce sont des toits et des pignons,
> En vols pliés, sur les maisons;
> C'est la ville tentaculaire.

Later, less worried by rural depopulation and more impressed by industrial progress, Verhaeren added a human dimension to this shell. The above extract, from one of his more venturesome pieces, is a successful description of the breathless and scattered tempo of urban life, which is further served by the division of paragraphs into irregular lines with some rhymes; but it has none of the necessary coherence that makes a piece of writing into a poem. The accumulation of details slowly leading up to the central image 'ville tentaculaire' is interesting but lacks shape; as the poem develops, Verhaeren places too many words, such as 'cab', 'naphte', 'rails', merely for the sake of neologism and too obviously tries to squeeze as many metaphors as he can from each detail in his landscape. In his excitement and his truly cosmic optimism at the new prospects of mankind, he failed not only to find transcendental formulas but even to create a truly literary response to the new ideas, and did not wholly avoid the pitfalls of scientific and humanitarian poetry, well explored by Sully Prudhomme and Jean Richepin before him.

Between 1903 and 1914 a minor, but extremely influential poetic movement grew out of an odd intellectual community, intended to resemble a minute 'phalanstère',[1] which began at the abbey of Créteil and is depicted in Duhamel's novel *Le Désert de Bièvres*. Its members called themselves 'unanimistes' after Jules Romains's book of poems, *La Vie unanime*. Romains has described how he rediscovered the existence of humanity one day in 1903 as he was taking a walk near the Gare Saint-Lazare. He suddenly realized that the people in the street were part of a huge composite being, a crowd, with a rhythm and a consciousness of its own representing more than the sum of its component souls. His earliest—and best—poetry stems from the tension between conventional lyrical interests and his new sense of belonging to the city: it 'individualizes' forms of corporate experience, such as a funeral procession, a theatrical performance, a school outing. Such beings have a life of their own, which must be felt to be free from the observer: Romains tried to bend the alexandrine to this purpose by emphasizing its inner rhythmical life and intricate patterns of assonance rather than the crystalline rhyme that appears imposed by an ever-present poet. In the following extract from *Odes et prières*, where the soul of a town rises into being, the contrast between the complexity of detail and the grandeur of the overall feeling is particularly well expressed by the form:

> Tandis que des quartiers se boursouflent et font,
> Sous la brume qui tombe avant la fin du jour,

[1] An experimental self-supporting community of 1,632 people advocated by Charles Fourier as an answer to the social problems of the 1830s. In the mid nineteenth century several *phalanstères* were set up in North America. Hawthorne describes one in *The Blithedale Romance* (1852).

Partir, en un soudain épanouissement
De leur centre qu'un feu par le dedans tourmente
Vers ce qui souffre seul dans les derniers faubourgs
Plusieurs bourrelets mous qui grossissent, qui roulent,
Qui noient de glu les tas avant de les dissoudre,
Qui cerclent peu à peu de leur anneau plus grand
Plus de chair, étirant les groupes reployés
Pressant les carrefours et les rassemblements,
La rue en marche et la famille qui se chauffe
Pour qu'ils deviennent tous une ceinture accrue
Autour de l'âme en bloc qui se pense au milieu
Et que jusqu'au rempart la ville soit un dieu. . . .

A ghostly being slowly appears and emerges from the streets. The unanimists prefigured some of the basic principles of sociology, and thus remained 'ahead' or abreast of scientific inquiry, in this case that of Lévy-Bruhl and Durkheim (whom Romains claimed not to have read until much later). They had a long-standing influence on such later figures as André Spire and Pierre-Jean Jouve. Unanimism, like Whitman, has been a fomenter of ideas. But in itself it was only a minor poetic movement. It is significant that Romains and Duhamel both turned to the novel. The introduction of everyday reality into poetry was a welcome reaction against symbolism and its 'aesthetic' themes; but one at least of the lessons of symbolism should have been heeded—that, in order to justify its pretentious formal claims, poetry needs to remain aloof from the perceived world, though it thereby aims at penetrating it more intimately. When impressionistic reporting is put to verse, however sophisticated the metaphoric structure used, we remain 'outside' reality.

The same reservations can be made concerning the poems of Blaise Cendrars and Valery Larbaud, and some of Apollinaire's work. The first two are interesting in that they broadened their inspiration geographically by describing the complex nostalgias and hopes of globe-trotters. Cendrars, different in this from the poets of the nineteenth century whose voyages were imaginary, really did travel by train to Manchuria (as an agent for a dealer in diamonds) before writing the long piece provocatively entitled 'Prose du Transsibérien et de la petite Jehanne de France'. It is indeed a prose account divided into irregular lines that have lost all poetic function apart from that of stressing the words on which they pause and therefore slowing down the reading. Cendrars's theme is the multiplicity of the impressions he remembers from his trip: the many new things that struck him as a stranger in Moscow, the variety of passengers on the famous weekly transcontinental train, the diversity of lands this oddly assembled community travelled through. His technique is a literary collage, which associates impressions for the sake of contrasts and surprises, with accident or simultaneity as an excuse. Thus:

Moi, le mauvais poète qui ne voulais aller nulle part, je pouvais aller
    partout
Et aussi les marchands avaient encore assez d'argent
Pour aller tenter faire fortune.
Leur train partait tous les vendredis matin.
On disait qu'il y avait beaucoup de morts.
L'un emportait cent caisses de réveils et de coucous de la Forêt-Noire
Un autre, des boîtes à chapeaux, des cylindres et un assortiment de tire-
    bouchons de Sheffield
Un autre, des cercueils de Malmoe remplis de boîtes de conserve et de
    sardines à l'huile
Puis il y avait beaucoup de femmes
Des femmes des entre-jambes à louer qui pouvaient aussi servir
De cercueils
Elles étaient toutes patentées
On disait qu'il y avait beaucoup de morts là-bas
Elles voyageaient à prix réduits
Et avaient toutes un compte courant à la banque.

The actual widening of horizons in Cendrars's case does not provide him with a poetically coherent vision. As the 'Prose du Transsibérien' wanders on, he becomes increasingly nostalgic for his home country and for a girl called Jeanne he met by chance just before leaving. His collections of poems, *Du monde entier . . .* or *Kodak*, are merely accounts of the flotsam of the traveller's impressions, the fool's paradise of the perpetual tourist. The same impression arises from the poetry of Valery Larbaud, who is concerned with the apparatus of travel rather than with its destination. Luxury trains, synchronized clocks, aerodromes, the clink of foreign names provide the imaginary multi-millionaire A. O. Barnabooth with easy exotic thrills and a superficial nostalgia of times and places. But the cosmopolitan existence as seen here is merely a rootless one, and the experience no better than the fast-paling pleasure of the travelogue.

'Simultanéisme' was to be more influential as a technique for gathering impressions about reality than as a means of expressing a broader experience. It was used at about the same time by Apollinaire in his long poem 'Zone', which expresses similar feelings of nostalgia and rootlessness against the same bewildering background. But, as with Cendrars, it is not so much on the breadth of experience as on the technique itself that the poet finally concentrates. 'Zone' develops into an increasingly serious blurring of reality ending on the jarring discord 'Soleil cou coupé', which was to be one of the starting-points of surrealism. Although of course all modern poetry has absorbed and often makes use of the collage of impressions, revealing and provocative in detail, one cannot expect of it any more permanent or universal image of the world. It is essentially destructive, and it is also basically a lyrical view: the random wandering of the poet's gaze or the associations in his mind are its only excuse. Though he is now a cosmopolitan and a free agent in society, this only makes him the more rootless, friendless, and aimless and his writing expresses defeat.

Péguy's poetry, in complete opposition to these examples, begins from firm convictions; he develops and generalizes them confidently into a universal system, underwritten by the vigorous personality of Péguy himself, a Catholic and a Frenchman. His roots in the workaday peasantry of the Beauce, and his ideals, the Christian virtues of Faith, Hope, and Charity, are both symbolized by the cathedral which at Chartres seems to grow out of the fields, and professed by the two saints, Jeanne d'Arc and Sainte Geneviève. Whereas his earlier works are little more than gushes of lyrical faith, the 'tapestries' are attempts to weave together in an arduous, patient, repetitive process, similar to the labour of the peasant, the religious symbols and the everyday virtues they stand for. The roots of the

F

peasant or the pilgrim, are also national, and so patriotic feeling is as important as religious feeling: Péguy's is the last great cry, at times frankly heretical, of Catholic gallicanism.

The form springs out of 'La tapisserie de Sainte Geneviève et de Jeanne d'Arc', written in small daily sections as if during a period of meditation, when the poet could modify and develop his thought progressively like an unhurried artisan. The second tapestry takes a similar shape, which was finally to flower in Péguy's most successful work, *Ève*. The logical structure of this poem is its least important aspect. It is an invocation by Jesus, who gradually develops into a first person plural speaking, for the whole of mankind, in praise of the first woman, mankind's mother. Her difficult life after the Fall from Paradise is evoked, and she becomes the symbol of womanhood struggling to impose system and order and having to overcome the faults of men. This struggle widens, for no particular reason, except that this is the way thoughts develop, into a panorama of the gradual progress of Christianity in the Western world, and finally into a comparison between the arduous but simple and rewarding existence in the traditional world, and over-legalized, over-industrialized, over-commercialized modern life. This in turn becomes a comprehensive review of the moral issues that face mankind, pleading for a whole system of life in danger of being forgotten by modern materialistic city-dwellers.

The form Péguy uses is highly original. The poem consists of 1,911 stanzas made up of four alexandrines rhyming in pairs, and arranged in long sequences of up to several dozen. Each stanza may only differ slightly from the one before: within the same phrase pattern, a word or a group of words, sometimes as little as a syllable, is modified, and the poet continues his gropings and explorations of a pattern through as many as fifty stanzas until, it seems, he has written one composite stanza, including all the possible echoes and variations on the original shape: 'Aucune phrase', Gide remarked, 'ne suffit à exprimer la pleine touffe de la pensée. . . . Chaque mot, de chaque phrase de Péguy aussitôt dite débandée, court après tout ce qu'il a laissé fuir.'

> Et ce n'est pas leurs poids dans ces cages de verre
> Qui pèseront le sang qui fut versé pour nous.

Ce n'est pas leur balance avec des caoutchoucs
Qui pèsera le sang versé sur le Calvaire.

Et ce n'est pas leurs poids chez les pharmaciens
Qui pèseront l'offense et le péché mortel.
Et ce n'est pas leurs lois chez les praticiens
Qui laveront le sang sur le dernier autel.

Et ce n'est pas leurs poids dans les laboratoires
Qui pèseront la chute et la rédemption.
Et ce n'est pas leurs lois dans les conservatoires
Qui fermeront la lutte et la contrition.

Et ce n'est pas leurs poids dans leurs laboratoires
Qui pèseront l'orgueil et la contention.
Et ce n'est pas leurs lois dans leurs conservatoires
Qui fermeront le seuil sur la prescription.

Ce n'est pas leurs bocaux chez les pharmaciens
Qui recevront le sang qui fut versé pour nous.
Ce n'est pas leurs bocaux chez les praticiens
Qui recevront le pli de nos humbles genoux.

Ce n'est pas leurs balances de pharmaciens
Qui diront notre poids quand nous serons pesés.
Ce n'est pas leurs sentences de praticiens
Qui diront notre sort quand nous serons dosés.

Ce n'est pas leurs balances de précision
Qui diront notre poids quand nous serons pesés.
Ce n'est pas leur sentence et leur décision
Qui diront notre sort quand nous seront dosés.

No extract can do more than suggest all the echoes and variations that a complete reading brings out: this pattern 'Ce n'est pas. . . . Qui. . . .', which pits the need for spiritual rearmament against modern gadgetry, has already at this point been repeated for forty stanzas, and continues for four hundred more, while certain key words, 'leurs poids', and 'notre sort' have already been part of previous sets of variations and will recur again, as threads in a tapestry blend, disappear, and reassert themselves in different places.

The reader who has learned to expect of poetry a crystalline expression of idea or experience may feel here that he is witnessing no more than poetry in the making: instead of correcting himself, Péguy rewrites a stanza in a slightly different shape, in a kind of insult to 'good literature'. But his quest was more meaningful: it was precisely his mistrust of crystalline language and the carefully fenced-in ideas it expresses that led him to break with academic literature. The ideas he is trying to convey are closer to 'intuitions' in the Bergsonian sense: single words or concepts may 'fall between' them, and categories fail to do justice to their complexity. Joyce merges old words together; Péguy presents them in a spray, as if afraid of leaving out anything and thereby imposing personal and temporal limitations on the associative vastness of a thought.

Yet he can hardly avoid the thought being his own, and we never lose sight of his compulsive personality. His retreat from the difficulties of the modern world into the womb of Christian hagiography and myth, the simplification of this myth into an appeal by a boy Jesus to such mother figures as Eve, Sainte Geneviève, and Sainte Jeanne, the desperate regularity of the form in which his world is poetically enclosed, are all clear instances of privation play.

There is no such thing as a Catholic poet; there are only poets who are Catholics. For one could hardly imagine a more different type of verse than that of Claudel, who, in this protest against hermetic writing, abandons the regular support of rhyme and orthodox rhythm:

Poète, tu nous trahis! Porte-parole, où portes-tu cette parole que nous t'avons confiée?

Voici que tu passes à l'ennemi! Voici que tu es devenu comme la nature et ton langage autour de nous aussi privé d'attention pour nous que les collines.

Nous demandions que tu achèves avec ton esprit ces choses ici qui ne sont pas complètes.

Il n'arrive pas ce qu'il faudrait. Joie ou douleur, personne jusqu'au bout.

Toi, raconte-nous l'histoire, et fais trembler la scène sous le déchaîne-
ment de la parfaite comédie!

Est-ce que tu trahis notre cause? La parole du moins était à nous! Et toi,
est-ce pour cela que nous avons payé tes trimestres au lycée,

Afin que tu accroisses de tes runes la quantité de ces choses que nous ne
comprenons pas?

Where Péguy's style could be compared to that of a litany, the
rhythm of these long, winding sentences from Claudel's *Cinq
Grandes Odes*, with their apparently arbitrary division into over-
flowing lines, is similar to that of a psalm. They are invocatory,
repetitive, and digressive, and thus removed from the laws of prose;
yet, leaving aside the occasional poetic short cut, such as that in the
fourth line above, they could be spoken as normal speech, in a con-
versational tone. On the other hand, their logic is not quite that of
unwritten speech, though they reproduce its groping, leaping
progress and its tendency to catch briefly the fever of eloquence.
They could be situated at a more primitive stage, that at which our
ideas and feelings slip into words and phrases, which we select and
organize before uttering them, and which the conscious mind calls
its thoughts. Claudel creates the impression that he is setting these
straight down, in the form of spurts, or pulsations, and he himself
has said that the rhythm used is intended to imitate that of breathing, assumed to be the regulator of all the other bodily acts: each
line would thus represent the thoughts contained in one breath,
would vary in length according to their emotional colour, and above
all, would catch the 'thought line' before it has been parsed into
alexandrines.

Both the form and content of these lines show clearly, if we consider that they were written in 1908, that their author was reacting
against symbolism, while still trying to protect the poet's art from
the inroads of utilitarian prose. The accusation made here by the
'voice of the public' according to which the poet has retreated into
a closed house, is answered by the very words chosen by Claudel,
for nothing could be less hermetic and Mallarméan than this
reprimand for having wasted the money spent on his education.
On the other hand the everyday phrases take on a solemnity and

resonance that would not be found in everyday speech. In this
Claudel was underlining his own spiritual progress, for he had
begun his literary career under the joint influence of positivism and
symbolism, but cast them both off. Where Mallarmé considers
objects singularly in order to cull associations and meanings,
Claudel's verse uses plural nouns, and is concerned with the
multiplicity of things. If his poetry is symbolic, it is so in the
Goethean sense: it attempts to mirror the real impressions real
things make, and let the poem grow out of the relationships that
appear almost spontaneously between the poet and the world:

Que mon vers ne soit rien d'esclave! mais tel que l'aigle marin qui s'est
   jeté sur un grand poisson,
Et l'on ne voit rien qu'un éclatant tourbillon d'ailes et l'éclaboussement
   de l'écume.

Claudel also rejected 'le bagne matérialiste' in which he claimed
to have grown up, under influences such as those of Comte and
Renan. Like Rimbaud, he became convinced that there really was
a spiritual world to be perceived beyond the material one, but he
identified it much more clearly as the universal coexistence of things
created by the hand of God. Unlike Rimbaud, he built his attitude
on a firm philosophical basis, drawn mainly from Aristotle and
Aquinas. This appears clearly in the cosmology outlined in his main
theoretical work, *Art poétique*. The first part, 'Connaissance du
temps', develops imaginatively some classical objections against
any form of idealism, and notably that implied by scientific
generalization: the concepts of cause and effect are arbitrary, science
will never succeed in knowing the individual, as opposed to the
theoretical phenomenon, and time and movement are unexplain-
able in purely materialistic terms. The second part, 'Traité de la
co-naissance au monde et de soi-même', answers this partly
Aristotelian view with a system based on Aquinas's *Summa*, according to which the universe can be grasped as a synthetic whole
whose parts are defined and preserved by their interdependence
and infused with the spirit of God. He stresses, through the
etymological pun on 'connaissance', the fact that Man, born into
the same world as all material things, becomes the appointed centre

of the universe through his faculty of knowledge, denied to all other beings: this godlike quality places him apart, yet he still shares in the universal interdependence of existence. It is this privileged apprehension that the poet must try to express. His appointed role consists in reviewing through cosmic (Claudel prefers the word 'comic') juxtaposition and apprehension the variety and unity of Creation:

Ainsi quand tu parles, ô poète, dans une énumération délectable
Proférant de chaque chose le nom,
Comme un père tu l'appelles mystérieusement dans son principe, et
selon que jadis
Tu participas à sa création, tu coopères à son existence.

The *Cinq Grandes Odes*, followed by a 'Processional pour saluer le siècle nouveau', are, in their very form, a synthesis of the poetic and the liturgic. They begin with a classical invocation to the Muses, yet as they progress the poet's Muse becomes an invocation of divine Grace and what had been a search through his experience for inspiration becomes a hymn to the meaningful multiplicity of the universe. Claudel brings together a wealth of Biblical references and another set of terms borrowed from classical antiquity, but he also situates his poem with reference to Homer, Virgil, Dante, and the humanist tradition of epic poetry, while not forgetting the heritage of medieval liturgy, so often neglected in modern humanist literature, and separating it clearly from the theological tradition; there are also many traces of influence from Chinese and Japanese and South American cultures (the work was written largely in China). The first ode is concerned with broadening the scope of poetry: as Claudel appeals in turn to the nine Muses depicted on a sarcophagus in the Louvre, he gathers all the skills they represent and remembers all the most famous examples of their arts as if to combine their virtues into his projected work. The second ode finds in the pervasive presence throughout the world of water a principle with which to scan the whole of creation and symbolize the equally pervasive presence of the spirit: again, the ode has a definite setting, the diplomatic quarter of Peking in which Claudel feels imprisoned, and it progresses from a diversity of material objects towards spiritual apprehension. His point of view is extra-historic, for he sees himself as coming after 'La poudre qui fut Sodome, et les empires d'Égypte et des Perses, et Paris, et Tadmar et Babylone', as well as super-geographic, for when he imagines himself travelling along water, this is immediately identified as 'all the great rivers':

> . . . le Gange, le Mississippi,
> L'épaisse touffe de l'Orénoque, le long fil du Rhin, le Nil avec sa double vessie.

From the third ode onwards, Claudel begins to identify his poetic review of the cosmos with the act of divine creation, and he moves, much as in the Japanese poetic tradition, towards a multiple series of meanings. In writing of the inspiration to compose these odes, he is also speaking of his poetic vocation and his discovery of religion; as he re-creates the world in the poem he repeats and thus praises the act of its original creator, for if the world contains the image of its creator, so will the poem in its turn. 'La poésie', Claudel wrote in *Positions et propositions*, 'doit inclure le tout de Dieu, le tout du langage.' In keeping with this aim, Claudel successfully, though violently, brings the many-stranded world together within a poem in a way opposed to, yet as ambitious as, that of Mallarmé. But most of his later pieces either are trivial or abandon the cosmic view for that of the professional patriot, who misguidedly believes everything he says about his country in his speeches: his war poetry does not stress the devotion of the masses to a common purpose, which could be admirable, but the political excellence of their cause.

One is thus forced to consider the *Cinq Grandes Odes* as an isolated achievement, and it must be recognized that the work is seriously deficient in one important respect. The poet states that there is a cosmic harmony, and presents us with impelling lyrical insights into it; yet what does it consist of? For the reader who cannot refer to a shared religious system, the surge of divine creation is not a sufficient answer. True, there is the suggestion that Man himself has the attribute of Aquinas's God: of being wherever he is a centre with no circumference. But this has always been a commonplace of European mystics, and the *Grandes Odes*, ever preoccupied with the act of writing poetry, do not actually create or develop a modern vision of Man and his world. From this point of view they are no more than a prelude to a work that never materialized as a poem. Fragments of it are found in Claudel's early drama. *Tête d'Or* and *La Ville* introduce the universal, timeless setting that the *Cinq Grandes Odes* announce: the characters in *Tête d'Or* are a Warrior and a Young Man, and the opening scene takes place in front of the Town.

The 'chanson' with which Saint-John Perse opens his enigmatic *Anabase*, illustrates, rather than reflects on, the existence of a cosmic harmony within which Man has a place:

Il naissait un poulain sous les feuilles de bronze. Un homme mit des baies amères dans nos mains. Étranger. Qui passait. Et voici qu'il est bruit d'autres provinces à mon gré. . . . 'Je vous salue, ma fille, sous le plus grand des arbres de l'année.'

Car le soleil entre au Lion et l'Étranger a mis son doigt dans la bouche des morts. Étranger. Qui riait. Et nous parle d'une herbe. Ah! tant de souffles aux provinces! Qu'il est d'aisance dans nos voies! que la trompette m'est délice, et la plume savante au scandale de l'aile! . . . 'Mon âme, grande fille, vous aviez vos façons qui ne sont pas les nôtres.'

Il naquit un poulain sous les feuilles de bronze. Un homme mit ces baies amères dans nos mains. Étranger. Qui passait. Et voici d'un grand bruit dans un arbre de bronze. Bitume et roses, don du chant! Tonnerre et flûtes dans les chambres! Ah! tant d'aisance dans nos voies, ah! tant d'histoires à l'année, et l'Étranger à ses façons par les chemins de toute la terre! . . . 'Je vous salue, ma fille, sous la plus belle robe de l'année.'

The absence of any didactic or narrative meaning is at first disarming: the author avoids being the sole guarantor of his poem and offers us instead an abstract theme—here death and renewal, and the periodicity of Creation—which takes shape in a series of images with a symbolic charge but also suggestive in their own right. The reader does not think of the idea of a colt being foaled: he imagines it vividly, as he does the mysterious Stranger (medicine man or bringer of disease?) who leaves behind him the taste of sour berries and the desire to find a rare herb, while also introducing the odours of death and embalming, funereal bitumen and roses. Then in a second stage, we associate the two images and draw our own conclusions as to the idea of renewal through death and birth. It is the same with the late-summer splendour of the tree, and the powerful and majestic lion that appears in the sky during that season; while the desire to write a poem, to make a fresh departure, arises out of the very rites of death: these objects exist fully on the mythical scene where the poem is set.

There is thus no 'one for one' relationship of images to ideas: not only are a whole range of phenomena mustered, from the cycles of days, of seasons, of life-spans, to illustrate periodicity, but some of them—in *Anabase* mainly those connected with horses and nomadic journeys—gather multiple meanings during the course of the poem. Critics interested in the genesis of the poem point out that these latter were the grains of experience around which the poet collected suggestive clusters of facts and events: as its title suggests etymologically, the poem was conceived during journeys on horseback from Peking up to a temple on the edge of the great caravan trails of the Gobi desert. As in the work of Rimbaud, the metaphorical scenery here is brought to life with such vividness that one only remains faintly conscious of its matrix in the poet's personal experience and reflections. Saint-John Perse, however, adds a sense of the tangible reality of this scenery by regularly rejoicing in lengthy encyclopedic surveys of its constituent parts. The apparently enigmatic quality of this poetry, it will be found, is due more to its resisting attempts by the mind to make it into a story or a set of ciphers, than to any mystery in the images themselves: these are only slightly refined ('arbre de bronze' for 'arbre aux feuilles de bronze') or wary of the abstract, of which Saint-John Perse has a deep mistrust (as with 'la plume savante, au scandale de l'aile', which merely means 'for writing', and 'plucked from the wing').

From the complex thematic standpoint thus established—maturity, mobility, omens of death, and the desire for rebirth—*Anabase* develops into what is, on the outermost level, an account of a large collective enterprise—an expedition, a civilization, the building of a city on the coast—by an ambiguous narrator, inhabited at times with the personality of a soldier-emperor reminiscent of Tamburlaine, and at others with that of a poet, historian, or astrologer glorifying his achievements. But the rise, fall, and renewal referred to are wider even than this: the asiatic flavour of the poem is only incidental, for its setting is the world and human history seen from an anthropological point of view. It is related to the comparative histories of civilizations and religions of the time, as Eliot's *Waste Land* was to *The Golden Bough*. With its bias towards primitive cultures, which was so common in the 1920s and relates Saint-John Perse to Picasso and Stravinsky, it borrows material from classical, medieval, and oriental, but not industrial, civilizations. It describes the will to organize and conquer, the growth of customs and beliefs and laws, the diversity of human crowds, and the restlessness that impels Man to destroy and begin again when he appears to have reached fulfilment. It is also at one, in a way Claudel never quite achieved, with its own creation, for the recurrent birth is also that of the poem, and the restlessness is the urge of the poet to begin yet another work or spur his horse yet again towards the desert.

Saint-John Perse's descriptions of the world, for his poems are all enumerative and encyclopedic, have been compared with journeys which, instead of following recognized roads or currents, might follow isobars or isotherms, hitherto unsuspected yet real paths. Within this world man loses some of his privileges: he is only a part of the natural forces and harmonies that run through all things, and he is treated no differently from the birds and the plants which Saint-John Perse knows so well. *Exil* mentions a seafarer who turns over instinctively in his sleep as the tide changes, the wind veers, and his ship swings on to a new tack. This sense of the wondrous fullness of the world leads the poet, even during the sad experience of exile in America, to a meticulous precision, sometimes at the cost of immediate clarity, and to a sustained pitch of almost incantatory high praise. Saint-John Perse said once that *Éloges*, the title of his second major poem, should be his only title. In a world whose main lines of force are so comprehensive and so complex, all things are equally worthy of note, and it would be artificial to limit one's vision, in the traditional manner of the short poem, to one trivial, albeit significant, coincidence. Perse's 'verse', in outward appearance similar to that of Claudel, in fact starts from a more rigid framework, for his long, apparently flexible paragraphs are often built around alexandrines, still the instinctive pattern of French poetry. But they burst out of these formal limits for the same reason that leads Péguy to continue writing over and over again the same quatrain: because every path that occurs in Nature must be included in the poem.

It would, however, be wrong to seek anywhere in his work for a definitive encyclopedia—a *grand œuvre*; for in spite of their vast scope all his poems are only examples of far-ranging series, and they are all closely informed by the author's private theme: *Images à Crusoé*, with its contrast between the flowering of the City and the flowers of Nature, suggests the impressions of the poet on arriving in a French town from his childhood spent on a West Indian island; *La Gloire des rois* is concerned, as was the young diplomat, with the ritual role of the leader of men; *Exil* with the cruel exclusions in Nature as well as with Alexis Léger's flight from the Vichy regime in 1940; *Vents* with migrations and the discovery of new worlds— or the New World; *Neiges* with winter, stillness, despair at his mother's death; *Pluies* with purification by water and the renewal of poetic inspiration; *Chronique* with the old age of the poet and with that of his civilization and of mankind, combined into a song of human achievement. Perhaps the most ambitious, as well as the most successful of his works is *Amers*, where the relationship of the sea and the land, and that of a lover and his beloved, are evoked: the 'sea-marks' referred to in the title, objects and sightings that help navigation but are visible and meaningful only to the mariner, are a perfect symbol for Perse's principles of organization.

Saint-John Perse is the poet of a time when everyone's knowledge is *potentially* universal: though many things he mentions are unusual they are all verifiable, whether through sociology, history, botany, or geology. They are at once members of series as rambling and global as those of Péguy, and challenges to the reader not to forget, as Péguy's reader might, that the richest part of our experience is that of the outside world. In this Perse is an epic poet, not in the sense we have given to the word because of our Homeric heritage—there is no story here and no individual, only generic personalities, whose names (le Conteur, le Prince, le Maître d'Astres et de Navigation) refer to the grasp they have on the world —but according to the definition Hegel suggested for the epic: the adventures of Man in contact with Nature. Here Man is confident in his total harmony with Nature, and describes lavishly, not his whole kingdom, too vast to be compressed into a poem, but a route through its plurality past the sea-marks he loves.

NOTE

Poetry is increasingly approached through anthologies and these are particularly useful where they include substantial commentaries on a large selection of poets. Anthologies of this type relevant to this chapter include R. Bertelé, *Panorama de la jeune poésie française* (1942) (for the ten years immediately preceding the Second World War); W. Fowlie, *Mid-Century French Poets* (1955) (a limited selection); G.-E. Clancier, *De Rimbaud au surréalisme* (1959); J. Rousselot, *Les Nouveaux Poètes français* (1959) (follows on from Clancier). Mention should also be made of J. Onimus, *La Connaissance poétique* (1966), a general work with many suggestive bibliographical notes.

ÉMILE VERHAEREN, 1855-1916, a native of Flanders and a student at Louvain, was a professional man of letters throughout his life, in touch with the literary circles of both Brussels and Paris. He published some fifty volumes of verse. The type of poem discussed in the preceding chapter is best represented in *Les Villes tentaculaires* (1895), *Les Forces tumultueuses* (1902), and *La Multiple Splendeur* (1906). Critical works on Verhaeren include E. Estève, *Un Grand Poète de la vie moderne, Verhaeren* (1929); F. Hellens, *Verhaeren* (1952); P. Mansell Jones, *Verhaeren* (1957).

JULES ROMAINS is the pseudonym of LOUIS FARIGOULE who was born in 1885 in the Cevennes but was brought up in Paris. His volumes of poetry that stand most chance of survival are: *L'Âme des hommes* (1904), *La Vie unanime* (1908), *Un Être en marche* (1910), *Europe* (1919), and *L'Homme blanc* (1919). The poetry of Romains and the unanimists is studied in G. Guisan, *Poésie et collectivité 1890-1914: le message social des œuvres poétiques de l'unanimisme et de l'Abbaye* (1938). BLAISE CENDRARS's poetry is contained in the first volume of his *Œuvres complètes* (1963) and was originally published as *Prose du Transsibérien* (1913), *Du monde entier* and *Au cœur du monde* (1919), *Dix-neuf poèmes élastiques* (1919), and *Kodak* (1924). The work of VALERY LARBAUD referred to in this chapter is *Poésies de A. O. Barnabooth* (1913).

CHARLES PÉGUY, 1873–1914. For a brief biographical note, together with details of the major critical essays on Péguy, see the previous volume in this series (*The Late Nineteenth Century*), chapter 11, pp. 195 and 197. Most of Péguy's poems appeared in the *Cahiers de la Quinzaine* (1900–14) of which he was editor, some written avowedly as stopgaps during periods of financial difficulty. After experimental pieces, of which the most interesting is *Le Porche du mystère de la deuxième vertu* (1911), he published his best works which he called 'tapestries': *La Tapisserie de Sainte Geneviève et de Jeanne d'Arc* (1912), *La Tapisserie de Notre-Dame* (1913), *Ève* (1913). All are collected in the Pléiade *Œuvres poétiques complètes* (new edn., 1958).

PAUL CLAUDEL, 1868–1955. For brief biographical notes on Claudel, together with details of the major critical studies of his work, see the Note to chapter 5 of the present volume and chapter 11 of the previous volume (*The Late Nineteenth Century*). Claudel's major poetic work, apart from his plays, is his *Cinq Grandes Odes suivies d'un Processional pour saluer le siècle nouveau* (1910). His *Cantate à trois voix* (1913) was an interesting experiment but nothing more. There are some poems of worth in the collections *Poèmes de guerre 1914–1916* (1922), *Feuilles de saints* (1925), and *Visages radieux* (1945). All these are in vols. 1 and 2 of the Gallimard *Œuvres complètes* (26 vols. up to 1967). Vols. 5 and 15 of the same collected edition contain his major works on poetry: *Art poétique* (1907) and the first vol. of *Positions et propositions* (1928). The symbolist and aquinist backgrounds are particularly well described in E. Friche, *Études claudéliennes* (1943); and there are interesting stylistic analyses in G. Antoine, *Les Cinq grandes odes de Claudel, ou la poésie de la répétition* (1959).

SAINT-JOHN PERSE is the pseudonym of ALEXIS LÉGER. He was born in Guadeloupe in 1887 and this Caribbean island provided the setting of his first major book, *Éloges* (1911), written while studying in Pau and Bordeaux. He then entered the French foreign service and was first sent to Peking, where he wrote *Anabase* (1922) and *Amitié du Prince* (1924). He later held high positions at the Quai d'Orsay of which he was permanent head from 1937 to 1940, when he went into exile. Deprived of his nationality by Vichy, he has since lived mainly in the U.S.A., where he has written his central works, *Exil* (1942), *Pluies* (1943), *Neiges* (1944), *Vents* (1946), and *Amers* (1957). He was awarded the Nobel Prize in 1960 for his last poem, *Chronique* (1959). See *Œuvre poétique* (2 vols., 1960) and *Poésie* (1961) (his Nobel Prize speech). As an exile he did not, until the Nobel Prize, receive the amount of commentary he deserved from French critics. Important studies include: R. Caillois, *Poétique de Saint-John Perse* (1954); J. Paulhan, 'Enigmes de Perse', *Nouvelle Revue Française*, 1 Nov. 1962; G. Poulet, 'St.-J. Perse', in *Le Point de départ* (1964); A. Knodel, *Saint-John Perse: a Study of his Poetry* (1966); M. Maxence, 'Saint-John Perse ou la tentation de la démesure', *Tel Quel*, iv.

The type of poetry studied here could be followed into contemporary literature. The shorter poems of Supervielle (though he writes more within the South

American poetic view of Nature than as part of the French tradition) are set in a scene that appears to mirror the universal aspiration of Claudel and Saint-John Perse, though not their real cosmic ambitions. Various other pre-war poets such as Pierre Mac-Orlan, André Salmon, Paul Morand, are comparable though far less successful. There are also echoes of the 'monomyth' even in such individualistic poetry as that of Henri Michaux (see for instance 'Quelque part quelqu'un', *Nouvelle Revue Française*, Oct. 1938).

Three contemporaries, all returning to religious, rather than humanist myths, may come to be regarded as of similar stature: Patrice de la Tour du Pin, Pierre Emmanuel, and Pierre-Jean Jouve. And there are various poets writing in French from former colonies (Aimé Césaire, Edouard Glissant, Kateb Yacine) who may be placed in the same line.

10. Theatres of Escape

FRENCH theatre in the twentieth century resembles a kaleido-scope. It has suffered changing modes, constant experimentation in form, production, and style of acting; it has endured wave upon wave of new ideas, enjoyed foreign masterpieces and survived competition from the screen. It follows then that any attempt in the space of a single chapter to give coherence to the bewildering medley of names, interests, and forms is, inevitably, highly selective and personal.

Going to the theatre is surrounded with artificiality. Before we go our expectations are aroused towards some kind of emotional, and perhaps intellectual, experience. We expect to be 'taken out of ourselves' while sharing in the feelings and dilemmas of the charac-ters on the stage. Recognizing the importance of using the spec-tator's anticipation in order to direct his response, and reacting healthily against the uninspiring and constricting naturalism which Zola and his followers had for years imposed upon the theatre, play-wrights of the 1920s and 1930s made their works seem as far removed from reality as possible.

Jean Cocteau, rendered virtually dizzy by the variety of his artistic gifts, was one of the first of these dramatists to take his audience into unfamiliar surroundings. Often sustaining simul-taneously roles as playwright, actor, choreographer, poet, and film director, he kept the spectator constantly amazed and amused by his manifold transformations. The element of surprise lay at the centre of his art. The very forms he used to present his ideas changed with each production. Monologues came in quick succession to the ballet *Parade* (1919); a chronicle play, *Les Chevaliers de la Table Ronde* (1937), had been preceded by a melodrama, *Les Parents terribles* (1936), and followed by a verse tragedy, *Renaud et Armide* (1943); intermingled were adaptations of Greek plays and of

Shakespeare. Almost every new work was prefaced by Cocteau's declaration that he had showered a witty radiance upon old forms and ideas, and that, in his surprise presentation of well-known people and stories, he had revealed new significances which would inspire his contemporaries.

Wit and ingenuity are easy to find in any play of Cocteau; new significances, however, make themselves exceedingly obscure. Theatrical convention accepts that flowers and birds speak human language as in *Les Chevaliers de la Table Ronde*; it also allows for Gauvain's magic-carpet journeys in the same play. It does not challenge the character's right to walk through liquefying mirrors, or to hang unsupported in the air (*Orphée*). Anything is possible as long as the scene designer can make such unusual happenings credible. But if such elements are also to be meaningful, if they are to carry 'new significance', then they must have some kind of tangible relevance in their context. A play like *Les Chevaliers de la Table Ronde* unquestionably creates a strange atmosphere of enchantment with its distant, mysterious, historical setting; and speaking flowers, magic carpets, and conjurations clearly belong to such a world. Thus far it is possible to follow Cocteau and appreciate his effort. What is not clear, however, is the significance which the spectator is supposed to attach to this play. As entertainment it is delightful, even disarming. Outside the theatre the experience quickly fades as one realizes that admiration should more properly be directed at the scene designer's ingenious achievements. Astonishment, then, seems to have been the main response that Cocteau solicited. In front of his plays the spectator is essentially passive.

A similar cloudiness of intention surrounds the well-known figure of Orphée, who gives the impression that he is a symbol of great portent for Cocteau, while there are few hints for the spectator to direct his own interpretation of this myth. In spite of the haunting effect of the play, and particularly of the film, *Orphée*, the problems which concern Cocteau there—death and the struggle of the poet—seem only potentially interesting. Once the dazzling wrappers have been removed from his ideas, they seem somehow trivial. In spite of his jokes and the mischievously distorted situations, Cocteau himself no doubt felt the seriousness of his undertakings, but it is a concern which he was unable to communicate. The world he creates remains idiosyncratic, and suggests that he was primarily indulging his own private need to escape from the real world. He seems to be consoling himself rather than revealing anything to us.

This impression is also valid for his best-known play, *La Machine infernale* (1932). On the one hand, this work sets out to demonstrate the careful and mathematical destruction of a human being— to use Cocteau's own terms. On the other hand, Cocteau chooses to transform the Oedipus myth into a rollicking satire of heroes and gods, and he does this so successfully that the first supposedly serious intention is totally undermined. His Oedipus is no more than a robot. His Jocasta is full of petty, bourgeois concerns. Tiresias, the powerful and august prophet of Sophocles, becomes a doddering old uncle 'Zizi'. Not only has the original grandeur of conception of these characters been lost, their words diminish them further; there has probably never been a play so full of puns.

Cocteau's idea of bringing Greek myth up to date is really another concealed opportunity to indulge his own irresistible desire to joke. This fact can be seen in his manipulation of the story itself. He chooses to elaborate the most sensational aspects of the myth— those moments which present the stage designers with especial difficulty and which, furthermore, provoke the greatest degree of emotionalism in the audience. Apart from the very end of the play, which is bathed in a 'lumière de peste', the entire action takes place at the bewitching hour of night. The first happening is the pathetic and comical appearance of Laius' ghost against the cold wall of the castle battlements. The traditionally enigmatic sphinx, unexpectedly portrayed as a beautiful woman, is displayed for all to see in the second act. The third act, set on the wedding night in the bridal chamber itself, is the most sensational scene of all. (It also has the ingredients of a truly dramatic scene.) The room itself is heavy with an atmosphere of gruesome expectation. Jocasta and Oedipus are drugged with fatigue. In their drowsiness they do not comprehend the revelations about their future fate which are sucked out of them to underline the horrible nature of their union for the audience. The spectators, knowing the details of the myth in advance, do understand. Had Cocteau so constructed his play that this scene coincided with the climax, then the emotional force of these unwilling avowals would be difficult to resist. But the tone of previous scenes and the dwindling significance of even the main characters provide, on the contrary, a context in which such admissions are made to seem (no doubt deliberately) completely ridiculous. Cocteau's escape into jokes, witticisms, and sensation is perhaps more self-revealing than he intended. Unknowingly, in 1938, he had already prepared his own critical epitaph: 'Dans une époque aussi intelligente que la nôtre, il n'y a plus à redouter qu'excès de finesse.'

A similar accusation, rather differently slanted, could be made against Cocteau's prolific contemporary, Jean Anouilh, whose first of some thirty plays was performed in 1932. From the start he argued a very sour view of man's lot. The most powerful of his early plays are all concerned with poverty and its excesses. He indignantly and crudely denounced its stifling effects in *L'Hermine* (1932); he made Thérèse consciously submit to its inevitability in *La Sauvage* (1938). Even when he moved into pleasanter surroundings, his concern was to reveal, savagely, the unattainability of human desires. Ideals of love, friendship, and companionship are shown to have no part in real life. The kind of compromise which Créon is prepared to accept in *Antigone* (1944) is just acceptable, rationally— but the very fact that he proposes such a course demonstrates the degrading effects of living. Increasingly, Anouilh turned to the view that a reasonable existence could only be artificially created and imposed. As the Count explains in *La Répétition* (1950), life is a question of studied aesthetics: 'C'est très joli la vie, mais cela n'a pas de forme. L'art a pour objet de lui en donner une précisément, et de faire par tous les artifices possibles plus vrai que le vrai.'

Anouilh's theatrical sense, his technical mastery, and his witty word-play are particularly suited to such a view. With these skills he can create a glittering, sophisticated world of illusion, where human beings are replaced by brilliant talking marionettes. These 'characters' only very occasionally allow a glimpse of the emptiness behind their shallow, puppet-like faces. In constant fear of being bored or boring, they expend enormous energy chasing whims and fancies, mounting complicated mascarades as in *Le Bal des voleurs* (1937), or creating the ideal atmosphere evoked in *Léocadia* (1939) —an Alice-in-Wonderland place where anything can happen, where everything is out of time and full of surprises. The atmosphere they generate is never relaxed. Perpetual motion does away with the need to think, but produces strain. Their witticisms, which form a shield against any deep penetration of personality, are often sharp rather than gay; they are endowed with the bitty irony of the Countess's sinister aphorisms in *La Répétition* (1950) which gives their talk a brittle edge; the laughter they provoke is uneasy. Protecting this merry world from the cracks of intruding reality is a desperate business.

Giving life a form—that is covering up its sordid parts with a froth of witticisms and a thin veil of mascarade—seems, however, a rather poor solution to Anouilh's problem. It is merely a way of opting out. It does not try to come to terms with real life, it simply rejects it in all its aspects, offering instead a moment's relief, artificially contrived. In an early play, *Le Voyageur sans bagages* (1937), the hero has made no effort to understand his past, he has simply dismissed it. By 1950, with *La Répétition*, Anouilh has got no further forward. Weaving lines of Marivaux skilfully into his own, he avoids analysis of situations; keeping his 'characters' involved in an endless whirl of activity, he leaves no time for exploration of ideas, of feelings, or of personality. Increasingly, his plays have become sleek, bitter-sweet performances, where even the technical skills are showing signs of wear. His plays seem too long, straining an idea beyond its limits. At the outset, for example, *Pauvre Bitos* (1958) looks as though it is going to explore the character and motivations of the hero by drawing a parallel to his nature and situation in the historical figure of Robespierre. In the event, such expectation is shown to have been falsely aroused. Anouilh never really tries to make Bitos and Robespierre correspond. The original idea for the play was a clever one; its execution is disappointing.

Both Anouilh and Cocteau evoke traditional great themes of the theatre. Their plays bring up repeatedly the words 'love', 'life', 'death', 'liberty', and 'war'. Yet somehow the finer problems inherent in these themes are never discussed. Either their importance is reduced to brittle cocktail-talk (in the case of Anouilh) or (for Cocteau) they become concepts to be flirted with: the mystery of death, for example, presented as a beautiful woman. A kind of quixotic or cynical humour has pride of place at the expense of these themes whose richness is correspondingly diminished. Exceptionally gifted, these two playwrights are both victims of their technical brilliance. Their fantasies fulfil a private need where the challenge of surprise and of technical difficulties to be overcome is most prominent. However impressive the initial impact of their productions may be, I find their magic has no lasting qualities and their verbal felicities are quickly forgotten.

The vital element which Anouilh and Cocteau overlooked in their attempt to dazzle their public continuously by swift changes of scene and complicated plots flawlessly handled was that the theatre is primarily a speaking art. Fundamentally, a play's power of communication depends on the quality of its language. Most of Shakespeare's or Molière's plays have interest, however amateurish the production, because of the powerful resonance of the words they employ. It could be argued that the tradition of doing honour to language in the theatre is nowhere better established than in France. There the theatre audience, nourished relentlessly from early childhood on the noble beauties of French classical plays, expect every time they go to the theatre to take part in some form of public speaking. They are not afraid of rhetoric; education and long years of training have taught them to enjoy plays where the language itself is strikingly persuasive. They remain unmoved by the accusations of foreign critics that their dramas are over-rhetorical on the one hand and often too remote from reality on the other.

Not only education but personal preference had given Jean Giraudoux a particularly thorough knowledge of both classical and French theatre traditions. He had a very clear and noble idea of the art of the theatre, and has explained his views on innumerable occasions, perhaps most clearly in *Littérature* (1931) and

L'Impromptu de Paris (1937). In general, he saw it as 'la seule forme d'éducation morale ou artistique d'une nation'. Such a view implies the will to communicate his thoughts on matters relevant to the audience in ways which are both aesthetically pleasing and thought-provoking. His handling of themes is never trivial or restrictedly entertaining. In *La Guerre de Troie n'aura pas lieu* (1935), for instance, he provided an analysis of the theme of war which was not only peculiarly relevant to that particular moment of history; it also tells us something positive about human beings confronted with the possibility of war, and their efforts to avoid it, in a manner which continues to concern us. The problem is stripped down to its basic elements. War is exhaustively discussed and its emotional and rational repercussions examined. The theme is treated with humour and nobility. The well-known myth gives the discussion a possibility of application to any age, while the most searching analysis is provided in the solemn words of the majestic figures of Hector and Ulysses. The noble nature of their magnificent verbal battle which constitutes the climax of the play is thrown into sharper relief by the trite quarrel of Demokos which precipitates the war. The theme loses neither its grandeur nor its horror in spite of Helen's fickleness, the lascivious looks of the old men of Troy, and the jokes of Paris. These refreshing reinterpretations of the myth give a new, living quality to the story; they are timed and ordered so that they almost become laughing asides within the more solemn, rhythmic speeches of Andromache, Hector, and Ulysses.

In this play Giraudoux succeeds in linking together two elements which one would not have thought could coexist in the same work: frivolous entertainment and purposeful solemnity. Like his favourite poet, La Fontaine, he realized that thoughts strike deeper on an audience if you give them an extra spice, a humour and attractiveness which are far more persuasive than dull, high-minded sobriety. While Cocteau and Anouilh made excessive play with words and jokes and turned them into faults, Giraudoux employed similar elements threading them more expertly into a nobler conception which sought to achieve a certain balance between the amusing and the serious.

The delicate weighting of two such diverse tones was not always successfully managed. There are moments of strain even in *La Guerre de Troie*. When Giraudoux tried to maintain a consistently serious tone in a play (in his tragedy *Judith* (1931), for example), his thoughts on war seem something of a rhetorical exercise. Overplayed or misplaced jokes in *Électre* (1937) make his vast themes of liberty and compromise dwindle into personal and often incomprehensible comment. He had to find a language which would permit the successful blending of two such contrasting tones, frivolity and seriousness, a way of making them work together to affect the spectator. Giraudoux knew that to make an impact upon his audience he had to arouse them intellectually and emotionally. He also knew that the deepest impression is made when the spectator has been encouraged to give attention willingly. Theatrical experience he described as 'un spectacle et un filtre'; the audience, he thought, expects to experience some kind of enchantment in the theatre and it was the dramatist's role to satisfy such anticipation by creating an atmosphere which at first sight might seem a deliberate escape from reality. Since, as the 'droguiste' explains in *Intermezzo* (1933), the theatre is a place which permits 'le passage d'un niveau de vie à un autre', Giraudoux determined that, in front of his plays, our minds and sensibilities should immediately be alerted to a different quality of living from that which we normally experience. Only then, caught on a higher and more intense level of feeling and response, could we consciously appreciate the nuances of changing tones which carry his thought.

Thus, at all times Giraudoux tries to mark and emphasize the difference between the lives we lead and the ones we perceive through the filter of the theatre. He constantly reminds us that we are in the theatre and that we are experiencing something special. This privilege is underlined by the gardener in *Électre* and by the 'droguiste' in *Intermezzo*. Mercure does not let us forget our role as spectators in *Amphitryon* (1938), and the illusionist's skill in *Ondine* (1939) virtually warns us of the limits of what the theatre technician's art can accomplish. Conscious participation in a theatrical event is an important part of Giraudoux's moral purpose;

since he wishes to persuade, he cannot allow the traditional magic of the theatre spectacle to absorb us into passivity.

The atmosphere evoked at the beginning of his plays has always something odd about it, something which immediately challenges our interest and involves us. *Intermezzo* begins, for example, with the exclamations of the Mayor: 'Oh! Oh! évidemment l'endroit est étrange — ne trouvez-vous pas que l'acoustique de ce pré a je ne sais quoi de trouble, d'inquiétant.' The place is indeed strange. The field is vague and empty, made even more mysterious in the falling dusk when shadows play tricks with the eyes, and the lines of the countryside are muted and transformed. The disquiet of the Mayor is quickly communicated and we feel no stir of protest when the 'droguiste' pronounces 'notre ville est en délire poétique'. Giraudoux often heightens our feeling of the strangeness by introducing a certain sense of timelessness. In *La Guerre de Troie* he pitches his drama in the distant past; he knows, however, that the events of the Trojan War are well known to most people; and he calculates that his spectators, surprised by the familiar, bourgeois features of his characters, will be forced to think about the particular historical and political events of 1935. It is quite usual for dramatists to choose a historical period or well-known myth to parallel contemporary events in order to put forward their own opinions in detail. Giraudoux, however, goes far beyond this common practice. His is a double achievement. By encouraging his spectator to reflect simultaneously upon two historical conditions, in reality set far apart in time, he gives the impression that what is being thought is relevant to all time. In *La Guerre de Troie* it is the thoughts which Giraudoux induces in the spectator which provoke the feeling of timelessness; in *Ondine* the illusionist takes over this role, and so muddles our notions of time and place that we are ready to believe ourselves not only on a different plane of being but in a different world entirely. In the first case our minds produce the effect, in the second we are carried along on the marvels invented by art.

There is never anything lugubrious in the strangeness we experience. Certain words—'beauté', 'charme', 'crépuscule', 'aurore'— containing in themselves the power to suggest a privileged moment of time or an exceptionally happy state of mind, recur throughout Giraudoux's work, creating the dominant tone. They are repeated by the sparkling, gay young heroines who are endowed with an extraordinary capacity to extract warmth and poetry from the most common things of life. The 'petites filles' in *Intermezzo*, for instance, make the daisy into 'la plus noble conquête de l'homme'. We are quite ready to see the world from their point of view since they speak with such verve and their adversary, 'Monsieur l'Inspecteur', is so pompous and almost antipathetic. Gradually, through statements such as those of the 'petites filles', which in any other context would seem simply ridiculous, the nature of the world Giraudoux builds in his theatre becomes clear. It is a rather complex view, which at one and the same time recognizes the importance of the real world in which we live and reveals the presence and desirability of an idealized world. The ideal exists primarily in the imagination of Giraudoux's characters. It is perceived in only a shadowy way by Isabelle in *Intermezzo*, where the ghost represents both the mysterious nature and the fragility of an existence which can only be glimpsed by the mind. It is evoked nostalgically in the eloquence of Hector and Ulysses (in *La Guerre de Troie*). It is given its most powerful expression in *Ondine*, where the more-than-human heroine demonstrates the urgency and the exclusive nature of ideal love. Such ideals are never presented by Giraudoux as unattainable; he suggests that, since they do exist in the mind, they can be given a reality which will reflect back upon our lives in the real world. They exist to be reached for and can be obtained with difficulty, if one recognizes that the real world itself provides the rich material; its attractions are manifold, and these can be revealed and transmuted if one possesses the eloquence of the 'Contrôleur' in *Intermezzo*.

The remarkable power of language given to the 'Contrôleur', to persuade us of both the beauty and the nobility of much that surrounds us, is a gift which other characters of Giraudoux share; he could not always hope to convince through the simplicity and naïvety of 'petites filles'. Judith, for example, is confident in her ability to tackle Holofernes because she has eloquence, as she explains: 'mon arme la plus dangereuse, c'est mon langage.' In addition to eloquence, his characters all possess a fine capacity for concentrating thought and feeling. Électre both puzzles and attracts by the force of aphorisms such as 'le seul bonheur que j'ai connu en ce monde est l'attente'. When Alcmène concludes succinctly 'Il est plus facile de revêtir l'uniforme de la guerre que celui de l'absence', she is summarizing the wealth of feeling, the tenderness, and the affliction felt by a wife whose husband's thoughts are turned to the prospects and glory of war.

With such exceptional talent for using words these characters can build upon fragments from reality, transforming them in such a way that the vision they eventually produce can seem artificial and over-idealized, particularly if it is taken out of context. Agnès, in *L'Apollon de Bellac* (1942), provides a good example. Words rescue her from shyness and clumsiness. She learns to use her linguistic resources skilfully, and enjoys the exhilaration of actually creating something of value while, at the same time, awakening herself and others to beauties hitherto ignored or unseen. Her first attempt to gain confidence by experiencing the persuasive power of words for herself is practised on a chandelier. Her task is to bring this object to life. At first her compliments are simple; gradually the sentence builds up as her confidence grows; then, as her enthusiasm heightens, her words become more complex and more colourful:

Comme tu es beau, mon petit, mon grand lustre! Plus beau quand tu es allumé? ne dis pas cela. . . . Les autres lustres, oui. Les lampadaires, les becs de gaz, toi pas. Regarde, le soleil joue sur toi, tu es le lustre à soleil. La lampe pigeon a besoin d'être allumée, ou l'étoile. Toi pas. Voilà ce que je voulais dire. Tu es beau comme une constellation, comme une constellation le serait, si, au lieu d'être un faux lustre, pendu dans l'éternité, avec ses feux mal distants, elle était ce monument de merveilleux laiton, de splendide carton huilé, de bobèches en faux Baccarat des Vosges et des montagnes disposées à espace égal qui sont ton visage et ton corps. (*Le lustre s'allume de lui-même.*)

Out of context the words of this passage might well seem precious and illogical; placed in the theatre atmosphere ready to receive them, they delight uncritically—Apollon's pupil has just achieved perfection.

This steady process of building up an imaginative world is seen at its most simple with Agnès. But already it is apparent that the beings who achieve such feats of expression are by no means ordinary. In fact, looked at closely, Giraudoux's characters are most unnatural. They are exquisitely intelligent, extraordinarily eloquent, extremely sensitive and percipient; and, with all that, they are charming. Even the barbarous Holofernes is depicted as sensitive, heroic, and worthy of love. The young heroines somehow know that they are different, better than others—and perhaps what makes them so is not only their power of language, but also the fact that they all obstinately remain true to their idea of themselves and to their pursuit of a single end. Électre is defined by her passion for her father, and Judith by the role history has given her; Alcmène is obsessed by her notions of fidelity, and Ondine dies unable to modify her idea of love.

These characters might well seem totally alien to us, were we not drawn knowingly into their world from the beginning and kept aware of the process of transmutation, and also of the distance separating the ideals these characters cherish and represent, and the aspects of reality which we know to have sparked off their imaginations. This consciousness of distance is kept before us through Giraudoux's irony which underscores almost every speech and every situation in his plays.

The very title *La Guerre de Troie n'aura pas lieu* presents an ironical challenge. We know the historical war did take place and we know that war was imminent in Europe in 1935. These two facts allow Giraudoux to control the progress of the debate and con-centrate attention on the brilliance of the exchanges. In *Amphitryon* even the king of the gods is not spared Giraudoux's irony. Mercure's role seems especially designed to show up Jupiter in his most ridiculous light. His divinity is laughed at because it is too perfect, since it cannot by itself conceive of a hybrid passion such as friend-ship. In this respect human beings are less limited than gods; in an upside-down way, the relative world seems to offer more scope than absolutes, since it allows the imagination full flight. As soon as one has conveniently established the primacy of the human over the divine world, one begins to suspect that the matter is more complex. Just as Molière, in his *Amphitryon*, subtly maintained a balance between the laughs he had at Jupiter/Louis XIV's expense and the compliments he paid the King's divinity, so Giraudoux puts certain limits on human endeavour. Your human mind can pretend to itself that it is better than the divine, you can make your memory blot out certain experiences, you can encourage your mind to fashion a reality of its own, but Jupiter does, after all, in spite of the merriment, triumph over Alcmène and Hercules will be born. Thus the meaning of the play is deliberately kept ambiguous, so that the spectator is forced into a state of alert participation and directed reflection.

The irony is not always as boisterous as this. Even Medusa becomes less horrifying as Alcmène sees the proud eyes of Amphitryon sparkling through his mask. Électre, on the other hand, bitterly attacks the irony of the gods whose artistry makes the most beautiful visual moments always coincide with disaster: 'une belle lueur sur un incendie, un beau gazon sur un champ de bataille, voilà pour eux la justice.' Such an illogical state cannot be tolerated. A beautiful moment, imaginatively constructed, must be seen to start from the recognizably real and to proceed in such a way that the mind can still perceive that reality.

It is a cruel irony which brings the prosaic world of the clumsy Ritter Hans von Wittenstein zu Wittenstein into contact with the water-sprite Ondine. From the first moment of their encounter it is obvious that the distance between their worlds is too immense to be bridged. Hans never ceases to flounder through the fairy-tale happenings of the play. His so-called spirit of adventure is shown to be more ridiculous than the excessive imaginings of Don Quixote, as his blundering dull mind halts wonderingly before the strangeness of sudden metamorphoses and natural elements endowed with human speech. Total absence of any sort of emotional sensitivity prevents him from appreciating the true nature of Ondine's regard, while she is so absolutely absorbed by her love for Hans that she will sacrifice it entirely rather than let anything contaminate it. Her unrelenting obsession not only makes *Ondine* the most emotionally charged of all Giraudoux's plays; it also allows him scope for the most beautiful evocations of a perfect love. At one and the same time Ondine embodies all the qualities needed for such a state—

generosity, sensitivity, beauty, desire, and a sense of sacrifice—and, in her contact with Hans, she demonstrates the impossibility for ordinary human beings of ever attaining such an absolute. Nevertheless, the irony which brought these two worlds together has given us a glimpse of the potential which human love possesses, it tempts us to strain towards ideals of beauty, order, love, and decorum, for it has put us in touch with the absolute.

At first glance Giraudoux's irony seems designed merely to add a further dimension of amusement, to seal the characters off in their world of make-believe. A closer look, however, reveals that far from distancing that world from us, we are drawn further into it through the ambiguity which is created and by seeing, at close range, the manner in which his characters' imagination proceeds. Irony is an important instrument with which Giraudoux engages our minds. By providing delights which are left open to interpretation it forces questions, incites our imagination to work along similar lines, and, in the end, persuades both of the significance and the relevance of such stretching of our mental resources. Entry into Giraudoux's theatre first implies an ability to respond to the charms of the atmosphere with which his language surrounds us, it then encourages that alertness of mind and sensitivity which the author considered of lasting value: 'c'est très bien d'illuminer la Tour Eiffel, mais ne crois-tu pas que c'est mieux d'illuminer les cerveaux?' (*Impromptu*, 1937). Anouilh and Cocteau would have been content with the first action; Giraudoux beguiles us out of such passivity.

In the final analysis it is our ability to recognize and define a 'style' in an author which permits us to separate him off as greater than other writers. By 'style' I do not simply mean a way of writing (although this is vitally important); I include the power to create a world which impinges upon us in such a way that our sensibilities are automatically sharpened and our imagination set in motion. Cocteau and Anouilh, while being able to write in a way which can be described as characteristically 'theirs', seem unable to set an audience alight except perhaps once, or fleetingly. Giraudoux can arouse in the spectator a quality of thought and feeling which has possibilities of permanent renewal.

NOTE

JEAN COCTEAU (1889–1963), born into a family of comfortable means, of artistic interests and ability, spent the largest part of his life in Paris, hating every kind of discipline and cherishing excitement. He escaped from the Lycée Condorcet and from successive tutors, and instead sought after plays, concerts, pictures, operas, and ballets. By 1912 he had met and begun to work with Diaghilev, Nijinsky, and Stravinsky, he had corresponded with Proust and met Gide. Within two years he had made friends of Picasso, Modigliani, Braque, and Chirico, as well as Apollinaire and Reverdy. Thereafter the story of his life moves through a glittering array of personalities and artists: ballets made with Massine, music experiments with Poulenc, Honegger, Auric, and Darius Milhaud (in the 1920s), collaboration with Charles Dullin at the Vieux Colombier (1922), a close personal relationship (1919–23) with the young poet Radiguet, a quarrel with Jacques Maritain (1925–6), friendship with Chaplin (1930s), collaboration with Jouvet (1934), with Jean Marais, Marlene Dietrich, Jean Genet, and so on. Such activities brought him much notoriety and some honours. He was received into the Académie française in 1955 and was given an honorary degree by the University of Oxford in 1956. He long outlived his age.

Major Dramatic Works. Parade (1919), *Le Bœuf sur le toit* (1920), *Les Mariés de la Tour Eiffel* (1924), *Roméo et Juliette* (1926), *Orphée* (1927), *Œdipe Roi* (1928), *Antigone* (1928), *La Voix humaine* (1930), *La Machine infernale* (1934), *Les Chevaliers de la Table Ronde* (1937), *Les Parents terribles* (1938), *Les Monstres sacrés* (1940), *Le Bel Indifférent* (1940), *La Machine à écrire* (1941), *Renaud et Armide* (1943), *L'Aigle à deux têtes* (1946).

Criticism. His most recent biography is by Elizabeth Sprigge and J.-J. Kihm, *Jean Cocteau: the Man and the Mirror* (1968). Historical approaches to his life and work are by Margaret Crosland, *Jean Cocteau* (1955), and Wallace Fowlie, *Jean Cocteau: the History of a Poet's Age* (1966). Useful studies of his theatre include P. Dubourg, *Dramaturgie de Jean Cocteau* (1954), and N. Oxelhandler, *Scandal and Parade: the Theatre of Jean Cocteau* (1957).

JEAN ANOUILH (1910–   ). Born in Bordeaux, he has always been very reticent about his life. He started writing plays at the age of twelve, but it was not until he went to Paris in 1928 that his dramatic career really began. There he met Giraudoux who introduced him to Jouvet. Anouilh became this great actor's company secretary until commercial success relieved him of the need for such employment. Success came quickly, especially after Anouilh met the Pitoëffs in 1937. Since that time Anouilh has presented the world with at least one play a year and has also tried his hand at producing; he still pursues both these enthusiasms.

Major Dramatic Works. L'Hermine (1932), *Y avait un prisonnier* (1935), *Le Voyageur sans bagages* (1937), *La Sauvage* (1938), *Le Bal des voleurs* (1938), *Léocadia* (1939), *Le Rendez-vous de Senlis* (1941), *Eurydice* (1942), *Antigone* (1944), *L'Invitation au château* (1947), *Ardèle* (1948), *La Répétition* (1950), *Colombe* (1951), *La Valse des toréadors* (1952), *L'Alouette* (1953), *Médée* (1953), *Cécile* (1954), *Ornifle* (1955), *Pauvre Bitos* (1956), *L'Hurluberlu* (1959), *La Petite Molière* (1959), *Beckett* (1959), *La Grotte* (1961), *L'Orchestre* (1961), *La Foire d'Empoigne* (1962).

Criticism. A fairly comprehensive study of the plays can be found in L. C. Pronko, *The World of Jean Anouilh* (1961). An attempt to describe his method has been made by J. Harvey, *Anouilh: a Study in Theatrics* (1964). A helpful essay on the importance Anouilh attaches to an aesthetic interpretation of the theatre is provided by B. Pingaud, 'Anouilh ou la tentation de la frivolité', *La Table Ronde*, February 1952.

JEAN GIRAUDOUX (1882-1944) was born in Bellac (a little country town which figures prominently in his writings). He had a brilliant school career first at Châteauroux and then, from 1903, at the École Normale. After some months in Munich and a year at Harvard, Giraudoux returned to Paris in 1907; finally in 1910 he entered the Diplomatic Corps and there, fulfilling his wish to spend long periods of time in Paris, he passed a relatively quiet and leisurely career only interrupted by active service in the First World War. His duties often took him abroad (Turkey, Berlin, Harvard) and, as he became increasingly popular, he travelled even more widely on lecture tours. The most important event of his artistic career was his meeting with Louis Jouvet in 1928; in that year began a collaboration which was to be broken only by the coming of the Second World War and which can be said to be at the source of Giraudoux's entire dramatic output.

Dramatic Works. Siegfried (1928), *Amphitryon 38* (1929), *Judith* (1931), *Intermezzo* (1933), *Tessa* (1934), *Supplément au voyage de Cook* (1935), *La Guerre de Troie n'aura pas lieu* (1935), *Impromptu de Paris* (1937), *Électre* (1937), *Cantique des cantiques* (1938), *Ondine* (1939), *L'Apollon de Bellac* (1942), *Sodome et Gomorrhe* (1943). There are two posthumous plays: *La Folle de Chaillot*, performed first in 1945, and *Pour Lucrèce* (1953). Editions of all these plays are easily available. Giraudoux's main critical writings, including *Littérature* (1931), have been collected and published by Grasset under the title *Œuvres littéraires diverses* (1958).

Criticism. C. Marker, *Giraudoux par lui-même* (1952), and L. LeSage, *Jean Giraudoux, his life and works* (1959) present straightforward accounts of Giraudoux's career. A thematic approach to his theatre is provided by Marianne Mercier-Campiche, *Le Théâtre de Giraudoux et la condition humaine* (1954). Sound analyses of his plays can be found in D. Inskip, *Jean Giraudoux: the Making of a Dramatist* (1958). Marie-Jeanne Durry's essay *L'Univers de Giraudoux* (1961) is very illuminating.

General works and essays on these and other twentieth-century dramatists are legion. They range from superficial surveys to minute investigations of a particular theme or technique. Some books in which I have found chapters or essays helpful and sometimes suggestive are listed here. D. I. Grossvogel, *Twentieth Century French Drama* (1958); J. Jacquot (ed.), *Le Théâtre moderne: hommes et tendances* (1958); P. Surer, *Le Théâtre français contemporain* (1964); T. Boyard and W. I. Oliver (eds.), *Modern Drama: Essays in Criticism* (1965); Dorothy Knowles, *French Drama in the Inter-War Years 1918–1939* (1967).

11. The Novel and Christian Belief

GUSTAV JANOUCH, in the course of his conversations with Kafka, reports the latter as saying: 'The man of faith cannot speak and the man of no faith ought not to speak.' This statement indicates a double problem once we relate it to the work of novelists who write out of Christian conviction. On the one hand, the writer who is a Christian—for the purposes of this chapter, the novelist who is a Catholic—attempts, as an artist, to give his readers a convincing picture of some aspect of human experience. As a believer, however, he regards no portrayal of human experience as complete unless it takes into account an element of divine transcendence operative in human affairs. He is thus faced with the formally paradoxical task of translating the ineffable into words, of setting forth convincing human evidence of divine providence. On the other hand, the critic who reads these novels meets difficulties of a similar kind. At the simplest level all critics, both Christian and non-Christian, will meet cases where conversions, miracles, or the promptings of the Holy Ghost are as much the refuge of a second-rate talent as are the improbable coincidences and convenient deaths of purely secular writers. At a more serious level, the non-Christian critic will reject the basic assumptions of the Christian novelist however considerable the latter's literary talents may be. He may then go on to accuse the novelist in question of artistic inadequacy, of relying on the supernatural at points where he, the critic, would only be convinced by 'normal' psychological motivation. Such criticism may be deemed irrelevant in the sense that the critic disqualifies himself by regarding as unacceptable the fundamental assumptions from which such a novelist starts. He is incapable of 'entering' the fictional world which he seeks to evaluate. It can be argued that in such a case the critic, strictly as a literary critic, 'ought not to speak' about novels of this kind. In a word, then, the whole concept of

G

a novel that reflects aspects of doctrinal Christianity poses severe problems for both writer and critic. Both may be tempted to give up their tasks: the writer, because of the difficulty of making his faith acceptable in aesthetic terms; the critic, because of the difficulty of forming aesthetic judgements that remain independent of his unbelief.

The three novelists discussed in this chapter—Mauriac, Bernanos, and Julien Green—have all managed to command a wide readership while producing a considerable body of work in which they have written consciously as Catholics. Mauriac, in a frequently quoted passage from his *Journal 1932–39*, describes himself as 'un métaphysicien qui travaille dans le concret', and adds: '. . . j'essaye de rendre sensible, tangible, odorant, l'univers catholique du mal. Ce pécheur dont les théologiens nous donnent une idée abstraite, je l'incarne.' The emphasis in Bernanos is more positive. His novels give expression to his conviction that 'la vie, même avec la gloire . . . est une chose vide et sans saveur, quand on n'y mêle pas, toujours, absolument, Dieu.' Green, in his *Journal* for 1947, claims a similar concern, as a novelist, with the presence of God in human affairs: 'Mes romans laissent entrevoir dans de grands remous ce que je crois être le fond de l'âme et qui échappe toujours à l'observation psychologique, la région secrète où Dieu travaille.'

This last quotation refers to the distinction already made above between divine action and a satisfactory psychological rendering of that action. It is not surprising that if all three novelists have tried to embody Christian truth in their work, all three have also spoken either of the impossibility, or the severe difficulty, of such a task. Mauriac writes: 'Rien de moins saisissable que le doigt de Dieu dans le cours d'une destinée.' Bernanos firmly asserts (despite herculean efforts to prove the contrary) that 'l'expérience de l'amour divin n'est pas du domaine du roman'. Wrestling with the same problem Green admits: 'Je crois de moins en moins à la réalité objective du monde extérieur', and indeed his novels are notable for their visionary 'réalisme magique'. Even in cases of partial success, however, words remain inadequate for his vision. He refers to 'quelque chose d'inexprimable dans ce que nous essayons de décrire' and adds: '. . . pour moi écrire c'est faire allusion, rien de plus.' This last remark points to the beginnings of a solution often found in both Mauriac and Green. At the artistic level their strong religious sense is implied rather than stated and works more by significant understatement or tentative allusion than by positive assertion.

The aims which these Catholic novelists pursue, and the problems which they encounter, perhaps differ more in intensity than in kind from those of novelists generally. This intensity is important, however, and can lead, as already suggested, to a despairing contemplation of renunciation and silence. The area in which the Christian novelist works is a shrinking one. What he sees as the religious and the metaphysical is increasingly viewed by a majority of readers in psychological and social terms. The ground on which he takes his stand is occupied by a growing band of natural scientists, social anthropologists, sociologists of religion, etc. Here again, of course, the problem is part of a general malaise which prompts those inquiries into 'the death of the novel' that are a regular feature of the French critical scene. Happily, however, novels of all kinds continue to be written, novels with a distinctive Christian background being no exception. Indeed, where the Christian novelist is concerned, the danger has not been silence so much as the writing of manuals of piety. Mauriac comes close to this danger in certain novels, but such a criticism cannot be levelled against either Bernanos or Green. With typical verve, Bernanos inveighs against novels peopled by 'des hommes non décantés, de pieux jeunes gens inquiétants, des maris chastes, procédant liturgiquement à l'acte matrimonial, et prêts à conter avec attendrissement leurs édifiantes voluptés . . .'. In rather different terms, Green makes a similar point: 'Je n'essaie pas de faire de mes livres des romans catholiques. Cela me fait horreur. Mais je crois que tous mes livres, si loin qu'ils puissent paraître de la religiosité ordinaire et reçue, n'en sont pas moins religieux dans leur essence.'

This avoidance of naïve religious didacticism, notable in Mauriac's best work as well as in the novels of Bernanos and Green, goes some way towards explaining the considerable appeal of all three to a largely secular-minded public. They are not concerned to illustrate religious dogmas but to respond to their faith in imaginative and human terms. More particularly, they respond to the element of mystery in human experience, setting hints of transcendence against the drab rationalism and surburban scientism of the age. A powerful writer like Bernanos may not command the 'philosophic belief' of his readers, but he often compels their 'poetic assent'. He may not fill that 'God-shaped blank' which Huxley finds even in the secular mind, but he often arouses a response in it. In the final analysis, Mauriac, Bernanos, and Green are all worth reading because, if they sometimes appear to diminish man, they do not trivialize the experience of living. They do not restrict belief to what can be seen and touched. They do not confuse knowledge and belief. They do not make of the individual a mere socio-political abstraction or a psychoanalytical case-history.

Thérèse Desqueyroux (1927), beautifully written and richly textured, is typical of Mauriac's best fiction. As in so many of his novels, he uncovers the egotism, materialism, prejudice, insensitivity, scandal-mongering, and hypocrisy in the lives of Catholic property-owners in the region around Bordeaux. He does this with such a magnificent sense of place that the heavily shuttered houses, the sultry weather, the forest fires, the whole flat landscape of the Landes, seem to be in league with the prejudices and passions of his characters. Thérèse enters into a marriage which makes good financial and business sense but remains loveless. Eventually, she attempts to poison her husband, Bernard, prompted by impulses which she cannot account for adequately. Bernard recovers and testifies in her favour in order to save the family reputation. The examining magistrate decides, with doubtful legality, that there is no case to answer and to this extent the scandal is hushed up. The novel opens with Thérèse leaving the Palais de Justice to return home to her husband. The rest of the book is a mixture of narrative and elaborate interior monologue as Thérèse attempts to account for her behaviour. Later, when the scandal is dying down, she leaves Bernard, with his agreement, to begin a new life in Paris.

It would be perfectly possible to read this novel and remain unaware that Mauriac writes consciously as a Catholic. There are few overt references to Christian ideas apart from Thérèse's brief discussion with Jean Azévédo about mysticism and the search for

God. On this she comments: 'Je crois bien que je vomirais aujourd'hui ce ragoût.' Naturally, the absence of specific religious references does not in itself make the novel a secular one, but Mauriac's attitude to his characters strengthens this impression. Thérèse, who rejects Christian belief, who attempts to murder her husband, and who experiences a dissatisfaction which she can neither understand nor assuage, clearly has Mauriac's sympathy and is meant to possess moral superiority over the formally religious *bien-pensants* among whom she lives. It could be argued, however, that a novel writtten in a truly Christian spirit would extend the principle of loving the sinner while hating the sin to Thérèse's small-minded relatives as well as to herself. As it stands, Mauriac's attitude differs little from that associated with a familiar radical, and anticlerical, tradition.

Mauriac's other major novels published before 1930—*Le Baiser au lépreux* (1922), *Genitrix* (1923), and *Le Désert de l'amour* (1925)—are all open to the kind of criticism just made. They were attacked by the orthodox for their apparent complicity with certain sins while also implying that the church-going pillars of society are inevitably hypocrites and sadists. In *Le Romancier et ses personnages* (1933), in which Mauriac discusses his own practice as a novelist, he replied that his heroes and heroines 'aussi horribles qu'ils apparaissent, sont dépourvus de la seule chose que je haïsse au monde et que j'ai peine à supporter dans une créature humaine, et qui est la complaisance et la satisfaction. Ils ne sont pas contents d'eux-mêmes, ils connaissent leur misère.'

In addition to repeated attacks on the complacency inherent in a certain kind of Catholic conformism, Mauriac constantly returns to another theme—the vanity of human love and the bestial nature of sex ('cette chiennerie du sexe'). *Le Baisir au lépreux* harshly analyses the failure of a middle-class Christian marriage. *Genitrix* is the nightmarish study of a man of fifty whose marriage proves a disaster because of the devouringly possessive love of his mother. *Le Désert de l'amour* centres on a 'kept woman', Maria Cross, who becomes a focus both for Dr. Courrèges, fearfully seeking to assuage needs his marriage does not satisfy, and his schoolboy son Raymond, crudely attempting a short cut to sexual experience. Ironically, the social position of Maria Cross gives a false impression of her nature. She is romantic ('elle rêvasse toute la journée') but she has no enthusiasm for sexual contacts. Her lover, Larrousselle, says: 'Entre nous, elle n'aime pas ça . . . vous me comprenez, hein? Elle le supporte quand c'est moi parce que tout de même, c'est moi.' Thérèse Desqueyroux has a similar dislike of physical love-making: 'Il [Bernard] était enfermé dans son plaisir comme ces jeunes porcs charmants . . . lorsqu'ils reniflent de bonheur dans une auge ("c'était moi, l'auge", songe Thérèse).' It would seem that in Mauriac's eyes his heroines' view of sex as bestial and degrading is as much a virtue as their lack of complacency.

This theme is so all-pervasive in the novels mentioned above that it strongly suggests a deep, private obsession in Mauriac. More importantly, it points to a sense in which these novels are much more religious, if rather obliquely so, than at first appears. Mauriac is writing, in fact, out of an extreme puritanism. He avoids the 'manuel de piété' temptation by concentrating in his novels on a harshly uncompromising picture of 'la misère de l'homme sans Dieu'. Christianity is largely absent in explicit form. The formal observance of religious rites is shown to be a sham in many cases. But the frustration, the unhappiness, even the horror, which fill these novels, reflect the misery of a world that ignores God and in which true Christian values play no part. The novels are, in fact, a concealed plea, an indirect apologia, for Christianity. There are occasional hints of this stratagem, notably in *Le Désert de l'amour*. Maria Cross, after her attempted suicide, shows a sense of what is missing in her life, and in those of Paul and Raymond Courrèges, when she says: 'Songez qu'il n'est aucune route entre nous et les êtres que toucher, qu'étreindre . . . la volupté enfin! . . . Oui, comprenez-vous, nous empruntons la seule route possible, mais qui n'a pas été frayée vers ce que nous cherchons . . .' Shortly afterwards she speculates vaguely on the possible existence of 'un être que nous pourrions atteindre, posséder — mais non dans la chair . . . par qui nous serions possédés'. At the very end of the novel Mauriac reveals his hand, perhaps rather clumsily, in speaking of the passions of Dr. Courrèges and his son: 'Il faudrait qu'avant la mort du père et du fils se révèle à eux enfin Celui qui à leur insu appelle, attire, du plus profond de leur être, cette marée brûlante.' This type of authorial intervention, if doctrinally sound, is aesthetically suspect. The 'manuel de piété' temptation is close at hand.

For many readers, the type of statement by Mauriac quoted above bore disturbing resemblance to a pious afterthought. They noticed that sin seemed to bring out the best in Mauriac the writer. Despite his discouraging presentation of sexual love, 'l'univers catholique du mal' was invested with considerable glamour. The artist in Mauriac seemed to get the better of the theologian. He became acutely aware of this problem himself, and was deeply disturbed by it. He admitted: 'Rien ne pourra faire que le péché ne soit l'élément de l'homme de lettres et les passions du cœur le pain et le vin dont chaque jour il se délecte.' This is the problem which caused Mauriac to undergo a severe personal crisis in 1929. The determination to solve it resulted in the more orthodox, charitable, and explicitly Christian novels of his 'second period'.

Some critics have argued that this effort by Mauriac to 'purify the source' of his novels has weakened his literary gifts. They claim that he allowed the theologian to dominate at the expense of the artist and lost the creative dynamic previously supplied by the tension between a humanly impossible desire for purity and a theologically dubious fascination with sin. It is true that *Le Mystère Frontenac* (1933), in which the orthodox values of the Catholic bourgeoisie are sympathetically presented, shows a slackness and a sentimentality notably absent from his earlier work. It is also true that in *La Fin de la nuit* (1936), a novel dealing with Thérèse Desqueyroux's final conversion (a symbolic purging of his earlier work), Mauriac has to intervene heavily. In doing so, he robbed his heroine of the artistic integrity with which she was portrayed in 1927—and he also provoked the damaging criticisms of a now famous essay by Sartre. Nevertheless, Mauriac also wrote some impressive novels after 1929, chief among them being *Le Nœud de vipères* (1932) and *La Pharisienne* (1941).

Both these novels, in contrast to the interlude of *Le Mystère Frontenac*, return to the mean sins of the provincial Catholic middle-classes. But they move from 'la misère de l'homme sans Dieu' to 'la félicité de l'homme avec Dieu' in the sense that, like *La Fin de la nuit*, they are novels of conversion. For the Christian novelist, specifically as a novelist, the phenomenon of religious conversion is both an immense challenge and a likely source of complete disaster. Mauriac no doubt had this problem in mind when he wrote, in the phrase quoted near the beginning of this chapter: 'Rien de moins saisissable que le doigt de Dieu dans le cours d'une destinée.' In the event he fails signally in *La Pharisienne*, despite this novel's other qualities, and the didacticism accompanying the conversion of Brigitte Pian is pinpointed by the two final sentences. He has gone well beyond even the closing intervention of *Le Désert de l'amour* when he writes: 'Au soir de sa vie, Brigitte Pian avait découvert enfin qu'il ne faut pas être semblable à un serviteur orgueilleux, soucieux d'éblouir le maître en lui payant son dû jusqu'à la dernière obole, et que Notre Père n'attend pas de nous que nous soyons les comptables minutieux de nos propres mérites. Elle savait maintenant que ce n'est pas de mériter qui importe mais d'aimer.'

Le Nœud de vipères is an impressive novel on all counts. It has Mauriac's special gifts of physical atmosphere linked to spiritual drama. The 'generations of vipers' surrounding the free-thinking Louis are acutely observed and the spiritual air which they breathe is reflected in the constant references to heat, stuffiness, closed shutters, a generally stifling atmosphere. Significantly, Mauriac does not intervene as the omniscient narrator. Louis himself meditates on his life and his conversion develops within the specificity of the novel's own terms. It is made clear at an early stage that his generally anti-religious attitude has been partly social, partly political. He has had no confrontation with authentic Christianity. The first suggestion that he might change comes with his reference to an occasion when 'j'eus soudain la sensation aiguë, la certitude presque physique qu'il existait un autre monde, une réalité dont nous ne connaissons que l'ombre . . .'. Later, it is clear that his criticism of his family's religious life comes from a more demanding idea than theirs of what belief ought to entail: 'Vos adversaires se font en secret de la religion une idée beaucoup plus haute que vous ne l'imaginez et qu'ils ne le croient eux-mêmes.' A third possibility of change comes after his response to the 'faveur touchante' of the child Marie and the priest's comment: 'Vous êtes bon.' Louis possesses the sense of need, the marked absence of 'la satisfaction de soi', which must precede salvation: 'Je connais mon cœur, ce cœur, ce nœud de vipères.' He goes on growing in self-knowledge and his diary stops in mid sentence: '. . . cet amour dont je connais enfin le nom ador . . .'. The meaning we are meant to give this phrase is made quite clear when Louis's granddaughter says: 'Grand-père est le seul homme religieux que j'aie jamais rencontré.' Louis's illumination is at once psychologically convincing and spiritually moving.

To turn from the novels of Mauriac to those of Bernanos is to realize something of the great range of attitudes and talents enclosed within the inadequate term 'Catholic novelist'. It is true that Bernanos, in his non-fictional polemical writings, displays reactions also found in Mauriac. In *La Grande Peur des bien-pensants* (1931) he attacked the materialism of the Catholic bourgeoisie, in *Les Grands Cimetières sous la lune* (1938) the Franco forces in Spain, and in essays such as 'Réflexions sur le cas de conscience français' (1943) the Vichy regime. With the novels, however, dramatic differences appear. Mauriac, through the stratagem of the concealed apologia, seeks to share common ground with the non-Christian reader. With Bernanos, we enter a violent, incoherent, visionary, and obsessional world in which he seems to concentrate all his resources of poetry and passion in a desperate bid for the reader's soul. He throws down the challenge of the supernatural, deals in terms of personified evil and sanctity, and practises a form of shock therapy on his audience. He sees the world as the theatre of a titanic struggle between good and evil. This struggle is also reflected in the double thrust of individual human beings—'une effusion d'amour, qui fait de la souffrance et du renoncement l'objet même du désir' and '[le] goût mystérieux de l'avilissement . . . le vertige de l'animalité'. As several critics have pointed out, the fictional world of Bernanos, with its figures of pure evil and its 'saintly fools', places him much nearer in spirit to Dostoevsky than to Mauriac.

At a more formal level also, Mauriac and Bernanos have written quite different types of novel. Mauriac is very much the

professionally competent novelist possessing a wide range of technical skills placed in the service of his beliefs. The theologian and the
writer, though related, have separate roles in his work and sometimes
come into sharp conflict. Bernanos, by contrast, engulfs and absorbs
the artist in the religious thinker. At the level of craftsmanship, his
novels sometimes become formless and disjointed under the pressure of his intense spiritual vision. They are pulled out of shape by
long and urgent statements addressed to the reader. Ostensibly,
these impassioned speeches are made by characters in the novels;
in fact, they frequently possess qualities of expression and insight
inappropriate to the speaker in question. It is Bernanos's own voice
which dominates. The fictional integrity of his characters becomes
a secondary consideration. With Mauriac, the writing of novels is
a profession; with Bernanos, a vocation. Mauriac constructs novels
of psychological analysis; Bernanos generates sagas of transcendental
exploration: '. . . le métier d'écrivain n'est plus un métier, c'est une
aventure, et d'abord une aventure spirituelle.' These are novels
designed to catch the danger and the drama of a world in which
God and Satan wrestle for mastery in human lives.

Bernanos admired Balzac and considered himself a novelist in
the same tradition. Some of his main characters certainly resemble
those of Balzac in the sense that they take on a grandiose stature in
pursuit of a single passion. Abbé Cénabre in *L'Imposture* (1927)
and the eponymous hero of *Monsieur Ouine* (1943) devote themselves single-mindedly to evil; Abbé Donissan of *Sous le soleil de
Satan* (1926) and Chantal de Clergerie in *La Joie* (1929) follow a
steep and ruggedly heroic path to sainthood. The grandiose element
associated with such characters is also reflected in constant features
of the Bernanosian vocabulary—the repetition of such adjectives
as 'surnaturel', 'singulier', 'ineffable', 'mystérieux', 'fulgurant',
'démesuré', and their synonyms. Another Balzacian aspect is the
realistic treatment of the background against which these larger-
than-life characters move. With Bernanos this background is most
often a harsh peasant milieu of ignorance, poverty, cruelty, drunken-
ness, and debauchery. It is the only life known to the fourteen-year-
old Mouchette in *Nouvelle Histoire de Mouchette* (1937) and the
atmosphere in which the country priest of Ambricourt must live

and work (*Journal d'un curé de campagne*, 1936). Finally, modern criticism of Balzac not only notes his preoccupation with 'surface realism' of this kind but emphasizes his sense of a larger 'religious' or 'sub-religious' experience in which supernatural forces operate.[1] The same awareness, heightened and intensified by a profound religious conviction, is to be found in Bernanos. 'Realism', as he uses the term, means responsiveness to the life of the spirit as well as of the flesh and must encompass both the seen and unseen worlds. In the unseen world God and Satan exist. In the seen world they work through human beings and their reality is manifest in the presence of both grace and evil. For Bernanos, the seen and unseen worlds are inseparable.

Bernanos describes the metaphysical schema with which he works when he writes: 'Le monde du péché fait face au monde de la grâce ainsi que l'image reflétée d'un paysage, au bord d'une eau noire et profonde. Il y a une communion des saints, il y a aussi une communion des pécheurs.' He is not at all inhibited by the fact that the modern, dechristianized world rejects such an account of human reality. He believes passionately both in pure evil and in pure grace. His fictional world is peopled by heroic individuals who go to the utmost limits, whether in the service of sin or in the search for salvation. At the same time, his major characters seldom display unredeemed malignity (though the pure evil of M. Ouine is an example to the contrary). More usually, characters show Satan's influence through a despairing sinfulness and this sinfulness can be overcome by good. In fact, Bernanos establishes a vital relationship between sin and salvation: 'Nul ne peut offenser Dieu cruellement qui ne porte en lui de quoi l'aimer et le servir.' This is the same doctrine which Péguy expressed: 'Ceux qui sont bons pour le péché sont de la même nature, du même règne que ceux qui sont bons pour la grâce.' The sinner who goes to the utmost limits has his own form of thirst for an absolute. If he genuinely plumbs the depths of despair he will become aware of his dependence and need —the first step in the search for God. As Bernanos puts it: 'Quand on va jusqu'au bout de la nuit, on rencontre une autre aurore.' Only the indifferent or the lukewarm, lacking both passion and

[1] See the essay on Balzac in Vol. 4 of this series, *The Early Nineteenth Century*, pp. 114–31.

imagination, risk putting themselves beyond the reach of grace. They represent that majority described, again by Péguy, as a people 'qui ensemble n'est bon ni pour le péché ni pour la grâce'. Bernanos finds them equally numerous inside and outside the Church.

It is the saints and sinners, not the lukewarm conformists, who serve as vehicles for the spiritual dramas played out in Bernanos's novels. In most cases a priest plays a central role since, by the nature of his calling, he represents a vital point of contact between the seen and unseen worlds. Inevitably, there are lukewarm priests just as there are lukewarm laymen, and Bernanos adopts the same attitude of disgust towards them: 'Le prêtre médiocre est laid.' The priests he chooses as heroes, particularly Abbé Donissan and the parish priest of Ambricourt, are passionate, imprudent, and nonconformist by temperament. They are simple men, physically and socially awkward, living a life of material poverty yet possessing spiritual riches. They are the 'pure in heart' who take the teaching of Christ seriously. Abbé Menou-Segrais describes the external gracelessness of the young Abbé Donissan, destined to become 'le saint de Lumbres':

. . . un grand garçon aux larges épaules, d'une bonne volonté ingénue à faire grincer les dents, plus assommant encore d'être discret, de dérober ses mains rouges, d'appuyer prudemment ses talons ferrés, d'adoucir une voix faite pour les chevaux et les bœufs. . . . Mon petit setter le flaire avec dégoût, ma gouvernante est lasse de détacher ou de ravauder celle de ses deux soutanes qui garde un aspect décent. . . . D'éducation, pas l'ombre. De science, guère plus qu'il n'en faut pour lire passablement le bréviaire. Sans doute, il dit sa messe avec une piété louable, mais si lentement, avec une application si gauche, que j'en sue dans ma stalle, où il fait pourtant diablement froid!

Similarly, the dean of Blangermont ranks the priest of Ambricourt with those who are 'une épreuve pour l'Église avant d'en devenir la gloire'.

It is only priests such as these who prove capable of great spiritual distinction by living out in their lives something akin to the agony and suffering of Christ. They make of their humility and their spiritual torment something of redemptive value for others. In fact, the Catholic doctrine of the reversibility of merits is central to much of Bernanos's fiction. In *Sous le soleil de Satan* the juxtaposition of two lives—that of Germaine Malorthy who kills her lover and whose child is stillborn, and that of Abbé Donissan who wrestles with the Devil and penetrates the secret of Germaine's crime and pride—suggests that Donissan undergoes the torments of temptation and despair on her behalf. More explicitly, in *Journal d'un curé de campagne*, the country priest suffers torments as the price by which he purchases the peace of others—particularly the countess—in an agonizing process of exchange and substitution. The same theological pattern shapes *La Joie*, but in this case the girl Chantal de Clergerie achieves a degree of sanctity prior to being murdered which enables Abbé Cénabre (the malignant priest of *L'Imposture*) to be delivered from evil.

Between the twin poles of degradation and sublimity Bernanos locates human dramas that occasionally come close to *grand guignol* and have been criticized for their 'spiritual staginess'. There are numerous murders and suicides and these, together with rape and what is in effect a lynching, are used to carry strong religious significance. Something like a mystique of crime and suffering (again recalling Dostoevsky) is the major means by which Bernanos dramatizes the conflict between evil and sanctity central to his vision of life. For many readers this will remain an alien world; for all readers it must be a disturbing and uncomfortable one. In his first major novel, *Sous le soleil de Satan*, the conflict is perhaps too crudely presented and evil too obviously identified as Satan in the form of a sly horse-dealer. The last novel which Bernanos wrote, *Monsieur Ouine*, makes an advance in his ability to give artistic form to his spiritual insights. Here the very ordinary, yet enigmatic, Ouine himself strikingly embodies the elusive and equivocal quality of evil. In some ways, *Nouvelle Histoire de Mouchette* is Bernanos's most satisfactory artistic achievement with its deeply compassionate account of an unloved, and superficially unlovable, child. The religious significance is implied rather than stated positively, yet implied with both delicacy and boldness, as the tragic suffering of a fourteen-year-old girl points to Christ's passion. The other major novel and Bernanos's best-known work, *Journal d'un curé de campagne*, is relatively free from violence and shows Bernanos's ability to deal directly with religious themes. The country priest's diary is a convincingly human and richly spiritual document in which his meditations on poverty and love, doubt and faith, humility and death, are woven into the fabric of his life in a parish cursed by 'la fermentation d'un christianisme décomposé'. At first sight, the picture of life contained in all these difficult and sometimes obscure novels seems one of gloom and despair. We shall only begin to decipher their message aright when they enable us, on the contrary, to share Bernanos's own confidence that the day will come when 'les doux posséderont la terre, simplement parce qu'ils n'auront pas perdu l'habitude de l'espérance dans un monde de désespérés'.

Julien Green's novels are less widely known than those of Mauriac and Bernanos. Many of them are impressive and haunting works, however, revealing both an original sensibility and a distinctive talent. At the same time, some of Green's basic attitudes recall those of his two elders. He shares Mauriac's strong dislike of the flesh—it is a critical commonplace to speak of his 'puritan' reaction to sexuality—and like Bernanos he has a dramatic sense of an invisible, spiritual world behind external phenomena. Many of his novels have a claustrophobic atmosphere and portray a hopeless, loveless, faithless world which Mauriac's more desperate characters would recognize as their own. It is also a violent world in which murder and rape, madness and suicide, continue and intensify the more dramatic tendencies of Bernanos. Green's novels are powerfully conceived meditations on fear, death, cruelty, madness, violence, loneliness, and self-disgust. Behind these emotions lies an unseen world of horror and fatality. Green writes: 'Il n'y a de vérité ni d'absolu que dans l'invisible.' This invisible world, particularly in his earlier novels, can take on a terrifying power that has prompted comparisons with Hawthorne and Poe, as well as with the Gothic novel.

The peculiar strength and character of Green's novels have clearly been formed by a deep and complex inner experience on the author's own part. This experience differs most obviously from that of Mauriac and Bernanos in the sense that he was not born a Catholic but had a Protestant (largely Presbyterian) upbringing which coloured his subsequent Catholicism. Green became a Catholic convert in his teens, lost his faith (again unlike Mauriac and Bernanos) during part of the 1920s and 1930s, turned to Buddhism for a number of years, and finally became a convinced Catholic in 1939. This spiritual evolution is reflected in various ways in most of his novels.

The earliest novels, which are among the most compelling, include *Adrienne Mesurat* (1927), *Léviathan* (1929), and *Épaves* (1932). In all these novels we enter a cruel, sinister, hopeless world in which both family life and wider social contacts produce horror and loneliness ('Que d'abîmes d'une âme à une autre!'). The only characters that arouse our sympathy, Adrienne Mesurat herself or Guéret (in *Léviathan*), are gauche and timid individuals desperately searching for a love and reassurance that are denied them. Yet if other characters conspire against them, their real tragedy is more mysterious. They appear to be the helpless playthings of a wanton and malevolent fate presiding over all human life. Adrienne is trapped in an 'espèce de cycle dans lequel le désespoir succédait à l'espoir et la crainte à la joie'. Guéret is similarly caught in a vicious circle: 'Souffrir pour un être qu'il oublierait un jour comme il avait oublié tant d'autres et quitter cet être pour porter ailleurs ses désirs, toujours les mêmes désirs, quelle destinée rebutante!' It is Adrienne's destiny to kill her father and lose her reason. It is Guéret's destiny to commit rape and murder. Neither Adrienne nor Guéret can account rationally for their actions.

In this world of fatality, mental suffering and fear of death are recurring themes. They haunt Philippe Cléry as he walks beside the Seine with his small son and contemplates suicide (in *Épaves*). They dominate most characters in *Léviathan*. Mme Grosgeorge cries 'n'espérez rien, n'espérez jamais' and Angèle adds: 'On ne sait jamais quand la vie va vous trahir; inutile de compter sur le lendemain, ni même sur l'heure qui va suivre; il n'y a de certain que la mort.' It is also Angèle who appears to sum up the final verdict in these novels on the unseen world: 'Il n'y a pas de hasard, il n'y a que des méchancetés du sort et ses perfidies, préparées de longue main, n'ont cette apparence fortuite que parce que les dessous nous en échappent.'

It is quite clear, however, that Green himself does not turn his back on religion at this period because of his lack of faith. The novels contain unobtrusive, but significant, indications of the disbelief or religious indifference of most of the characters. The one character who seems to manage to live outside the circles of the Inferno is Dr. Maurecourt (in *Adrienne Mesurat*) who possesses the gift of faith. In short, these early novels strongly suggest the private dilemmas of a writer who had an acute religious sensibility unsupported by belief, a writer who was tortured by the apparent absence of that very divine purpose which could alone make life acceptable to him.

The novels of what might be termed Green's 'middle period' show the development of his struggle with faith and also his interest in Buddhism. He wrote at this time: '. . . la vie ne m'a jamais paru tout à fait réelle', and in *Le Visionnaire* (1934), *Minuit* (1936), and *Varouna* (1940) the earlier world of cruelty and sordid reality persists—but accompanied by a new dimension of fantasy, vision, and mysticism. *Le Visionnaire* is typical of the new element in Green's work with its central section containing a strange dream, significantly mingling sexuality and death, in which the youthful Manuel gives himself over to a fantasy world 'qui aurait pu être'. Manuel's cousin, Marie-Thérèse, seems to express Green's own conviction at the time when she says: 'Je me demande si le visionnaire, après tout, ne jette pas sur cette terre un regard plus aigu que le nôtre et si, en un monde qui baigne dans l'invisible, les prestiges du désir et de la mort n'ont pas autant de sens que nos réalités illusoires.' The influence of Buddhist thought is suggested by M. Edme's preoccupation with *nirvana* (in *Minuit*) while *Varouna* is built round the doctrine of the transmigration of souls. This latter idea seems to have helped Green to accept the fact of death somewhat more easily, as well as pointing the way towards the Catholic doctrine of the communion of saints. Buddhism was not to prove satisfactory, but *Varouna* hints at the way in which it prepared Green's return to Catholicism.

The main novels written by Green the believer are *Moïra* (1950) and *Chaque homme dans sa nuit* (1960). The first of these is a striking analysis of a puritanical young American student, Joseph Day— the setting is the University of Virginia in 1920—who is fascinated by the very sexuality which he so vehemently denounces ('Je désire horriblement ce péché que je ne commets pas'). The attitude to the unseen world in this novel is strikingly different from that in *Léviathan*. Joseph is upset by the constant swearing of his fellow students and Green comments:

La seule réalité, c'était ce nom qu'on ne prononçait, même dans un blasphème, qu'avec la permission divine. L'autre réalité, la réalité de la chair, la réalité du désir, si cruelle qu'elle fût à certaines heures, paraissait illusoire en cet instant. Il y avait deux royaumes: celui de Dieu et celui du monde, et ces deux royaumes s'expulsaient l'un l'autre du cœur de l'homme; et ces garçons qui blasphémaient le Christ, rétablissaient sans le savoir un ordre invisible.

It is this invisible world, ordered by God, in which Green now believes. Joseph Day's tragedy results from the fact that he believed in it too, yet could not maintain in the seen world what he interpreted as the consequences of this belief.

A fierce conflict between the flesh and the spirit is also central to *Chaque homme dans sa nuit*. In this case, however, the central character, Wilfred, achieves faith and completes, as it were, the quotation from Hugo of which the first half provides Green's title: 'Chaque homme dans sa nuit s'en va vers sa lumière.' Green, commenting on this his first 'optimistic' novel, emphasizes the existence of a divine meaning beyond the life of suffering and failure, cruelty and solitariness, which is his conception of the human condition and which he has repeatedly described over a period of more than forty years. He expresses the final lesson offered by Mauriac and Bernanos, as well as by himself, when he writes: '. . . notre vie apparaît comme un roman dont nous n'arrivons pas à trouver le titre, mais Dieu trouve le titre.'

NOTE

General background. Among the many books and articles in English dealing with the general relationship between literature and religion the following titles are particularly useful: M. H. Abrams (ed.), *Literature and Belief* (1957), T. S. Eliot, 'Religion and Literature' in *Essays Ancient and Modern* (1936), S. R. Hopper (ed.), *Spiritual Problems in Contemporary Literature* (1952), M. Jarrett-Kerr, *Studies in Literature and Belief* (1954), G. A. Panichas (ed.), *Mansions of the Spirit: Essays in Religion and Literature* (1967), N. A. Scott (ed.), *The Tragic Vision and the Christian Faith* (1957), and M. Turnell, *Modern Literature and Christian Faith* (1961). A spirited recent discussion of these problems, particularly in relation to Mauriac and Bernanos, will be found in A. Sonnenfeld, 'The Catholic Novelist and the Supernatural', *French Studies*, xxii, no. 4 (October 1968), and E. Beaumont, 'The Supernatural in Dostoyevsky and Bernanos: a reply to Professor Sonnenfield', *French Studies*, xxiii, no. 3 (July 1969). Relevant books in French include L. Barjon, *Le Silence de Dieu dans la littérature contemporaine* (1956), A. Blanchet, *Le Prêtre dans le roman d'aujourd'hui* (1955), and three works by J.-L. Prévost: *Le Prêtre, ce héros de roman* (2 vols., 1952–3), *Satan et le romancier* (1954), *Le Roman catholique a cent ans* (1958).

FRANÇOIS MAURIAC was born in 1885 in Bordeaux where he attended school and university. During the First World War he spent two years as a hospital orderly in the *services sanitaires* before being invalided out, at Salonika, in 1917. His career as a major novelist began in the early 1920s, he was elected to the Académie Française in 1933, and he received the Nobel Prize for Literature in 1952. He remained in France and published clandestinely during the Occupation. Apart from his success as a novelist and dramatist, he has written much liberal political journalism and a variety of books on religious topics.

Novels and short stories. *L'Enfant chargé de chaînes* (1913), *La Robe prétexte* (1914), *La Chair et le sang* (1920), *Préséances* (1921), *Le Baiser au lépreux* (1922), *Le Fleuve de feu* (1923), *Genitrix* (1923), *Le Désert de l'amour* (1925), *Thérèse Desqueyroux* (1927), *Destins* (1928), *Trois récits* (1929), *Ce qui était perdu* (1930), *Le Nœud de vipères* (1932), *Le Mystère Frontenac* (1933), *La Fin de la nuit* (1936), *Les Anges noirs* (1936), *Plongées* (1938), *Les Chemins de la mer* (1939), *La Pharisienne* (1941), *Le Sagouin* (1951), *Galigaï* (1952), *L'Agneau* (1954), *Un Adolescent d'autrefois* (1969). There is a very useful edition of *Thérèse Desqueyroux* by C. Jenkins (1964).

Criticism. Many of the problems raised in the foregoing chapter are discussed at more length by N. Cormeau, *L'Art de François Mauriac* (1951), C. Du Bos, *François Mauriac et le problème du romancier catholique* (1933), J. E. Flower, *Intention and Achievement: an Essay on the Novels of François Mauriac* (1969), G. Hourdin, *Mauriac, romancier catholique* (1945), J. Majault, *Mauriac et l'art du roman* (1946), M. F. Moloney, *François Mauriac* (1958), R. J. North, *Le*

Catholicisme dans l'œuvre de François Mauriac (1950), A. Palante, *Mauriac, le roman et la vie* (1946), and P.-H. Simon, *Mauriac par lui-même* (1953). A sympathetic but intelligently critical study is C. Jenkins, *Mauriac* (1965). The critical reaction against Mauriac takes different forms in M. Jarrett-Kerr, *François Mauriac* (1954), in 'D. O'Donnell' (Conor Cruise O'Brien), *Maria Cross* (1954), in M. Turnell, *The Art of French Fiction* (1959), and in J.-P. Sartre, *Situations I* (1947).

GEORGES BERNANOS, 1888–1948, was born in Paris. As a student he became involved in the affairs of the Action Française, joining the monarchist *camelots du roi*. With the outbreak of the First World War he enlisted in the army, was wounded on active service and decorated for gallantry. After the war he worked in insurance until 1926 when the success of *Sous le soleil de Satan* encouraged him to devote himself entirely to writing. He broke with the Action Française in 1932, denounced Franco and the Spanish Church in 1938, and emigrated to South America where he continued to live during the Occupation. Apart from his novels and a play, *Dialogues des Carmélites* (1949), he wrote several books of highly personal political and moral comment.

Novels and short stories. The major works are conveniently collected in a Pléiade edition: *Œuvres romanesques suivies de Dialogues des Carmélites* (1961). The publication dates of the various works of fiction are as follows: three short stories published in 1913 are *La Tombe refermée, La Mort avantageuse du chevalier de Lorges, La Muette*. A further short story, *Madame Dargent*, was published in 1922. The major novels are: *Sous le soleil de Satan* (1926), *L'Imposture* (1927), *La Joie* (1929), *Un Crime* (1935), *Journal d'un curé de campagne* (1936), *Nouvelle Histoire de Mouchette* (1937), *Monsieur Ouine* (1943), *Un mauvais rêve* (posth. publ. 1950). There is a useful edition of *Journal d'un curé de campagne* by Eithne M. O'Sharkey (1969).

Criticism. The major study remains H. U. von Balthasar, *Le Chrétien Bernanos* (trs. from German by M. de Gandillac, 1956). There is much useful material in A. Béguin (*et al.*), *Georges Bernanos: essais et témoignages* (1949), and A. Béguin, *Bernanos par lui-même* (1954). The *Études bernanosiennes* which began in 1960 are also a source of much important information. Studies in French include W. Bush, *Souffrance et expiation dans la pensée de Bernanos* (1962), L. Chaigne, *Bernanos* (1960), M. Estève, *Le Sens de l'amour dans les romans de Bernanos* (1959), J. de Fabrègues, *Bernanos tel qu'il était* (1963), G. Gaucher, *Le Thème de la mort dans les romans de Bernanos* (1955), Jessie L. Gillespie, *Le Tragique dans l'œuvre de Georges Bernanos* (1960), B. Halda, *Bernanos: le scandale de croire* (1965), F. Lefèvre, *Georges Bernanos* (1926), C. Moeller, 'Bernanos' in *Littérature du XXᵉ siècle et christianisme*, vol. 1 (1954), G. Picon, *Georges Bernanos* (1948), and J. Scheidegger, *Georges Bernanos romancier* (1956). The main studies in English are: E. Beaumont, 'Georges Bernanos' in J. Cruickshank (ed.), *The Novelist as Philosopher: Studies in French Fiction 1935–1960* (1962), Gerda Blumenthal, *The Poetic Imagination of Georges Bernanos: an Essay in*

Interpretation (1966), and P. Hebblethwaite, *Bernanos* (1965). Mention should also be made of a more specialized work: W. Bush, *L'Angoisse du mystère: essai sur Bernanos et 'Monsieur Ouine'* (1966).

JULIEN GREEN was born in Paris of American parents in 1900. He went to school in France and attended the University of Virginia for three years. He regards himself as French and, apart from one autobiographical work (*Memories of Happy Days*, 1942), his entire literary output has been written in French. Towards the end of the First World War he was sent by the American Red Cross to the Italian front. He spent much of the Second World War in America, served for a time in the American army, and returned to Paris in 1945. His post-war plays, particularly *Sud* (1953) and *L'Ennemi* (1954), enjoyed considerable success but, apart from his novels, his major work is the *Journal*, volumes of which have been published at intervals since 1938.

Novels and short stories. These are included, along with the *Journal* and the plays, in the *Œuvres complètes* of which 10 vols. have been published since 1954. The publication dates of individual works of fiction are as follows: Short stories and novellas: *Le Voyageur sur la terre* (1927), *Les Clefs de la mort* (1928), *Christine* (1928), *Léviathan* (1928), *L'autre aommeil* (1931); novels: *Mont-Cinère* (1926), *Adrienne Mesurat* (1927), *Léviathan* (1929), *Épaves* (1932), *Le Visionnaire* (1934), *Minuit* (1936), *Varouna* (1940), *Si j'étais vous* (1947), *Moïra* (1950), *Le Malfaiteur* (1956), *Chaque homme dans sa nuit* (1960).

Criticism. The chief books are: J.-C. Brisville, *A la rencontre de Julien Green* (1947), P. Brodin, *Julien Green* (1956), M. Eigeldinger, *Julien Green ou la tentation de l'irréel* (1947), A. Fongaro, *L'Existence dans les romans de Julien Green* (1954), M. Gorkine, *Julien Green, essai* (1956), J.-L. Prévost, *Julien Green ou l'âme engagée* (1960), G. N. Rousseau, *Sur le chemin de Julien Green* (1965), R. de Saint-Jean, *Julien Green par lui-même* (1967), J. Sémolué, *Julien Green ou l'obsession du mal* (1964), and S. Stokes, *Julien Green and the Thorn of Puritanism* (1955). Attention should also be drawn to the long essay on Green in C. Moeller, *Littérature du XXᵉ siècle et christianisme*, vol. 1 (1954), and to B. T. Fitch (ed.), *Julien Green: configuration critique* (1966). This volume contains excellent critical essays by P. C. Hoy, Annette Lavers, C. R. P. May, and the editor.

12. Vichy France, 1940–1944: The Literary Image

> En ce temps-là, la France était un radeau à la dérive emportant des naufragés, et les vivres manquaient, les enfants étaient pâles, les femmes déchiraient le ciel de leurs cris; des hommes, si maigres qu'on voyait leurs douleurs, fixaient sur les lointains sans voiles la malédiction de leurs yeux secs.... Enfin vous pouvez à votre loisir parachever l'allégorie de la nouvelle Méduse . . .

So Aragon, in the preface he contributed to the clandestine edition of Jean Cassou's *33 Sonnets composés au secret* (1944). Certainly the image of German-occupied France as another 'raft of the Medusa' not only serves, in a way characteristic of Aragon's wartime writings, to recall the French to their own cultural heritage (in the shape of Géricault's great painting), but also crystallizes the privations and despair of the period. The printer's note appended to Cassou's sonnet-sequence conjures up the historical moment more directly, but no less movingly: 'Ce volume publié aux dépens de quelques lettrés patriotes a été achevé d'imprimer sous l'oppression à Paris, le 15 mai 1944.' Yet, though the raft of the Medusa may offer a haunting symbol of the plight of occupied France, it does not convey the profound sense of ambiguity which so frequently penetrates the loyalties and the moral and political choices of French society at this time, and which envelops the tracts and poems, novels, plays, and private diaries that reflect the vicissitudes of occupied France. It is this pervasive ambiguity that gives to the internecine struggles of Vichy France a truly tragic dimension, in the sense in which Hegel defines tragedy as a conflict of rights.

The sense of the ambiguities inherent in all aspects of French life under the German occupation is nowhere more insistently present than in what Sartre writes about the period. It is there in the striking paradox which opens 'La République du silence' (1944) evoking an extreme situation in which human agents are compelled to come to terms with the nature of their own freedom: 'Jamais nous n'avons été plus libres que sous l'occupation allemande.' It is spelt out more explicitly still in the pages of 'Paris sous l'occupation' (1945): 'Chacun de nos actes était ambigu. . . . Le mal était partout, tout choix était mauvais et pourtant il fallait choisir et nous étions responsables . . .' Such formulations, though they breathe the voluntarism native to Sartre's thought, can be applied to issues ranging from the armistice signed on 22 June 1940 and the British navy's deliberate sinking of the French squadron at Mers-el-Kebir on 3 July 1940 to the shifts and stratagems of the French Communist Party between 1939 and 1941, Vichy policy on the Jews and forced labour, and the use of violence by Resistance patriots. Already, scarcely more than a quarter of a century later, it requires an effort of imagination on our parts to enter into that specific community of fear, suffering, and hope; to gauge its moral climate and to reconstitute, in their full complexity, the temporizing, degradation, heroism, and total disarray of the time.

The moral and political dilemmas begin with the armistice itself. How was a French soldier of the regular army to judge where his duty lay? An obscure tank officer recently promoted to brigadier had gone into voluntary exile in London and was calling on French patriots to continue the fight against Nazi Germany, in spite of the catastrophic military collapse of May–June 1940 and the chaos inside France. Such an appeal had to contend with rooted French distrust of Britain (reinforced by the successful evacuation of British troops at Dunkirk on 4 June 1940 and the withdrawal of British air-support); a historical tradition which identified 'emigration' with treason; and the highly legalistic habits of mind prevalent among French officers and officials who tended, in words Churchill was to use later, to judge the 'direct, unbroken chain of lawful command' as more important than 'moral, national or international considerations'. To accept that de Gaulle was right and a patriot was to accept that every French officer who had obeyed the instruction of the legally constituted government of Vichy was wrong and a traitor. In the circumstances, it is not hard to see how, in the summer of 1940, the majority of French officers, confused and lost in what Saint-Exupéry describes as 'le ventre aveugle d'une administration', preferred to be 'realistic', to accept defeat and dismiss de Gaulle as a visionary and a deserter in flagrant defiance of his rightful government. Precisely where realism lay was difficult to determine but, with the knowledge of hindsight, pamphleteers have subsequently tended to be scathing of Vichy's brand of it. Such is the case with Jean Dutourd's polemical *Les Taxis de la Marne* (1956):

> D'un côté le raffinement, l'élégance, le conformisme, le *réalisme*: c'était Vichy, où se rua tout ce que la France comptait d'esprits distingués, de politiques adroits et de militaires ambitieux; de l'autre, le geste insensé, apparemment inutile, le poncif de l'image d'Épinal et du manuel d'instruction pour écoles communales: c'était de Gaulle, dressé sur la petite île britannique et rappelant la France aux armes.

Yet the Vichy regime could not have been established, nor could it have survived, unless there had been widespread doubt, confusion, and uncertainty about the 'right' course of action for France to follow. This is reflected in the very heterogeneous elements which initially supported the regime: families hoping for the early return of French prisoners of war; patriots hoping Pétain's prestige would save something from the wreck; soldiers dreaming of using the ex-servicemen's organization, the Légion des Anciens Combattants, as the nucleus of a new French army; doctrinaire Fascists and anti-semites; renegade socialists believing the nascent 'new order' would benefit organized labour; pacifists who preferred German occupation to what they conceived to be the greater evil of a continuing war; bishops who saw in Vichy the hope of a Catholic revival; farmers and businessmen who viewed it as a solid bulwark against communism; and unscrupulous opportunists in all walks of life. The French public was, in fact, shattered by defeat and very vulnerable to the promptings of guilt which Vichy propaganda did its best to stimulate in the pages of the licensed press. Urged to believe that their tribulations were a just chastisement for the incorrigible depravity they had displayed in peacetime by frequenting bars, cinemas, and restaurants during the corrupting leisure of the forty-hour week provided by the Popular Front government of 1936, the bewildered French citizens of autumn 1940 were in no position to question the logic by which a pagan state, founded in police terror and religious persecution, could be presented as the avenging arm of the Lord. A residue of guilt made it difficult, even for those Frenchmen who recognized the confidence-trick, to dismiss out of hand what Sartre later described as 'cette immonde image qu'ils voulaient nous donner de nous-mêmes'. Such ambiguities became more acutely painful with the passage of time.

In effect, the conduct of the war being waged beyond the borders of France produced increasingly harsh repercussions on French internal affairs. Vichy identified collaboration and 'realism' and derived both from the assumption that the German victory in Europe was permanent. This assumption was undermined when Hitler decided to invade the Soviet Union on 22 June 1941; was further rocked by America's entry into the war after the attack on Pearl Harbour in December 1941; and finally dissipated when the tide of war turned against Germany in the winter of 1942. Vichy had also justified its policies by pointing to the freedom of action it had retained, notably over the 'Free Zone'. This argument too was shattered when, in response to the Allied landings in North Africa, German troops crossed the demarcation line and occupied the whole of France on 11 November 1942. These events not only destroyed the credibility of Vichy as an autonomous regime and disillusioned many of its supporters, but also placed new and fearful strains on German manpower and war-production and so made it inevitable that an even more ruthless bleeding of the French economy and labour-force would follow. The attack on the Soviet Union had a further direct impact on French internal politics: it brought the French Communist Party, as an organized force, into resistance and, with it, a new strain of militancy. In fact, the party was peculiarly well equipped, by its cellular structure and discipline, ideological coherence, and previous experience of underground activity, to play a leading role in a resistance movement which, up until then, had been very much an affair of isolated individuals and small groups attesting their personal commitment to France. The entry of the Communist Party into resistance, the heavier material exactions of the occupying power, and the growing resentment of the French at the sacrifices demanded of them, all conspired to make the struggle within France more savage and unrelenting. Thus, from the winter of 1941 onwards, the stage is set for the most exacerbated of moral and political dilemmas, and it is the echoes of these which reverberate through the literature created under the German occupation or inspired by it.

Vichy had claimed to protect the interests of Frenchmen against their military conquerors and argued that its very existence saved the nation from the fate of countries like Poland which were ruled directly by Nazi *gauleiters*. There was some truth in this argument, but a truth everywhere distorted by the actions and policies which Vichy condoned and which were often indistinguishable from the Nazi policies prevailing elsewhere in Europe. The anti-Jewish legislation of 3 October 1940 was a case in point, in that it went beyond any demands the German authorities were making on the French at that juncture. These laws made it impossible for Jews to own or be employed by newspapers, magazines, broadcasting or film companies, forbade them to handle securities, foreign exchange, or real estate, and limited their entry into the liberal professions. The government were empowered to intern foreign or stateless Jews and, in fact, no fewer than 20,000 of these, most of whom had fled to France precisely to escape Nazi persecution, were to be found in internment camps in the unoccupied zone by the end of 1940. Vichy did not demur in May 1942 when an ordinance prescribed the wearing of the star of David, nor did it seriously interfere in July 1942 when a series of decrees banned Jews from almost all public places and restricted their movements about the streets. In July 1942 the Vichy government and police effected, on their own initiative, a round-up of Jews in the Paris area which resulted in the internment of nearly 13,000 foreign and stateless Jews, subsequently deported to concentration camps in Germany as part of the Nazis' 'final solution'. By early September 1942, 27,000 Jews had been deported from France with the active co-operation of the French government and police. Laval's defence of French action against the Jews was to claim that by agreeing to the deportation of foreign and stateless Jews, he had protected the lives of French

Jews. Laval expressed the dilemma at the level of public policy but, for the Jews themselves, the dilemma cut deeper. A French Jew might owe his survival to the deportation of a foreign Jew no less innocent or he might, like M. René Mayer, have to decide whether he could serve his people best by staying with de Gaulle in London or by returning to France with the risk of sharing in the fate of his co-religionists.

The French skilled worker, unemployed or on short-time in 1942 because of allied bombing of his factory, was also confronted with harsh conflicts of loyalty. He might resist the appeal of the pro-paganda posters on the walls in the spring of 1942, inviting French-men to volunteer for work in Germany, only to be faced with Laval's broadcast of 22 June 1942 initiating the 'Relève' scheme, by which 50,000 French prisoners-of-war were to be gradually released in exchange for 150,000 specialist workers. If the factory-worker accepted, his wages would go up, at a moment when rationing and the black market were making life very hard for his family, and he would also be performing a patriotic act in helping to release a fellow countryman. Unhappily, his skill would certainly aid the German war-effort and the weapons he made might well be used to destroy the Soviet 'homeland of the workers' on which, as a trade-unionist, he might have pinned his hopes. When, on 16 February 1943, a new law fixed the period of forced labour service ('service du travail obligatoire') at two years, the worker was con-fronted with the choice of escaping into the *maquis* and abandoning his family or else of complying with the law, supported as it was with a propaganda campaign in which posters of a happy mother and child, with an exultant factory worker standing behind them, beamed their message to the French public: 'Finis les mauvais jours! Papa gagne de l'argent en Allemagne!'

The Resistance itself was riddled with moral and political ambiguities. Its ranks included devout Catholics and anti-clerical socialists, soldiers who had belonged to the pre-war fascist 'Cagoule' and communists who had been active in the anti-fascist campaigns of the thirties only to accept an apparently cynical reversal of policy when the Nazi–Soviet Pact of 23 August 1939 was signed. The Resistance was first and foremost a patriotic struggle to liberate the homeland from foreign oppressors, but since the enemy was also the instrument of a brutal ideology, Resistance groups inevitably tended to link their patriotism to a contrary ideology and to the vision of a regenerated society that would spring from the ashes of war. Much of this ideology was socialistic in character and resisters who were neither socialist nor communist often gave tacit support to these doctrines rather than risk splitting resistance unity. Many resisters were deeply idealistic—their political manifestos show it—and one can gain some sense of it from a letter addressed by a *maquis* group to French prisoners in Germany. It is quoted under an entry for 25 March 1944 in Jean Guéhenno's *Journal des années noires* (1947):

Rejetés de la communauté, nous avons à loisir comme vous médité sur la médiocrité et les erreurs qui nous ont conduits à ce desastre. Et comme vous avez dû le faire, nous nous sommes juré de travailler à reconstruire une cité forte et libre qui mette sa force au service d'une juste paix.

This resembles nothing so much as the language of Camus's 'meurtriers délicats' in *Les Justes* (1949), the play he devoted to exploring the problem of ends and means.

Of course, the language does not hold good for all members of the *maquis*, some of whom were on the run from the law for offences quite unconnected with civil disobedience or patriotic activity against the occupying forces. In any event, lawlessness and minor brigandage were a necessary condition of the lives of even the most idealistic members of the *maquis*, if only when they stole food from farms to keep themselves alive. The Resistance was confronted with more severe ordeals of conscience than this. Just as there were Frenchmen in Vichy's special police, the 'Milice', prepared to hunt down, torture, and execute other Frenchmen in the name of the loyalty they owed to a French government, so members of the Resistance had to be prepared to sabotage trains carrying innocent passengers and often driven by workers sympathetic to the Resistance cause, in order to prevent food or soldiers reaching their destination. Worse, they had to balance the killing of German soldiers against the death of French hostages, often chosen deliberately by the

Germans from among Jews and communists, like the fifty shot on 22 October 1941 as a reprisal for the killing of a German officer at Nantes. Worse still, after a decree of 10 July 1942, members of the Resistance knew that to be caught in acts of sabotage was to involve their male relatives in execution, their female relatives in hard labour, and their children (under the age of 17) in forcible removal to an approved school. These appalling dilemmas exemplify in the most vivid way the difficulty of deciding on good and evil in the conditions of 1940–4, and they could be framed by a score of less dramatic predicaments.

Such was the pattern of life, such the ambiguities of choice with which the literature written about the occupation concerns itself. France was often near to hunger and always in the shadow of arbitrary arrest and imprisonment, torture and the taking of hostages, forced labour and mass-executions, requisitioning and looting, police raids, burning of farms and villages, break-up of families, threat and reality of deportation and concentration camp. Inevitably, there is no single way of rendering the experience of this society in imaginative terms. Most of what is written about occupation and resistance at the time it is happening hardly rises to the level of literature. It is the reign of the document. The 'document' may be a message scratched on the wall of a death-cell or a scrap of paper smuggled out of a prison-camp like Drancy. In the early months of occupation it is more likely to be an information sheet, like the first clandestine news-sheet, *Pantagruel*, which appeared in October 1940. Later, between 1942 and 1944, the smudged mimeographed sheets passed round a handful of readers give way to major Resistance newspapers—*Combat*, *Défense de la France*, *Franc-Tireur*—well produced, efficiently distributed, and reaching circulations varying from 100,000 to 300,000. These concentrate on information and propaganda and, not surprisingly, much of the imaginative writing created under the conditions of occupation is also consciously propagandist in tendency. It conforms to the model suggested by Jean-Marie Domenach in *Le Retour du tragique* (1967): 'Le sang inspire les poètes, mais à distance. Il y a le pressentiment, l'annonce, la prophétie, — et puis le souvenir, la réinterprétation. Mais sur le moment, l'Histoire bouscule l'écrivain:

il se tait, ou il fait de la propagande.' This critic might have added, however, that a writer can deliberately mask his meaning in fable or myth and so effectively transcend the limits of mere propaganda. In some degree, this is what happens with works like Vercors's *Le Silence de la mer* which first appeared in a clandestine edition of 350 copies in February 1942, and with the eight octavo pages of Aragon's *Le Musée Grévin* published secretly in October 1943.

In fact, all efforts to convey the experiences of occupation and resistance imaginatively (which is to say, by distancing and re-ordering the raw material of history) are, at the same time, attempts to invent forms capable of rendering the ambiguities of the period. The forms vary but some of the most 'distanced' works (in the sense that the actual events of Vichy France do not constitute the centre of the narrative or do not figure in it at all) often come closest to creating the feel of the period and its moral complexities. For instance, it could be said that Aragon's *La Semaine sainte* (1958), with its constant shuttling between the Hundred Days of 1815 and the June days of 1940, communicates more persuasively than the communist stereotypes of his novel-sequence, *Les Communistes* (1949–51), an epic sense of national destiny and an almost Michelet-like feeling for the grandeur of the common people. In a similar way, Jean Anouilh's *La Foire d'empoigne* (1962), with its implied defence of compromise and moderation in the unromantic person of Louis XVIII, makes a statement about political fanaticism and purges that reflects the experiences of 1940–4 as sharply as the debate contained in *Antigone* (1944). Perhaps, too, Sartre's play *Les Séquestrés d'Altona* (1959) represents a more powerful and complex exploration of the problems of torture and historical violence (as the Resistance encountered them) than *Les Morts sans sépulture* (1947), written so much closer to the events it describes. The process need not be retrospective. More insight into the magnetism exercised by Nazism over the mind of a certain type of French intellectual can be gleaned from the pages of Robert Brasillach's pre-war novel, *Les Sept Couleurs* (1939)—and especially from Patrice's reactions to a Nazi rally: 'C'est aujourd'hui un grand pays étrange, plus loin de nous que l'Inde et que la Chine'—

than from the reflections contained in his *Journal d'un homme occupé* (published posthumously in 1956).

Writers, then, employ different forms of distancing their material in order to render the experiences of occupied France. At one end of the spectrum is the journal or report, the fictive form nearest to autobiography. Emmanuel d'Astier's *Sept fois sept jours* (1945) is an admirable example. It is clearly rooted in the autobiographical record of one man's experience of the Resistance but its episodes are so shaped, its overall structure so elegantly ironic, that one is forced to recognize the degree to which personal experience has been expanded in a fictive way, in order to play up the sense of ambiguity that resides in even the most purposeful action. One has only to note, for example, how the narrative is framed between an early moment of disillusion when d'Astier eats peaches in the sun-drenched south of France after the armistice has been signed—'Nous avons l'impression d'avoir été roulés depuis des mois' — and the disenchanted final judgement which echoes this moment near the end of the book—'La montagne a accouché d'une souris: nous avons assisté à une médiocre Restauration'. *Sept fois sept jours* is an exceptionally vivid and convincing picture of the loneliness, risk, fear, and fatigue of the resister's life, especially in early 1941:

De nos voyages ont disparu les sentiments habituels, l'anxiété ou l'élan des départs, la satisfaction ou la jeunesse des arrivées. Nous ne quittons plus des êtres ou des lieux plus ou moins chers, une forme de vie pour une autre. Je chemine à travers des lieux qui ne sont que des décors sans habitudes, parmi des personnes qui entrent et sortent comme au théâtre. Et le voyage, sans joie ni tristesse, sans curiosité, est une lutte contre la distance, la fatigue et la menace.

The stage imagery here neatly emphasizes the shifting and unreal character of events. This is the world of action seen, at first hand, by a subtle and inquiring mind given to introspection, endowed with an almost Stendhalian degree of lucidity and detachment, and strongly aware of the complex nature of human behaviour. This makes it all the more striking when d'Astier manages the transition to another plane (his discovery of the fraternity of men engaged in a common, risky enterprise) without mawkishness or recourse to facile rhetoric:

... j'ai découvert en France des hommes nouveaux, animés soudain d'une passion, dépouillés de l'algèbre des formes sociales, rendus aux actes et aux pensées, et qui inventaient chaque jour d'autres hommes à leur image en leur touchant la main, en leur demandant quelque chose qui ne se payât pas et en leur décernant un nom.

Though *Sept fois sept jours* has this vein of reflection and keeps focused on the dilemmas of Resistance activity, it persistently communicates a vivid sense of movement and adventure. By contrast, Saint-Exupéry's *Pilote de guerre* (1942) alternates between two quite different modes. It is a graphic document on the military defeat of 1940, as seen from the air, and a spiritual testament. The document is alive with narrative energy and its concrete notation of episodes is sharp and memorable—burning villages seen from the sky, tracer bullets piercing the fuselage of planes and rattling like 'hail on a drum', choked roads like slow-flowing treacle:

Je survole donc des routes noires de l'interminable sirop qui n'en finit plus de couler. On évacue, dit-on, les populations. Ce n'est déjà plus vrai. Elles s'évacuent d'elles-mêmes. Il est une contagion démente dans cet exode. Car où vont-ils, ces vagabonds? ... Où vont-ils? Ils ne savent pas! Ils marchent vers des escales fantômes, car à peine cette caravane aborde-t-elle une oasis, que déjà il n'est plus d'oasis. Chaque oasis craque à son tour, et à son tour se déverse dans la caravane ...

These physical images, drawn from the memory of events actually experienced, are linked to a set of moral reflections on the nature of defeat, courage, and responsibility. The raw material of military failure is used to ask questions about the human condition and to press home difficult truths. There is an attempt at an ambitious restatement of humanism, often obscure and mystical in tendency, and deriving its strength from a large conception of self-sacrifice which rests on experience of war and acceptance of common responsibility for defeat:

Ainsi je ne me désolidariserai pas d'une défaite qui, souvent, m'humiliera. Je suis de France. ... La défaite divise. La défaite défait ce qui était fait. Il y a, là, menace de mort: je ne contribuerai pas à ces divisions, en rejetant la responsabilité du désastre sur ceux des miens qui pensent autrement que moi. Il n'est rien à tirer de ces procès sans juge. Nous avons tous été vaincus . . .

It is not easy to decide here whether the dominant tone is one of humility or of a kind of pride by which the natural leader agrees to identify himself with the common run of men. As a statement of faith, it survives by blurring important issues: whether, for example, some of those who 'think differently from me' (like certain pre-war fascist groups) did not set out deliberately to destroy French institutions from ideological motives. One can, at least, see how this mystique of defeat, sacrifice, and regeneration could have been reconciled in 1942 with the prevailing Vichy cult of 'national contrition'. In important respects, *Pilote de guerre* mirrors the moral ambiguity of Vichy's posture.

More 'distanced' than these near-autobiographical accounts is the novel in which the strains and ambiguities of occupied France are subdued to a consciously invented narrative, and where imaginary characters (sometimes, no doubt, trailing the qualities and idiosyncrasies of 'real' people) move within a fictionally self-consistent world. In spite of their fictive characters and situations, some of these novels stick close to the actual texture of life in Vichy France. Their technique is realistic, well anchored in concrete particulars. They reproduce the 'properties' of the period, so to speak (forged papers, the difficulties of rationing, articles in the licensed press, etc.), and the exploration of the social, political, and moral conflicts of this society represents the centre of gravity of such novels.

Such is Jean-Louis Curtis's *Les Forêts de la nuit* (1947), in which the specific conflicts of occupied France are skilfully woven into a dense, pre-existing web of personal and family relationships, rivalries, and animosities in the little town of Saint-Clar situated close to the line of demarcation between the occupied and unoccupied zones. A comprehensive yet detached sympathy plays over the characters of this novel and over their choked resentments, open or covert loyalties, and the tyranny of habit and memory which, in varying degrees, holds them prisoner. Perhaps no single novel about the period excels *Les Forêts de la nuit* in suggesting how attitudes rooted in the past, in social patterns, and in the local terrain colour the choices of French citizens under the German occupation. There is the malicious Mme Costellot whose snobbery and pre-war anglophobia incline her naturally to collaboration with the German intelligence officer, von Brackner, and the gentle and credulous Mme Delahaye, widow of a composer, who has to conciliate her genuine patriotism with the human claims made on her by the gentle and musical lieutenant Rustiger, and who pays for her human weakness at the Liberation by having her hair shaved while the local profiteers jeer in the crowd. There is also Francis de Balansun, an idealistic boy from an impoverished family of the local nobility, who helps resisters cross the demarcation line and is eventually betrayed to the Germans by Mme Costellot, then tortured and shot while trying to escape from the French secret police. Moving adroitly among all the factions in the town is the opportunistic Darricade who successfully insures himself against the future by his flexibility and discretion. Nothing in the fate of these individuals suggests the triumph of justice; everything points to the complexity of their motives. Philippe Arréguy, wastrel son of a sluttish mother, is a black marketeer and works hand in glove with the Gestapo, but he proves sexually irresistible to Francis's virgin sister, Hélène, and is moved by enough human sympathy to try and rescue Francis from his tormentors. His mother, who has lived off a German lover during the occupation, has enough courage to defy and insult her 'judges' at the Liberation. A page of the novel makes explicit what is implied in their lives:

L'opinion officielle distinguait deux camps: celui des bons et des mauvais, des félons et des héros, des parjures et des fidèles. Ce n'était pas tout à fait aussi simple que cela: d'une attitude extrême à l'autre attitude extrême, il y avait des moyens termes; il pouvait se produire d'innombrables glissements, des interférences. Sous les étiquettes grossières que l'on collait au dos des gens, il y avait mille et mille nuances possibles.

What distinguishes *Les Forêts de la nuit* is both the sense of equity it brings to the scrutiny of human motives and its acute feeling for the dilemmas of a closed political situation. The individual choice is constantly seen in terms of its social repercussions. There is nothing here of that strong whiff of romantic impersonation

H

which characterizes certain novels having the activities of *maquis* or resistance groups as their central preoccupation—Jacques Perret's *Bande à part* (1951), for example, with its racy, demotic dialogue, rapid action, and strong admixture of broad comedy; or even Roger Vailland's *Drôle de jeu* (1945), in which the histrionically named 'Marat' is both libertine and adventurer and acts out his emotional needs within the framework of a resistance movement. No doubt, resistance activity was, for some, a unique opportunity for self-realization through violent action, and there are novels set in the period in which the ideological and social conflicts of Vichy France represent nothing more than a vivid background against which purely private obsessions are played out.

There is, for example, no serious attempt to explore the moral and political implications of resistance and collaboration in Roger Nimier's *Les Épées* (1948). Francis Sanders, the young, disaffected son of a professional soldier, passes from membership of a Resistance group to that of Darnand's militia, casually recommending the death penalty for his former colleague and sexual partner, 'Louisiane', and impassively viewing her execution in the barrack yard. The almost glacial elegance of tone and the glancing obliquity of the narrative confirm this as an ironic exercise in which all is filtered through the sensibility and intelligence of a self-absorbed and deeply egotistical narrator for whom all creeds and persons, except for his hated soldier-father and his sister, Claude, whom he surrounds with a radiance that stems from his own, implicitly acknowledged, incestuous passion, are simply pretexts through which he explores and defines his own moral nature and tests out his feelings. The narrator allows ferocious mockery to play impartially over what he conceives to be the 'antics' of both resisters and collaborators. Resistance is simply an antidote to boredom; he joins 'pour secouer le temps' and notes, with disenchantment, its 'romantic' air, its 'complexe de Jeanne d'Arc'. He views the members of the militia, with equal detachment, as a motley crew imprisoned within their own slogans: 'Fils de famille en rupture d'idéal, ouvriers fascistes tuberculeux, bretons amateurs de chouannerie et quelques repris de justice — le sel de la terre, comme on dit.' Nothing interests him as much as himself: occupying

Germans, Frenchmen who resist or collaborate only make up the shifting and unreal decor against which he plays out his private tensions and fantasies.

As marked a form of distancing occurs in the satires devoted to the period. There is, for example, the truculent ironic verve of Marcel Aymé's *Uranus* (1948), in which the folly of mere ideology is paraded before us in the persons of a zealous Resistance sympathizer and a fervent Fascist, conveniently brought together under the same roof as a result of an allied bombing attack on the town of 'Blémont'. There is, above all, the dairy-shop of Jean Dutourd's *Au Bon Beurre* (1952), where the novelist creates, in the proprietor and his loyal helpmeet, two of the most memorable comic characters in the literature of Vichy France. Charles-Hubert and Julie Poissonard are odious in their cynicism, greed, and opportunism and their career between 1940 and 1944 is counterpointed, with fine comic aplomb, to the economic and political vicissitudes of the period. By acquiring vast reserve stocks early on, and by keeping their nerve and releasing them only when enemy requisitioning of French food has led to severe shortages and rationing, the Poissonards find themselves uniquely placed to exploit their customers and to direct extensive black-market operations. With the money so acquired, they buy gold and property, end with a fortune, and marry off their awful daughter to a climbing aristocratic deputy as opportunistic as themselves.

Charles-Hubert's politics are fluid and circumspect and he deals indifferently with occupying Germans or a dispossessed Jewish businessman on the run from the Gestapo, so long as they provide him with a profit or insurance against the future. Sensitive to changes in the political climate, he veers from a nicely judged admiration for Pétain to a judiciously timed expression of Gaullist sympathies when the German cause is obviously faltering in 1943 and when his adulteration of milk and butter has earned him a fine and the temporary closure of his premises by the Vichy authorities. The novel is never less than ironically cool and detached in its treatment of human cowardice and selfishness, but the trouble with such unvarying irony is that all human aspiration emerges from it as irremediably tainted with folly, greed, and self-interest.

Consequently, it is not surprising that the political loyalties of the period are subjected to the same corrosive treatment, embodied in caricatures which cancel each other out. The credulity of the pro-Gaullist Mme Lécuyer is balanced by the confused moralizing of the Pétainist M. Lebugle, while the quality of Léon Lécuyer's resistance activities is sadly undermined by the fact that he is a booby, ingenuous to the point of fatuity, and the prisoner of his own bookish rhetoric. His picaresque adventures cannot, however, discredit him in the way that a choice piece of comedy destroys the mystique of Pétainism. In a hilarious scene the time-serving Poissonards visit Vichy and present the Marshal with a box of fresh eggs, a scene subsequently written up by Pétain's official chronicler, René Benjamin, in an article invented by Dutourd to caricature the abject and fulsome vacuity of Vichy propaganda:

Ce sont des poules qui les ont pondus, monsieur le Maréchal. De simples poules de chez nous. Elles savaient que vous les mangeriez! On le leur avait dit! Voilà pourquoi ils sont si gros. Ces œufs, c'est l'acte de foi des poules de France!

Perhaps, after all, that scene, together with the ironies which accumulate elsewhere, shifts the comic balance of the novel decisively and damages the Vichy regime more lethally than other loyalties and principles exposed to ridicule in the work.

By contrast, there is fiction which, while remaining close to the concrete particulars of occupation and resistance, displays the process of distancing simply by its creation of idealized images of political virtue. Such is one of the tales in Aragon's *Servitude et grandeur des français* (1945), in which a priest is compelled to recognize in a young communist resister a faith as vital as his own. Similar is Elsa Triolet's story, 'Les Amants d'Avignon' (published clandestinely in October 1943 and reprinted in *Le Premier Accroc coûte deux cents francs*, 1945), in which Juliette Noël's ravishing good looks, courage, unaffected simplicity, appetite for life, gaiety, and quick wits are clearly the lineaments of an exemplary 'daughter of the people', ideally equipped to outwit the cruel and stupid Vichy police. This image is even more naïvely rendered in Roger Vailland's *Un Jeune Homme seul* (1951), where the solitary and despairing engineer, Eugène-Marie Favart, is contrasted with the engine-driver, Pierre Madru, the head of the local Resistance network who is accidentally killed while planting explosives in the railway yards which come under Favart's control. At Madru's funeral, the mourners paint a picture of 'un vrai bolchevik' who is a paragon of private and social virtues. His qualities are echoed in Favart's resolute, Spanish-born wife, a Party member of long standing, who behaves with dignity and courage when interrogated by the Vichy secret police. The moral lesson is plain: the Communist Party is the 'saine partie de la nation', and Madru's sacrifice breaks down the solitude and nihilism of Favart, humanizes him, and offers him a model of heroic commitment. The Resistance is implicitly identified with the Communist Party and the Party seen as the source of all heroism, integrity, and humane virtue. The schematic plotting of the novel and the sentimentality of some of the language simply support a fictive structure that is an ideological demonstration, not an exploration of experience.

Perhaps the most developed form of distancing is that of the fable or myth. Paradoxically, this is even true of a fable like Vercors's *Le Silence de la mer* (1942) that is set among the humdrum routine of life in a French family obliged to lodge a German officer. Only faint echoes reach us of the violence and hatred outside. The 'real' world is held in abeyance and what *lives* for us is a single stylized image: the firelight in the parlour, the almost palpable silence, and the stiff, embarrassed movements of uncle, niece, and von Ebrennac. The implacable silence of the French couple is an echo of a literary convention: the patriotism of Maupassant's mute peasants under an earlier occupation. Von Ebrennac's passion for the music of Bach, and its power to reveal 'la nature . . . désinvestie . . . de l'âme humaine', is another. He personifies the idealism of the great cultural tradition which exerted such a magnetic hold over Renan and Romain Rolland. His illusion is to believe this tradition compatible with Nazism, and his volunteering for the Russian front is the admission that he has been grossly deceived. The human sympathy of the fable is transparent: while refusing to turn von Ebrennac into a monster, it presses home the truth that even 'good' Germans are either dupes or victims, though it is questionable whether such a moral was very effective propaganda in the harsh conditions of the winter of 1941-2. Ironically, the fervently patriotic naturalized Frenchman, Thomas Muritz, of Vercors's *La Marche à l'étoile* (1943) is as blind an idealist as von Ebrennac and cannot survive the savage realities of the age.

The most ambitious literary myth corresponding to the experience of occupied France is that of Albert Camus's *La Peste* (1947). It functions at several levels. It is a plain tale, full of action and involving a variety of characters; it has strong elements of tension and suspense and paints a detailed picture of a society in the throes of fear and recklessness. But this plain tale has specific features that point to the circumstances of occupation and resistance—the gagging of the press, the separation of Oran from the rest of the country (in the manner of the two zones), the growing power of the police, the special camps (recalling those for Jews and political resisters), the sanitary squads which resemble Resistance groups, the black market, and, in the early sermons of Paneloux, something close to Vichy policies of 'national contrition'. The generality of the symbol of the plague is valuable in the sense that it keeps open the possibility of plural meanings and so powerfully enhances the suggestiveness and ambiguity of the experience related. The weakness inherent in using the plague as a symbol of evil is that it confuses human agency (and hence, moral responsibility) with a natural disaster that cannot be appropriately regarded in moral terms. Perhaps, after all, *La Peste* is best seen as only obliquely connected with the occupation of France, and not as a conscious attempt to embody that *particular* experience in novel form. It makes a more general statement about human suffering and perhaps fulfils the need of a declared pagan for a statement of large significance about life that can effectively displace the received myths of Christianity. In this sense, the plague is a myth about salvation, but salvation conceived in terms of human solidarity, and the novel is evidence of a desire to replace the figure of the saviour who sacrifices himself for those who reject him and do not understand him, by the figure of a man (Dr. Rieux) among other men, recognized and accepted by them and differing from them only in the quality of his solidarity and service.

At the very least, this kind of myth can be seen as having a definite community of interest with the dilemmas of occupied France. In the end, it affirms the power of human goodness and offers itself as the antithesis of those frightening images through which L.-F. Céline conveys his own hatreds and his hysterical fear of the collapse of European civilization. In *Féerie pour une autre fois, I* (1952) and *Normance* (*Féerie pour une autre fois, II*) (1954), we see the Paris of 1940-4 in a distorting mirror. In *Normance* the mutilated sculptor, Jules, whose picaresque career of vice we are introduced to in *Féerie pour une autre fois, I*, reappears as a sinister and evil figure. He seems to be directing the R.A.F. planes, in their bombing of Montmartre, from the roof of that palace of fun, the Moulin de la Galette. Indeed, the bombing scene is a prolonged and maniacal farce and, in the course of it, the huge porter Normance has his head smashed in by the rioting tenants of a block of flats and bleeds to death silently while the tenants guzzle stolen liquor. The dying Normance lies in the hallway of the block of flats until the tenants throw him down the lift-shaft, in a gesture clearly intended to symbolize the death of France.

Both *D'un château l'autre* (1957) and *Nord* (1960) reflect the collapse of Germany from July 1944 to March 1945, and they constantly move beyond the residual, documentary fact toward a heightened satiric fantasy used as the vehicle of a comprehensive hatred and disgust. Characteristically, the unifying metaphor of *Nord* is a cesspool, and in both novels, death is surrounded with gothic imagery. In *D'un château l'autre* the last survivor of the house of Hohenzollern is half-witch, half-mole; an insane surgeon operates on a patient without benefit of anaesthetic and to the blood-thirsty shouts of an audience; Aïcha, the female executioner, stalks through the novel in blood-red boots and presides over 'Room 36' where the damned are dragged to their destruction. In one episode of *Nord* the camp-following prostitutes stream like vengeful maenads across the ruined landscape; in another, there is an elaborate burial ceremony like a parody of Wagnerian opera. The horrors of real life in war-torn Europe progressively merge with horrific fantasy, and the rapid, uneven rhythm of the prose, the atomized syntax, the swift, episodic movement of the narrative, with its ellipses and sudden transitions, all convey incoherence and collapse. This fictive apocalypse takes the facts of history for its starting-point but goes beyond them. Céline's novels represent the revenge of the imagination on the hated 'real' world. No imaginative reordering of events can go further without falling into total delirium.

NOTE

The selection of books which follows corresponds to the particular perspective chosen in this chapter.

The basic collection of documents is: *Les Événements survenus en France de 1933 à 1945* (11 vols., 1947 ff.). The best short survey of the Vichy regime remains A. Cobban, 'Vichy France' in *Hitler's Europe* (1954). P. Farmer, *Vichy: Political Dilemma* (1955), is a judicious introduction that may be supplemented by the impressionistic Robert Aron, *Histoire de Vichy* (1954).

On the French defeat of 1940 and the origins of the Vichy government, the most useful studies are: M. Bloch, *L'Étrange Défaite* (1948); A. Horne, *To Lose a Battle* (1969); H. Michel, *Vichy, année 40* (1966), and J. Vidalenc, *L'Exode de mai-juin 1940* (1958).

Illuminating for life under the German occupation are the studies of P. Arnoult *et al.*, *La France sous l'occupation* (1959), and M. Baudot, *L'Opinion publique sous l'occupation* (1960).

Valuable general studies of collaboration include: M. Cotta, *La Collaboration: 1940-1944* (1964); E. Jäckel, *Frankreich in Hitlers Europa* (1966; French trans., 1968), and J. Plumyène & R. Lasierra, *Les Fascismes français: 1923-1963* (1963).

The treatment of the Jews is specifically dealt with in H. Monneray (ed.), *La Persécution des juifs en France et dans les autres pays de l'ouest* (1947), and the case of the deportees in *La Déportation* (1967).

Useful studies on Pétain are: d'Argenson, *Pétain et le Pétinisme* (1953), and J. Plumyène, *Pétain* (1964), while the most important studies of Laval are: G. Bechtel, *Laval 20 ans après* (1963), D. Thomson, *Two Frenchmen: Pierre Laval and Charles de Gaulle* (1951), and G. Warner, *Pierre Laval and the Eclipse of France* (1968). Of great interest are the transcripts of the trials of prominent collaborators—Pétain (2 vols., 1945), Laval (1946), Maurras (1946)—and the examination of the post-war purges made by P. Novick, *The Resistance versus Vichy* (1968).

Essential general studies of the Resistance include: R. Hostache, *Le Conseil national de la Résistance: les institutions de la clandestinité* (1958), and H. Michel, *Histoire de la Résistance* (2nd edn., 1958) and *Les Courants de pensée de la Résistance* (1962). The role of the communists from 1939 to 1941 is defended by A. Lecœur,

Le Parti communiste et la Résistance: août 1939-juin 1941 (1968), and G. Willard, *La Drôle de guerre et la trahison de Vichy* (1960), and examined sceptically and critically by A. J. Rieber, *Stalin and the French Communist Party: 1941-1947* (1962), and A. Rossi, *La Guerres des papillons: quatre ans de politique communiste, 1940-1944* (1954). A useful introduction to the Resistance press is C. Bellanger, *Presse clandestine: 1940-1944* (1961), while P. Bourget & C. Lacretelle's *Sur les murs de Paris: 1940-1944* (1959) gives a vivid account of the posters of the period.

Light is thrown on the conditions of clandestine writing by H. Josephson and M. Cowley, *Aragon: Poet of the French Resistance* (1945), and Vercors, *La Bataille du silence* (1967), and on the writings of collaborators by P. Sérant, *Le Romantisme fasciste* (1959).

13. Revolt and Revolution: Camus and Sartre

THE vigorous discussion of fundamental political questions is a major activity in France. Both the nature and subject of the discussion have long been affected by the fact that the country possesses a revolutionary tradition originating in the events of 1789 and sustained by those of 1830, 1848, 1871, and 1968. Furthermore, French political debate in this century has been sharpened by a series of experiences and memories relating to the bitter ideological clash over the Dreyfus Affair, the hopes and fears roused by the formation of the Popular Front government in 1934, the heroism and betrayal associated with the German Occupation, and the deeply divided national conscience during the Algerian war which lasted from 1954 to 1962 and cost the lives of 12,000 regular French troops together with something like ten times as many Moslem dead.

Against this general background of political drama, writers have always occupied a distinctive position in France. Even those who have taken no active part in politics have often been expected to express their views publicly. In the case of artists who have written directly about political issues, the attention paid to their statements has been serious and widespread. And perhaps France alone could have provided the situation which arose in 1958 when Malraux, then Minister of Information, suggested that three winners of the Nobel Prize for Literature (Roger Martin du Gard, Mauriac, and Camus) should go to Algeria to investigate allegations that the French army was making regular use of torture against prisoners. It was as though in America, at some point during the Vietnam war, someone like Hemingway had held an equivalent government post to that of Malraux and had proposed sending Steinbeck,

Faulkner, and Pearl Buck to Saigon. It is only rarely that the assumptions underlying this kind of proposal have been questioned by French writers themselves. Camus, as it happens, is one of the few examples. As early as 1938 he said of Gide, whose work he greatly admired, that his political ideas were no more worthy of attention than those of any reasonably educated and liberal-minded Frenchman.

The fact remains, however, that most French writers have regarded it as natural that they should comment in detail, and from a certain privileged position, on political affairs. Many in this century have done so, including Péguy, Valéry, Rolland, Gide, Bernanos, Mauriac, and Malraux. Two of the most influential recent figures, arguing from fundamentally different standpoints, have been Camus and Sartre. In the minds of many readers their literary achievements have even become inseparable from their political attitudes. Certainly, between them, they represent much that was most intellectually exciting in France in the first twenty years that followed the Second World War. It seems appropriate, therefore, to outline the political ideas of each in turn and then to discuss their famous quarrel of 1952 which points to several fundamental issues which have continued to underlie political debate since that time.

In 1913 Albert Camus was born into an impoverished European family in the French colony of Algeria. He reached manhood in the 1930s which were dominated, as far as public events are concerned, by a severe economic crisis, the rise of fascism and nazism, and the Spanish Civil War. In such circumstances it is not surprising that he became involved in politics by the time he reached his twenties. Two or three years earlier he had decided, very consciously, to become a writer and he took his dedication to literature —which he interpreted not as vague aestheticism but as devotion to truth—very seriously. Camus had thus set himself a problem at the outset of his career—the problem of reconciling the claims of art, as he conceived them, with those of political responsibility. His work as a writer meant putting a premium on his own personal sense of truth with all that this involves in terms of seeing many issues in various shades of grey rather than in black and white. This attitude inhibited his political loyalties in the sense that it conflicted with the moral compromises and conscious simplifications often associated with a 'realistic' or 'practical' party line. Indeed, he soon experienced the nature of the clash in a disturbing form. In 1934, largely at the prompting of his friend and teacher Jean Grenier, he joined the Communist Party; within months he had left it again following a tactical change in the Algerian Communist Party's opposition to French colonial policy, a change which appears to have been ordered by Moscow as a result of Laval's mission there in May 1935. The problem which he had met in this practical form continued to preoccupy Camus and we find him writing of it in 1939: 'L'artiste aujourd'hui doit, d'une façon ou d'une autre, lui trouver une solution. C'est à la fois sa servitude et sa grandeur.' It is significant that this same question concerning the nature and limits of the writer's political commitment was to form the theme of his Nobel Prize speech in 1957. About one thing, however, Camus was already clear. Literary quality should neither be divorced from nor sacrificed to political considerations. He went further and stated positively that quality of thought and quality of expression are inseparable in this sphere:

. . . il n'est point d'œuvre révolutionnaire sans qualité artistique. Ceci peut paraître paradoxal. Mais je crois que si l'époque nous enseigne quelque chose à cet égard, c'est que l'art révolutionnaire ne peut se passer de grandeur artistique, sans retomber aux formes les plus humiliées de la pensée.

Camus's political ideas were formed by three sets of experiences: those in Algeria up to the outbreak of the Second World War; those in France during the Occupation and Resistance; those in the post-war France of the Fourth Republic. It is hardly necessary to add that he related his own more immediate experiences, chiefly as a journalist, to the wider European and world scene. It will be clear also, from what has already been said, that the situation in pre-war Algeria was crucial in laying the foundations for those political positions which he formulated in more detail later. Towards the end of this first period he worked for the left-wing daily *Alger-*

Républicain and briefly edited *Soir-Républicain*. Many of the articles he wrote at this time already show that high-minded humanity which was later to irritate both right-wing and Communist opponents. It was in 1939, for example, that he wrote an important series of articles on the famine existing among the Moslem population in the Kabylia region of Algeria. He did so at a time when the Communist Party offered a diet of ideology to the starving Kabylians. He himself avoided ideology, gave a detailed analysis of the situation, provided facts and figures, and outlined precise, practical measures in connection with wages, housing, agricultural reforms, etc. An extract from his final article conveys the spirit in which he wrote:

> Mon rôle n'est d'ailleurs point de chercher d'illusoires responsables. Je ne trouve pas de goût au métier d'accusateur. Et si même je m'y sentais porté, beaucoup de choses m'arrêteraient. Je sais trop, d'une part, ce que la crise économique a pu apporter à la détresse de la Kabylie pour en charger absurdement quelques victimes. Mais je sais trop aussi quelles résistances rencontrent les initiatives généreuses, de si haut qu'elles viennent quelquefois. Et je sais trop, enfin, comment une volonté, bonne en son principe, peut se trouver déformée dans ses applications.

A few lines later he adds:

> Ce n'est pas pour un parti que ceci est écrit, mais pour des hommes. Et si je voulais donner à cette enquête le sens qu'il faudrait qu'on lui reconnaisse, je dirais qu'elle n'essaie pas de dire: 'Voyez ce que vous avez fait de la Kabylie', mais: 'Voyez ce que vous n'avez pas fait de la Kabylie'.

It is wholly typical of Camus that he should have refused in this way to make party political capital out of the suffering of his fellow-Algerians.

We find this same 'human' rather than 'party-political' stand in his post-war writings on Algeria. He severely condemned the brutal repression of the rising at Sétif in 1945 and emphasized the seriousness of both the economic and political situations in the country. Ten years in advance, and unlike many who were to criticize him later, he foresaw the approaching Algerian crisis and tried to rouse French public opinion. When the Algerian war broke out in 1954, this foresight gave Camus a certain moral prestige, though characteristically he did not exploit it. And it was consistent with his attitude during the previous twenty years that he should refuse to adopt the unquestioning pro-F.L.N.[1] position of extreme left-wing intellectuals such as Sartre. Thus he wrote in 1958: '. . . il faut cesser de considérer en bloc les Arabes d'Algérie comme un peuple de massacreurs. La grande masse d'entre eux, exposée à tous les coups, souffre d'une douleur que personne n'exprime pour elle', but he added:

. . . il faut cesser aussi de porter condamnation en bloc sur les Français d'Algérie. Une certaine opinion métropolitaine, qui ne se lasse pas de les haïr, doit être rappelée à la décence. Quand un partisan du F.L.N. ose écrire que les Français d'Algérie ont toujours considéré la France comme une prostituée à exploiter, il faut rappeler à cet irresponsable qu'il parle d'hommes dont les grands-parents, par exemple, ont opté pour la France en 1871 et quitté leur terre d'Alsace pour l'Algérie, dont les pères sont morts en masse dans l'est de la France en 1914 et qui, eux-mêmes, deux fois mobilisés dans la dernière guerre, n'ont cessé, avec des centaines de milliers de musulmans, de se battre sur tous les fronts pour cette prostituée. . . . Je résume ici l'histoire des hommes de ma famille qui, de surcroît, étant pauvres et sans haine, n'ont jamais exploité ni opprimé personne.

As Camus refused to apply the all-too-easy colonialist and class stereotypes to the population of Algeria, he also refused to condone violence from whatever source it might come. He condemned those units of the French army which carried out 'les représailles contre les populations civiles et les pratiques de torture', and added: 'Mais, pour être utile autant qu'équitable, nous devons condamner avec la même force, et sans précautions de langage, le terrorisme appliqué par le F.L.N. aux civils français comme, d'ailleurs, et dans une proportion plus grande, aux civils arabes.' Because he was born and grew up in Algeria, because he was one of the people, and because he felt a loyalty both to Algeria and to France, Camus could not accept a highly selective and partisan liberalism. His personal circumstances ensured that he saw the problem in its full human dimension, not in terms of political abstraction. He rejected both

[1] The Algerian Front de Libération Nationale.

right-wing colonialism and F.L.N. nationalism, supporting a federal solution which would have given Algeria government by Algerians in union with France.

Between his first and last writings on the Algerian problem Camus joined the French Resistance and worked for the clandestine newspaper run by the 'Combat' group. A number of the earliest commentators on his work, largely unaware of his pre-war political writings, found it surprising that he should have left Algeria for this purpose. Some later readers, confused by the many clichés used to present Camus as a 'prophet of the absurd', have thought his action illogical. In fact, prior to the outbreak of the Second World War, he had followed political events in Europe with deep interest, identifying himself with the main liberal and left-wing positions. In any case, quite apart from the fact that radical absurdism could make participating in the Resistance no more illogical than opting out, his analysis of contemporary nihilism had been carried on with a view to discovering a positive, humanist alternative. In the course of this analysis he was well aware that the purely quantitative ethic discussed in *Le Mythe de Sisyphe* would be inadequate in the face of human suffering and need. Again, the growth of fascism and Nazism in the thirties had made it clear that the nihilism derived from a certain interpretation of the absurd leads to terrible human disasters. Finally, the absurd as a concept can only be meaningful in relation to an implied standard of human coherence and justice.

Inevitably, the Occupation was a period during which plans were made and ideals discussed which would ensure a political rebirth of France once the war was over. The bonds of comradeship forged in adversity would be maintained, justice and truth would prevail, there would be no return to the betrayals and hypocrisies associated with the Third Republic. With the Liberation, Camus appeared as editor of the daily *Combat*, a post which he held until 1947, and he expressed his militant hopes and enthusiasms in a series of editorials. The following passage from one of them is typical:

Nous voulons réaliser sans délai une vraie démocratie populaire et ouvrière . . . une Constitution où la liberté et la justice recouvrent toutes leurs garanties, les réformes de structure profondes sans lesquelles une politique de liberté est une duperie, la destruction impitoyable des trusts et des puissances d'argent, la définition d'une politique étrangère basée sur l'honneur et la fidélité à tous nos alliés sans exception.

Statements such as these were accompanied by the assertion that the revolution he envisaged need not be a violent one, and Camus, for a time at least, emerged as the spokesman of many non-Communist *résistants*.

This period of political euphoria did not last. Many of Camus's ideals failed to be realized and he gradually grew more disillusioned both by the resurgence of strength from the Right and by the tactical manœuvres of the Communists. He was also appalled by the continuing totalitarian regime within the U.S.S.R., by Soviet foreign policy, and by the crushing of both the workers' rising in East Berlin and the Hungarian revolt of 1956. In 1951 he had exposed, in *L'Homme révolté*, what he considered to be the injustice, violence, and dishonesty inherent in Marxism. From this time onwards he began to give increasingly unambiguous expression to his anti-Communism, culminating in his references to 'le nouvel impérialisme qui menace la liberté de la France et de l'Occident', to the fact that socialism, as readily as capitalism, can give rise to war, and to his conviction that no evil which (Communist) totalitarianism claims to remedy is worse than totalitarianism itself. These views, which first received detailed and systematic expression in *L'Homme révolté*, were still an important element in his political thought at the time of his death in 1960.

As a young man Sartre was much less involved in political activity than Camus. Although eight years the latter's senior, he appears to have been relatively unaffected by the international crises of the twenties and thirties. Unlike many of his contemporaries, he took no part in the Spanish Civil War. Also, the fact that he failed to vote either in 1932 or 1936 was almost certainly due to indifference rather than to any conscious rejection of basic democratic procedures. At the same time, Sartre possessed an acute moral conscience and a puritanical strain no doubt derived from his half Alsatian origins and his family connection with the Schweitzers (Albert Schweitzer was a cousin). Although he rejected all formal religion at an early stage, he continued to look for solutions to his problems in philosophy, and particularly in ethics and psychology. The conclusions he had reached by the end of the thirties laid the foundations of his particular brand of existentialism which is characterized, above all, by high moral seriousness. The puritan conscience is notably at work in *L'Être et le néant* (1943). It was this fundamental characteristic of his temperament, increasingly affected by his experience of Occupied France followed by the France of the 'cold war' years, which gradually focused his attention on political problems. In the 1950s and 1960s he turned his back more and more on literary writing in order to concentrate on political analysis.

Like Camus, Sartre had to face the problem of the writer's political responsibilities once he began to publish novels and plays at the end of the Second World War. With much more certainty than Camus, he argued that the writer must be committed to left-wing causes. This certainty is expressed in various essays including his introduction to the first number of *Les Temps Modernes* (October 1945) and the long 'Qu'est-ce que la littérature?' of 1947. It is also reflected in the notable difference between the explicit political content of such novels and plays as *Les Chemins de la liberté* (1945–9), *La Putain respectueuse* (1946), *Les Mains sales* (1948), and Camus's *L'Étranger* (1942), *La Peste* (1947), and *Le Malentendu* (1944) or *Caligula* (1944). Starting from the statement 'nous ne voulons rien manquer de notre temps', Sartre rejected a purely aesthetic interpretation of the writer's revolutionary role: 'Il ne s'agit plus d'allumer des incendies dans les brousses du langage, de marier des "mots qui se brûlent" et d'atteindre à l'absolu par la combustion du dictionnaire.' He insisted that the writer, by the very nature of his occupation as one who communicates with an audience, is committed in any case: '. . . l'écrivain n'est ni Vestale, ni Ariel: il est "dans le coup"', and adds: '. . . il faut parier, l'abstention est un choix.' Thus he held Flaubert and the Goncourt brothers responsible for the crushing of the Paris Commune in the sense that, by not writing against it, they gave it their tacit support. The political responsibility of the writer, therefore, cannot be evaded. It is the role of the true artist to give society a guilty conscience.

All this implies a certain confidence in the political efficacy of literature as such. It is perhaps not inconsistent with the ending of *La Nausée* (1938) which has been interpreted as a (rather uncertain) form of salvation through art. But this ending, as several critics have pointed out, hardly accords with our general impression of Sartre's thought and seems more like a convenient technical device for ending the novel than a seriously thought-out solution to the philosophical problems which it raises. In fact, Sartre was soon unable to find political satisfaction in purely literary work. By its nature it involves a certain 'distancing' of reality, a certain abstraction and remoteness from the very material with which it deals. In the late 1940s he moved rapidly from the idea of justification through art to that of salvation through politics. The extent to which he now rejects the doctrine of artistic commitment as inadequate can be seen in this extract from an interview with Madeleine Chapsal published in 1960:

J'ai bien perdu des illusions littéraires: que la littérature ait une valeur absolue, qu'elle puisse sauver un homme ou simplement changer des hommes (sauf en des circonstances spéciales), tout cela me paraît aujourd'hui périmé: l'écrivain continue à écrire, une fois les illusions perdues, parce qu'il a, comme disent les psychanalystes, tout investi dans l'écriture.[1]

In 1948 Sartre took the practical step of forming not a new party but a 'rally' of left-wing groups, the Rassemblement Démocratique Révolutionnaire. He envisaged the eventual creation of a European federation which, while distinct from both the U.S.A. and the U.S.S.R., would be strongly *communisant* and have a firm proletarian basis. The grouping had a short life, mainly as the result of a combination of internal dissension and lack of working-class support. The activities and ideals of the R.D.R., however, gave rise to *Entretiens sur la politique* (1949), written in collaboration with David Rousset and Gérard Rosenthal. Sartre's contributions to these 'conversations' show that he was very unwilling to criticize the U.S.S.R. (against Sartre Rousset argued, as Camus was to do, that the Soviet system had simply replaced capitalist exploitation by a ruthless system of state control), that he considered the proletariat to be the sole source of salvation, and that he accepted the

[1] M. Chapsal, *Les Écrivains en personne*, Paris, 1960, p. 232.

theory of historical materialism. He interpreted politics not in terms of moral absolutes but in accordance with historical and social relativity. Although fiercely attacked by Communist theorists since his emergence as an existentialist at the end of the war, Sartre's adherence to Marxist fundamentals was clear. His chief quarrel was with some aspects of the Communist interpretation of Marxist theory. And now, with the failure of the R.D.R., he became convinced that the Communist Party alone could effectively represent and pursue the true interests of the working class. More generally, he wrote: 'Le communisme nous apparaît, malgré tout, comme le seul mouvement qui porte en lui les chances du socialisme.'

From this point onwards he commented constantly, and often at enormous length, on both domestic and foreign policy. In articles collected in the various volumes of *Situations* (particularly 'Matérialisme et Révolution', 'Les Communistes et la paix', and 'Le Fantôme de Staline') he defended the U.S.S.R. and the Marxist cause generally, going so far as to say of Eastern Europe: '. . . on juge de ce qu'elle fait au nom de ce qu'elle veut, de ses moyens au nom de sa fin.' This view that political systems should be judged by their theoretical aims rather than by their deeds—a view, incidentally, which Sartre was not prepared to apply to the U.S.A. —is some indication of the strong theoretical bias underlying his judgements. It is this theoretical position which he has been mainly concerned to elaborate in recent years. The first part of his attempt to do so was published in 1960 as *Critique de la raison dialectique I: Théorie des ensembles pratiques.*

This is a very large work—half as long again as *L'Être et le néant* and at least as difficult to read. It is written with several purposes in mind, among them being an analysis of the relationship between existentialism and Marxism, a total understanding of historical process, and the addition of a sociological, and even an anthropological, dimension to Sartre's political theory. On the first of these points it is evident that existentialism and Marxism start from very different theoretical positions. Existentialism begins with individual apprehension of the world, Marxism with collectivist and class realities; existentialism emphasizes indeterminacy and individual freedom, Marxism assimilates freedom to necessity; existentialism is Kierkegaardian where Marxism is Hegelian. Sartre thus set himself the task of showing that to pass from the individual to the group, from consciousness to history, is logical and inevitable once the truths of existentialism and Marxism have been properly grasped. This movement of *totalisation* is in fact natural, according to Sartre, for if man is a 'project', a *pour-soi* in the terminology of *L'Être et le néant*, this project is none the less exposed to a set of external conditions. Existentialist freedom means, in the end, that the individual is at liberty in the sense that he can accept, modify, or transcend a situation which he has been given. Existentialism and Marxism combine to underline the individual's 'freedom within necessity'.

Again, Sartre's existentialist writings had emphasized the element of conflict in human relationships resulting from the juxtaposition of free individuals and their inevitable treatment of one another as objects. This feature of existential psychology made relatively easy the transition to Marxist instrumentalism, the concept of class antagonism, and the justification of human means by abstract ends. The movement is one from a predominantly metaphysical view of human relationships to an economic one which pictures a hostile universe of scarcity and, indeed, regards scarcity as 'the motor of history'. At the same time, Sartre considers that Marxism, unlike existentialism, has paid insufficient attention to psychological factors, particularly those associated with the psychoanalytical account of childhood. Having complained that 'les marxistes d'aujourd'hui n'ont souci que des adultes', he praises psychoanalysis for discovering 'le point d'insertion de l'homme dans sa classe, c'est-à-dire la famille singulière comme médiation entre la classe universelle et l'individu'.

In connection with one aspect of historical process Sartre distinguishes between existentialism—which he terms an ideology—and Marxism—which he distinguishes as a philosophy. It is a philosophy in the same sense as Cartesianism or Hegelianism because it 'totalizes' knowledge, methodology, social impact, and a world view. As such it cannot be transcended since philosophies, as distinct from ideologies, 'sont indépassables tant que le moment historique dont elles sont l'expression n'a pas été dépassé'. Thus, for Sartre, anti-Marxist arguments are literally non-progressive.

In the nature of historical development they cannot be more than a refurbishing of pre-Marxist ideas whose day, by Marxist definition, is past. The role of existentialism as an ideology will thus be confined to adding a new dimension to certain features of Marxist theory. And Sartre adds: 'A partir du jour où la recherche marxiste prendra la dimension humaine . . . comme le fondement du Savoir anthropologique, l'existentialisme n'aura plus de raison d'être.'

As regards a new anthropology and sociology, Sartre bases them on an evaluation of human relationships as either sadistic or masochistic owing to the fact of scarcity and the unabating struggle against it. 'Scarcity' is a central idea in Sartre's current thinking and he analyses the idea at some length. It provides the modern sense in which 'men are everywhere in chains': '. . . les hommes sont tous esclaves en tant que leur expérience vitale se déroule dans le champ practico-inerte et dans la mesure expresse où ce champ est originellement conditionné par la rareté.' This is a situation which Marxism alone can remedy. Men can only overcome scarcity by joining a group entered into by a 'pledge' and further held together by fear and terror. This important concept of a 'pledged group', as distinct from a 'serial' or disparate collection of competing individuals, appears to resemble closely the apparatus of the Communist Party and Sartre does not hesitate to defend violence in the pursuance of its ends. His neo-Marxism, which perhaps uses Marx to modernize existentialism as much as it uses existentialism to clarify Marx, subsumes individual freedom within historical necessity in an effort to demonstrate the dialectical inevitability (aided by rational violence) of a new man and a new social reality.

It will now be clear that Camus and Sartre have little in common as political theorists, apart from the genuine moral concern of each and their desire that society should be different. Camus advocated democratic socialism; Sartre preaches a form of authoritarian Marxism. Where Camus was reformist and gradualist, Sartre is revolutionary and violent (see his Introduction to Fanon's *Les Damnés de la terre*). Camus wrote from a position of moral intransigence; Sartre writes from a readiness to 'soil his hands' in the pursuit of long-term moral aims. Where Camus argued the need for revolt, a revolt with concrete and immediate values, Sartre maintains the need for violent revolution, a revolution with formal and historical values. Camus's conception of revolt is an ethical theory which lacks a distinctive sociology; Sartre's conception of revolution puts historical and sociological realities before ethics. The gulf between them, which is something much more fundamental than a mere semantic disagreement, emerges clearly enough from the statement by Sartre quoted by Simone de Beauvoir: 'La morale, c'est un ensemble de trucs idéalistes pour vous aider à vivre ce que la pénurie des ressources et la carence des techniques vous impose [sic].' Despite their post-war friendship, Camus and Sartre were bound to clash politically. This clash came in 1952 following the publication of Camus's L'Homme révolté in 1951.

According to Camus's analysis in L'Homme révolté, the three main forms of revolution known to modern times have ended in injustice, inhumanity, and violence. The French Revolution of 1789, starting from high secular ideals of reason, freedom, and human rights, developed into a 'reign of terror'. Despite the initial abolition of capital punishment, thousands of victims were soon to be guillotined. A more nihilistic form of revolution, activated by the belief that there are no absolutes and showing contempt for both reason and humane values, is exemplified by the violence of both nazi practice and surrealist theory. We are familiar enough with the world of torture and oppression created by Nazism. At a more theoretical level the surrealist leader André Breton had claimed, during his most militant phase, that to discharge a revolver arbitrarily in a crowded street would be a genuinely surrealist act. Both these revolutions, the 'Jacobin' and the 'nihilistic', were forms of metaphysical rebellion representing 'une expédition démesurée contre le ciel'. The third example of revolution, the Russian Revolution of 1917, is the first major example of 'historical' rebellion. It is based on the conviction that truth, equality, and justice are located in future time and will be realized by a discernible and dialectical historical process. This is the doctrine on which Camus focuses much of his attention. He reminds his readers of that nightmare world of torture and purges, of labour camps and enforced collectivization, of secret police and rigid Party control, which has been the lot of large areas of Europe in recent years. How are we to react to an ideology which proclaims, in apparently blatant contradiction to its actual treatment of men and women, that human well-being is its goal? Is it inevitable that the doctrine of historical determinism, which is central to Marxism, should result in terrorism and tyranny?

Camus's answer to this last question is in the affirmative. Nevertheless, he is far from indulging in facile anti-Communist propaganda. He praises Marx for having uncovered in a systematic way the social hypocrisy of the nineteenth-century bourgeoisie. He also emphasizes the more general moral impulses which motivated Marx and quotes the latter's statement that 'an end requiring unjust means is not a just end'. The value of such a statement obviously depends on the meaning one gives to the terms 'just' and 'unjust', but Camus takes them at their face value. He does not relate this assertion to another celebrated Marxian claim: that 'violence is the midwife of progress'. Nevertheless, what appals him most in the Communist application of Marxist theory is in fact a drawing of the full consequences of this second statement. According to Camus's analysis, Marxism has simply replaced the absolutism of 'vertical' transcendence—belief in an omnipotent God—by the absolutism of 'horizontal' transcendence—faith in that historical inevitability which has become 'la seule transcendance des hommes sans Dieu'. Communism involves the use of terror and the exercise of tyranny because it depends on a philosophy which deifies history and, in practice, 'se condamne à toutes les servitudes pour fabriquer un oui rejeté à l'extrémité des temps'. Furthermore, Camus maintains that Marx's ideas and methods were unscientific, that his writings confuse determinism and prophecy, practical analysis and private wish-fulfilment. L'Homme révolté asserts that, at the theoretical level, a considerable number of Marx's prophecies have been denied by the turn of historical events. At the practical level, there has been a direct connection between his absolutist view of history and the methodical terrorism of Communist regimes.

Since Camus's criticisms of Communist practice are closely related to Marxist theory, he is bound to reject the whole system as irremediably dogmatic and violent. This is why he pleads for what he calls 'revolt' in place of historically obsessed revolutionary action. Shortly after the last war Sartre had drawn a distinction between the rebel and the revolutionary: '. . . au contraire du révolté qui est seul, le révolutionnaire ne se comprend que dans ses rapports de solidarité avec sa classe.' Camus rejected this distinction, insisted on the fraternal nature of revolt ('je me révolte, donc nous sommes'), and added: 'Apparemment négative, puisqu'elle ne crée rien, la révolte est profondément positive puisqu'elle révèle ce qui, en l'homme, est toujours à défendre.' This is why his own distinction between revolt and revolution takes such a different form from that of Sartre. He writes: 'La revendication de la révolte est l'unité, la revendication de la révolution historique la totalité. La première part du non appuyé sur un oui, la second part de la néga- tion absolue. . . . L'une est créatrice, l'autre nihiliste.' Revolt, as Camus conceives it, is a political doctrine which emphasizes the sanctity of human life and the need to translate justice, compassion, freedom, and honour into practical realities. Revolt is the basis of an approach to politics which rejects what Yeats called 'the thoughts men think in the mind alone' and sees society in terms of immediate human needs rather than according to abstract dogmas.

   L'Homme révolté is essentially an analytical work. Camus's pur- pose was to examine the ideological aspects of revolution rather than to write a political programme. Some readers of the book have interpreted this as evidence of the political impracticality of Camus's moral position; others have claimed that the first essential task was to expose the inherent weaknesses of Marxist theory; yet others find in *L'Homme révolté* the basis for an effective social democracy with strong syndicalist elements. Whatever the truth of these con- flicting reactions, it was clearly an important part of Camus's aim to expose what he considered to be a new *trahison des clercs*, a betrayal by those twentieth-century intellectuals who have placed their faith in a doctrine that defends the murder of certain opponents and the rigid mental disciplining of adherents on the grounds that a final and future justice will redeem such procedures.

   Reactions from many of these intellectuals were not slow in coming. One such reaction was a harsh review of *L'Homme révolté* by Francis Jeanson in *Les Temps Modernes* of May 1952. Jeanson took the line that Camus was an 'âme pure'—too morally fastidious to contribute in a practical way to the fight against social injustice. This, of course, was monstrously unfair, and Sartre invited Camus to write a reply. The latter did so in a 'Lettre au directeur des *Temps Modernes*'. He claimed that Jeanson had misinterpreted *L'Homme révolté* and had argued from Marxist assumptions while failing completely to answer the objections to Marxist theory set out in the book. Camus also argued that the Marxist theory of necessary historical goals was incompatible with the fundamental philosophical position of existentialism. Camus's letter was published in the August issue of *Les Temps Modernes* accompanied by replies from both Sartre and Jeanson. While Sartre opted for the efficacy of collective 'historical' endeavour, whatever its moral failures, Camus emphasized the values of the individual conscience and consciousness independent of history. Inevitably, Sartre repeated the essence of Jeanson's earlier criticisms when he wrote: '. . . je ne vois qu'une solution pour vous: les îles Galapagos.' To Camus's question whether or not Sartre and Jeanson regarded the Soviet regime as representing a satisfactory application of Marxist philosophy, Jeanson replied, somewhat uneasily, that the Soviet state was not authentically revolutionary but had the inestimable merit of being the only system of government attempting to be so. As regards the contrast made by Camus between the 'closed' Marxist view of history and the 'open' existentialist one, Sartre replied in orthodox fashion that Marx only ascribed a foreseeable end to 'prehistory' (i.e. history up to the establishment of the authentically Marxist state). This hardly answers the dilemma which Camus outlined:

> Si l'homme n'a pas de fin qu'on puisse élire en règle de valeur, comment l'histoire aurait-elle un sens dès maintenant perceptible? Si elle en a un, pourquoi l'homme n'en ferait-il pas sa fin? Et s'il le fait, comment serait-il dans la terrible et incessante liberté dont vous parlez?

The fact that Sartre saw the point of Camus's criticism and took it seriously is indicated by the long subsequent meditations, in *Critique de la raison dialectique*, on the sense in which history can be said to have an end and on the general relationship between existentialism and Marxism.

The debate initiated in this way by Camus and Sartre was important in 1952 (year VII of the cold war, as Raymond Aron put it) and has continuing relevance. It is relevant as an element in the central political debate of our time—the debate between Marxism and the non-Marxist Left. And it is important because this particular exchange of viewpoints between Camus and Sartre clearly shows that the issue is not simply one of conflicting political policies but has to do with fundamental moral and philosophical issues. The political writings of Camus and Sartre, with their contrasting philosophies of moral revolt and violent revolution, show how wide a gap exists between these two positions. They also provide essential prior reading for any discussion of the desirability, and the possibility, of a genuinely liberal and effectively humane alternative to Marxist dogmatics.

NOTE

ALBERT CAMUS, 1913–60, grew up in Algeria, worked for the clandestine press in France during the Occupation, edited the daily *Combat* in the immediate post-war years, and was killed in a car accident at the age of 47. During the 1940s and 1950s he built up a world-wide reputation as an essayist, novelist, and moral force generally, as well as writing and adapting plays. His major intervention in the Algerian War was an unsuccessful truce appeal in 1956 in which he urged both the French army and the nationalist F.L.N. to cease their violence against the civilian population. Camus was very much the spokesman and mentor of the immediate post-war generation, arguing against cynicism and nihilism and in favour of a liberal alternative to Marxism. He was awarded the Nobel Prize for Literature in 1957.

JEAN-PAUL SARTRE was born in Paris in 1905. He was trained as a philosopher and studied in pre-war Germany as well as in France. With the Fall of France in 1940 he was a prisoner-of-war for a brief period. After his release he took part in Resistance activities and also returned to his pre-war profession of teacher of philosophy in various French *lycées*. In 1945 he emerged as the leading French exponent of existentialism, founded the monthly *Les Temps Modernes*, and wrote a number of important and influential plays, novels, and essays. He has become increasingly preoccupied by politics, seeking to synthesize existentialism and Marxism in a revolutionary doctrine for his times. He declined the award of the Nobel Prize for Literature in 1964.

Works. Camus's major works are: fiction: *L'Étranger* (1942), *La Peste* (1947), *La Chute* (1956), and *L'Exil et le royaume* (short stories, 1957); plays: *Le Malentendu* (1944), *Caligula* (1944), *Les Justes* (1950); essays: *Le Mythe de Sisyphe* (1942), *L'Homme révolté* (1951), *L'Été* (1954), 3 vols. of *Actuelles* (1950-8), and 2 vols. of *Carnets* (1962 and 1964).

Sartre's major works are: fiction: *La Nausée* (1938), *Le Mur* (short stories, 1939), *Les Chemins de la liberté* (*L'Âge de raison*, 1945; *Le Sursis*, 1945; *La Mort dans l'âme*, 1949); plays: *Les Mouches* (1943), *Théâtre* (containing *Les Mouches*, *Huis clos*, *Morts sans sépulture*, and *La Putain respectueuse*, 1947), *Les Mains sales* (1948), *Le Diable et le bon Dieu* (1951), *Les Séquestrés d'Altona* (1956); essays: *L'Être et le néant: essai d'ontologie phénoménologique* (1943), *Réflexions sur la question juive* (1946), *Saint Genet, comédien et martyr* (1952), *Critique de la raison dialectique, I* (1960), 7 vols., so far, of *Situations* (1947-65); and the first part of an autobiography, *Les Mots* (1964).

Criticism. The reader is referred to the bibliographical Note accompanying Chapter 14 for details of some of the more illuminating items among the many books written on Camus and on Sartre. It seems most useful here to indicate general background reading to the politically coloured intellectual debates of the 1940s and 1950s in France. The books listed represent, between them, a wide coverage of the political spectrum. Factual background: E. Behr, *The Algerian Problem* (1962), J. Chapsal, *La Vie politique en France depuis 1940* (1966), A. Cobban, *A History of Modern France* (esp. vol. 3, 1965), F. Fauvet, *La Quatrième République* (1959), D. Johnson, *France* (1969), H. Michel and B. Guetzévitch, *Les Idées politiques et sociales de la Résistance* (1954), P. Williams, *Politics in Post-War France* (1954). Ideas: R. Aron, *L'Opium des intellectuels* (which includes a discussion of the Camus/Sartre quarrel, 1955), L. Casanova, *Le Parti communiste, les intellectuels et la nation* (1949), P. Hervé, *La Révolution et les fétiches* (1956), F. Jeanson, *Notre Guerre* (1960), B. de Jouvenel, *De la politique pure* (1963), J. Kanapa, *Situation de l'intellectuel* (1957), M. Merleau-Ponty, *Humanisme et terreur: essai sur le problème communiste* (1947), J. Moch, *Confrontations* (1952), E. Mounier, *Révolution personnaliste et communautaire* (1935) and *La petite peur du XXe siècle* (1948), Simone Weil, *Oppression et liberté* (1955). To these should be added, of course, the writings of Camus and Sartre discussed in the above chapter.

14. The Novel of Action

THE collective consciousness of Europe in the twentieth century bears the scars of two cataclysmic wars and of violent and extreme ideologies. It is perhaps not surprising that much of its literature reflects the anguish, intellectual doubt, and self-questioning associated with and intensified by political events. This is particularly true of the works we shall be discussing later. For the moment we should consider the political perspectives and the related changes in social and moral values.

The First World War was responsible, in large measure, for the feeling of the collapse of an old order; and the ideal of liberal humanism crumbled in the face of violence and the disdain for individual life. The spiritual foundations of European civilization were severely shaken, resulting in a loss of identity. If Nietzsche had proclaimed God to be dead in the nineteenth century, the disintegration of cultural and religious values was now experienced collectively. Idealism and the notion of scientific progress had been similarly shattered, and in a turmoil of conflicting beliefs and ideas the intellectual attempted to reinterpret the world. In a frenzy of self-examination he surveyed his past glory and exhausted himself. The destructive dadaist movement and its successor surrealism preached the bankruptcy of society, language, and the intellect and looked to a spiritual dimension of life in the 'surréel' beyond the superficial crust of reality. Equally important was the impact of Freud's theories of human behaviour which emphasized the latent forces in man's unconscious. And in literature writers such as Proust and Pirandello described the personality in terms of a succession of unco-ordinated thoughts, actions, and feelings, often resulting in the breakdown of the idea of a stable 'moi'.

Yet even within the climate of bankruptcy and fragmentation one senses man's awareness that he has the power to change the world;

that he has within him the idea of something better which he may achieve through his intellect, his art, or his actions. In his striking essay on Western civilization, *La Tentation de l'Occident* (1926), Malraux talks of crumbling individualism, propped by a slender structure of negations, and man's desire for a 'raison d'être' to underpin his actions. He describes the whirlwind succession of art forms as 'madness aware of itself' and the sense of anguish dominating a Western consciousness invaded by the past and present of the whole world. The old defences and barriers gone, and with no force strong enough to impose itself, the European is simply in conflict with his own civilization. And it is this conflict which prepares him for 'les royaumes métalliques de l'absurdité'. And for Malraux the death of man as a meaningful entity is closely related to the death of God, since the idea of God previously resolved man's inner contradictions. Malraux, the intellectual consciousness, is therefore left with the image of Europe and, by implication, of himself as 'ma gloire morte et ma souffrance vivante'. And yet in the midst of anguish and absurdity Malraux describes himself in these terms: 'Lucidité avide, je brûle encore devant toi, flamme solitaire et droite.' The witness of man's situation will turn to action within that situation in order to try to leave his mark on the world.

Malraux is an outstanding figure of this period, for he acknowledges with lucidity and courage the absurdity of man's condition and thereby implies the difficulties and limitations of action. In this brief survey one should, however, also take into account other significant literary figures. For in the late 20s and 30s various writers attempted to establish the notion of something permanent in man, something which might transcend his historical presence. Giono's early novels proclaimed a primitive and mysterious depth of life which unified man and nature, and the novels of Catholic writers like Bernanos and Mauriac were concerned with the fate of individual souls. The problem of human action which centred around the concepts of 'disponibilité', remaining open to all possibilities, and that of choice, which would limit those possibilities, though it had been posed earlier by André Gide, was still an important issue. But the spirit of optimism and the renewal of humanism were more frequently tempered by a sense of futility and despair. Montherlant's cult of heroic self-fulfilment and Drieu la Rochelle's will to power, which led him to seek a sense of exaltation and communion in fascism—'une action dans le désespoir'—both reveal a fundamental pessimism in action.

The economic crisis of 1929-30, the developing pressure of political events, and the atmosphere of impending catastrophe contributed to the growth of commitment and the political orientation of literature. The revolutionary spirit of the age inspired writers and intellectuals to sign manifestos and align themselves in ideological debate on internationalism, fascism, and communism. And Marxism, the major ideological force among the intellectuals, focused attention on immediate social and political problems. But as Victor Brombert points out, there was a difference between 'ideological commitment and nostalgia for heroic rebellion', exemplified in the arguments of many French intellectuals at the International Congress of Revolutionary Writers held in Paris in 1935. Whilst acknowledging the positive role of communist writing, they stressed the need to safeguard the rights of the critical mind and of man's inner life and to express the isolation and anguish of the individual. And thus they posed very clearly the dilemma which confronted them, that of reconciling the claims of their individuality with their desire to achieve some meaning beyond that individuality in a historical context.

The problem outlined here of the relationship between the individual's self-awareness and personal destiny and his involvement and action in a collective historical situation is at the heart of the novels under consideration. In *La Tentation de l'Occident* Malraux emphasizes the importance of action for Western man as a means of conquering and transforming the world and of thereby achieving individuality through self-possession in this action: 'Il veut se soumettre le monde, et trouve dans son action une fierté d'autant plus grande qu'il croit le posséder davantage.' The action of the adventurer is then an affirmation of energy and virile passion. In more metaphysical terms, the desire to surpass himself is a way of transforming the anguish of his isolation. By committing himself in action he escapes his solitude and joins his fellow men in assuming the suffering and responsibility of human destiny. But the intellectual's commitment, as a quasi-Marxist, is a chosen way of escaping the bankruptcy of his bourgeois cultural values. As the product of a certain class his sense of social and political guilt may lead him to identify himself with the proletarian cause. He is, however, an object of suspicion for the militant proletariat who believe he espouses their cause for personal ends and as a means of justifying his life and ultimately his death. The intellectual's dilemma is heightened still further by the fact that he is himself fully conscious of his situation and analyses his sense of guilt and inadequacy in a self-accusatory manner. And in his Preface to Roger Stéphane's *Portrait de l'aventurier* (1950) J.-P. Sartre considers the most important elements of this dilemma.

Distinguishing the militant from the man of action, Sartre says that the former is constituted and defined in class and historical terms through his adherence to the Communist Party. He is absorbed in that collectivity of actions directed towards a goal which constitutes the Party:

Soutenu et continuellement recréé par ce projet qui le dépasse, le militant se trouve protégé contre la mort: l'entreprise qui le définit excède de loin la durée d'une vie; il travaille donc sans cesse au-delà de sa propre mort et sa disparition ne modifiera pas le processus historique, pas plus que son apparition ne l'a modifiée.

The adventurer, on the other hand, is a heroic parasite who cherishes his individuality, wanting others to acknowledge it, and yet seeks to escape his isolation in action. But it is only in his death, when he finally fulfils the destiny he has created in his life, that he can achieve the consummation and consecration of himself in the eyes of others. By relating that life to a political cause he seeks to intensify it, but in the end his attempt both to justify himself and to communicate with his fellow men through action is doomed and his isolation is merely intensified. For the double irony of his death and isolation lies in the physical and metaphysical separation of this final moment.

Though Sartre recognizes the historical and moral rightness of the militant cause, he adds significantly: '. . . c'est l'aventurier que je suivrai dans sa solitude. Il a vécu jusqu'au bout une condition impossible.' Furthermore he maintains that the Marxist should adopt the adventurer's sense of personal freedom and critical mind, combining them with his own commitment to achieve his historical ends: 'Il faut rétablir la négativité, l'inquiétude et l'auto-critique dans la discipline. Nous ne gagnerons que si nous tirons toutes les conséquences de ce cercle vicieux: l'homme est à faire et c'est l'homme qui seul peut faire l'homme.' Though the novelists under discussion are not militantly committed to the Marxist cause, except perhaps for Sartre, they are on the whole deeply concerned with the political issues of their time. Almost more important, however, is their concern with man's tragic and absurd experience of his existence in a Godless universe. With different emphases Saint-Exupéry, Malraux, Camus, and Sartre all confront these problems. The term 'novels of action' does not, however, imply that they transpose in fictional terms clear-cut solutions to given problems. For the strength of their novels lies in fact in the tension which exists in the individual's anguished attempt both to create some meaning for his life and to seek fulfilment in a historical situation which transcends and limits his individuality. He exists both as an individual and within a social framework, and wrestles with both metaphysical and political problems.

Whilst Saint-Exupéry does in some respects conform to this pattern, he is essentially different from the others in that he is not an intellectual in the sense of the term as one applies it to Sartre and perhaps to Malraux. For, whilst he is a thoughtful and reflective writer, he does not make the same determined effort to grasp the totality of the world within some kind of conceptual framework, as do the others in their respective ways. His novels are little more than episodic and loosely structured sequences of memories, incidents, and meditations written in simple and direct language which, however, achieve considerable poetic intensity in the pilot's descriptions of earth and sky. Central to each novel is the figure of the pilot whose plane, like the peasant's plough, brings him face to face with the elemental and secret forces of the universe. Flying, as Saint-Exupéry describes it, is a privileged activity in which the pilot is a pioneer, for he not only opens up new channels of air-mail communication but, more important, is engaged in a cosmic battle on the edge of the known and unknown in the name of man. From the cockpit he dominates the world, seeing himself as a shepherd watching over the flock who live their lives in simple happiness which he both envies and despises for its cosy regularity and security. Out of his plane he feels awkward and cut off from ordinary people; but within the airline or the squadron he experiences a sense of real communion in danger and his life takes on a meaning beyond his individual death. It is this willingness to face danger, the submission to the group and the idea of self-sacrifice for a higher ideal beyond the futile missions of 1940, which is emphasized in the novel of war-time experiences *Pilote de guerre*.

Out of this collective gesture of risk and his experience of the absurdity of his action and that of his comrades in defeat, Saint-Exupéry develops his idea of the need for a wider collective acceptance of defeat for the renewal of France. He stresses men's need to fulfil themselves and he looks beyond conflicting factions and ideologies to a communion of men which subsumes the individual. If his ideal civilization presumes an essence of man in which Christian principles are adapted to the new humanism, it can only exist if the individual sacrifices himself to the ideal through action. In trying to give once more some real meaning to the notions of man and of humanism, Saint-Exupéry stresses the idea of sacrifice, since, in his view, real fraternity can only exist when men give themselves together to something bigger than both their individuality and their collective identity as a group of individuals: 'Collectivité est mot vide de signification tant que la Collectivité ne se noue pas en quelque chose. Une somme n'est pas un Être.' Saint-Exupéry looks then beyond the masses and the state, the individual and the social good to an ideal of man, 'qui s'était vidé de substance', which he sees as a cathedral or a 'Citadelle'. And if 'l'homme est d'abord celui qui crée', the edifice he helps to build is 'l'Homme', an edifice which alone, for Saint-Exupéry, can establish meaningful equality and liberty. And this liberty is understood in turn as 'celle de l'ascension de l'Homme'. The individual's equality, freedom, and growth are thus attainable within and through that

I

gesture of sacrifice by which he participates in the construction of the new humanism. The ideal, beyond both the value of the individual or the social good, is the 'Citadelle' which men must construct together to achieve the freedom to grow.

This ultimate answer to man's ill-defined hunger bypasses social and political considerations and is developed in terms of a mystical humanistic abstraction. Only in *Vol de nuit* does a coherent social pattern in a real situation emerge. The airmail company described is a hierarchical organization, controlled by a ruthless leader, Rivière, to whom everyone—pilots, inspectors, ground-crew—submits. What is essentially a commercial enterprise is inflated and elevated almost to the level of an absolute in which the pilots achieve a higher destiny. In Rivière's hands the human clay is moulded through discipline, self-sacrifice, and danger and given a will and a soul. The men therefore mask their love and fear in a cult of moral and physical toughness in action. Submission to the leader is essential for he looks beyond the individual towards the creation of the collective monument which, like a temple or a pyramid, preserves the men from oblivion. But this insistence on self-sacrifice to the leader's vague ideal of greatness is disturbing if one transfers it to the political sphere. And the implications of such an attitude are further reinforced by the description of Fabien's death. An individual pilot's death must cause no disruption to the services of the airline, and further, by allowing the night flights to continue, 'Rivière-le-Grand, Rivière-le-Victorieux' uses that death as a stepping-stone towards the final victory of the airline, and victory here means commercial success. And on yet another level of the narrative Saint-Exupéry poeticizes Fabien's death in his description of it as an innocent and beautiful journey into the unknown: 'On avait dénoué ses liens, comme ceux d'un prisonnier qu'on laisse marcher seul, un temps, parmi les fleurs.' Death is then distorted and falsified, to some extent, in both material and metaphysical terms to justify the private vision of the leader.

Les Noyers de l'Altenburg, Malraux's last novel, explores at some length possible conceptions of the permanence of man across

civilizations. In his consciousness of his life and death as an individual, Western man experiences his destiny as something independent of the world. And this profound self-awareness is intensified
within the Christian tradition through what Malraux describes as
the interiorization and the relation to human nature of certain fatal
forces. In this perspective psychology has become the major process
by which we seek to unravel this fatality and thereby the sense of
our destiny. If, as a result, man seeks to reconstruct the world on
his own scale, art is perhaps one means by which he can build
something in the face of the 'néant' of his existence:

> Le plus grand mystère n'est pas que nous soyons jetés au hasard entre
> la profusion de la matière et celle des astres; c'est que, dans cette prison,
> nous tirions de nous-mêmes des images assez puissantes pour nier notre
> néant.

But art, like history and action, is discussed in *Les Noyers de
l'Altenburg* in relative, conceptual terms as the possible basis and
justification for belief in a notion of man. But there is seemingly no
solid foundation on which to build, and all men's constructions are
surpassed by the walnut tree which draws its strength from the
earth and achieves a certain weight and reality which is denied to
man. Yet in the end, just as the old peasant woman sees beyond life
to death with calm resignation, so, in a similar way, the artist can
perhaps oppose death with his creation: 'Mais je sais que certaines
œuvres résistent au vertige qui naît de la contemplation de nos
morts, du ciel étoilé, de l'histoire.'
    In the first place, however, it is the anguished sense of their finite
nature which intensifies the attempt of Malraux's heroes to leave
their scar on the world, and they frequently choose to act in extreme
situations—revolution, war, the jungle. For in these situations
death is an imminent danger which they confront in a desperate bid
to achieve a final consummation of their destiny. The heroic
suicide is then a way of bridging the absurd gap between life and
death by making it the supreme moment of the life it ends. This
attitude is exemplified in the characters of Hong (*Les Conquérants*)
and Tchen (*La Condition humaine*). Both are terrorists who become
locked inside their form of political action which operates as an

opiate against a feeling of fatality. They are obsessed with their death and isolation and are impelled by 'une force aveugle'. The final irony of Tchen's martyrdom as he hurls himself at Chiang Kai-shek's car clutching a bomb lies in the fact that Chiang is not in the car and that Tchen finally shoots himself as he is kicked by a policeman and not at a moment of his choosing. Death is not always presented by Malraux as a heroic suicide but is also, in the words of Lucien Goldmann, 'une menace permanente, étrangère à tout problème de l'action'. The destiny of the individual, and above all his death, are perhaps the dominant features of Malraux's fiction. The political framework of the novels is not therefore that of a revolutionary writer whose characters take part in a struggle of historical inevitability. It is rather an arena in which they commit themselves as individuals seeking to satisfy that inner urge which Garine talks of in *Les Conquérants*: 'Il y a une passion plus profonde que les autres, une passion pour laquelle les objets à conquérir ne sont plus rien. Une passion parfaitement désespérée — un des plus puissants soutiens de la force.'

Both Garine and Perken, the hero of *La Voie royale*, impelled by such a force to gamble with their lives, display energy and passion with little concern for objectives or results. In a revolutionary context Garine clashes with the communist ideal of constructing a new society and rejects the notion of progress. If political action distracts him temporarily from his illness and imminent death, the sense of absurdity returns as his health deteriorates, ironically, at the moment of political victory. Similarly, in his battles to secure a 'kingdom' in the Indo-chinese jungle, Perken's principal concern is to avoid the death which he dreads most, in 'déchéance' and impotence: '. . . il se peut que faire sa mort me semble beaucoup plus important que faire sa vie.' Faced by possible death at the hands of natives he prefers to confront the danger in a kind of metaphysical self-assertion against the absurd universe. In assuming the responsibility for one's death it becomes the ultimate stake in a dangerous way of life and an attempt at total self-possession against possible 'déchéance'. But like Garine, Perken fails, for he stumbles on a poisoned arrow and is thus robbed in a sense of a chosen death, suffering instead within his body a physical decline which reveals to him in his isolation the full horror of death.

The ideas and characters in *La Condition humaine* and *L'Espoir* are developed on a much larger scale and set in more complex political situations. The former is, however, a more obviously controlled and schematic novel in which the characters work out their destiny in terms of action and death in clearly defined ways— Kyo and Katow as revolutionaries, Tchen as a terrorist, Ferral in business, Gisors through his opium, and Clappique as a gambling mythomaniac. Each is essentially aware of his individuality and isolation and, though they are all caught up in the 1927 *coup d'état* in Shanghai, their adventures are essentially private and parallel strands which Malraux weaves together. For Kyo and Katow, captured with their comrades by Chiang Kai-shek's forces, death becomes 'un acte exalté, la suprême expression d'une vie à quoi cette mort ressemble tant' and 'la légende sanglante dont se font les légendes dorées'. Only Katow's gesture, in the face of torture, of giving his cyanide capsule away partly redeems this intense individualism. But it is the final perspective created in the novel and imposed by Gisors, the ex-Marxist lecturer who has turned to opium, which emphasizes the metaphysical significance of the private quest in *La Condition humaine*. Having lived through his son Kyo, he finally renounces the world for 'des mondes de contemplation où tout est vain'.

Malraux fought in the Spanish Civil War and this perhaps accounts in part for the epic qualities, the richness and vividness of so many scenes in *L'Espoir*, which are exemplified in the combination of panoramic sweep and attention to detail in the description of infantry battles, the bombing of Madrid, the plane crash, and so on. He weaves together the fundamentally disparate strands of the anarchist, communist, catholic, and intellectual resistance to fascism without destroying the reality and complexity of the situation. In the course of the novel he also traces the development of a sense of discipline and organization around the communists which gradually grows out of necessity. If the goal for the communist Garcia is 'transformer en conscience une expérience aussi large que possible', the problem for the spontaneous revolutionary Manuel is to assume the responsibilities of leadership. As he moves closer to the Party and is given command of a brigade, his sense of isolation and of his impossible dilemma increases. Cut off from his former life by war, he nevertheless looks beyond men's involvement in the bloody struggle to 'la possibilité infinie de leur destin'. Through Manuel Malraux conveys, perhaps for the first time with the ring of truly authentic experience, the full significance of living 'jusqu'au bout une condition impossible':

Il était né à la guerre, né à la responsabilité de la mort. Comme le somnambule qui soudain s'éveille au bord du toit, ces notes descendantes et graves lui jetaient dans l'esprit la conscience de son terrible équilibre — de l'équilibre d'où on ne tombe que dans le sang.

Through the central figures of Roquentin in Sartre's *La Nausée* and Meursault in Camus's *L'Étranger* we return to a fundamental experience of the absurdity of existence and the contingency of the world. In different ways both authors pare down that experience to the point at which the minds of the characters are seen almost as *tabulae rasae* in the face of the world around them which has no built-in moral order, or purpose. Roquentin and Meursault invent defences for themselves in their isolation which provide an essentially private solution to the experience which is described in a first-person narrative. Whilst Roquentin is both intelligent and self-analytical, Meursault is an impulsive and spontaneous sensualist who only comes alive in the sun and sea. His physical self-indulgence and brutishness contrast with Roquentin's horror of his body and all that 'exists'—'cette ignoble marmelade' which covers everything.

With considerable clarity and economy Camus conveys the sense of boredom and meaninglessness through Meursault's fragmented thoughts, feelings, and impressions. And the only relief from that meaninglessness lies in the brief moments of pleasure he enjoys, sunbathing, swimming, and making love with Marie. To that extent Meursault resembles the young gods who spend their summer on Algerian beaches and who are described by Camus in that essay of praise to the senses, 'L'Été à Alger'. Yet the pleasures and beauties of the physical world which they enjoy offer no defence against death and may even intensify the realization of the fact of human mortality. Man thus remains essentially the outsider and perhaps the victim within his physicality: 'Je sais seulement que ce ciel durera plus que moi. Et qu'appellerais-je éternité sinon ce qui continuera après ma mort?' And in *L'Étranger* the intensity of Meursault's experience of the sun, the sea, and the beach, which were the very source of his pleasure, forces him to the point at which he destroys the equilibrium and the silence in the murder of the Arab. But this insistence on physical sensations, making Meursault the victim of sunlight and heat, which are transformed into deterministic forces, would seem to oversimplify the issues of the novel, as they relate to the individual's experience of the world, and the implications of that experience. For Camus seems to recreate the notion of fatality within the limited dimensions of sensual experience and to express that fatality in the novel in the metaphor of the sensualist crushed by cosmic forces. This has the effect perhaps of reducing, to some extent, the artistic representation of the absurd to a particular kind of metaphysical experience. And the symbolic trial and judgement, though they convey the absurdity of a legal and social interpretation of individual experience and motives, nevertheless serve to reinforce the overall cosmic absurdity of Meursault's experience. After the judgement he is therefore placed in a position in which, with an unlikely display of lucidity, he conveys a somewhat mystical sense of coincidence with the indifference of the world in the face of death.

The combination of physical nausea, arising from a heightened awareness of objects and the incoherence of the world, and a penetrating intellect which intensifies this experience, contribute to Roquentin's sense of alienation. In a number of highly ironical passages he mocks various social poses ranging from Dr. Rogé's 'experience of life', 'the rights and duties' of the civic dignitaries, the social manners of the 'bons bourgeois' of Bouville, to those of the adventurer, the lovers in the café, and the humanist 'autodidacte'. Roquentin suggests that these people invent false meaning for their lives: 'Il n'y a que les salauds qui croient gagner', but he constantly questions and analyses his own motives. Reawakened from the falseness of his historical research to an intense experience of his physicality, his existence, he discovers the irreducibility and contingency of physical objects. He becomes absorbed in the momentary experience of the tree root and yet is instantly separated from it by his consciousness. As he probes his sense-impressions of the tree root in its colour and form, he realizes that the 'thing itself' is beneath the level of explanation; it is indivisible and irreducible: 'Noueuse, inerte, sans nom, elle me fascinait, m'emplissait les yeux, me ramenait sans cesse à sa propre existence.' But in his experience of the irreducibility of things and in a kind of ecstasy at the confusion and intangibility of his sensations, there arises within him the sensation of nausea. And within this total experience he becomes aware that the nature of existence is in its contingency; of the fact that to exist is simply to 'be there'. Almost as a direct result of this intense experience of the gratuitous and absurd nature of existence, Roquentin senses the absurd freedom of his life, cut off from his past, confronting the void of that freedom which resembles death. Yet, unlike Meursault, the natural animal condemned from above, Roquentin confronts the absurd in his most intense experience of the physical world and only seeks a solution in his own life through art. He believes that by writing he might free himself a little from his existence in the same way that the composer and singer of the banal ragtime tune 'se sont lavés du péché d'exister', for it is through art that he may in some way transform and escape his existence—'me purifier, me durcir, pour rendre enfin le son net et précis d'une note de saxophone'. But both the source of the inspiration and the sudden clutching at straws intensify the irony of this 'leap into art' with which the novel appears to end.

But one might now make a distinction between the subsequent fiction of Sartre and Camus and that of Saint-Exupéry and Malraux. For whilst both Sartre and Camus were active in a personal and political way in the Resistance, their fiction does not transpose lived experience in quite the same manner as that of Saint-Exupéry, nor does it present, on the whole, the individual's self-projection in action in the manner of many of Malraux's characters. Although their characters do act, often in extreme situations of plague or war or prison-camp, the novels are much more an exploration of situations and the bases, terms, and nature of possible action in the light of their understanding and presentation of that situation and of the absurd. Furthermore writing itself becomes a primary means of action; and when Sartre describes the prose-writer as someone who unmasks a situation and recreates the world in the very act of writing, the notion of 'engagement' is at once understood in its broadest sense: 'L'écrivain "engagé" sait que la parole est action: il sait que dévoiler c'est changer et qu'on ne peut dévoiler qu'en projetant de changer.' The novel is then one possible arena to which the writer can commit himself in order that no one should claim ignorance or innocence in the face of the world.

The setting of Camus's novel *La Peste* within the plague-stricken town of Oran provides him with an extreme situation in which the people are the victims of an unexpected scourge. Through his central character and narrator, Dr. Rieux, he traces their feelings, reactions, and behaviour in a situation which is both real and also a symbolic representation of the German Occupation of France and of the human condition in general. But the all-embracing metaphor of the plague imposes on the temporal and the political as well as on the changeless and universal in human life the uniform dimensions of cosmic injustice which elicit from man a blanket resistance in his experience of the absurd as an endless defeat. And it is above all the doctor whose attitude of total resistance to the fact of death in any circumstances and to 'la création telle qu'elle était' seems to lend weight to such an argument. His impatience with the inadequacy of the town's administration and his desire to face disaster and simply fight it head-on intensify the sense of man's relative impotence in an absurd struggle. And yet at the level of purely metaphysical conflict the novel coheres in a more meaningful way. But, as a key figure in the battle against the plague or disease in general, Rieux's medical tasks are clearly defined and, like those of Saint-Exupéry's pilots, his professional activities make him a special case. Both the circumstances and his job are therefore to some extent unrepresentative of a social and political situation, where man is constantly engaged in a struggle with his fellow men and where injustice, unlike the plague, does not remain quiescent 'pendant des dizaines d'années'. The image of the scourge which descends on man's head oversimplifies to some degree both the moral and political issues.

Yet through the various reactions of other characters to the plague Camus does imply that certain attitudes are more constructive than others. It is significant that Tarrou and Paneloux, whose reactions to life and suffering are similarly stark and absolute, should die, whilst characters like Grand, admired by Rieux for his quiet goodwill and simple nobility, and Rambert, who puts happiness above all else, should be saved. But Camus neither wholly justifies nor condemns a particular attitude in a world devoid of moral absolutes in which each man chooses his own course. He does, however, emphasize a common and fundamental desire for happiness, symbolized by the swim which Rieux and Tarrou take together and in the collective joy which reasserts itself once Oran is reopened. But just as Rambert experiences an irreconcilable clash between his personal happiness and the 'abstraction' of the plague, so the happiness of the people as a whole is defined in terms of the absurd. For if the just reward of happiness for those who depend only on man lies in sensual pleasure and human tenderness, that happiness acquires its particular intensity through the cosmic suffering which constantly threatens it. And though Camus finally reminds man that his battle is never won, it is as the 'doctor' of a total and circular human condition rather than in a perspective of historical events that he calls on him to act.

In the three volumes, and the fragment of a fourth, comprising *Les Chemins de la liberté*, Sartre both describes the attempts of various characters to achieve their freedom as an essentially individualistic quest and sets this pattern of individual and inter-related lives in a political context. *L'Âge de raison* (vol. 1) is centred mainly on one of the major characters of the whole work, Mathieu, who is a philosophy teacher, and on his desire to preserve his personal liberty. This attitude keeps him from committing himself to anything or anyone and leads to a profound sense of dissatisfaction in his life. The events of Munich week in 1938 provide a framework in *Le Sursis* (vol. 2) and also the background to the lives of the many characters who appear. Sartre uses a technique in this particular novel which closely resembles that of the American novelist, John Dos Passos. In *La Mort dans l'âme* (vol. 3) Sartre traces the lives of various characters who were introduced in *L'Âge de raison*—Mathieu, who is now a soldier, the communist Brunet, and the homosexual Daniel, amongst others—through the months of May and June 1940 and the fall of France.

Though there are references to the Spanish Civil War in *L'Âge de raison* and Brunet tries to persuade Mathieu to renounce his liberty and join the Party, the action of this novel is largely concerned with private problems and relationships as they affect Mathieu and his curiously assorted group of acquaintances. Much of it is taken up with Mathieu's own relationship with his mistress, Marcelle, and with his attempts to raise money for her to have an abortion. And though his attitude to Marcelle, to the young girl Ivich, and to the fact that he has been unable to commit himself in the Spanish Civil War is in some ways extraordinarily immature, Mathieu, like Roquentin, is remarkably lucid and self-analytical. He is conscious above all of the gap between his projected desires to achieve a meaningful life by engaging his liberty and the reality of that life, in which he tends to act impulsively. As a result of this gap the significance of his actions eludes him. In a somewhat involved narrative, and with a style which often prefigures that of the 'new novel', Sartre shows the complex interrelation of the thoughts, feelings, and gestures of his characters, using images and detailed observation; and explores the cowardice, lies, and self-deception which characterize much of their behaviour. For apart from Brunet, whose life has some purpose, they are all shown to be the victims of their own 'bad faith', from Lola, the ageing night-club singer, and Jacques, Mathieu's comfortable bourgeois brother, to the dramatic Boris and Ivich who cocoon themselves inside their youth, and Daniel, the homosexual who deliberately punishes himself by marrying Marcelle. Theirs is then essentially a small world of private problems, tensions, and frustrations in which positive relationships are impossible.

The events of Munich week and their implications dominate the lives of the characters in *Le Sursis*. Personal problems of course remain but Sartre attempts above all to convey the pressure of events from which the politicians themselves are not immune and which impresses Mathieu and his sister-in-law Odette with a sense of their own anonymity:

> La guerre: chacun est libre et pourtant les jeux sont faits. Elle est là, elle est partout, c'est la totalité de toutes mes pensées, de toutes les paroles d'Hitler, de tous les actes de Gomez: mais personne n'est là pour faire le total.

And Sartre himself will not 'faire le total' as a novelist, preferring to move rapidly across individual destinies, impressions, and political events to suggest the weight and density of history. Though the structure is perhaps not strong enough to make the patchwork of experience fully convincing, Sartre does convey the helplessness of the individual for whom past, present, and future are modified by the perspective of mobilization and war. The lives of the young pacifist Philippe, the illiterate shepherd Gros-Louis, and Gomez, who feels himself come alive in the Spanish Civil War, are all radically changed by the superior forces of history. Within this new perspective even the philosopher Mathieu becomes more intensely aware of the duality of his being and his separation from the world and that he is condemned to be free, but 'free for nothing'. Even as he reads the notice announcing his call-up, he is aware that his life has suddenly changed: the past and all his former projects for the future fall away behind him, leaving him floating in an uncertain present. If war cuts Mathieu off from himself in a historical or temporal sense, that feeling of separation achieves its full intensity as he stands looking at his hand on the stone balustrade of the Pont-Neuf and becomes aware in existential terms of his separation from himself and from the world:

> Aussi inséparable du monde que la lumière et pourtant exilé, comme la lumière, glissant à la surface des pierres et de l'eau, sans que rien, jamais, ne m'accroche ou ne m'ensable. Dehors. Dehors. Hors du monde, hors du passé, hors de moi-même: la liberté c'est l'exil et je suis condamné à être libre.

At the collapse of the army and the fall of France, described in *La Mort dans l'âme*, all Mathieu's feelings of inadequacy and helplessness are heightened in the face of a defeat which he, and the other ordinary soldiers, are forced to take upon themselves. He is particularly angry that they will be judged as 'les vaincus de 40', and at the ease with which some of his fellow soldiers can seemingly accept defeat. Again it is Mathieu's lucidity itself and his relentless analysis of the situation which isolate him from the others and constantly reveal to him his own shortcomings and the impossibility of his position. And in a mood of complete frustration the intellectual, who has clung to his concept of personal freedom to the last, now longs to lose himself in action: 'S'enfoncer dans un acte inconnu comme dans une forêt. Un acte. Un acte qui engage et qu'on ne comprend jamais tout à fait.' Mathieu does in fact take part in a last-ditch stand against the invading German army, but the final flurry of shots which he fires from the church tower is described as an orgy of symbolic destruction and despair in which he fulfils himself in a completely negative manner: 'Je décide que la mort était le sens secret de ma vie, que j'ai vécu pour mourir; je meurs pour témoigner qu'il est impossible de vivre. . . .' But the last part of this volume and the fragment of the uncompleted volume 4 (*La Dernière Chance*) largely centre on the political clash between Brunet and Schneider in the prisoner-of-war camp. Schneider, the ex-communist who left the Party because of the Soviet-Nazi pact, attacks the Party and its newspaper, *L'Humanité*, for destroying with their abstractions the workers' ability to defend themselves and their situation. He also attacks Brunet's commitment to a party-line of which he cannot be sure. Brunet is a tough, self-disciplined man wanting to make his fellow prisoners face the horror of their situation, whilst they are more concerned with 'leur petit bonheur têtu'. But his trust in the U.S.S.R. and his desire to use the situation in which he finds himself are shaken by news of the pact. And his sense of personal loss at Schneider's death as they try to escape finally overrides his sense of political loyalty.

Though Brunet finally awakens, through this friendship, to a feeling of personal suffering which tempers and perhaps necessarily undermines unflinching political commitment, he cannot be judged on the same scale as the individualistic Mathieu. Sartre may have felt unable to develop his novel in terms of positive political action in which the individual would achieve meaning in his life, but he does leave one of his central characters poised on the knife-edge of a fuller and deeper personal and historical awareness where Malraux's Manuel stands. And such a moment compensates in some measure for the artistic unevenness of the work. For the intensity of such experience and the complex dimensions of the situation combine to give the 'novel of action' a range and power which has too rarely been achieved in more recent French fiction.

NOTE

ANTOINE DE SAINT-EXUPÉRY, 1900–44, was born in Lyons, educated in Paris, and joined an aviation regiment for his national service in 1921. His passion for flying dates from this period and in 1926 he joined the Compagnie Générale d'Entreprises Aéronautiques which was beginning long-distance commercial flights. He flew on the Toulouse–Casablanca airmail service and went to South America in 1929 as the director of the Aeroposta Argentina service from Buenos Aires to Punta Arenas. With the success of *Vol de nuit* (1931) he decided to spend more time writing. He visited Moscow and Spain as a journalist (1935–7) and also tried to break two air records in 1935 and 1938 but crashed on both occasions. In 1939 he returned to flying with 2/33 squadron in northern France and later Algeria. In 1941 he went to the United States but rejoined his old squadron in 1942. Having been allowed five more flights after a crash-landing, he was shot down over Corsica on his ninth mission.

ANDRÉ MALRAUX was born in Paris in 1901 and educated there. He visited Cambodia in 1923–4 on an archaeological expedition with his first wife, Clara, and was sentenced to three years' imprisonment for removing statues from a Buddhist temple. He was subsequently granted a stay of execution. In 1925–6 he returned to Indo-China, helped to found a revolutionary newspaper, and also visited China very briefly. He went back to China in 1931 and again in 1934. He also attended the Writers' Congress in Moscow in the latter year. He fought in the International Brigade in the Spanish Civil War and then toured the United States on behalf of the Republican cause. He was captured at the fall of France (1940) but escaped and joined the Resistance. In 1944 he served as a brigade commander in Alsace and was Minister of Information in de Gaulle's Provisional Government in 1945. When de Gaulle returned to power in May 1958 Malraux soon became Minister of State for Cultural Affairs, a post which he held until de Gaulle's resignation in 1969.

Biographical details for Camus and Sartre will be found in the Note at the end of chapter 13 of the present volume.

Editions. A Pléiade edition of Saint-Exupéry's works was published in 1954 and this includes the novels together with *Le Petit Prince*, *Citadelle*, and *Lettre à un otage*. The novels are also readily available in Livre de Poche editions. Two collections of letters have been published: *Lettres de Jeunesse* (1953) and *Lettres à sa mère* (1955).

There is no complete edition of Malraux's works, but *Les Conquérants* (1928), *La Voie royale* (1930), *La Condition humaine* (1933), and *L'Espoir* (1937) have been published by Gallimard in the 'Collection Soleil' together with the first volume of his *Antimémoires* (1967). The major novels are also available in Livre de Poche and an edition of *La Condition humaine*, with a useful introduction by C. Jenkins, was published in 1968. There are two other novels: *Le Temps du mépris* (1935) and *Les Noyers de l'Altenburg* (1943). Malraux has also published two important essays, *La Tentation de l'Occident* (1926) and *D'une jeunesse européenne* (1927), and a number of works on various aspects of art: *La Psychologie de l'art* (1947-9) which was reissued with revisions as *Les Voix du silence* (1951), *Le Musée imaginaire de la sculpture mondiale* (3 vols., 1952-4), and *La Métamorphose des dieux* (1957).

An edition of Camus's works, which includes his novels and plays, together with his literary, philosophical, and political essays, was published in six volumes in 1962 by L'Imprimerie nationale Sauret. There is also a two-volume Pléiade edition, *Théâtre, récits et nouvelles* and *Essais*, edited by R. Quilliot (1962-5). *L'Étranger* (1942) and *La Peste* (1947) are again available in Livre de Poche and an edition of *La Peste* (ed. W. Strachan) was published by Methuen in 1959. Camus's two major philosophical essays, *Le Mythe de Sisyphe* (1942) and *L'Homme révolté* (1951), are available in the Gallimard 'Idées' series. Two volumes of *Carnets* have also been published (1962 and 1964).

Sartre's novels, which were first published by Gallimard, are available in Livre de Poche. A volume of 'mémoires', *Les Mots*, describing his childhood, appeared in 1964. Of his plays *Les Mouches* (1943), *Huis clos* (1945), *Morts sans sépulture* and *La Putain respectueuse* (1946), *Les Mains sales* (1948), *Le Diable et le bon Dieu* (1951), and *Les Séquestrés d'Altona* (1959) are likewise available in Livre de Poche. His major philosophical works are *L'Être et le Néant* (1943) and *Critique de la raison dialectique* (1960). Important literary and political essays are contained in the various volumes of *Situations*. In *Situations I* (1947) there are essays on Faulkner, Mauriac, and Camus amongst others and *Situations II* (1948) contains the long essay, 'Qu'est-ce que la littérature?', in which Sartre discusses the notion of 'committed' writing.

Criticism. The following list of critical works represents no more than a selection from the many books which are concerned with the various philosophical, political, and literary problems raised by so much twentieth-century literature. Among those which deal with writers in a largely political or general intellectual framework the following are particularly recommended: M. Adereth, *Commitment in Modern French Literature* (1967); R.-M. Albérès, *L'Aventure intellectuelle du*

XXᵉ siècle (1950); V. Brombert, *The Intellectual Hero* (1960); D. Caute, *Communism and the French Intellectuals* (1964); R. Pierce, *Contemporary French Political Thought* (1966), and R. Stéphane, *Portrait de l'aventurier* (1950). There are also a number of critical studies which provide a useful historical perspective or emphasize a number of problems of a broadly existential nature and they include: R.-M. Albérès, *La Révolte des écrivains d'aujourd'hui* (1949); P. de Boisdeffre, *Métamorphose de la littérature* (2 vols., 1950); P.-H. Simon's *L'Homme en procès* (1949), *Témoins de l'Homme* (1951), and his two-volume study *Histoire de la littérature française au XXᵉ siècle* (1957); and C. Sénéchal, *Les Grands Courants de la littérature française contemporaine* (1934), which contains useful material on the 1920s. Mention should also be made of B. T. Fitch, *Le Sentiment d'étrangeté chez Malraux, Sartre, Camus et Simone de Beauvoir* (1964). Finally, essays or chapters devoted to the novelists under discussion are contained in these books on the modern novel: G. Brée and M. Guiton, *An Age of Fiction* (1957); J. Cruickshank (ed.), *The Novelist as Philosopher* (1962); H. Peyre, *The Contemporary French Novel* (1955).

I have again selected only a few of the books devoted specifically to the four authors. The three English and three French books on Malraux cover various aspects of his work: D. Boak, *André Malraux* (1968); W. M. Frohock, *André Malraux and the Tragic Imagination* (1952); D. Wilkinson, *Malraux: an Essay in Political Criticism* (1967); J. Hoffmann, *L'Humanisme de Malraux* (1963); C. Mauriac, *Malraux ou le mal du héros* (1945); G. Picon, *Malraux par lui-même* (1953).

The following books provide a fairly balanced view of Saint-Exupéry: R.-M. Albérès, *Saint-Exupéry* (1961); L. Estang, *Saint-Exupéry par lui-même* (1956); J.-C. Ibert, *Saint-Exupéry* (1960). There is also an interesting chapter on Saint-Exupéry in E. W. Knight, *Literature considered as Philosophy: the French Example* (1957).

Several of the following books on Camus deal at some length with both politics and literature: G. Brée, *Camus* (1957); J. Cruickshank, *Albert Camus and the Literature of Revolt* (1959); E. Parker, *The Artist in the Arena* (1965); N. A. Scott, *Camus* (1962); P. Thody, *A. Camus: a Study of his Work* (1957).

Colette Audry's book, *Sartre* (1966), provides a helpful introduction to the most important elements of his philosophy. General studies of both Sartre's philosophy and literature recommended for further reading are: M. Cranston, *Sartre* (1962); F. Jeanson, *Sartre par lui-même* (1955); A. R. Manser, *Sartre: a Philosophical Study* (1966); I. Murdoch, *Sartre* (1953); and P. Thody, *Sartre: a Literary and Political Study* (1960).

15. A Theatre of Victims: The Contemporary French Avant-Garde

'AFTER us the Savage God.' It is tempting to see in W. B. Yeats's remark on the first performance of Alfred Jarry's *Ubu Roi* (11 December 1896) a brilliant guess about the future of the European *avant-garde* theatre. It would be to exaggerate the quality of the play's insights to view it (as some have done) as a prophetic allegory of the excesses of the totalitarian state but, in certain significant respects, it can properly be said to prefigure our contemporary 'drama of the absurd'. This is not to argue that Beckett or Ionesco, Adamov, Arrabal or Tardieu are directly indebted to *Ubu Roi* or show any particular awareness of it as a model, but simply that it opens up ways of staging, modes of 'theatricalizing' experience from which they have profited. The casual savagery of the plot already suggests something of the character of this novel farce. In *Ubu Roi* a gross, cowardly, and grotesque buffoon, Ubu, egged on by his monstrous wife, turns on his king, murders him and most of the royal family, proclaims himself king of Poland and inaugurates a reign of terror with the help of a 'disembraining' machine. Ubu is eventually defeated by the army of the Russian Czar and forced to take refuge in a cave in Lithuania before escaping to France, presumably to resume his activities there.

The broad farcical tone and the hectic tempo of the action are crucial to the distinctive effects produced by *Ubu Roi*. As a play, it radicalizes the medium by inflating the role of violence and making it one of the central and unifying metaphors of the theatrical experience and by using the stage as a weapon for thoroughly unnerving the polite audience. It also marks something of a revolution in the aesthetics of the modern stage, in the sense that it exploits a stylized set of conventions in which heavy simplification (both visual and of character) combines with metaphoric suggestiveness to displace the literalness of naturalistic drama, and in which traditional techniques of clowning, reminiscent of the *commedia dell' arte* and the music-hall, are revived so as to reinforce the moral outrage implicit in the action. For example, Jarry specifies a mask for Père Ubu, cardboard horses' heads for the Russian cavalry, and the adoption of a single plain set or back-drop against which a 'formally dressed' actor can carry on a printed placard (in the manner of the Elizabethan stage) so as to indicate the precise location of the action. He also recommends reducing crowds to one or two actors so that battles or public gatherings can be conventionally suggested rather than actually represented. He further urges the claims of 'neutral' costumes in place of elaborate confections designed with an eye to 'local colour' and historical accuracy.

Jarry's characters echo the anti-realistic style of his settings: they are incongruous or frankly grotesque, closer to animated puppets than to the real-life facsimiles of naturalistic drama. Of course, the legendary and dream-like heroes of symbolist plays (Maeterlinck's *La Princesse Maleine*, 1889, or *Pelléas et Mélisande*, 1892) had already undermined traditional notions of character in the drama, but the degree to which Jarry, in the figures of Ubu and his wife, tends to diminish 'character', so far as that implies moral and psychological complexity, and to give expression to fantasy and obsession, seems to anticipate our contemporary French *avant-garde*. Besides, the blithe cruelty and the elements of coarse verbal inventiveness ('merdre', 'cornegidouille'), parody and punning help to maintain the puppet characters within a consciously unreal framework. It is true that by drawing on his own eccentric style of life Jarry succeeds in bathing Ubu's antics in an atmosphere of gross but natural and spontaneous fun and, in this respect, *Ubu Roi* differs from the jokes of Jarry's dadaist and surrealist imitators of the 1920s, which seem more self-consciously created in the shadow of Freudian theory. This criticism does not, however, apply to Jarry's contemporary admirer, Guillaume Apollinaire, who revived his techniques, together with their strain of sheer exuberance, in the riotously inconsequential scenes of *Les Mamelles de Tirésias* (1917). This fantasy presents us with a 'collective person' who stands for the people of Zanzibar, an animated newspaper kiosk, jingles and music 'off', and a blue-faced heroine, Thérèse, who has toy balloons for breasts and changes sex when these become detached and float into the air. *Les Mamelles de Tirésias*, like *Ubu Roi*, is characterized by nonchalant eruptions of violence, as when Thérèse, disguised as a fortune-teller, claws and strangles the Policeman who threatens to arrest her, a dramatization of the clash between the claims of instinct and the claims of external authority.

Ubu Roi, with its spirit of anarchy, levity, and schoolboy smut understandably shocked its 90s public. In the uninhibited way in which it allows the predatory and destructive instincts to run riot, it can properly be called subversive and, for this reason, the play's vein of infantilism must be seen not simply as an effect of temperament but also as a flash of insight into the nature of the subconscious self, and as a deliberate tactic for demolishing the 'serious' world of the bourgeoisie. The play offers a vivid metaphor of the lust for power, is rooted in a swollen caricature of the bourgeoisie's acquisitive appetites and moral vacuity, and presents us with a parody of the nature of public authority. However, *Ubu Roi* is also very much centred on the destructive possibilities of the individual personality and, consequently, Jarry's Ubu emerges less as a symbol of the corruption of bourgeois society than as a stage image of the disruptive Freudian *Id* which actually anticipates the general diffusion of Freud's ideas. In retrospect, the slapstick and rather relentless jokiness we encounter in *Ubu Roi* and *Les Mamelles de Tirésias* and which survive, though less spontaneously, in some surrealist fantasies of the 1920s—Tristan Tzara's *Le Cœur à gaz* (1920), for example, or Cocteau's *Les Mariés de la Tour Eiffel* (1921)—impress one by the energy, resilience, even optimism that they imply. Indeed, compared with the 'black' jokes of Beckett and Ionesco, the menace of the early Adamov plays, or the almost demented cruelty of Arrabal (to take a sample of French dramatists of the current theatrical *avant-garde*), Jarry, Apollinaire, and the surrealist playwrights of the 1920s emerge as 'playboys of the Western World' engaged in a familiar, and not too serious, anti-bourgeois game.

Beckett and his contemporaries occupy a very different territory and it might be useful to speculate on how they have got there.

The crucial difference of *temper* between the dadaist and surrealist theatre and the work of today's *avant-garde* playwrights in France stems from the latter's fuller and more intense imaginative awareness of the uniquely revolutionary and destructive character of the thirty years of European history culminating in 1945. Our contemporary dramatists have responded, though with the indirection and distortion characteristic of art, to what can conveniently be called a persuasive 'myth' about the plight of European man since the First World War, the 'Great War' as it is still known, with what we have come to recognize as pardonable hyperbole. By 'myth' here I mean an image of the world which imaginatively embodies the deepest hopes, fears, and needs of a particular society, and which is widely accepted as true and shared by its intellectuals and creative artists. The elements which compose this myth are the product of pressures at work in twentieth-century European society.

These pressures are of two sorts: one physical and the other deriving from scientific theories, the findings of which may be distinguished, in Arnold Toynbee's phrase, as a 'series of morally subversive discoveries'. Of the physical pressures the most noteworthy are: the scale and destructive power of modern warfare, the dramatic growth of urbanization and technology, the impact of large-scale economic crises, and the ruthless organization of the coercive power of the state to serve secular ideologies like nazism and communism. Many of these factors were already prevalent in the late nineteenth century but were dangerously aggravated in the twentieth. For example, the wars of 1914-18 and 1939-45 occasioned human and material losses unparalleled until then, while mass-society is largely a creation of the inter-war period when an accelerated process of urbanization was combined with revolutionary developments in mass-communications, with all that these imply of distortion of language for purposes of political propaganda. In a comparable way, mass-unemployment, with its generalization of despair, is a product of the ruinous inflation precipitated in Germany by the ending of the First World War and the breakdown of the economic system which occurred in the wake of the American depression of 1929.

These events and forces had profound repercussions on political, social, and moral values. Many sensitive and alert minds felt not only that men were in danger of being depersonalized and de-humanized by their environment, but also that they were victims of forces they could control only imperfectly. The 'Great War' itself was often seen as representing the liquidation of traditional values, and the Bolshevik Revolution of 1917 and the wide diffusion among the European intelligentsia of the Marxist critique of the capitalist system undermined confidence in the rationality of Western European society. New scientific theories seemed to challenge still further man's assumptions about his own nature and situation. Among these one must count the implications of Freud for the idea of the self, and theories about the structure of the physical universe, notably those of Einstein in his 'General Theory of Relativity' (1915). It is true that, outside specialist circles, the influence of these ideas was often in inverse proportion to any exact understanding of them, as Saint-Exupéry noted with dismay in comparing the reactions of the educated public to Pirandello's plays and Einstein's scientific concepts: 'Ils ne voulaient plus rien comprendre à rien, éprouver un grand désarroi, sentir l'aile de l'inconnu.' Though it was by no means clear what new world-picture was going to emerge from the welter of revolutionary theories, such ideas were widely held to confirm the dissolution of traditional values and beliefs about the nature of man and his place in the world.

Here there was already latent a notion of the 'absurd', not as an elaborate philosophic position (in the manner of Camus's *Le Mythe de Sisyphe*) but as a kind of intense intuition that the world no longer made sense. Man, whether conceived as the prey of un-conscious impulses or as adrift in a universe which had ceased to offer the intelligible structure of the mechanistic universe of the nineteenth century, seemed to have lost density and stability. The mood was often one of bafflement and confusion, as was natural in the face of rapid technical and social change and the breakdown of traditional political systems. The sense of being victims, which was engendered by war and economic crisis, was reinforced by man's estrangement from the machines his ingenuity had created. Fear of the machine inhabits Expressionistic drama of the 1920s, provides the graphic imagery of the Čapeks' robot play *RUR* (1921), and feeds the satiric energy of Chaplin's classic film, *Modern Times* (1936). The notion of the impending collapse of European civilization, implied in Spengler's study of the mortality of civilizations, *The Decline of the West* (1918-22), seemed increasingly to be borne out by the systematic terror practised by the totalitarian states of Italy, Germany, and the Soviet Union; by Nazi persecution of the Jews and other 'inferior' races; and by the prospect of global destruction made possible through the invention of nuclear weapons.

The interplay of these forces gives birth to a vision of the world marked by violence, incoherence, and desolation, and it is to this vision, lacking any ultimate revelation of meaning and magnifying the loneliness, vulnerability, despair, and inhumanity of men, that dramatists like Beckett, Ionesco, Adamov, and Arrabal respond. Though deeply subjective, it is also a persuasive vision. These playwrights invent imaginary forms for expressing fears, doubts, and anxieties which may well be rooted in private obsession but which transcend the experience of the individual and speak of our common lot, of the situation of our society. If I do not think of Jean Genet's plays as touching our common humanity in quite the same way, it is because I find that the sado-masochistic rituals of his homosexual outcasts and the inflated poetic conceits of his language stylize human conflict and despair in too narrow and narcissistic a spirit. I am not led by these perverted rites to an illumination of the larger predicaments in which men find themselves as masters and slaves, leaders and led, victims and executioners.

The image of man which is so often embodied in the plays of Beckett and the others, and which is communicated to us in tones varying from the anguished to the balefully comic, is that of a *victim* in an ambiguous world deprived of acceptable systems of value and belief. This figure experiences suffering (or, at the very least, harsh misunderstanding) and knows the anxiety which comes from the fear of losing personal identity and human dignity. The spirit of such plays is far from the playful anarchism of Jarry, Apollinaire, and the surrealist playwrights of the 1920s. It is equally remote from the way in which dramatists of the interwar years like Gide, Cocteau, and Giraudoux (if we except the almost apocalyptic vision of his *Sodome et Gomorrhe*, 1943) revive and rehandle ancient myths. Such drama is the vehicle of self-conscious irony and detachment; it reflects the sceptical dance of intelligence, and Cocteau's reworking of the legend of Oedipus in *La Machine infernale* (1934) is symptomatic of it. He boldly emphasizes the incestuous nature of the bond between Oedipus and Jocasta and, in the process, signals knowingly over the heads of the actors to an audience modishly attuned to Freudian concepts.

In exploiting Biblical or Greek myths, Gide, Cocteau, and Giraudoux appealed to a tradition of educated discourse and assumed the frame of reference of a common, inherited culture— their natural audience would be drawn from those who had passed through lycées and universities. What characterizes the imagined worlds of Beckett, Ionesco, the early Adamov, and Arrabal is their greater *immediacy*, the way in which they confront us with a more intensely personal and idiosyncratic vision of experience and expect us to take it on trust, on its own terms. Of course, Cocteau and Giraudoux do have their own language, sensibility, and characteristic way of looking at the world, and we respond to them, gratefully recognizing and enjoying the stylized image of life they set forth on the stage but feeling too that, in spite of their acknowledged individuality, we are *at home* in much of the universe they have created. By comparison, the worlds of Beckett and the others are more radically strange and autonomous. This is true even though scholars constantly detect erudite echoes in Beckett—Dante's 'Marsh of Styx' in *En attendant Godot*, for example, or Zeno's 'heap of millet' in *Happy Days*[1]—for our understanding of the nature of the experience embodied in these plays in no sense depends on our identifying the philosophic echoes or recognizing their significance. They survive, perhaps, as a private joke in the text but

[1] I quote the titles of plays in the language in which they were originally written, though Beckett has versions of them in French and English.

they do not affect the feeling produced in us of entering unknown territory.

All the theatre of Samuel Beckett (1906-   ), and notably *En attendant Godot* (1953), *Fin de partie* (1957), and *Happy Days* (1961), is a sustained meditation on death. His familiarity with a long tradition of metaphysical speculation ranging from Democritus to Augustine, Aquinas, Dante, and Descartes, lies behind his manner of leading his audience towards sudden and unnerving confrontations with the haunting reality of death and decay. His breathtaking originality is to have vitalized this meditation and to have made his own radical pessimism communicable and bearable to a modern public by harnessing it to the techniques of the circus and the music-hall, and by investing the patter, 'props', and 'business' of the cross-talk comedian with the power to shock us into an awareness of our mortality, our 'naked and unaccommodated' state.

A concern with man's physical and spiritual indigence is central to this theatre and is coupled with a fierce and unrelenting scepticism about all kinds of optimistic rationalism that tend to mask man's metaphysical plight as a lonely and impotent creature in a hostile universe. Beckett's chosen metaphors for conveying that plight—tramps, invalids, victims, cell-like rooms or barren landscapes—have the generality necessary to a dramatist who never ceases to see man in the light of eternity, but they also seem to me to carry with them an aura, a weight of implication, an emotional charge that are specific to our time. These, however much they lie at the back of our minds, help to produce the shock of recognition we experience and the paradoxical sense of involvement we feel with creatures apparently so remote from us. Behind the tramps there are at least the shadows of those refugees made homeless by war or change of political regime; behind the bare, confining rooms an echo, at least, of prison cells; behind Pozzo's whipping of Lucky in *En attendant Godot*, Hamm's malignant treatment of his parents in *Fin de partie*, or Winnie's suffering under constant burning light in *Happy Days*, a fleeting image of the camps and torture-chambers of modern Europe; behind the birdless and desolate terrain glimpsed through the window in *Fin de partie*, a prefiguration of nuclear war.

Not that the waste outside the window can be confidently interpreted in that way alone. Like many of Beckett's images, it is plurivalent: it is a device for intensifying the isolation and despair of the men in the room; an image of the gap between the finite mind and the mystery of the universe; and, finally, an allusion to nuclear devastation: 'Mais enfin quel est votre espoir? Que la terre renaisse au printemps? Que la mer et les rivières redeviennent poissonneuses . . .?' All that need be said here is that, though Beckett's integral pessimism is almost certainly native to him and prior to the great public catastrophes of this century, his plays reveal, in the graphic force of their central images, the degree to which this pessimism has been sensitized by the specific horrors and excesses of our time.

Beckett's stage world is a world of stasis, a closed system in which the same themes and situations persistently recur and in which all activity tends to end in a necessary failure. The ritual of failure is what gives the plays their circular structure—the identical phrase closing the first and last acts of *En attendant Godot*, the almost hieratic image of Hamm, with bloodstained handkerchief over his face, brooding over the opening and closing of the action in *Fin de partie*. There is no progress, little technology (except for the car and locomotive in *All that Fall*, 1957), and such consumer goods as survive—the tape-recorder in *Krapp's Last Tape* (1958) or the contents of Winnie's handbag in *Happy Days*—only serve to stress the general privation. The human body shares in this indigence. At best, it is an incompetent and failing mechanism, the source of scatological jokes—Krapp's constipation, for example, or Vladimir's bladder trouble in *En attendant Godot*. At worst, it is diseased, decaying, afflicted with blindness, paralysed (as with Hamm), or mutilated—the case of Nagg and Nell, Hamm's parents. By these deliberate exercises in the grotesque, Beckett compels us to assent to the tyranny of our physical nature, perhaps so as to reaffirm the essential misery of man even in sophisticated societies. His characters appear in degrading postures: on all fours, stuffed into bins or jars, roped like performing animals (Lucky in *En attendant Godot*), and all inhabiting what has been called a 'paradise of indignity', the very image of man's inhumanity to man.

They are set down in featureless wastes which mock their frailty—the desolate beach of the radio-play, *Cascando* (1963), the mound in which Winnie is embedded—or else, pent up in cells—Krapp's squalid room, the dimly lit refuge that contains Hamm and his shambling servant, Clov. The image of men in cells is taken to the point of caricature in the dust-bins in which Hamm confines his clownish parents or the three grey urns in which husband, wife, and mistress are trapped in *Play* (performed in German translation in 1963, but first staged in English in 1964).

All these characters suffer or inflict suffering, and are usually linked together in a double-act: master and slave, victim and torturer—a relationship, in the case of Vladimir and Estragon, Hamm and Clov, vaguely reminiscent of the film comedians Laurel and Hardy. The characters who make up these couples insult each other, quarrel, even persecute one another, but are inextricably bound together. Each partner exists as a mirror for the other and depends òn the other for his own sense of being alive. So important, in Beckett's theatre, is another person to share one's predicament, so strong the need for a witness to one's own life, that, if no partner exists, it becomes necessary to invent him. So Krapp rescues himself from his solitary state and reaffirms his own identity by setting the tape-recorder in motion.

Beckett's is a world haunted by time; and Estragon, one of the tramps in *En attendant Godot*, typifies it. His memory is poor and confused; he blurs past and present and experiences time as an endless continuum, a kind of agony. Though time perpetually threatens to seize up or congeal, it never quite does. It lapses slowly and encapsulates the characters in an elastic 'here and now'. 'Ils ne bougent pas', say the stage directions at the close of the first and last acts of *En attendant Godot*, and Vladimir and Estragon do not move—because there is nowhere to go in Beckett's world. All they can do is wait, learn patience, endure the slow attrition of time, though their waiting is listless and unsupported by any vital faith. Waiting is nothing more than the hope that identity and meaning will reveal themselves in the world, just as wisdom is stoically learning to expect nothing. No revelation is ever vouchsafed to Beckett's characters: Godot never comes. Perhaps Lucky is so called because his experience of the arbitrariness and cruelty of life at Pozzo's hands has deprived him of expectations.

Caught in this monotonous world, on the edge of silence and timelessness, Beckett's characters fight the inertia with anything that comes to hand. The tramps of *En attendant Godot* respond with horseplay, physical jerks, clownish games with bowler hats. Others handle language, that most distinctively human gift, with a kind of creative brio. In fact, they become involved in Pascalian 'diversion' or 'distraction', so as to avoid confronting the fact of their mortality. The tramps' puns and jokes, Krapp's tenderly poetic evocation of the loved girl in the boat, Hamm's story about the starving man who presents himself at the rich man's door, Winnie's sentimental recapturing of the past, are all consciously rhetorical devices for masking the progress of bodily decay, redeeming the insignificance of life, and holding death at bay. The *vox humana* sounds over a darkening world peopled with victims, but that voice is stoical to the end and is epitomized in Winnie's half-remembered literary tag: 'laughing wild amid severest woe'.

Though the energy of stoic laughter may rescue Beckett's theatre from total gloom, it remains an implacable world, and the exceptional verbal and structural economy which characterizes it reinforces this impression. By comparison, the plays of Eugène Ionesco (1912–   ), though strikingly consistent in theme and imagery, present a more elaborate and expansive creation. There is certainly a persistent vein of metaphysical anguish present in Ionesco's plays—they have their obsessions and nightmares—but they also have their pockets of genial fun and are often aerated by a sense of wonder and a spontaneous comic fantasy. These he supports with all the mechanical resources of the stage: bold visual metaphors, as when Jean, in a profane transcription of the iconography of the Sacred Heart, draws the branch of briar out of his heart in *La Soif et la faim* (1966); visual jokes, like Roberte II's three noses in *Jacques ou la soumission* (1955); choreographic groupings; and complicated lighting plots for varying mood and perspective, as in the contrast between the triumphal brilliance bathing the 'Emperor's' entrance in *Les Chaises* (1952) and the dim, aqueous light of the 'end of time' which falls over the closing scene. Ionesco's plays are, in fact, heavily stylized, reposing on the principle that theatre, true to its own nature, should 'theatricalize' experience; that is, magnify, exaggerate, and distort effects so as to create a novel synthesis of the real and the imaginary. The idiom is concrete and highly responsive to the visual possibilities of the stage. Ionesco puts the matter succinctly in his collection of essays, *Notes et contre-notes* (1962): theatre is

... une construction, une architecture mouvante d'images scéniques. ... Tout est permis au théâtre: incarner des personnages, mais aussi matérialiser des angoisses, des présences intérieures. Il est donc non seulement permis, mais recommandé de faire jouer les accessoires, faire vivre les objets, animer les décors, concrétiser les symboles.

His practice is faithful to his prescriptions. In *Amédée ou comment s'en débarrasser* (1954), the enormous corpse growing in the room next door makes tangible, in the most surprising and direct way, the remorse and sterility in the relationship between Amédée and his wife Madeleine, for whom love is dead, just as the multiplying rhinoceroses of *Rhinocéros* (1960) make concrete, in the most vivid fashion, man's alienation from himself through collective hysteria. The motive power behind the plays conceived within this aesthetic framework derives from Ionesco's conviction that the common humanity we share can be identified with our 'anguish', our 'unfathomable longings', our fear of death and our striving for the absolute. Consequently, his plays are intended to appeal from the depths of his own subjectivity to the subjectivity of others, a process which risks exaggerating the interest and significance of certain private obsessions and converting the play into a therapeutic exercise, of value chiefly to the dramatist. Ionesco reposes considerable faith in the virtues of the dreaming mind because he prizes inwardness as the counter to the purely social realm, viewed by him as uniquely sterile, the source of fraud, lies, violence, and empty or 'automatic' behaviour.

The typical conflict in Ionesco's plays is, therefore, between a social medium which dehumanizes and alienates man, with the aid of political ideology and the manipulation of language, and the lonely individual, prey to anguish and depression, but capable of transcending the cruelty and banality of life in moments of creativity and love, brief epiphanies of joy. This conflict is sometimes expressed in terms of an 'Everyman', an archetype who embodies the continuing concerns and needs of all men everywhere, and a stereotype who is the product of a particular society, wholly assimilated to it, and the prisoner of its values. 'Bérenger', who appears in several of Ionesco's plays, and so helps to create the sense of a self-consistent mythical world, is Ionesco's preferred archetype. He is sacrificed to the Killer, the embodiment of radical and irreducible evil, in *Tueur sans gages* (1959), and returns in *Rhinocéros* as the solitary human survivor in a society of wild beasts. Here, Ionesco's passion for concrete visual detail has its dangers. To see the mindlessness of fascist ideology in terms of a society of stupid pachyderms is one thing; to make the metaphor literal and change men into rhinoceroses on stage is to risk destroying the metaphor in a welter of pantomime. Only Bérenger's distraught perseverance in his human condition saves the day. Alone on the stage, surrounded by the trumpeting of beasts from every quarter, his agony and vulnerability compel our involvement and help us accept the bizarre stage effects as a necessary means of throwing his humanity into relief.

Elsewhere, the passion pays off less equivocally. For example, Ionesco uses concrete forms to support a metaphoric system which underlies much of his work: the dichotomy between 'évanescence ou lourdeur . . . transparence ou opacité . . . du vide et du trop de présence'. These metaphors express the swing between two poles of experience which characterize Ionesco's view of life: elation and despair; sense of transcendence and sense of mortality; bliss and banality. He manipulates these metaphors scenically, setting the blue sky, radiant flowers, and serene light of the 'cité radieuse' in *Tueur sans gages* against the dark and joyless clutter of Bérenger's own room (his social home), or the magical silver bridge of *Le Piéton de l'air* (1963) against Bérenger's vision of endless marching columns of headless victims or his wife Josephine's nightmare encounter in which 'John Bull' executes English children with a machine-gun. This dichotomy of images is epitomized in the contrast between Amédée's final ascent into the sky (*Amédée*) or

Bérenger's levitation (*Le Piéton de l'air*) and the hectic prolifera-
tion of objects we meet elsewhere in Ionesco's theatre: chairs in
Les Chaises; mushrooms in *Amédée*; furniture and ornaments in
Le Nouveau locataire (1955); noses in *Jacques ou la soumission*. These
are, perhaps, tangible stage metaphors for the variety of impedi-
ments which human beings confront in their struggle to achieve
happiness and integrity. They may respectively suggest wild
dreams of power; guilt and remorse; suffocation by material pos-
sessions and technology; surrender to social convention and
hysteria.

Cumulatively, they point to a theatre in which a surrealistic verve
of invention is exploited to communicate vivid fears about personal
identity and mortality which, increasingly in Ionesco's theatre, are
coloured by problems particular to our epoch: the encroachments
of centralized society, the terrorism of totalitarian states, the threat
of nuclear holocaust. It may well be that Ionesco is a naturally
religious spirit—there are mystical strains in his autobiographical
writings, as in the moving attempt to 'live' the experience of dying
which forms the core of *Le Roi se meurt* (1962)—but these metaphysical aspirations are given particular intensity and forlorness
through being set against a menacing world in which social order
and authority are shown to be dangerous shams, and in which
degradation and falsification of language, in cliché, platitude, and
propaganda, lead to degradation of feeling and thought.

Clichés and distorted proverbs (the signs of conventional
wisdom) accumulate like a dead language in *La Cantatrice chauve*
(1950) but they do not simply imply the impoverishment of the
moral and emotional lives of those interchangeable identities, the
Smiths and the Martins. They point also to language as the mask
and instrument of aggression and to social man as an aggressive and
lubricious animal. The violence of *La Cantatrice chauve* is verbal
and the apparently nonsensical formulas, puns, etc., are weapons
of aggression, not means of rational communication. After all, the
invading Martins oust the occupying Smiths. This idea is given its
most explicit political resonance in *La Leçon* (1951) where the
Professor's pupil succumbs to his *verbal* rape, a metaphor for the
triumph of propaganda since, in several productions, the Maid

slips a swastika armband over the Professor's arm. She thus relieves him of remorse, the armband acting as a charm which 'legitimizes' man's aggressive nature through political ideology. In a similar way, the scene, in *Victimes du devoir* (1953), where Choubert's mouth is ruthlessly stuffed with bread, is, among other things, a scene of torture imposed by Authority, in the shape of the Policeman, and connived at by the public (Nicolas and Madeleine) who stand by indifferently. One critic plausibly thinks of this scene as an echo of the Italian Fascists' practice of dosing their victims with castor oil. Examples could be multiplied to show how much of Ionesco's theatre, for all its charge of private obsession, is also a theatre of *public* themes, from the coffins and mass-murder hinted at in *La Leçon* and the suggestion of a devastated world surrounding the island in *Les Chaises*, to the fable about fascism in *Rhinocéros* and the bombing and destruction glimpsed by Bérenger in the visionary moments of *Le Piéton de l'air*. In this theatre, man is repeatedly humiliated, threatened, or tortured; a victim striving to escape a world of aggression when he is not himself its agent.

As with all deeply idiosyncratic creators, the danger facing Beckett and Ionesco is that of self-parody. Deprived of the metaphysical anguish that moves his major plays, the idiom and properties assembled by Beckett begin to wear an air of contrivance. What begins in *En attendant Godot* as a manner of despairing, ends, in the outlandish 'eternal triangle' of *Play*, as a mannered despair. In much the same way, what begins as an original comic fancy in *La Cantatrice chauve* or *Amédée*, declines, with the 'faery' properties and effects of *Le Piéton de l'air*, into a feyness and whimsicality worthy of J. M. Barrie. This risk of self-parody is also implicit in the oppressively narrow imaginary worlds conjured up by Adamov and Arrabal, worlds in which echoes of Kafka are insistently present.

In his early plays (up to *Le Ping-Pong*, 1955) Arthur Adamov (1908–   ) acts out the obsessions of a profoundly disturbed mind and confronts us with an image of life that is moved by guilt, fear of unmerited punishment, and anxiety about the reality of the individual self. In *Le Sens de la marche* (1953) and *Les Retrouvailles* (1955), the self is prey to the tyranny of parental love. In the first, the son revenges himself by murdering his grotesque father's companion and *alter ego*; in the second, the son is wholly subjected to the power of the mother, a fact symbolized by the burlesque violence of the final scene in which she wheels him off in a perambulator. These themes are orchestrated in larger, public contexts which reflect Adamov's acute awareness of the catastrophes of our time, and which reaffirm the helplessness and isolation of man. In the ferocious allegory of *La grande et la petite manœuvre* (1950), the 'Mutilated One', the eternal victim, is caught between rival factions which reduce him to a mere trunk in a wheel-chair, while in *Tous contre tous* (1953) the war waged against the people who limp by antagonists who are barely distinguishable from them, is a transparent image of the cruel and senseless persecution of the Jews.

The strong sense of human suffering and impotence which animates Adamov's theatre is intensified in the savage rituals which mark the plays of Fernando Arrabal (1932–   ), plays rooted in Arrabal's own experience of civil war and dictatorship in Spain, with their accompanying terror, coercion, torture, and betrayal. What Arrabal does is to reorder that experience within the framework of a fantasy-world owing much to the vision of Goya and Kafka. This world is peopled exclusively by victims and executioners and dominated by characters with the mentality of perverse children, who veer between spontaneous tenderness and shocking violence and who yet raise, in paradoxical (and sometimes blasphemous) fashion, problems of good and evil. They are, in the popular sense, 'holy terrors', but without being at all 'holy simpletons'. In *Fando et Lis*, Fando beats his paralysed girl, Lis, to death because she has broken his little drum, but, faithful to his promise, he turns up at the cemetery with dog and flower to salute her memory. In *Picque-nique en campagne* (1959), Zapo's parents are too simple to grasp the horrors of modern war and so join him on the battlefield, where they are wiped out by gunfire at their picnic. The parody of the Passion of Christ which forms the core of *Le Cimetière des voitures*, and which ends with the trumpet-player Emanou (Emmanuel) dying with his arms outstretched on the handles of a bicycle, only serves to emphasize

the tragic impossibility of pursuing goodness in a world conspicuously devoid of an ethical sense. Over each of these plays,
and over *Les Deux Bourreaux*, where Maurice is eventually led
to accept his mother's torture of his father as morally right, falls
the shadow of the moral confusions, irrational cruelties, and divided
loyalties of modern European war and politics.

The experimental playlets of Jean Tardieu (1903–   ) rehandle
many of these themes and reflect the vision of man as victim of a
hostile world, object of undefined menace, and slave of mechanical
social conventions. The humiliation of the pompous professor in *La
Politesse inutile* (1950), who is assaulted by a shabby and sinister
visitor, not only prefigures the arbitrary humiliation of the scholar
accused of obscene conduct in Adamov's *Le Professeur Taranne*
(1953) but epitomizes a shifting and treacherous world where men
are never safe or certain. *Qui est là?* (1940) is even more obviously
haunted, as Tardieu himself avers, 'by the profound sense of
tragedy inspired by our still-recent history (after the mass-
extermination of men could Man still be saved?)'. In this play, a
depersonalized family in a bare room is invaded by a mysterious
strangler who murders the father in an eerily dream-like sequence.
The son subsequently summons the father from the dead and he
moves in a strange light through a countryside littered with corpses
—perhaps an image of the world of total war and concentration
camps. The tone in such playlets tends to be portentous and the
plays are structurally too brief and schematic to bear quite the
weight of social and metaphysical implication they are asked to
carry, but, in their glancing, oblique way, they belong with the
more developed creations of Beckett, Ionesco, Adamov, and
Arrabal. The plays of all these dramatists are preeminently theatrical 'games', as distinct from thesis-plays, but they unmistakably
reflect our current concerns. Compared with the *jeux d'esprit* of
Jarry and Apollinaire, they are *jeux d'angoisse*, perhaps the only
drama our time deserves.

K

NOTE

SAMUEL BECKETT was born in 1906 at Foxrock, Dublin, of a Protestant middle-class family, and educated at Trinity College, Dublin, where he took a degree in French and Italian in 1927. He spent the years 1928-30 as *lecteur d'anglais* at the École Normale Supérieur, entered the literary life of Paris, and began a difficult but fruitful association with James Joyce and his experiments with language. After a brief period (1931) as a lecturer in French literature at Trinity College, Dublin, Beckett resigned and travelled about France and Germany before settling in Paris in 1937. He spent part of the German occupation of France hiding from the Gestapo in the Vaucluze countryside. His international fame began with the Paris production of *En attendant Godot* (1953). He was awarded the Nobel prize for literature in 1969.

EUGÈNE IONESCO was born in 1912 in Slatina (Romania) of a French mother, and spent his childhood in France before returning to Romania in 1925. He subsequently took his degree at the University of Bucharest and, from 1936 to 1938, taught French at the lycée in Bucharest, at which point he was awarded a scholarship for research in France, since when he has lived in France. At their original performances his early plays were a complete failure with the public, but in 1953 a laudatory article by Jean Anouilh helped to change the public mood. Ionesco's plays now reach an international audience.

ARTHUR ADAMOV was born in 1908 of a rich family at Kislovodsk in the Caucasus, and educated in schools at Geneva and Mayence before settling as a young man in Paris. Between the wars he participated in the surrealist movement and was a friend of Paul Éluard's. He was interned for a year under the Vichy regime. *L'Aveu* (1946) is a frank account of the fears and obsessions of a profoundly neurotic personality. After 1958 Adamov became an active member of the French Communist Party and his later plays reflect his politics.

Editions. There is no collected edition of Beckett's plays. Apart from the plays mentioned in the chapter, the following have also been produced: *Acte sans paroles I* (1957); *Embers* (1959); *Act without words II* (1960); *Words and Music* (1962); *Eh Joe* (1966); *Va et viens* (1966); and a film scenario, *Film* (1965). An admirably informed edition is *En attendant Godot*, ed. C. Duckworth (1966).

Ionesco's plays are conveniently available in *Théâtre* (4 vols., 1954-66), but valuable insights are contained in his other writings: *La Photo du colonel* (*Nouvelles*) (1962); *Notes et contre-notes* (1962); *Journal en miettes* (1967); *Présent passé, Passé présent* (1968). A useful edition is *Le Roi se meurt*, ed. R. J. North (1966).

Adamov's plays have been collected in *Théâtre* (4 vols., 1953-68) while *Off Limits* (1969) has appeared separately. Autobiographical material which throws light on his early plays is contained in *L'Aveu* (1946) and *L'Homme et l'enfant* (1968). His theories of the stage are to be found in *Ici et maintenant* (1964).

The plays of Arrabal are currently available in *Théâtre* (6 vols., 1958–69), vol. v appearing as *Théâtre panique* (1967).

Jean Tardieu's playlets have been collected in two volumes: *Théâtre de chambre I* (1955; 2nd enlarged edn. 1966) and *Poèmes à jouer: Théâtre II* (1960).

Criticism. Relevant studies of the contemporary European theatre, which include treatment of these dramatists, are: L. Abel, *Metatheatre: a New View of Dramatic Form* (1963); R. N. Coe et al., *Aspects of Drama and the Theatre* (1965); M. Corvin, *Le Théâtre nouveau* (1963); M. Esslin, *The Theatre of the Absurd* (1961); D. I. Grossvogel, *Four Playwrights and a Postscript* (1962); J. Guicharnaud, *Modern French Theatre* (1961; revised edn. 1967); J. Jacquot (ed.), *Le Théâtre moderne: II. Depuis la deuxième guerre mondiale* (1967); P. L. Mignon, *Le Théâtre d'aujourd'hui de A jusqu'à Z* (1966); L. C. Pronko, *Avant-Garde: the experimental theatre in France* (1962); G. Serreau, *Histoire du nouveau théâtre* (1966); J. L. Styan, *The Dark Comedy: the Development of Modern Comic Tragedy* (1962); P. Surer, *Le Théâtre français contemporain* (1964); G. E. Wellwarth, *The Theatre of Protest and Paradox* (1964); Raymond Williams, *Modern Tragedy* (1966).

On the forerunners of the current French *avant-garde* theatre, the most useful studies are: H. Béhar, *Étude sur le théâtre dada et surréaliste* (1967); Dorothy Knowles, *French Drama of the Inter-War Years, 1918–39* (1967); R. Shattuck, *The Banquet Years: the Arts in France, 1885–1918* (1958; paperback edn. 1968).

On Beckett, helpful and illuminating studies include: R. N. Coe, *Samuel Beckett* (1964); Ruby Cohn, *Samuel Beckett: the Comic Gamut* (1962); M. Esslin (ed.), *Samuel Beckett: a collection of critical essays* (1965); J. Fletcher, *Samuel Beckett's Art* (1967); H. Kenner, *Samuel Beckett: a critical study* (1962); A. Marissel, *Beckett* (1963); P. Mélèse, *Beckett* (1966); J. Onimus, *Beckett* (1968); A. Reid, *All I can manage, more than I could: an approach to the plays of Samuel Beckett* (1968); N. A. Scott, *Samuel Beckett* (1965); W. Tindall, *Samuel Beckett* (1964). There are useful, though scattered, insights in the symposium, *Beckett at 60* (1967), and some valuable essays in M. J. Friedmann (ed.), *Configuration critique: Samuel Beckett* (1964).

On Ionesco, sympathetic and interesting essays have been written by: S. Benmussa, *Ionesco* (1966); F. Bradesco, *Le Monde étrange de Ionesco* (1967); R. N. Coe, *Ionesco* (1961); J.-H. Donnard, *Ionesco dramaturge ou l'artisan et le démon* (1966); L. C. Pronko, *Ionesco* (1965); P. Sénart, *Ionesco* (1964).

Valuable for Ionesco's views on the theatre is: C. Bonnefoy, *Entretiens avec Eugène Ionesco* (1966).

Useful for understanding Arrabal is: A. Schifres, *Entretiens avec Arrabal* (1969).

16. The 'Nouveau roman'

THE term *nouveau roman* has been freely used since the late 1950s to describe the novels of writers whose careers in some cases stretch back almost twenty years beyond that date. This time-lag may suggest that the *nouveau roman* is simply a convenient invention of the publicists, a label intended to bring both order and a touch of drama to an otherwise confused and uninteresting situation. But for all the differences which separate the writers labelled *nouveaux romanciers* the term is, as we shall hope to show, a useful and appropriate one.

As far back as 1947 Jean-Paul Sartre had seen that something new was taking place in the French novel. In his preface to Nathalie Sarraute's *Portrait d'un inconnu* he signals the arrival of what he calls the *anti-roman*, thus reviving a term first used in the seventeenth century. The characteristic of the *anti-roman* is that it sets out to question the validity of the novel-form not from without but from within; it is a fictional meditation on the difficulties and, more vitally, the dishonesties of writing a novel. Sartre makes a significant connection between this new manifestation and the temper of the age which produced it: 'Ces œuvres étranges et difficilement classables ne témoignent pas de la faiblesse du genre romanesque, elles marquent seulement que nous vivons à une époque de réflexion et que le roman est en train de réfléchir sur lui-même.'

Sartre's approach to the *anti-roman* is an excellent starting-point for any discussion of the *nouveau roman*, and all that the polemicists of the latter movement might want to add is that the birth of a new form of fiction *does* in fact argue the weakness of the old. Those who practise the *nouveau roman* do so primarily because they consider it impossible or inappropriate today to write novels indistinguishable in form from those of the last century. To do so, as they rightly maintain, is to ignore the innovations of novelists like Proust, Joyce, Kafka, Henry James, and Roussel.

The *nouveau roman*, then, does not decry tradition, it depends on it. Its aim is to show that the novel is a form which needs to evolve, which needs to be brought into line with the other arts, and whose development in this century can equally be interpreted as constituting an organized reflection on the creative process. What we must guard against is the tendency to suppose that the structure of the novel was fixed once and for all by the writers of the nineteenth century, with their consistent 'characters' and logically unfurled 'plots'. The *nouveau roman* belongs to that tradition, often Marxist in inspiration, which sees this confidence and stability as reflecting the complacency and will to exploitation of the middle classes, and itself proposes an art-form which disturbs rather than reassures its public that, in the Victorian poet's words, 'God's in his heaven—All's right with the world.'

The justification for this profound shift is not simply social, of course, but also philosophical. Sustaining the traditional forms of the novel is a philosophy often referred to as naïve realism, which treats the qualities and even the values of the natural world as existing independently of the observer. The nineteenth-century novel is therefore essentialist, convinced that significance is a lasting attribute of persons and things, having been bestowed on them either by God or by a commonly accepted social ethic. Its sequence of events moreover is one of simple cause and effect, reflecting the mechanistic models of contemporary physics and developed in accordance with the public time-scale of the calendar or the clock.

None of this survives in the *nouveau roman*; naïve realism has been replaced by the subjective realism of the phenomenologists, which is, epistemologically speaking, an attempt to resolve the old antinomy of realism and idealism. The phenomenologists do not exalt either the perceiver or the perceived at the expense of the other, but instead fix our awareness on the links which connect them at the moment of perception. This involves what they generally refer to as an 'eidetic reduction' or 'bracketing' of the natural world, which can no longer be allowed to have the field of consciousness entirely to itself, since it must be seen as existing in this time and place. And just as the mind can be partly withdrawn from the object of its attention in order to grasp at the nature of the links joining it to that object, so it can also be partly withdrawn from the processes of public or 'cosmic' time, which the phenomenologists contrast with private or 'phenomenological' time. What enables us to be partly though no wholly free from 'cosmic' time is of course our memory, or capacity for retention, which transforms mere sequence into a duration.

As far as the *nouveau roman* is concerned, the viewpoint *is* the view, and an existential order must replace the old essential one. Significance is no longer given *to* the individual mind but *by* it, on its journey through 'cosmic' time. But acts of signification will escape our attention unless we exploit the limited freedom which the constitution of our minds allows and withdraw it from the flux of experience. For the practitioner of the *nouveau roman*, writing a novel has become an exemplary activity because it mimics the daily activity of the human mind itself, called upon to bestow an order on chaos. The aims of fiction are no longer sociological, therefore, but ontological.

In order to fulfil its task of creating order, of building a 'world' about it, the human mind cannot hope to rely on knowledge alone, in the sense of verifiable facts. The imagination will also be required, perhaps to project more 'facts' beyond those that are verifiable or simply to posit connections between them. Thus fictions are born, and in order to understand the *nouveau roman* properly it is important to bear in mind the fundamental distinction between fact and fiction, or knowledge and imagination. The novel is, by definition, a work of imagination, which is why Michel Butor has called it 'le domaine phénoménologique par excellence', meaning that nothing which takes place in a novel is susceptible of verification. A novel therefore comes into being through ignorance and is a specifically human undertaking, since an omniscient God could produce only textbooks, never fictions. Butor makes this point delicately in one of his own novels, *Degrés* (1960), where the ambitious narrator sets out on the task of writing a total description of a whole class of schoolboys. At first he attempts to verify every piece of information he has about them, until he finds that the time this takes makes it impossible for him to acquire more information; henceforward he must invent. Butor's point is that novels are born of our imprisonment in time and space.

In a way then, the *nouveau roman* represents a rearguard action against the various scientific disciplines which have invaded the traditional spheres of the creative writer. If we want information about our own or other societies it is presumably more rational in our own day and age to get it from sociologists and anthropologists, rather than novelists; and the same can be said for information about the individual human psyche, which is the department of psychologists and psychoanalysts. In the twentieth century the scientific fact has acquired a great charisma, so it is not surprising that there should ultimately arise a school of novelists who refuse to tell lies with an easy conscience.

The doctrine of the *nouveau roman* is that the novel not only tells lies but must be seen to tell lies, and this is a doctrine with obvious moral implications. Since no reasonable person would deny that we use our imaginations constantly in our everyday life, it clearly matters a great deal that we should recognize what in our world is fact and what fiction. If the traditional novel teaches its readers to see 'plots' and 'characters' all round them this may be dangerous, and the *nouveau roman* offers a corrective. But it does so without suggesting that fiction has no value; by the study of our fictions we learn nothing about the external world, but we learn a great deal about our own most intimate obsessions, since it is often obscure emotional needs which are expressed in the patterns of an imaginary reality. To this extent fictions are dreams, and there are close links between what the *nouveau roman* is doing and the therapeutic programme of psychoanalysis.

It is the basic theory of the *nouveau roman* that fiction exists by virtue of the ambiguity of single facts, or the discontinuity between sets of facts. Facts (it might be more helpful in this context to talk of images, or facts that have become the mental property of the individual) must be seen as motives inducing a movement or disturbance in the mind. A novel, for the *nouveaux romanciers*, is very largely a journey round the mind, which may well give the impression of being autonomous, since the narrator does not always seem to have been granted the power to stop the machinery of association once it has been set going. But it is vital to see this movement as a dialectical one, rather than as a coherent progress from point A to point B, because what is involved is a struggle between a number of facts (or images) and fictional attempts to account for them.

A simple example should clarify this dialectical pattern between the visible and invisible worlds. One of the images which keeps recurring in Claude Simon's novel, *La Route des Flandres* (1960), is that of four horsemen riding across the devastated countryside of Flanders after the rout of the French army in 1940. One of these horsemen is in fact the narrator of the novel, which consists almost entirely of memory images, and the other three all play a big part in the events of the 'story'. One of the last invocations of this particular image is very revealing about the structure of the book as a whole: 'les quatre hommes reliés entre eux par un invisible et complexe réseau de forces d'impulsions d'attractions ou de répulsions . . .'.

The visible fact is here clearly separated from the invisible fiction, and the fog of possible motives from the contours of the actual event. There is of course nothing in the least revolutionary about this distinction, which is one novelists have been making for a long time—one might instance a title like Balzac's *L'Envers de l'histoire contemporaine* as a comparable example—but Simon's originality lies in his refusal to accord the same status to the invisible 'facts' as to the visible one. In the passage quoted he hints at the complex or even contradictory nature of the relationships linking these four men, and the novel which explores them is full of proliferating alternative explanations for the same set of phenomena. From the point of view of the *nouveau roman* the traditional novel is now dishonest when it suggests that only one sequence of events is possible, because this denies the ultimate gratuity of fiction, which is really free to make connections in any way it pleases.

This freedom is both a pleasure and a burden, a pleasure because it represents a limited escape from the external or contingent world, and a burden because its exercise implies choice and responsibility. Now the privileged area where a choice is made is the individual consciousness and the *nouveau roman* has provoked confusion where critics have failed to keep in mind that the world of each novel is a mental world, a reflection of the real world and therefore an exercise of a certain freedom. This is the world of which each individual is king, and one can find various more or less direct references to this important concept of private sovereignty in the *nouveau roman*. In Robbe-Grillet these references have a sly humour which many readers may never have glimpsed. In his first novel, for example, *Les Gommes* (1953), he appears thinly disguised in the text as Roy-Dauzet, a mythomaniac Minister of the Interior given to seeing 'plots' wherever he looks. In a later book, *La Maison de rendez-vous* (1965), mention is made of mad King Boris who can sometimes be heard ferrying to and fro in an upstairs room. The novelist, therefore, the creator of myths and hence a madman, is king of his own country—the 'interior' or the 'upstairs room', i.e. the mind. Similar references occur in the novels of Michel Butor, again conveyed in the names of certain characters; a good example is a boy called Régnier in *Degrés*, a *doublant* forced by illness to repeat a school year and accorded as a consequence certain privileges when it comes to the organization of images—his stamp collection is a model of systematic arrangement.

The *nouveau roman* does not try to conceal the fact that it operates, as literature must, on the level of the reflective consciousness and not on that of direct observation. On the contrary there are all sorts of clues, at any rate in Butor and Robbe-Grillet, that the novel represents a partial or total withdrawal of the mind and body from any active participation in the real world. Butor for example introduces just such a withdrawal on the first page of his first novel, *Passage de Milan* (1954): 'Depuis des années que l'abbé observait au moment des pages brunissantes, renonçant lentement à fermer ses volets, avant de s'installer près de sa lampe à contempler le passage des vitres de la transparence à la réflection . . .'.

It is of course perfectly possible to offer a naturalistic explanation of this or any other episode in Butor, but to do so would be wholly misleading. It is ontology *before* it is sociology. It is in the mind of the *abbé* that the action of *Passage de Milan* must be seen as taking place, and the novel is therefore a prolonged act of reflection or, to introduce a very relevant moral dimension into the argument, an *acte de reprise*. The *abbé* in the passage quoted is reluctant to close his shutters, or begin his *acte de reprise*, because he foresees that it will lead him to acknowledge unwelcome things about himself. He will be returned to the real world at the end of the novel a changed man, aware that his Christian habit—the pun is intentional—conceals his adherence to a more fundamental and more pagan notion of the deity.

It might seem as though the *nouveau roman* was attempting in this way to exclude the contingent world altogether, at least until the end of the novel, but if it did this it would run the risk of being even more comprehensively misunderstood than is the actual case. Contingency, or the external world, is allowed to intrude in the course of the novel, in varying degrees. In *Passage de Milan* the structure of the *abbé*'s consciousness is fused with that of an *immeuble*; but a limited number of visitors are allowed to enter it from outside during the course of his reflection, in addition to those already inside, who circulate busily. Butor is anxious to offer us a precise working model of the human mind, whose structures have constantly to be adjusted as new evidence reaches it from outside.

In Robbe-Grillet the intrusion of the contingent world is very much more aggressive and arresting. Nowhere else in the *nouveau roman* is the dialectic between the visible and invisible worlds so methodically used. Before he became a novelist Robbe-Grillet was an agricultural scientist and he has preserved from his training the conviction that scientists alone today represent the same sort of homogenous community as the bourgeoisie represented in the middle of the last century. The values of science are public and assumed to be beyond dispute, and if we want to establish on a scientific basis the sort of connections which it is fiction's business to establish, then this can only be done by having recourse to geometry. If geometry were all, there could be no novels. But geometry is not all, as Robbe-Grillet is happy to admit.

An enormous amount of attention has been given to his use of geometrical references in his descriptions of insignificant objects, with the result that the vital point has often been overlooked that this precision is only one pole of the dialectic. The other pole consists in the elaboration of extravagant and banal myths, the usually erotic fantasies of the popular imagination of the 1950s and '6os. Thus Robbe-Grillet's novels and films depend on a tension, between the imagination's tendency to fabricate myths and its necessary recall to reality. Geometry therefore means the death of the myth just as the creation of the myth means the death of geometry. In this way Robbe-Grillet establishes a dialogue between the eye that measures and the eyelid that enables the mind to escape from the real world. There is a fine example of how this dialogue begins in Les Gommes, in a lengthy description of a tomato which has sometimes been quoted misleadingly to exemplify Robbe-Grillet's *purely* descriptive urges:

Un quartier de tomate en vérité sans défaut, découpé à la machine dans un fruit d'une symétrie parfaite. La chair périphérique, compacte et homogène, d'un beau rouge de chimie . . . les pépins, jaunes, bien calibrés, maintenus en place par une mince couche de gelée verdâtre le long d'un renflement du cœur. . . . Tout en haut, un accident à peine visible s'est produit: un coin de pelure, décollé de la chair sur un millimètre ou deux, se soulève imperceptiblement.

This is in fact an *impure* description, because as it proceeds a fault is discovered which is enough to nullify all the accumulated weight of scientific language, 'machine', 'périphérique', 'chimie', and so on. This fault, the tiny imperfection in the skin of the tomato, is quite simply the fiction itself. But Robbe-Grillet has already stated, in the first few words of the passage quoted, that in fact—'en vérité'—the tomato is without a fault, so we must conclude that the defect in its skin is the creation of the mind which has turned the tomato into an image and been enabled to make its escape from the restrictions of scientific measurement.

It can certainly be argued against Robbe-Grillet that he fails to acknowledge the mythical nature of geometry itself, which he often seems to equate with a standpoint of absolute and hence permanent validity *vis-à-vis* the natural world. He is not of course proposing that any man can live without creating his own myths, but he is proposing that we should not be allowed to live with myths so ingrained in us that we mistake them for something inherent in the structure of the universe. In a famous essay called 'Nature, humanisme, tragédie' he takes to task the many modern writers and thinkers who attempt to build some lasting bridge over the gap that separates man from nature, and attacks the anthropomorphic language often used to humanize our environment. Robbe-Grillet's quarrel is really one of prepositions; he objects to the human mind being projected *into* the external world, and shows in his own novels that it can only be projected *onto* it. The difference is vital, for in the second case the mind must be restored to its place in time, from which there is no final escape, and restored too to a sense of its responsibility: the need for constant vigilance in order to prevent a convenient fiction hardening into a reassuring habit. 'Les choses ne sont jamais définitivement en ordre', says Lady Ava, in *La Maison de rendez-vous*, a remark which might serve as a motto for Robbe-Grillet's whole *œuvre*, and for the *nouveau roman* itself as a coherent movement.

This profound desire to avoid finality faces the writers of the *nouveau roman* with a dilemma; how are they to write novels which never end? Robbe-Grillet's answer to this problem is to write several novels one after the other within the space of two hundred pages or so; each time that the mind of his narrator returns to an objective point of reference it is as if one novel had ended; each time it is prompted to set off on its imaginative journey again another one begins. Apart from this structural indication that the process of creation is an endless one, Robbe-Grillet also introduces objects and even trades whose function is one of elimination or erasure— the india-rubbers of *Les Gommes*, *La Jalousie* (1957), and *L'Immortelle* (1963), or the road-sweepers of *La Maison de rendez-vous*. The fact that within the limits of a single book the narrator's mind is constantly returning to a very limited set of phenomena, trying again and again to rearrange them in accordance with its emotional needs, is a simple indication that this mind is obsessed, so that there is often a suggestion in Robbe-Grillet that the stability which measurement offers comes as a great relief after the anxieties of myth-raking.

The open-endedness which the *nouveau roman* is seeking constitutes above all an attack on habits and clichés since these are systems of ordering reality that have lost their validity. Nathalie Sarraute, for example, brings this out with disturbing clarity by showing what a terrible perversion our everyday language and gestures are, once they are contrasted with the inarticulate movements in the unconscious which gave birth to them. In her books, spoken and behavioural platitudes plop regularly into view like tiny explosions of marsh gas rising from the depths; and what Nathalie Sarraute has done is to assault, by leading our minds into an area of human nature where science cannot as yet compete, all the comfortable foursquare notions still held about human personality. She leaves us not with a more profound knowledge of other minds but with a generalized suspicion about their deeper intentions, and because she is attempting to trap psychic movements at a stage preceding their verbal formulation she is naturally led to expressing herself in disturbing metaphors taken from the zoological or botanical worlds. Like the other writers of the *nouveau roman* she owes a great deal to Jean-Paul Sartre, who was arguably the first French novelist to use metaphors systematically to represent what would otherwise have to remain without intelligible form. Just as Nathalie Sarraute finds metaphors sidling like crabs about the depths of the human personality so Robbe-Grillet finds them in the sea of *Le Voyeur* (1955) or the river of *La Jalousie*; for him the writer of fiction is often symbolized by a lonely figure standing staring into the water.

In just the same way it is chaos which constantly threatens to triumph over order in the novels of Claude Simon, who has a medieval obsession with the destructiveness of Time. Here again stability, mirrored as it often is in the bourgeois institutions of Western society, is an illusion, and it is the task of the novelist to introduce us to another, secret world, where everything is in flux. With Simon, language preserves a very insecure foothold on the passage of memory-images through the mind, and has to be seen in the end as a somewhat derisory means of keeping chaos at bay. It is certainly no substitute for the intricacies and potential glories of the present moment as it is (or should be) lived and Claude Simon is much concerned, as are the *nouveaux romanciers* as a whole, with the creative writer's responsibility for returning his readers to real life refreshed and, as it were, purified of the idle habits which make them less than fully human.

Simon's first ambition, as it happens, was to be not a writer but a painter, and there is an important sense in which the *nouveau roman* has to be understood as dealing with pictures rather than words, and as setting its readers problems which are iconographical rather than verbal. The aspect of the *nouveau roman* which has perhaps caused more confusion than any other is its adoption of an implicit instead of the more usual explicit mode of narration. What each novel confronts its readers with is a sequence of mental images within the mind of the narrator, but this narrator has deliberately been shorn of his ability to reflect on these images and explain their significance to himself. The prolonged act of reflection required is now the responsibility of the reader, who is being asked as it were to re-write the novel, and being offered very literally an opportunity for re-creation. It should be stressed, however, that the order or significance which the reader finally imposes cannot be his own but must be that of the novelist, who has turned into a dictator. The reader knows, when he sets out on his task, that this significance has been predetermined, and that he is not permitted to distort the contents of the novel in any way, by adding or subtracting images, or altering the order in which they occur.

Useful analogies have been made between the *nouveau roman* and the detective story; one perceptive critic, Ludovic Janvier, has called it 'le roman policier pris au sérieux', the added dimension of seriousness being due to the suppression of the detective, a role which the reader is now forced to fill. The 'evidence' is all there, in the successive mental images of the narrator's mind, each one of which must be questioned and explained in order that its significance may be established for this mind at this moment. Thus the reader can be brought to share in a very direct way in the elaboration of the novelist's 'myth', and to learn the lesson of what his attitude should be towards the ambiguous, puzzling world which confronts him every moment of his waking and sometimes even of his sleeping life.

The task is a demanding one of course, and the writers of the *nouveau roman*, Robbe-Grillet and Butor especially, have often stressed the importance for them of discovering readers prepared to co-operate. This plea is made eloquently and obliquely by Butor within the structure of his novels, most obviously in *L'Emploi du temps* (1956), the theme of which is the desperate attempt of a Frenchman to understand his experiences in an English manufacturing town called Bleston. Far more important than the fact that this novel stemmed from Butor's own two years in Manchester as a university *lecteur*, is the fact that the basic situation of a foreigner exiled in a wholly ambiguous environment is a paradigm of the existentialist view of the human situation. In *L'Emploi du temps* a close parallel is established between Butor's own novel and a detective story called *Le Meurtre de Bleston*, with the vital difference that whereas the latter is bound to produce a final solution to the mystery, *L'Emploi du temps* itself is bound not to. The final solution to it can come only from the reader, and such is the complexity of this particular novel that one wonders whether any reader is yet confident of having exhausted it. Small wonder that one of the characters in *L'Emploi du temps* is mentioned as having read *Le Meurtre de Bleston* six times before he understood it.

From this it should be apparent that to interpret any particular *nouveau roman* naturalistically, i.e. by reference to a world of commonly accepted significance, is to misinterpret it seriously. Read as an exercise in naturalism a novel like *L'Emploi du temps* could only be a monstrous bore, since Butor has limited himself rigorously to the most ordinary aspects of everyday urban life, in order to teach us the desired lesson more persuasively, that the 'myth' is a creation of the everyday and uses the least melodramatic of ingredients. So skilful has Butor been, especially in a novel like *Degrés*, with its detailed evocation of life in a Paris *lycée*, in overlaying the public reality with the private myth, that he has obscured his intentions altogether, something which Robbe-Grillet has avoided, as we have seen, by exaggerating the distortions which the mythomaniac practises on the everyday world. But the attitudes of the two writers towards the value of myth are completely opposed, since Butor is positive and Robbe-Grillet mockingly negative, except where scientific myths are concerned.

The *nouveau roman* then offers its readers a perhaps unexpected or even unwanted opportunity for re-creation. It is concerned to teach us what to do with our freedom, in the epistemological sense.

Behind it lies the most influential distinction drawn by Sartre in *L'Être et le néant* between the necessity of being and the freedom of nothingness. 'Nous ne sommes séparés des choses par rien, sinon notre liberté', wrote Sartre in that book, and it is our freedom to manipulate a mental reality which the *nouveau roman* is above all exploring. If the external world of physical *praxis* is a machine, then the internal world of reflection represents the 'play' in that machine, and it is surely no longer eccentric, if indeed it ever was, to attribute to all the creative arts a therapeutic role in society. It might, for example, be helpful to look on the *nouveau roman* as offering us the free associations of a certain mind and asking its readers to act as analysts. Different writers of the movement naturally take different views as to the likely value of such therapy; Robbe-Grillet is often frivolous, Butor, a teacher by training, more committed, and constantly appealing to all men of goodwill to co-operate in the mass task of social hygiene. But even Robbe-Grillet's derision of fictional creation is a moral attitude and the many charges of Parnassianism that have been made against the *nouveau roman* are evidence of a lack of penetration in those making them. The latter are perhaps more used to novelists making a moral stand over specific issues than they are to this very ambitious attempt to reshape the moral consciousness as a whole.

It is the *nouveau roman*'s inevitable dependence on a generalized structure which raises questions as to its likely future. A novel by Simon may be unlike a novel by Butor, but it is abnormally like another novel by Simon. The only possibility which these writers have is to place their structures or 'grids' over different aspects of human life, but since what interests them are above all the conditions under which the chaos of that life can be transformed temporarily into the order of a fiction, it would seem that their structures must continue always to obtrude. No doubt some future synthesis with the traditional forms is possible, but it is to be hoped that the lessons of the *nouveau roman*, if and when they are generally grasped, will not be altogether lost on those many novelists whose own structures are the result of unquestioning expropriation.

NOTE

Theory. Useful essays on the theoretical basis of the *nouveau roman* can be found in Alain Robbe-Grillet, *Pour un nouveau roman* (1963), Nathalie Sarraute, *L'Ère du soupçon* (1956), and Michel Butor, *Essais sur le roman* (1969).

Practice. By 1967 about a dozen French novelists had adopted the techniques of the *nouveau roman* more or less systematically. The best known amongst them are:

ALAIN ROBBE-GRILLET (b. 1922), whose novels include *Les Gommes* (1953), *Le Voyeur* (1955), *La Jalousie* (1957), *Dans le labyrinthe* (1959), and *La Maison de rendez-vous* (1965), together with two *ciné-romans*, based on film scripts: *L'Année dernière à Marienbad* (1961) and *L'Immortelle* (1963).

MICHEL BUTOR (b. 1926), a prolific writer and critic. His novels include *Passage de Milan* (1954), *L'Emploi du temps* (1956), *La Modification* (1957), *Degrés* (1960), and *Portrait de l'artiste en jeune singe* (1967).

NATHALIE SARRAUTE (b. 1902), published her first novel, *Tropismes*, as long ago as 1939. Since then she has written *Portrait d'un inconnu* (1947), *Martereau* (1953), *Le Planétarium* (1959), *Les Fruits d'or* (1963), and *Entre la vie et la mort* (1968).

CLAUDE SIMON (b. 1913). Since becoming a true *nouveau romancier* he has published *Le Vent* (1957), *L'Herbe* (1958), *La Route des Flandres* (1960), *Le Palace* (1962), *Histoire* (1967), and *La Bataille de Pharsale* (1969).

Criticism. The best study of the movement as a whole, including essays on the four writers above, is L. Janvier, *Une Parole exigeante* (1964). A less sympathetic view is taken in J. Bloch-Michel, *Le Présent de l'indicatif* (1963). A more recent general study in English, dealing particularly with Simon, Butor, and Robbe-Grillet, is J. Sturrock, *The French New Novel* (1969).

One or two excellent studies of individual writers have been written, notably Olga Bernal, *Alain Robbe-Grillet: le roman de l'absence* (1964), B. Morrissette, *Les Romans de Robbe-Grillet* (1963), J. V. Alter, *La Vision du monde d'Alain Robbe-Grillet* (1966), and J. Roudaut, *Michel Butor ou le roman futur* (1964). In addition there are two volumes in the Bibliothèque Idéale series: *N. Sarraute* by M. Cranaki and Y. Belaval (1965), and *M. Butor* by G. Raillard (1968). Useful introductions to Robbe-Grillet, Butor, and Sarraute are available in the Classiques du vingtième siècle series.

CHRONOLOGY

History	French literature	Other literatures
Franco-Italian agreement on North African colonies, 1900	Rostand, *L'Aiglon* (1900) Barrès, *L'Appel au soldat* (1900)	Conrad, *Lord Jim* (1900) Shaw, *Three Plays for Puritans* (1900) Dreiser, *Sister Carrie* (1900)
Law on congregations: French Catholics given right to form associations, 1901	Bazin, *Les Oberlé* (1901)	Strindberg, *The Dance of Death* (1901) Yeats, *Poems* (1901) Butler, *Erewhon Revisited* (1901) Kipling, *Kim* (1901) Mann, *Buddenbrooks* (1901) Lagerlöf, *Jerusalem* (1901-2)
Government of Combes, 1902-5	Gide, *L'Immoraliste* (1902) Verhaeren, *Les Forces tumultueuses* (1902) Barrès, *Leurs Figures* (1902)	James, *Wings of the Dove* (1902) Chekhov, *Three Sisters* (1902) Bennett, *The Grand Babylon Hotel* (1902) Gorky, *The Lower Depths* (1902)
President Loubet of France and Edward VII exchange visits, 1903 *Entente Cordiale* established, 1903	Boylesve, *L'Enfant à la balustrade* (1903)	Butler, *The Way of All Flesh* (1903) Mann, *Tonio Kröger* (1903) *James, The Ambassadors* (1903) Shaw, *Man and Superman* (1903) Hofmannsthal, *Elektra* (1903)
Entente Cordiale strengthened, 1904 Franco-Spanish agreement on Morocco, 1904	Rolland, *Jean-Christophe* (1904-12)	Conrad, *Nostromo* (1904) Hardy, *The Dynasts* (1904) Chekhov, *The Cherry Orchard* (1904)
Founding of French Socialist Party, 1905 Separation of Church and State in France, 1905	Ramuz, *Aline* (1905)	Shaw, *Major Barbara* (1905) Wells, *Kipps* (1905) Synge, *Riders to the Sea* (1905) Rilke, *Das Stundenbuch* (1905) Hesse, *Unterm Rad* (1905)

Painting and music	Criticism and aesthetic theory	Ideas
Liebermann, 1847–1935 Janaček, 1854–1928, (*Katya Kabanova* (completed) 1921; *Sinfonietta*, 1925; *From the House of the Dead*, 1928)	Bergson, *Le Rire* (1900) Péguy founds *Cahiers de la quinzaine* (1900–14)	Freud, *The Interpretation of Dreams* (1900)
Elgar, 1857–1934 (*Dream of Gerontius*, 1900; *Violin Concerto*, 1910; *Falstaff*, 1913; *Cello Concerto*, 1919)	Saintsbury, *A History of Criticism and Literary Taste in Europe* (1901–4)	Freud, *The Psychopathology of Everyday Life* (1901)
Ethel Smyth, 1858–1944 (*The Wrecker*, 1906)		
Mahler, 1860–1911 (*Symphony No. 8*, 1907; *Das Lied von der Erde*, 1908)	Croce, *Estetica* (1902)	Pareto, *Les Systèmes socialistes* (1902) James, *Varieties of Religious Experience* (1902)
Ensor, 1860–1949		Moore, *Principia Ethica* (1903) Russell, *Principles of Mathematics* (1903)
Charpentier, 1860–1956 (*Louise*, 1900)		
Maillol, 1861–1944		
Debussy, 1862–1918 (*Pelléas et Mélisande*, 1902; *La Mer*, 1903–5; *Images*, 1906–12)	Gourmont, *Promenades littéraires* (1904–13)	Weber, *The Protestant Ethic and the Spirit of Capitalism* (1904–5)
	Dilthey, *Das Erlebnis und die Dichtung* (1905)	
Delius, 1862–1934 (*Sea Drift*, 1903; *Brigg Fair*, 1908)	Maurras, *L'Avenir de l'intelligence* (1905)	

History	French literature	Other literatures
Dreyfus finally declared innocent, 1906	Claudel, *Partage de midi* (1906)	Galsworthy, *The Man of Property* (1906)
Algeciras Conference recognizes French rights in Morocco, 1906	Verhaeren, *La Multiple Splendeur* (1906)	
Fallières president; government of Clemenceau, 1906	Barrès, *Le Voyage de Sparte* (1906)	
Triple Entente of France, Russia and Britain, 1907		Conrad, *The Secret Agent* (1907)
		Synge, *The Playboy of the Western World* (1907)
		Strindberg, *The Ghost Sonata* (1907)
		George, *Der siebente Ring* (1907)
Casablanca incident between France and Germany, 1908	France, *L'Île des pingouins* (1908)	Bennett, *The Old Wives' Tale* (1908)
L'Action Française becomes daily paper, 1908	Romains, *La Vie unanime* (1908)	Chesterton, *The Man who was Thursday* (1908)
	Psichari, *Terre de soleil et de sommeil* (1908)	
Wave of strikes in France, 1909	Barrès, *Colette Baudoche* (1909)	Wells, *Ann Veronica* and *Tono Bungay* (1909)
Franco–German agreement on Morocco, 1909	Gide, *La Porte étroite* (1909)	Galsworthy, *Strife* (1909)
	Maeterlinck, *L'Oiseau bleu* (1909)	
	Bloy, *Le Sang du pauvre* (1909)	
French railway strike broken by Briand, 1910	Claudel, *Cinq grandes odes* (1910)	Bennett, *Clayhanger* (1910)
	Péguy, *Le Mystère de la charité de Jeanne d'Arc* (1910)	Forster, *Howard's End* (1910)
		Wells, *History of Mr. Polly* (1910)
		Hauptmann, *Der Narr in Christo, Emanuel Quint* (1910)
		Löns, *Der Wehrwolf* (1910)
Agadir crisis, 1911	Colette, *La Vagabonde* (1911)	Beerbohm, *Zuleika Dobson* (1911)
	Claudel, *L'Otage* (1911)	Pound, *Canzoni* (1911)

Painting and music	Criticism and aesthetic theory	Ideas
German, 1862–1936 (*Merrie England*, 1902)		Sorel, *Réflexions sur la violence* (1906)
Sérusier, 1863–1935		Pareto, *Manuale di economia politica* (1906)
Signac, 1863–1935		
		Bergson, *L'Évolution créatrice* (1907)
Munch, 1863–1944		Jung, *The Psychology of Dementia Praecox* (1907)
Strauss, 1864–1949 (*Salomé*, 1905; *Elektra*, 1909; *Der Rosenkavalier*, 1911)	Gide, *Prétextes* (1908)	
Sibelius, 1865–1957 (*Violin Concerto*, 1903)	Bradley, *Lectures on Poetry* (1909)	Bergson, *Matière et mémoire* (1909)
Busoni, 1866–1924 (*Fantasia contrappuntistica*, 1910; *Sonatina seconda*, 1912; *Arlecchino*, 1916)	Founding of *Nouvelle Revue Française* (1909)	
	Marinetti's futurist manifesto published in *Le Figaro* (1909)	
Satie, 1866–1925 (*Parade*, 1917; *Socrate*, 1919)		Angell, *The Great Illusion* (1910)
		Péguy, *Notre Jeunesse* (1910)
Kandinsky, 1866–1944		
	Lanson, *La Méthode de l'histoire littéraire* (1911)	
Granados, 1867–1916		

History	French literature	Other literatures
	Larbaud, *Fermina Marquez* (1911)	Lawrence, *The White Peacock* (1911)
	Perse, *Éloges* (1911)	Masefield, *The Everlasting Mercy* (1911)
	Péguy, *Le Porche du mystère de la deuxième vertu* (1911)	Hauptmann, *Die Ratten* (1911)
		Hofmannsthal, *Jedermann* (1911)
French protectorate established over Morocco, 1912	France, *Les Dieux ont soif* (1912)	Barlach, *Der tote Tag* (1912)
	Claudel, *L'Annonce faite à Marie* (1912)	Shaw, *Androcles and the Lion* and *Pygmalion* (1912)
		Machado, *Campos de Castilla* (1912)
Poincaré becomes president, 1913–20	Barrès, *La Colline inspirée* (1913)	Lawrence, *Sons and Lovers* (1913)
French army bill: three years' military service becomes law, 1913	Alain-Fournier, *Le Grand Meaulnes* (1913)	Mann, *Der Tod in Venedig* (1913)
	Apollinaire, *Alcools* (1913)	Rilke, *Das Marienleben* (1913)
	Martin du Gard, *Jean Barois* (1913)	Trakl, *Gedichte* (1913)
	Proust, *A la recherche du temps perdu* (1913–22)	
	Larbaud, *Journal de A. O. Barnabooth* (1913)	
	Cendrars, *Prose du Trans-sibérien* (1913)	
	Péguy, *Ève* (1913)	
	Psichari, *L'Appel des armes* (1913)	
Assassination of Jaurès, 1914	Gide, *Les Caves du Vatican* (1914)	Joyce, *Dubliners* (1914)
French mobilization and outbreak of First World War, 1914		Shaw, *Misalliance* (1914)
Battle of the Marne, 1914		H. Mann, *Der Untertan* (1914)
Briand becomes French premier, 1915	Genevoix, *Ceux de Verdun* (1915–22)	Lawrence, *The Rainbow* (1915)
Second battle of Ypres, 1915		Maugham, *Of Human Bondage* (1915)
		Conrad, *Victory* (1915)
		Wassermann, *Das Gänsemännchen* (1915)

Painting and music	Criticism and aesthetic theory	Ideas
Bonnard, 1867–1947		
Nolde, 1867–1956	Gleizes and Metzinger, *Du cubisme* (1912) Faguet, *L'Art de lire* (1912) Kandinsky, *Concerning the Spiritual in Art* (1912)	Durkheim, *Les Formes élémentaires de la vie religieuse* (1912) Jung, *The Psychology of the Unconscious* (1912) Freud, *Totem and Taboo* (1912–13)
Vuillard, 1868–1940		
Matisse, 1869–1954	Kandinsky, *Rückblicke* (1913)	Unamuno, *Del Sentimiento Trágico de la Vida* (1913) Husserl, *Ideas: General Introduction to Pure Phenomenology* (1913)
Lehár, 1870–1948 (*Die lustige Witwe*, 1905)		
Rouault, 1871–1958		
Scriabin, 1872–1915		
Diaghilev, 1872–1929	James, *Notes on Novelists* (1914)	Russell, *Our Knowledge of the External World* (1914)
Mondrian, 1872–1944		
Vaughan Williams, 1872–1958 (*Hugh the Drover*, 1924; *Sinfonia Antartica*, 1953)		Frazer, *The Golden Bough* (completed 1915) Rolland, *Au-dessus de la mêlée* (1915)

History	French literature	Other literatures
Easter Rising, Dublin, 1916 Battle of Verdun and battle of the Somme, 1916 Battle of Jutland, 1916	Barbusse, *Le Feu* (1916) Jammes, *Cinq poèmes pour le temps de la guerre* (1916)	Joyce, *Portrait of the Artist as a Young Man* (1916) Kafka, *Die Verwandlung* (1916)
Balfour Declaration, 1917 Fall of Briand Government, 1917 Battle of Vimy Ridge, 1917 Russian Revolution, 1917 Clemenceau succeeds Painlevé as French premier, 1917	Valéry, *La Jeune Parque* (1917) Jacob, *Le Cornet à dés* (1917) Duhamel, *La Vie des martyrs* (1917) Apollinaire, *Les Mamelles de Tirésias* (1917)	Yeats, *The Wild Swans at Coole* (1917) Pirandello, *Cosi è, se vi pare* (1917) Eliot, *Prufrock and Other Observations* (1917)
Failure of Ludendorff offensive and successful counter-offensive by Foch, 1918 Armistice ends First World War, 1918	Apollinaire, *Caligrammes* (1918) Duhamel, *Civilisation* (1918) Benoit, *Königsmark* (1918) Claudel, *Le Pain dur* (1918)	Thomas, *Last Poems* (1918) Lawrence, *New Poems* (1918) Joyce, *Exiles* (1918)
Treaty of Versailles, 1919 Nazi party founded, 1919 Mussolini founds fascist movement, 1919	Dorgelès, *Les Croix de bois* (1919) Gide, *La Symphonie pastorale* (1919) Rolland, *Colas Breugnon* (1919) Cendrars, *Du monde entier* and *Au cœur du monde* (1919)	Maugham, *The Moon and Sixpence* (1919) Shaw, *Heartbreak House* (1919) Conrad, *The Arrow of Gold* (1919) Ungaretti, *L'Allegria* (1919) Anderson, *Winesburg, Ohio* (1919)
Sacco and Vanzetti murders, 1920 Deschanel defeats Clemenceau in French presidential election, 1920 Canonization of Jeanne d'Arc, 1920	Valéry, *Le Cimetière marin* (1920) Duhamel, *La Confession de minuit* (1920) Colette, *Chéri* (1920) Claudel, *Le Père humilié* (1920)	Pound, *Hugh Selwyn Mauberley* (1920) Toller, *Masse-Mensch* (1920) Lawrence, *Women in Love* (1920) Owen, *Poems* (1920) Lewis, *Main Street* (1920) Čapek, *R.U.R.* (1920)

ainting and music	Criticism and aesthetic theory	Ideas
eger, 1873–1916	Brémond, *Histoire littéraire du sentiment religieux en France* (1916–31)	Dewey, *Democracy and Education* (1916)
achmaninoff, 1873–1943		Pareto, *Tratto di sociologia generale* (1916)
		Freud, *Introductory Lectures on Psychoanalysis* (1916–17)
olst, 1874–1934 (*St. Paul's uite*, 1913; *The Planets*, 16)		
choenberg, 1874–1951 *urrelieder*, 1900; *Pierrot unaire*, 1912; *L'Histoire du dat*, 1918; *Serenade*, 1923; *Survivor from Warsaw*, 47; *Moses and Aaron* nfinished))	Le Corbusier and Ozenfant, *Après le cubisme* (1918)	Mann, *Betrachtungen eines Unpolitischen* (1918)
	Tzara, *Manifeste Dada 1918* (1918)	Strachey, *Eminent Victorians* (1918)
es, 1874–1954 (*Three Places New England*, 1914; mphony No. 4*, 1916)		Spengler, *The Decline of the West (I)* (1918)
		Adams, *The Education of Henry Adams* (1918)
	Babbitt, *Rousseau and Romanticism* (1919)	Keynes, *The Economic Consequences of the Peace* (1919)
oleridge-Taylor, 1875–1912 *iawatha*, 1900)		
vel, 1875–1937 (*Ma mère ye*, 1908; *Daphnis et Chloé*, 12; *L'Enfant et les sortilèges 20*; *Boléro*, 1928)	Mondrian, *Le Néo-Plasticisme* (1920)	Freud, *Beyond the Pleasure Principle* (1920)
	Lukács, *Theorie des Romans* (1920)	Pareto, *Fatti e theorie* (1920)
	Eliot, *The Sacred Wood* (1920)	
arquet, 1875–1947	Maritain, *Art et scolastique* (1920)	
	Weston, *From Ritual to Romance* (1920)	

History	French literature	Other literatures
French occupation of Ruhr, 1921 Crushing of anti-Bolshevik Kronstadt mutiny, 1921	Carco, *L'Homme traqué* (1921) Giraudoux, *Suzanne et le Pacifique* (1921) Toulet, *Les Contrerimes* (1921) Cocteau, *Les Mariés de la Tour Eiffel* (1921)	Pirandello, *Sei personaggi in cerca d'autore* (1921) O'Neill, *The Emperor Jones* (1921) Shaw, *Back to Methuselah* (1921) Huxley, *Crome Yellow* (1921)
Irish Civil War, 1922 End of Civil War in Russia, 1922 Poincaré succeeds Briand as French premier, 1922	Perse, *Anabase* (1922) Valéry, *Charmes* (1922) Mauriac, *Le Baiser au lépreux* (1922) Lacretelle, *Silbermann* (1922) Montherlant, *Le Songe* (1922) Giraudoux, *Siegfried et le limousin* (1922) Martin du Gard, *Les Thibault* (1922-40)	Toller, *Die Maschinen-stürmer* (1922) Pirandello, *Enrico IV* (1922) Eliot, *The Waste Land* (1922) Joyce, *Ulysses* (1922) Mansfield, *The Garden Party* (1922) Hesse, *Siddharta* (1922)
French again occupy Ruhr, 1923	Romains, *Knock* (1923) Radiguet, *Le Diable au corps* (1923) Cocteau, *Thomas l'imposteur* (1923) Larbaud, *Poésies de A. O. Barnabooth* (1923)	Lawrence, *Kangaroo* (1923) Bennett, *Riceyman Steps* (1923) Rilke, *Duineser Elegien* (1923)
Cartel des gauches defeats *bloc national* in French elections, 1924 Failure of Dawes Plan, 1924	Mauriac, *Genitrix* (1924) Radiguet, *Le Bal du comte d'Orgel* (1924) Cendrars, *Kodak* (1924) Perse, *Amitié du prince* (1924)	Forster, *A Passage to India* (1924) Shaw, *Saint Joan* (1924) Mann, *Der Zauberberg* (1924)

ainting and music	Criticism and aesthetic theory	Ideas
illon, 1875–1963	Lubbock, *The Craft of Fiction* (1921)	Alain, *Mars, ou la guerre jugée* (1921)
	Valéry, *L'Âme et la danse* (1921)	Blondel, *Le Procès de l'intelligence* (1921)
alla, 1876–1946 (*El amor rujo*, 1915; *El sombrero de es picos*, 1919)		Jung, *Psychological Types* (1921)
		Pareto, *Transformazione della democrazia* (1921)
laminck, 1876–1958		Wittgenstein, *Tractatus logico-philosophicus* (1921)
lalevich, 1878–1935	Murry, *The Problem of Style* (1922)	Spengler, *The Decline of the West (II)* (1922)
	The Criterion (1922–39)	
	Thibaudet, *Physiologie de la critique* (1922)	
espighi, 1879–1936 (*The irds*, 1927)		
lee, 1879–1940		
icabia, 1879–1953	Rudler, *Les Techniques de la critique et de l'histoire littéraire* (1923)	Santayana, *Scepticism and Animal Faith* (1923)
	Gide, *Dostoïevski* (1923)	Ortega y Gasset, *El tema de nuestro tiempo* (1923)
larc, 1880–1916		Buber, *I and Thou* (1923)
)erain, 1880–1954		Berdyaev, *The Meaning of History* (1923)
	Breton, *Manifeste du surréalisme* (1924)	Collingwood, *Speculum Mentis* (1924)
pstein, 1880–1959	Klee, *Über die moderne Kunst* (1924)	Hulme, *Speculations* (1924)
	Richard, *Principles of Literary Criticism* (1924)	
artók, 1881–1945 (*Fourteen agatelles*, 1908; *The Mira-lous Mandarin* (composed)19); *Piano Concerto No. 2*,)33)	Gide, *Incidences* (1924)	
	Valéry, *Variété I* (1924)	
	Marinetti, *Futurismo e fascismo* (1924)	

History	French literature	Other literatures
Briand foreign minister, 1925–32	Rolland, *Clérambault* (1925)	Dreiser, *An American Tragedy* (1925)
French begin evacuation of Ruhr, 1925	Gide, *Les Faux-monnayeurs* (1925)	Fitzgerald, *The Great Gatsby* (1925)
Locarno treaties, 1925		Huxley, *Those Barren Leaves* (1925)
Rebellion against French rule in Syria, 1925		Kafka, *Der Prozess* (1925)
		Dos Passos, *Manhattan Transfer* (1925)
General strike in Britain, 1926	Colette, *La Fin de Chéri* (1926)	Kafka, *Das Schloss* (1926)
Publication of papal condemnation of Action Française, 1926	Bernanos, *Sous le soleil de Satan* (1926)	Lawrence, *The Plumed Serpent* (1926)
	Giraudoux, *Bella* (1926)	Babel, *Konarmiya* (1926)
	Montherlant, *Les Bestiaires* (1926)	Hemingway, *Fiesta* (1926)
	Gide, *Si le grain ne meurt* (1926)	
	Éluard, *Capitale de la douleur* (1926)	
Lindbergh makes first solo crossing of Atlantic, 1927	Mauriac, *Thérèse Desqueyroux* (1927)	Hesse, *Der Steppenwolf* (1927)
	Bernanos, *L'Imposture* (1927)	Woolf, *To the Lighthouse* (1927)
	Green, *Adrienne Mesurat* (1927)	Wilder, *The Bridge of San Luis Rey* (1927)
	Guilloux, *La Maison du peuple* (1927)	Lewis, *Childermass* (1927)
French military service reduced to one year, 1928	Malraux, *Les Conquérants* (1928)	Lorca, *Romancero gitano* (1928)
Left parties win French elections, 1928	Giraudoux, *Siegfried* (1928)	Huxley, *Point Counter Point* (1928)
	Pagnol, *Topaze* (1928)	Lawrence, *Lady Chatterley's Lover* (1928)

Painting and music	Criticism and aesthetic theory	Ideas
	V. Woolf, *The Common Reader* (1925)	Hitler, *Mein Kampf* (1925–7)
Léger, 1881–1955	Brémond, *La Poésie pure* (1925)	
Picasso, b. 1881		
Boccioni, 1882–1916	Fernandez, 'De la critique philosophique' (1926)	Whitehead, *Science and the Modern World* (1926)
		Lawrence, *The Seven Pillars of Wisdom* (1926)
		Malraux, *La Tentation de l'Occident* (1926)
Braque, 1882–1963		Webb, *My Apprenticeship* (1926)
		Maritain, *Antimoderne* (1926)
Kodály, 1882–1967 (*Háry János*, 1927; *Dances of Galanta*, 1933; *Missa brevis*, 1945)		Tawney, *Religion and the Rise of Capitalism* (1926)
	Malevich, *Die Gegenstandlose Welt* (1927)	Benda, *La Trahison des clercs* (1927)
	Forster, *Aspects of the Novel* (1927)	Malraux, 'D'une jeunesse européenne' (1927)
Stravinsky, b. 1882 (*Firebird*, 1910; *Petrushka*, 1911; *Rite of Spring*, 1913; *Oedipus Rex*, 1927; *The Rake's Progress*, 1951; *Agon*, 1957)	Gide, *Le Journal des Faux-monnayeurs* (1927)	Maritain, *Primauté du spirituel* (1927)
	Brémond, *Prière et poésie* (1927)	Freud, *The Future of an Illusion* (1927)
		Heidegger, *Being and Time* (1927)
		Teilhard de Chardin, *Le Milieu divin* (1927)
Webern, 1883–1945 (*Symphony, Op. 21*, 1928; *Concerto, Op. 24*, 1934; *Piano Variations*, 1936; *Second Cantata*, 1945)	Breton, *Le Surréalisme et la peinture* (1928)	Eddington, *The Nature of the Physical World* (1928)
	Aragon, *Le Traité du style* (1928)	

History	French literature	Other literatures
Decision to build Maginot Line, 1928	Giono, *Colline* (1928) Saint-Exupéry, *Courrier Sud* (1928) Breton, *Nadja* (1928)	Brecht, *Dreigroschenoper* (1928) Waugh, *Decline and Fall* (1928) Woolf, *Orlando* (1928)
Briand proposes European federal union, 1929 Wall Street Crash, 1929 First all-fascist parliament in Italy, 1929	Pagnol, *Marius* (1929) Claudel, *Le Soulier de satin* (1929) Cocteau, *Les Enfants terribles* (1929) Giraudoux, *Amphitryon '38* (1929) Giono, *Un de Baumugnes* (1929) Bernanos, *La Joie* (1929) Green, *Leviathan* (1929)	Döblin, *Berlin-Alexanderplatz* (1929) Pirandello, *Lazzaro* (1929) Bridges, *The Testament of Beauty* (1929) Faulkner, *The Sound and the Fury* (1929) Hemingway, *A Farewell to Arms* (1929) Remarque, *Im Westen Nichts Neues* (1929)
French evacuation of Rhineland, 1930 107 Nazis elected to Reichstag, 1930	Giono, *Regain* (1930) Malraux, *La Voie royale* (1930) Michaux, *Un certain Plume* (1930)	Faulkner, *As I Lay Dying* (1930) Shaw, *The Apple Cart* (1930) Maugham, *Cakes and Ale* (1930) Eliot, *Ash Wednesday* (1930) Musil, *Der Mann ohne Eigenschaften* (1930-43)
Doumer elected French president and Laval French premier, 1931 Republic established in Spain, 1931	Obey, *Noé* (1931) Giraudoux, *Judith* (1931) Pagnol, *Fanny* (1931) Giono, *Le Grand Troupeau* (1931) Saint-Exupéry, *Vol de nuit* (1931) Drieu la Rochelle, *Le Feu follet* (1931) Nizan, *Aden Arabie* (1931)	Seferis, *Strophe* (1931) O'Neill, *Mourning becomes Electra* (1931) Faulkner, *Sanctuary* (1931) Buck, *The Good Earth* (1931) Compton-Burnett, *Men and Wives* (1931) Zuckmayer, *Der Hauptmann von Köpenick* (1931) Broch, *Die Schlafwandler* (1931-2)

Painting and music	Criticism and aesthetic theory	Ideas
Utrillo, 1883–1955		
	Richards, *Practical Criticism* (1929)	Husserl, *Formal and Transcendental Logic* (1929)
Modigliani, 1884–1920	Breton, *Manifeste du surréalisme (II)* (1929)	
Beckmann, 1884–1950	Claudel, *Positions et pro-positions* (1929)	
Berg, 1885–1936 (*Wozzeck*, 1921; *Lyric Suite*, 1926; *Violin Concerto*, 1935; *Lulu*, 1935)		
	Aragon, *La Peinture au défi* (1930)	Freud, *Civilization and its Discontents* (1930)
Delaunay, 1885–1941	Empson, *Seven Types of Ambiguity* (1930)	Ortega y Gasset, *La rebelión de las masas* (1929–30)
	Valéry, *Variété II* (1930)	
Varèse, 1885–1965 (*Ionisation*, 1931)	Burke, *Counter-Statement* (1931)	Bernanos, *La Grande Peur des bien-pensants* (1931)
	Eastman, *The Literary Mind: its Place in an Age of Science* (1931)	Valéry, *Regards sur le monde actuel* (1931)
Rivera, 1886–1957		Husserl, *Cartesian Meditations* (1931)
Kokoschka, b. 1886		

L

History	French literature	Other literatures
Doumer assassinated and Lebrun French president, 1932–40 Great hunger march to London, 1932 Nazis gain 230 seats in Reichstag, 1932	Céline, *Voyage au bout de la nuit* (1932) Breton, *Les Vases communicants* (1932) Mauriac, *Le Nœud de vipères* (1932) Romains, *Les Hommes de bonne volonté* (1932–46)	Caldwell, *Tobacco Road* (1932) Morgan, *The Fountain* (1932) Dos Passos, *1919* (1932) Faulkner, *Light in August* (1932)
Roosevelt's 'New Deal', 1933 Hitler comes to power, 1933 Stavisky scandal, 1933	Malraux, *La Condition humaine* (1933) Giraudoux, *Intermezzo* (1933) Aymé, *La Jument verte* (1933) Duhamel, *La Chronique des Pasquier* (1933–44) Aragon, *Les Cloches de Bâle* (1933) Queneau, *Le Chiendent* (1933)	Lorca, *Bodas de sangre* (1933) Silone, *Fontamara* (1933) Stein, *Autobiography of Alice B. Toklas* (1933) Mann, *Joseph und seine Brüder* (1933–43)
King Alexander of Yugoslavia and French foreign minister, Barthou, assassinated at Marseilles, 1934 Anti-republican riots in France, 1934 Laval French foreign minister, 1934	Montherlant, *Les Célibataires* (1934) Cocteau, *La Machine infernale* (1934) Green, *Le Visionnaire* (1934)	Dinesen, *Seven Gothic Tales* (1934) Lorca, *Yerma* (1934) Fitzgerald, *Tender is the Night* (1934)
Italian invasion of Abyssinia and Hoare–Laval pact, 1935 *Croix de feu* founded in France, 1935	Guilloux, *Le Sang noir* (1935) Giraudoux, *La Guerre de Troie n'aura pas lieu* (1935) Giono, *Que ma joie demeure* (1935) Bernanos, *Un Crime* (1935) Salacrou, *L'Inconnue d'Arras* (1935)	Canetti, *Die Blendung* (1935) Compton-Burnett, *A House and its Head* (1935) Eliot, *Murder in the Cathedral* (1935) Steinbeck, *Tortilla Flat* (1935)
Popular Front government in France under Blum, 1936 Germany reoccupies Rhineland, 1936 Spanish Civil War, 1936–39	Martin du Gard, *L'Été* (1936) Bernanos, *Journal d'un curé de campagne* (1936) Aragon, *Les beaux quartiers* (1936) Anouilh, *Le Voyageur sans bagages* (1936)	Auden and Isherwood, *The Ascent of F. 6* (1936) Thomas, *Twenty-five Poems* (1936) Morgan, *Sparkenbroke* (1936) Lorca, *La casa de Bernarda Alba* (1936)

Painting and music	Criticism and aesthetic theory	Ideas
	Scrutiny (1932-52)	Mussolini, *La Dottrina del Fascismo* (1932)
Gris, 1887-1927		Huxley, *Brave New World* (1932)
		Bergson, *Les deux sources de la morale et de la religion* (1932)
Dufy, 1887-1953		Maurras, *Dictionnaire politique et critique* (1932-4)
	Leavis (ed.), *Towards Standards of Criticism* (1933)	Jung, *Modern Man in Search of a Soul* (1933)
	Eliot, *The Use of Poetry and the Use of Criticism* (1933)	
Villa-Lobos, 1887-1959		
Arp, 1887-1966	James, *The Art of the Novel* (posth. publ. 1934)	Mumford, *Technics and Civilization* (1934)
		Whitehead, *Nature and Life* (1934)
Chagall, b. 1887		Toynbee, *A Study of History* (1934-54)
Duchamp, b. 1887	Empson, *Some Versions of Pastoral* (1935)	Jaspers, *Reason and Existenz* (1935)
	Claudel, *Positions et propositions (II)* (1935)	
Chirico, b. 1888	Raymond, *De Baudelaire au surréalisme* (1935)	
Nash, 1889-1946		
Gaudier-Brzeska, 1891-1915	Valéry, *Variété III* (1936)	Gide, *Retour de l'U.R.S.S.* (1936)
	Lovejoy, *The Great Chain of Being* (1936)	Ayer, *Language, Truth and Logic* (1936)
Prokofiev, 1891-1953 (*Sarcasmes*, 1911; *Romeo and Juliet*, 1935; *Peter and the Wolf*, 1936)		

History	French literature	Other literatures
	Green, *Minuit* (1936)	Dos Passos, *The Big Money* (1936)
	Montherlant, *Les Jeunes filles* (1936-9)	
Fall of Blum government, 1937	Giraudoux, *Électre* (1937)	Silone, *Pane e vino* (1937)
Failure of *cagoulard* plot in France, 1937	Pagnol, *César* (1937)	Steinbeck, *Of Mice and Men* (1937)
Formation of Rome–Berlin Axis, 1937	Bernanos, *Nouvelle Histoire de Mouchette* (1937)	
	Malraux, *L'Espoir* (1937)	
	Breton, *L'Amour fou* (1937)	
	Cocteau, *Les Chevaliers de la Table Ronde* (1937)	
Anschluss: Austria declared part of Germany, 1938	Cocteau, *Les Parents terribles* (1938)	Bowen, *The Death of the Heart* (1938)
Munich agreement, 1938	Salacrou, *La Terre est ronde* (1938)	Williams, *The Corn is Green* (1938)
	Sartre, *La Nausée* (1938)	Warner, *The Professor* (1938)
	Mauriac, *Asmodée* (1938)	Greene, *Brighton Rock* (1938)
	Supervielle, *La Fable du monde* (1938)	Kazantzakis, *I Odysseia* (1938)
	Jouhandeau, *Chroniques maritales* (1938)	Arbuzov, *Tanya* (1938)
	Anouilh, *Le Bal des voleurs* (1938)	
German occupation of Czechoslovakia, 1939	Gracq, *Au Château d'Argol* (1939)	Mann, *Lotte in Weimar* (1939)
French communist party supports Hitler–Stalin pact, 1939	Sarraute, *Tropismes* (1939)	Eliot, *The Family Reunion* (1939)
Outbreak of Second World War, 1939	Drieu la Rochelle, *Gilles* (1939)	Steinbeck, *The Grapes of Wrath* (1939)
	Sartre, *Le Mur* (1939)	Isherwood, *Goodbye to Berlin* (1939)
	Saint-Exupéry, *Terre des hommes* (1939)	Jünger, *Auf den Marmorklippen* (1939)
	Giraudoux, *Ondine* (1939)	
Dunkirk evacuation, 1940	Blanchot, *Thomas l'obscur* (1940)	Winters, *Poems* (1940)
Germans enter Paris, 1940		Thomas, *Portrait of the Artist as a Young Dog* (1940)
Battle of Britain, 1940		Hemingway, *For Whom the Bell Tolls* (1940)

inting and music	Criticism and aesthetic theory	Ideas
	Collingwood, *The Principles of Art* (1937)	Gide, *Retouches à mon Retour de l'U.R.S.S.* (1937)
pencer, 1891–1959	Boas, *A Primer for Critics* (1937)	Bonhoeffer, *The Cost of Discipleship* (1937)
liss, b. 1891 (*Miracle in the orbals*, 1944)	Béguin, *L'Âme romantique et le rêve* (1937)	
onegger, 1892–1955 (*Pacific 1, 1923; Jeanne d'Arc au cher*, 1938)	Artaud, *Le Théâtre et son double* (1938)	Bernanos, *Les Grands Cimetières sous la lune* (1938)
	Bachelard, *La Psychanalyse du feu* (1938)	Montherlant, *L'Équinoxe de septembre* (1938)
lilhaud, b. 1892 (*Le Bœuf r le toit*, 1919)	Pound, *Guide to Kulchur* (1938)	Bonhoeffer, *Life Together* (1938)
	Valéry, *Variété IV* (1938)	Teilhard de Chardin, *Le Phénomène humain* (1938–40)
	Du Bos, *Qu'est-ce que la littérature?* (1938)	
liró, b. 1893	Stravinsky, *Poetics of Music* (1939)	Gide, *Journal 1885–1939* (1939)
		Eliot, *The Idea of a Christian Society* (1939)
		Freud, *Moses and Monotheism* (1939)
outine, 1894–1943		Sartre, *Esquisse d'une théorie des émotions* (1939)
Jicholson, b. 1894	Maulnier, *Introduction à la poésie française* (1940)	Mumford, *The Culture of Cities* (1940)
	Blackmur, *The Expense of Greatness* (1940)	Mannheim, *Man and Society* (1940)
		Sartre, *L'Imaginaire* (1940)

History	French literature	Other literatures
French government moves to Vichy and Pétain becomes premier, 1940 De Gaulle calls on French to resist, 1940		Greene, *The Power and the Glory* (1940) Koestler, *Darkness at Noon* (1940) Lorca, *Poeta en Nueva York* (1940)
Japanese attack on Pearl Harbour, 1941 Beginnings of French Resistance, 1941	Supervielle, *Poèmes de la France malheureuse* (1941) Mauriac, *La Pharisienne* (1941) Aragon, *Le Crève-cœur* (1941)	Brecht, *Mutter Courage und ihre Kinder* (performed 1941) Warner, *The Aerodrome* (1941) Fitzgerald, *The Last Tycoon* (1941)
Battle of El Alamein, 1942 Allied landings in North Africa, 1942 French fleet scuttled at Toulon, 1942	Saint-Exupéry, *Pilote de guerre* (1942) Anouilh, *Eurydice* (1942) Camus, *L'Étranger* (1942) Éluard, *Poésie et vérité* (1942) Ponge, *Le Parti-pris des choses* (1942) Vercors, *Le Silence de la mer* (1942) Montherlant, *La Reine morte* (1942)	Eliot, *Four Quartets* (1942)
Allied invasion of Sicily, 1943 Germans surrender at Stalingrad, 1943 Committee of National Liberation formed in Algiers by De Gaulle and Giraud, 1943 Worker-priest movement started in France, 1943	Perse, *Pluies* (1943) Queneau, *Pierrot mon ami* (1943) Beauvoir, *L'Invitée* (1943) Saint-Exupéry, *Le petit prince* (1943)	
Allied landings in Normandy, 1944 Liberation of Paris, 1944 Ho Chi Minh declares Vietnam independent of France, 1944	Anouilh, *Antigone* (1944) Sartre, *Huis clos* (1944) Camus, *Caligula* (1944) Perse, *Neiges* (1944) Genet, *Notre Dame des fleurs* (1944) Montherlant, *Fils de personne* (1944)	Maugham, *The Razor's Edge* (1944) Cary, *The Horse's Mouth* (1944)

ainting and music	Criticism and aesthetic theory	Ideas
Hindemith, 1895–1963 (*Mathis der Maler*, 1933)		
Gerhard, 1896–1970	Paulhan, *Les Fleurs de Tarbes* (1941)	Waddington, *The Scientific Attitude* (1941)
Gershwin, 1889–1937 (*Rhapsody in Blue*, 1924; *Porgy and Bess*, 1935)	Ransom, *The New Criticism* (1941)	Montherlant, *Le Solstice de juin* (1941)
Moore, b. 1898	Bachelard, *L'Eau et les rêves* (1942)	Camus, *Le Mythe de Sisyphe* (1942)
	Langer, *Philosophy in a New Key* (1942)	Burnham, *The Managerial Revolution* (1942)
		Fromm, *Fear of Freedom* (1942)
Calder, b. 1898		
Poulenc, 1899–1963 (*Les Biches*, 1923; *La Figure humaine*, 1943)	Blanchot, *Faux pas* (1943)	Sartre, *L'Être et le néant* (1943)
	Bachelard, *L'Air et les songes* (1943)	
Weill, 1900–50 (*Dreigroschenoper*, 1928; *Aufstieg und Fall der Stadt Mahagonny*, 1929)	Founding of *Esprit* (1944)	
	Messiaen, *Technique de mon langage musical* (1944)	
Křenek, b. 1900 (*Jonny spielt auf*, 1927)		

History	French literature	Other literatures
Unconditional surrender of German army, 1945	Sartre, *L'Âge de raison* and *Le Sursis* (1945)	Broch, *Der Tod des Vergil* (1945)
French Third Republic ended by referendum, 1945	Gary, *Éducation européenne* (1945)	Orwell, *Animal Farm* (1945)
Execution of Laval, 1945	Bosco, *Le Mas Théotime* (1945)	Levi, *Cristo si è fermato ad Eboli* (1945)
	Beauvoir, *Le Sang des autres* (1945)	Williams, *The Glass Menagerie* (1945)
	Gracq, *Un Beau Ténébreux* (1945)	
Resignation of De Gaulle, 1946	La Tour du Pin, *Une Somme de poésie* (1946)	Zuckmayer, *Des Teufels General* (1946)
Establishment of French Fourth Republic, 1946	Char, *Feuillets d'Hypnos* (1946)	Thomas, *Deaths and Entrances* (1946)
French evacuation of Lebanon, 1946	Prévert, *Paroles* (1946)	Kazantzakis, *Zorba the Greek* (1946)
	Perse, *Vents* (1946)	
	Bernanos, *Monsieur Ouine* (1946)	
	Salacrou, *Les Nuits de la colère* (1946)	
	Sartre, *La Putain respectueuse* (1946)	
	Jouve, *La Vierge de Paris* (1946)	
	Genet, *Miracle de la rose* (1946)	
India Independence Act, 1947	Montherlant, *Le Maître de Santiago* (1947)	Moravio, *La Romana* (1947)
Auriol president of France, 1947	Camus, *La Peste* (1947)	Mann, *Doktor Faustus* (1947)
Revolt against French rule in Madagascar, 1947	Genet, *Les Bonnes* (1947)	Williams, *A Streetcar Named Desire* (1947)
Establishment of Gaullist Rassemblement du Peuple Français, 1947	Green, *Si j'étais vous* (1947)	
	Audiberti, *Le Mal court* (1947)	
	Sarraute, *Portrait d'un inconnu* (1947)	
	Cayrol, *Je vivrai l'amour des autres* (1947–50)	
Third Force formed in France, 1948	Sartre, *Les Mains sales* (1948)	Greene, *The Heart of the Matter* (1948)
Berlin air-lift, 1948	Prévert, *Histoires* (1948)	Mailer, *The Naked and the Dead* (1948)

ainting and music	Criticism and aesthetic theory	Ideas
	Valéry, *Variété V* (1945) Founding of *Les Temps Modernes* (1945) Magny, *Les Sandales d'Empédocle* (1945)	Koestler, *The Yogi and the Commissar* (1945) Popper, *The Open Society and its Enemies* (1945)
ush, b. 1900 (*Wat Tyler*, 953; *Men of Blackmoor*, 956)		
opland, b. 1900 (*Rodeo*, 942; *Appalachian Spring*, 944)	Auerbach, *Mimesis* (1946)	Hersey, *Hiroshima* (1946) Sartre, *L'Existentialisme est un humanisme* (1946) Sartre, *Réflexions sur la question juive* (1946)
iacometti, 1901-66		
ubbra, b. 1901		
)ubuffet, b. 1901	Malraux, *La Psychologie de l'art* (1947-50) Brooks, *The Well Wrought Urn* (1947) Tuve, *Elizabethan and Meta-physical Imagery* (1947) Sartre, *Baudelaire* (1947)	Merleau-Ponty, *Humanisme et terreur* (1947) Buber, *Between Man and Man* (1947)
Valton, b. 1902 (*Belshazzar's east*, 1931; *Façade*, 1931)		
	Bachelard, *La Terre et les rêveries de la volonté* and *La Terre et les rêveries du repos* (1948)	Mounier, *La Petite Peur du XXe siècle* (1948) Eliot, *Notes Towards the Definition of Culture* (1948)

History	French literature	Other literatures
Establishment of O.E.E.C., 1948	Reverdy, *Le Livre de mon bord* (1948)	
	Gary, *Le Grand Vestiaire* (1948)	
	Bazin, *Vipère au poing* (1948)	
	Malraux, *Les Noyers de l'Altenburg* (1948)	
North Atlantic Treaty signed, 1949	Tardieu, *Qui est là?* (1949)	Miller, *Death of a Salesman* (1949)
Adenauer first West German Chancellor, 1949	Sartre, *La Mort dans l'âme* (1949)	Orwell, *Nineteen Eighty-Four* (1949)
Council of Europe established, 1949	Bernanos, *Dialogues des carmélites* (1949)	Brecht, *Der Kaukasische Kreidekreis* (1949)
Laos independent state within French union, 1949		Fry, *The Lady's not for Burning* (1949)
		Pound, *The Pisan Cantos* (1949)
Schuman proposes coal and steel plan, 1950	Camus, *Les Justes* (1950)	Lagerkvist, *Barabbas* (1950)
Pleven plan for European army, 1950	Green, *Moïra* (1950)	Pavese, *La luna e i falò* (1950)
Korean War, 1950–1	Ionesco, *La Cantatrice chauve* (1950)	Böll, *Wanderer, Kommst du nach Spa* (1950)
	Duras, *Un Barrage contre le Pacifique* (1950)	Eliot, *The Cocktail Party* (1950)
	Anouilh, *La Répétition* (1950)	Broch, *Die Schuldlosen* (1950)
	Tardieu, *La Politesse inutile* (1950)	
Coal and steel agreement between France, Germany, Italy, and Benelux, 1951	Sartre, *Le Diable et le bon Dieu* (1951)	Snow, *The Masters* (1951)
	Giono, *Le Hussard sur le toit* (1951)	
	Gracq, *Le Rivage des Syrtes* (1951)	
	Beckett, *Molloy* and *Malone meurt* (1951)	
	Ionesco, *La Leçon* (1951)	
	Montherlant, *La Ville dont le prince est un enfant* (1951)	

inting and music	Criticism and aesthetic theory	Ideas
erkeley, b. 1903	Sartre, *Qu'est-ce que la littérature?* (1948) Spitzer, *Linguistics and Literary History* (1948)	Saint-Exupéry, *Citadelle* (posth. publ. 1948)
utherland, b. 1903	Fergusson, *The Idea of a Theatre* (1949) Warren and Wellek, *Theory of Literature* (1949) Blanchot, *La Part du feu* (1949)	Lévi-Strauss, *Les Structures élémentaires de la parenté* (1949) Weil, *L'Enracinement* (1949–50)
kalkottas, 1904–49		
allapiccola, b. 1904 (*Tre audi*, 1937; *Canti di libera-one*, 1955)	Poulet, *Études sur le temps humain* (1950) Mauron, *Introduction à la psychanalyse de Mallarmé* (1950)	Mounier, *Le Personnalisme* (1950) Riesman, *The Lonely Crowd* (1950)
ali, b. 1904		
ambert, 1905–51 (*The Rio rande*, 1929; *Horoscope*, ●38)	Empson, *The Structure of Complex Words* (1951) Malraux, *Les Voix du silence* (1951) Lukács, *Balzac und der französische Realismus* (1951)	Weil, *La Condition ouvrière* (1951) Camus, *L'Homme révolté* (1951)

History	French literature	Other literatures
Pinay government in France, 1952	Beckett, *En attendant Godot* (1952) Obey, *Lazare* (1952) Ionesco, *Les Chaises* (1952)	Muir, *Collected Poems* (1952) Faulkner, *Requiem for a Nun* (1952)
Beginning of Poujadist movement against taxes, 1953 Coty becomes president, 1953 Death of Stalin, 1953	Green, *Sud* (1953) Robbe-Grillet, *Les Gommes* (1953) Beckett, *L'Innommable* (1953) Anouilh, *L'Alouette* (1953) Bonnefoy, *Du Mouvement et de l'immobilité de Douve* (1953)	Hartley, *The Go-Between* (1953) Brecht, *Der gute Mensch von Sezuan* (1953) Eliot, *The Confidential Clerk* (1953)
Fall of Dien Bien Phu, 1954 Government of Mendès-France concludes Indo-Chinese settlement, 1954 National rebellion against France begins in Algeria, 1954	Michaux, *Mouvements* (1954) Green, *L'Ennemi* (1954) Sarraute, *Martereau* (1954) Beauvoir, *Les Mandarins* (1954) Butor, *Passage de Milan* (1954) Montherlant, *Port-Royal* (1954)	Golding, *Lord of the Flies* (1954) Thomas, *Under Milk Wood* (1954) Snow, *The New Men* (1954) Amis, *Lucky Jim* (1954) Murdoch, *Under the Net* (1954)
Agreement on self-government for Tunisia between Mendès-France government and Néo-Destour party, 1955	Robbe-Grillet, *Le Voyeur* (1955) Duras, *Le Square* (1955) Ionesco, *Jacques ou la soumission* (1955) Adamov, *Le Ping-Pong* (1955)	Brecht, *Leben des Galilei* (1955) Larkin, *The Less Deceived* (1955) Powell, *The Acceptance World* (1955)
Morocco granted independence, 1956 Anglo-French intervention in Suez, 1956 Nasser becomes Egyptian president, 1956	Gary, *Les Racines du ciel* (1956) Genet, *Le Balcon* (1956) Arrabal, *Le Labyrinthe* (1956) Camus, *La Chute* (1956) Sartre, *Les Séquestrés d'Altona* (1956)	Golding, *Pincher Martin* (1956) White, *The Tree of Man* (1956) Osborne, *Look Back in Anger* (1956) Wilson, *Anglo-Saxon Attitudes* (1956) Yevtushenko, *Zima Junction* (1956) Dürrenmatt, *Der Besuch der alten Dame* (1956)

Painting and music	Criticism and aesthetic theory	Ideas
Seiber, 1905–60 Tippett, b. 1905 (*A Child of Our Time*, 1944; *The Mid-summer Marriage*, 1955; *Symphony No. 2*, 1957)	Poulet, *La Distance intérieure* (1952)	Sartre, *Saint Genet comédien et martyr* (1952) Tillich, *The Courage to Be* (1952)
	Barthes, *Le Degré zéro de l'écriture* (1953)	Wittgenstein, *Philosophical Investigations* (1953)
Jolivet, b. 1905 (*Mana*, 1935) Shostakovich, b. 1906 (*Symphony No. 5*, 1937; *Symphony No. 9*, 1945)	Picon, *L'Écrivain et son ombre* (1953)	
Lutyens, b. 1906	Proust, *Contre Sainte-Beuve* (posth. publ. 1954)	Léautaud, *Journal Littéraire* (1954–66)
Messiaen, b. 1908 (*Quatuor pour la fin du temps*, 1940; *Mode de valeurs et d'intensités*, 1950; *Oiseaux exotiques*, 1956; *Premier catalogue des oiseaux*, 1957)	Richard, *Littérature et sensation* (1954) Wimsatt, *The Verbal Icon* (1954)	
Bacon, b. 1909	Lukács, *Der historische Roman* (1955)	Weil, *Oppression et liberté* (1955)
	Richard, *Poésie et profondeur* (1955)	Aron, *L'Opium des intellectuels* (1955)
Liebermann, b. 1910	Blanchot, *L'Espace littéraire* (1955)	Heisenberg, *The Physicist's Conception of Nature* (1955)
Pollock, 1912–56		Lévi-Strauss, *Tristes Tropiques* (1955)
	Sarraute, *L'Ère du soupçon* (1956)	Whyte, *The Organization Man* (1956)
	Goldmann, *Le Dieu caché* (1956)	
Cage, b. 1912 (*Music for Piano I*, 1951; *Aria*, 1958; *Theatre Piece*, 1960)	Delay, *La Jeunesse d'André Gide* (1956) Robbe-Grillet, *Pour un nouveau roman* (1956)	
Britten, b. 1913 (*Peter Grimes*, 1945; *A War Requiem*, 1962)		

History	French literature	Other literatures
French Assembly ratifies Rome treaties for Common Market, 1957 Fall of Mollet government and partial devaluation of franc, 1957	Vailland, *La Loi* (1957) Robbe-Grillet, *La Jalousie* (1957) Perse, *Amers* (1957) Butor, *L'Emploi du temps* (1957) Beckett, *Fin de partie* (1957) Camus, *L'Exil et le royaume* (1957)	Pasternak, *Doctor Zhivago* (1957) Durrell, *The Alexandria Quartet* (1957–60) White, *Voss* (1957) Pound, *Section: Rock-Drill* (1957)
Revolt of army and Europeans in Algeria, 1958 French Assembly accepts government of De Gaulle, 1958 De Gaulle elected French president, 1958 Devaluation of franc, 1958	Butor, *La Modification* (1958) Genet, *Les Nègres* (1958) Simon, *L'Herbe* (1958) Duras, *Moderato Cantabile* (1958) Bonnefoy, *Hier régnant désert* (1958) Anouilh, *Pauvre Bitos* (1958)	Lampedusa, *Il Gattopardo* (1958) Frisch, *Biedermann und die Brandstifter* (1958)
Castro overthrows Batista regime in Cuba, 1959	Sarraute, *Le Planétarium* (1959) Queneau, *Zazie dans le métro* (1959) Anouilh, *Becket, ou l'honneur de Dieu* (1959) Vian, *Les Bâtisseurs d'empire* (1959) Arrabel, *Picque-nique en campagne* (1959)	Grass, *Die Blechtrommel* (1959) Bellow, *Henderson the Rain King* (1959)
Introduction of French 'new franc', 1960 Explosion of first French nuclear bomb, 1960	Green, *Chaque homme dans sa nuit* (1960) Ionesco, *Rhinocéros* (1960) Simon, *La Route des Flandres* (1960) Montherlant, *Le Cardinal d'Espagne* (1960) Butor, *Degrés* (1960)	Enzensberger, *Landessprache* (1960) Quasimodo, *Tutte le poesie* (1960) Voznesensky, *Mozaika* and *Parabola* (1960)

Painting and music	Criticism and aesthetic theory	Ideas
	Bachelard, *La Poétique de l'espace* (1957)	Hoggart, *The Uses of Literacy* (1957)
Searle, b. 1915	Frye, *The Anatomy of Criticism* (1957)	
Nolan, b. 1917		
Soulages, b. 1919	Starobinski, *Jean-Jacques Rousseau, la transparence et l'obstacle* (1958)	Williams, *Culture and Society, 1780-1950* (1958) Popper, *The Poverty of Historicism* (1958)
Nono, b. 1924 (*Canto sospeso*, 1956)	Blanchot, *Le Livre à venir* (1959) Spitzer, *Romanische Literaturstudien* (1959)	
Boulez, b. 1925 (*Polyphonie X*, 1951; *Structures I*, 1952; *Pli selon pli*, 1960)		
Berio, b. 1925 (*Circles*, 1961)	Weber, *Genèse de l'œuvre poétique* (1960) Butor, *Répertoire* (1960) Bachelard, *La Poétique de la rêverie* (1960) Diéguez, *L'Écrivain et son langage* (1960)	Sartre, *Critique de la raison dialectique* (1960) Barzun, *The House of Intellect* (1960)

History	French literature	Other literatures
Army revolt collapses in Algeria, 1961	Beckett, *Comment c'est* (1961)	Naipaul, *A House for Mr. Biwas* (1961)
Gagarin orbits the earth, 1961	Genet, *Les Paravents* (1961) Robbe-Grillet, *L'Année dernière à Marienbad* (1961)	White, *Riders in the Chariot* (1961) Frisch, *Andorra* (1961)
Independence of Algeria proclaimed, 1962 Pompidou becomes French premier, 1962 Cuban missile crisis, 1962	Simon, *Le Palace* (1962) Ionesco, *Le Roi se meurt* (1962)	Solzhenitsin, *One Day in the Life of Ivan Denisovich* (1962) Dürrenmatt, *Die Physiker* (1962)

Painting and music	Criticism and aesthetic theory	Ideas
Henze, b. 1926 (*Undine*, 1956; *Elegy for Young Lovers*, 1961)	Founding of *Tel Quel* (1961) Poulet, *Les Métamorphoses du cercle* (1961) Starobinski, *L'Œil vivant* (1961)	
Stockhausen, b. 1928 (*Gesang der Jünglinge*, 1956; *Gruppen*, 1957; *Kontakte*, 1960; *Momente*, 1962)	Rousset, *Forme et signification* (1962) Richard, *L'Univers imaginaire de Mallarmé* (1962)	Lévi-Strauss, *La Pensée sauvage* (1962)

Index

Absolute, the, 132.

Action française, L, 104; formation and nature of, 131; Péguy and, 135; and Catholic revival, 137; and new Catholic writers, 138; condemnation of, 138, 139.

Adamov, Arthur, and *Ubu Roi*, 265; compared with surrealists, 267; vision to which he responds, 270; his idiosyncratic vision of experience, 271; his work considered, 279–80; Tardieu and, 281.

    Works: *La grande et la petite manœuvre*, 280; *Le Ping-Pong*, 279; *Le Professeur Taranne*, 281; *Les Retrouvailles*, 279–80; *Le Sens de la marche*, 279–80; *Tous contre tous*, 280; note on his other works, 282.

Alain (pen-name of Émile-Auguste Chartier), on the dangers of power, 67; his influence, 68; *Mars ou la guerre jugée*, 67.

Algerian War, 226, 229–30.

Anouilh, Jean, his work considered, 171–3; plays with words, 174; biographical note, 182; recommended works on, 183.

    Works: *Antigone*, 171, 213; *Le Bal des voleurs*, 172; *La Foire d'Empoigne*, 213; *L'Hermine*, 171; *Léocadia*, 172; *Pauvre Bitos*, 172; *La Répétition*, 171, 172; *La Sauvage*, 171; *Le Voyageur sans bagages*, 172.

Anti-roman, characteristic of, 284.

Apollinaire, Guillaume (name taken by Wilhelm Apollinaris de Kostrowitzky), 111, 144, 151; quality of his war poetry, 61–2; Chirico's portrait of, 117; basis of his inspiration, 143; on *l'esprit nouveau*, 145; and collective entities, 146; concentrates on technique, 153; Cocteau and, 182; and Jarry, 266; Beckett and, 271; his *jeux d'esprit*, 281.

    Works: *Les Mamelles de Tirésias*, 267; 'L'Adieu du cavalier', 61; 'Chef de section', 61–2; 'Fête', 62; 'Merveille de la guerre', 61; 'Zone', 153.

Aquinas, St. Thomas, Claudel and, 158; Beckett and, 272.

Aragon, Louis, and surrealism, 112, 123, 126; on surrealists, 119; becomes communist, 120; Russian influence on, 144; idealistic appeal of, 146; on France in years of occupation, 205; recommended work on, 225.

    Works: *Les Communistes*, 213; *Le Musée Grévin*, 213; *Le Paysan de Paris*, 127; *La Peinture au défi*, 127; *La Semaine sainte*, 213; *Servitude et grandeur des français*, 220; *Traité du style*, 127.

Architecture, and surrealism, 111.

Aristotle, 158.

Aron, Raymond, 242.

Arrabal, Fernando, and *Ubu Roi*, 265; compared with surrealists, 267; vision to which he responds, 270; his idiosyncratic vision of experience, 271; risks self-parody, 279; his work considered, 280–1; edition of his works, 282.

    Works: *Le Cimetière des voitures*, 280; *Les Deux Bourreaux*, 281; *Fando et Lis*, 280; *Picque-nique en campagne*, 280.

Artaud, Antonin, and surrealism, 123, 126.

Augustine, St. (Aurelius Augustinus), 272.

Auric, Georges, 182.

Automatic writing, 112.

Avant-garde, *Ubu Roi* anticipates, 266; French dramatists of, 267; imaginative awareness of playwrights of, 268; recommended works on, 282.

Aymé, Marcel, *Uranus*, 219.

Babbit, Irving, 131.

Bacon, Francis, on art, 18.

Balzac, Honoré (de), his influence on Bernanos, 194, 195; *L'Envers de l'histoire contemporaine*, 288.

Barbey d'Aurevilly, Jules-Amédée, 139.

Barbusse, Henri, denounces horrors of war, 63; effect of War on outlook of, 67; *Le Feu*, 63, 67.

Barrault, Jean-Louis, 73.

PRINTED IN GREAT BRITAIN
AT THE UNIVERSITY PRESS, OXFORD
BY VIVIAN RIDLER
PRINTER TO THE UNIVERSITY